GROWTH AND CRISES IN THE ASIAN PACIFIC RIM

Revised Edition

Edited by
Margaret Malixi

California State University, Bakersfield

cognella™
San Diego, CA

Bassim Hamadeh, CEO and Publisher
Christopher Foster, General Vice President
Michael Simpson, Vice President of Acquisitions
Jessica Knott, Managing Editor
Kevin Fahey, Cognella Marketing Manager
Jess Busch, Senior Graphic Designer
Marissa Applegate, Acquisitions Editor
Stephanie Sandler, Licensing Associate

First published in the United States of America in 2013 by Cognella, Inc.

Trademark Notice: Product or corporate names may be trademarks or registered trademarks, and are used only for identification and explanation without intent to infringe.

Printed in the United States of America

ISBN: 978-1-62131-311-3

www.cognella.com   800.200.3908

CONTENTS

Preface

China's ongoing transformation and expanding economic prowess has sustained interest in the models of Asian economic development. The earlier successes of the Asian Tiger economies of South Korea, Taiwan, Hong Kong, and Singapore and the historic and current preeminence of Japan as both a regional and world economic power inspire more in-depth and comparative studies of these Asian models.

The purpose of this book is to familiarize the reader with the various Asian models of development, exploring both strengths and weaknesses of these paradigms. The book is designed as a textbook for both undergraduate and graduate students and is accessible to readers with a rudimentary knowledge of economics. Although the book endeavors to explain the phenomenon of economic growth and development, the selections are written from various disciplinary perspectives such as economics, history, political science, sociology, anthropology, business, and international relations. It is appropriate for use in courses in other social science disciplines and business areas focused on the study of Asian Pacific Rim development. The general reader who wishes to understand the various modes of growth and development of rapidly developing regions such as the Asian Pacific Rim will find the book's selections illuminating.

Japan's astonishing and rapid transformation from a physically, economically, and politically devastated country following World War II to an advanced industrial economy by the early 1970s was an admirable accomplishment that commanded the world's attention. The Japanese Model became the basis for other successful Asian Pacific Rim paradigms, most notably those of the densely populated, resource-poor, but highly literate countries of South Korea, Taiwan, Hong Kong, and Singapore—the so-called Newly Industrializing Economies (NIEs). It seemed that the spread of rapid development throughout Asia was inevitable as the rest of Asia, including the resource-rich Southeast Asian nations, jumped on the development bandwagon. Most recently, the focus has been on China's transformation and expanding preeminence in the world economy and politics.

Although most of the discussion focuses on uncovering the underlying cause of and conditions behind the phenomenal success of the region's economies, the robustness of these models has also been challenged by economic crises, such as the bursting of the Japanese Bubble Economy, the Asian Currency Crisis, structural problems, aggressive protectionism, ecological disequilibrium, and rapidly rising wages, to name a few. In particular, Japan's experience with stagnation and eventual transformation is discussed. A discussion of the factors and policies that made some countries more vulnerable to the financial crisis while others escaped unscathed, as well as an evaluation of the lessons learned from the experience, is included in the readings on the Asian Currency Crisis. China's historical transformation from stagnant communist state to its experiment with market socialism and eventual transformation to a vibrant state capitalist economy is the subject of the final section of the book.

One of my favorite teaching assignments is a constantly evolving undergraduate course on the Pacific Rim Economies, which has happily been sustained throughout the years by healthy enrollments and an ever-growing student interest in East Asian development. Although the course has continuously evolved following the tide of change in East Asia, one constant has been student interest in the interplay of culture, institutions, state, markets, and other factors in the process of East Asian development and growth. My students' interest has inspired my work on this project, and for that I would like to thank them.

Chapter 1: Introduction

Growth and Crises in the Asian Pacific Rim

By Margaret Malixi

Asian Pacific Rim (APR) nations have remarkable records of sustained and rapid economic growth. Beginning with the momentum established by the Japanese Model in the 1950s and continuing with the astonishing transformations of the Newly Industrializing Economies (NIEs) of South Korea, Taiwan, Hong Kong, and Singapore, the promising potential of the resource-rich nations of Southeast Asia, and, finally, the ascent of modern China to economic and political preeminence, growth in APR nations has shocked the world. Yet their aggressive sprint towards economic prosperity has not been without challenges and significant setbacks.

THE JAPANESE MODEL

Rising oil prices brought the Japanese engine of growth to a halt in 1973 following record levels of high-speed growth, which was attributed to the successful design and implementation of the Japanese Model. Japan entered an era of slower growth in 1974, burdened by higher energy costs, slower capital formation and productivity growth, increasing costs of acquiring technology, reorientation of social goals influencing the reallocation of resources, a changing labor market, and a sluggish economic environment.

Sustained export competitiveness, despite the slowdown in growth, resulted in soaring Japanese trade surpluses and pressures from Japan's major trading partners for reciprocal policy initiatives to address the trade imbalances. Asset prices soared as enormous trade surpluses and savings were invested in the stock market, foreign equities, real estate, and foreign debt. As investment opportunities dried up at home, the Japanese extended their buying spree abroad. Japanese banks and investment houses purchased U.S. equities, real estate, and Treasuries, while Japanese corporations sought to gain market access and technology, lower labor costs, and avoid protectionism by setting up manufacturing plants in the Europe, the U.S., and Southeast Asia.[1] The result is what has become known as the Japanese Economic Bubble.

The eventual bursting of the "bubble" at the end of the 1980s, with its attendant financial crisis and deflation, significantly weakened the Japanese economy as it began what would be a lengthy period of stagnation. As Japan struggled to emerge from stagnation, doubts abounded concerning the survival of the Japanese Model and its crucial institutions in the evolving global environment. What has followed is an ongoing period of transformation, reform, deregulation, corporate and political restructuring, and shifting economic priorities.

THE NEWLY INDUSTRIALIZING ECONOMY (NIE) MODEL

Portions of the Japanese Model were replicated throughout Asia. The next tier of success stories were dubbed Asia's Tiger economies or Asia's Newly Industrializing Economies and were comprised of South Korea, Taiwan, Hong Kong, and Singapore. Robust economic performances from the NIEs reinforced the belief that following the Japanese export-oriented growth model was the key to sustaining the East Asian Miracle. The resource-rich countries of Southeast Asia—Malaysia, Indonesia, the Philippines, Thailand, and, to a certain extent, Vietnam—jumped on the bandwagon. The ride, however, has been a bumpy one. Adverse shifts in external conditions, threats of protectionism, rising labor costs, agricultural crises, environmental degradation, social unrest, and other distress signals have led to questions of the legitimacy of this export-oriented NIE Model.[2]

The spread of economic prosperity across East Asia seemed to be inevitable. "From 1945 to 1997 the Asian economic miracle fueled the greatest expansion of wealth for the largest number of persons, in the history of mankind."[3] The region's increasing dependence on international trade as an engine of growth and its growing reliance on bank loans used to finance high rates of new investments increased its vulnerability to speculative attacks on its currencies. The flood of large short-term capital inflows despite the dearth of productive investment opportunities, coupled with a sharp downturn in export revenues and rapidly expanding and unsupervised capital markets, provided the ingredients for the perfect storm. These factors clearly contributed to a reversal in creditor perceptions and rapid capital flight, sparking the Asian Financial Crisis in 1997.[4] The five countries significantly impacted by the crisis were Thailand, South Korea, Malaysia, the Philippines, and Indonesia. Dominant in the literature are two explanations of what caused the crisis: fundamental distortions and self-fulfilling prophesies. The fundamentalist view is that the Asian Currency Crisis was rooted in fundamental imbalances in the crisis-affected countries, while proponents of the self-fulfilling prophesies assert that the crisis was caused by inherent instabilities in international financial markets.[5]

Despite the widespread economic and social distress in the aftermath of the crisis, recent economic indicators, such as GDP growth, stabilization of currency values, and the steady return of capital, paint an optimistic picture of recovery from the crisis. Important catalysts, including financial injections from the International Monetary Fund (IMF), prudent monetary and fiscal policies, domestic fiscal stimuli, and an element of luck in the form of good weather, which yielded bumper crops of rice and other agricultural commodities, hastened the recovery.[6]

THE CHINA MODEL

China's transformation from socialist to market economy began with structural and institutional reform. "The structures and institutions of late Maoism had been abandoned in an attempt by Deng Xiaoping to create an economic system which combined elements of capitalism and socialism,"[7] later dubbed market socialism. As the market socialist vision waned with Deng's death in 1997, China completed significant price liberalization, implemented fiscal and monetary expansion, introduced stock markets, and accelerated the pace of opening up.[8] Although the role of the state in the economy remains large, it is apparent to most current China observers that socialism has, to all intents and purposes, been abandoned by China.[9] The transition to capitalism was characterized by structural changes on an unprecedented scale, including the abandonment of collective farming, the intensifying challenge to state-owned industry by local, state-owned enterprises based in the countryside, a vibrant private sector, and the removal of barriers to internal labor migration.[10] China's astounding transformation, however, does not ensure sustained rapid growth. Transparent governance, independent courts, enforceable property rights, and free information[11] are other desirable prerequisites to China's continued integration in the world economy.

Despite the significant momentum generated by the China Model, questions persist regarding the sustainability of the pace of economic expansion or "whether imbalances in the economy might slow growth, perhaps significantly."[12] China's transformation to capitalism is far from complete, and whether China can avoid what some analysts have identified as fault lines in its economic terrain remains to be seen.

ORGANIZATION OF THE BOOK

The book is organized along the same lines as these developments. Discussion of the Japanese Model begins with a historic overview of Japan's rapid growth phase (1950–1973) and the slowdown in growth (1974–1985) in Chapter 2. Aspects of Japanese corporate culture thought to intensify Japanese comparative advantage are explored in Chapter 3. Chapter 4 investigates the limitations of the Japanese Model, while Chapter 5 analyzes the development and demise of the Bubble Economy. An investigation into Japan's prolonged period of stagnation is the subject matter of Chapters 6. The various strategies for reform and recovery are laid out and analyzed in Chapters 7, 8, and 9.

The New Asian Capitalists adopted Japanese strategies and generated their own successful transformations. Chapters 10, 11, and 12 elaborate on various aspects of the NIE model. The Asian Currency Crisis rudely interrupted Asia's explosive growth and, in the process, revealed the kinks in what earlier appeared to be indestructible Asian armor. Chapter 13 investigates the roots of the crisis, while Chapter 14 explores the role of Asian values, previously viewed as strengths, in generating the crisis. Chapter 15 focuses on financial reforms, while Chapter 16 discusses other factors that contributed to economic recovery after the crisis.

The remaining chapters elaborate on China's transformation from socialism to capitalism. Chapter 17 explores China's experiment with market socialism, and its eventual march towards state capitalism is discussed in Chapter 18. Chapter 19 spells out the important features of the China Model, while Chapters 20 and 21 point out perceived weaknesses in the model that could slow the pace of China's growth significantly.

ENDNOTES

1. Richard H. K. Vietor, Globalization and Growth (Ohio: Thomson South-Western, (2005), p. 317–18.
2. Walden Bello and Stephanie Rosenfeld, Dragons in Distress (San Francisco: Institute for Food and Development Policy, 1990), p. 8–16.
3. Karl Jackson, Asian Contagion (Boulder: Westview Press, 1999), p.7.
4. Seiji Naya, Asian Development Experience (Tokyo: Asian Development Bank, 2002), p. 83–93.
5. Hafiz Akhand and Kanhaya Gupta, Economic Development in Pacific Asia (New York: Routledge, 2006), p. 68–71.
6. Shalendra Sharma, The Asian Financial Crisis (Manchester: Manchester University Press, 2003), p. 340–353.
7. Chris Bramall, Chinese Economic Development (New York: Routledge, 2009) p. 325.
8. Bramall, p. 350.
9. Bramall, p. 470.
10. Bramall, p. 490.
11. Rowan Callick, "The China Model," The American, November/December 2007: 1–9.
12. Jahangir Aziz and Steven Dunaway, "China's Rebalancing Act," Finance and Development, September 2007.

THE JAPANESE MODEL

Chapter 2: The Slowdown in Growth

By Edward J. Lincoln

J APAN burst upon the world in the 1960s and 1970s with a flood of high-quality, competitively priced manufactured products, the result of its postwar economic "miracle." This success has created an enduring image of the country as an unstoppable phenomenon of rapid growth. The reality, however, is that the Japanese economy has been growing at much more moderate rates for better than a decade. While Japan is still relatively successful, the era of extraordinarily high economic growth is gone and will not return.

THE ERA OF HIGH GROWTH

From 1950 to 1973 the annual real growth of Japan's gross national product *averaged* 10 percent, probably the highest sustained rate of increase that the world has ever seen. Although there were some fluctuations in this performance, at no point during these years did Japan suffer a recession. What the Japanese called recessions were years when the growth rate dropped to levels of 4 or 5 percent. Even some of these short-lived periods were not the result of a domestic business cycle but were deliberately caused by tight monetary policy when continuous rapid growth had pushed the country into balance-of-payments problems: short doses of slower growth were needed to curb the appetite for imports so that the government would not be forced to devalue the currency under the rules of the Bretton Woods system.

The industrialization and modernization that made rapid growth possible stretch back to the nineteenth century. It is often conveniently identified with the Meiji Restoration of 1868, an event that initiated the creation of the modern political nation-state. In fact, the roots of economic success can be traced back even farther to factors such as the high literacy rate prevailing by the time of the restoration. But these facts hardly diminish the luster of the extraordinary postwar economic performance.

Table 2–1. Sources of Growth in Japan, 1953–71

Percent

Sources	Contribution to growth[a]
National income growth rate	8.77
Labor	1.85
Employment	1.14
Hours	0.21
Age-sex composition	0.14
Education	0.34
Unallocated	0.02
Capital	2.10
Inventories	0.73
Nonresidential structures and equipment	1.07
Dwellings	0.30
International assets	0
Land	0
Productivity change	4.82
Advances in knowledge and "not elsewhere classified"	1.97
Improved resource allocation	0.95
Economies of scale	1.94
Irregular factors	−0.04

Source: Hugh Patrick and Henry Rosovsky, eds., *Asia's New Giant: How the Japanese Economy Works* (Brookings, 1976), p. 94.

a. Percentage points of total national income growth originating in each factor. For example, increased labor inputs contributed 1.85 percentage points to the 8.77 percent national income growth.

Causes of High Growth

One way to explain growth is to look at trends in the main factors of production: labor, capital, and growth of productivity, a term that encompasses a variety of elements, including technological change. In their work for *Asia's New Giant*, Edward Denison and William Chung found that five factors contributed more to growth in Japan than they did in ten other industrial countries: increased labor input, increased capital stock, advances in knowledge, reallocation of resources away from agriculture, and economies of scale. Their findings are summarized in table 2–1. Of the 8.77 percent average annual rise in real national income in the 1950s and 1960s, labor contributed 1.85 percentage points, capital 2.10 points, and changes in productivity 4.82 points. Thus the rising productivity of labor and capital accounted for more than half of the economic growth. What Denison and Chung called advances in knowledge (which might also be labeled technological change or the introduction of improved technology) was the most important source of productivity change, contributing 1.97 percentage points. Just slightly less important were economies of scale, representing the ability of industry to attain more efficient size as the Japanese market grew. Improved resource allocation, mainly the movement of resources out of agriculture, contributed another 0.95 percentage point to growth.[1]

Some of these developments are self-explanatory. Labor's contribution increased partly because population was increasing. The very success of growth itself allowed a reallocation of labor away from low-productivity work in agriculture. Growth and rising incomes also allowed for economies of scale in production. The key question, then, is why did capital stock and gains from improved technology grow so fast?

Capital stock lies at the center of the explanation of growth provided by Kazushi Ohkawa and Henry Rosovsky, an analysis that nicely pulls together the relationships among the various factors involved.[2] Their analysis rests on three principal observations: Japan lagged far behind the industrial countries in technology in the 1950s and 1960s, it had a large pool of labor eager to move out of agriculture, and it had the social capability to absorb and adapt foreign technology. The critical element, one largely beyond the bounds of traditional economic analysis, is the ability to absorb new technology from abroad. Many nations lag behind the developed countries and have large pools of underemployed labor, but few have been able to import technology efficiently and move up the industrial ladder.

Japan is a market economy; capital stock lies mostly in the hands of the private sector, and economic decisions about production, prices, and investments are motivated by a desire to earn profits. Direct government involvement has mainly been limited to railroads, telecommunications, and cigarette manufacture (and recent efforts have been made to get out even of these). In this private-sector setting, the lag in technology, the ready availability of labor, and the ability to absorb new technology stimulated investment after World War II. Corporations expected high profits from investments in new plant and equipment, bringing in foreign technology in the process and hiring from the pool of available workers without putting undue upward pressure on wages. Those expectations were realized, encouraging further investment. As investment expanded, the continued availability of workers meant that productivity tended to rise as fast or faster than wages, which helped keep corporate profits high. High profits do not normally accompany continuous rapid investment in a mature economy. During investment spurts, profits decline, bringing an eventual slowdown in investment activity. Thus what happened in Japan was unusual; the technological lag, the ability to absorb technology, and the pool of available labor allowed it to avoid this cyclical pattern.[3]

An additional cause of growth was that investing in manufacturing was more profitable than investing in agriculture, so that resources flowed out of agriculture. Agriculture lacked profitability because little of the capital-intensive foreign technology was appropriate to the fragmented land holdings in Japan and because the large families of farmers gave them little incentive to replace workers with tractors.

The gains that Denison and Chung attributed to advances in knowledge follow from this model of strong investment demand because the technology was incorporated in new plant and equipment. Ohkawa and Rosovsky supported these findings with evidence of a close correlation between investment spurts and productivity growth. Gains from economies of scale also follow from this investment model, since an important feature of new plant and equipment was production on a larger scale. The effect was more important in Japan than in other countries because capital stock was growing so quickly.

Rapid growth based on this model applies to both prewar and postwar Japan, with a widened technological gap between it and more developed countries at the beginning of the postwar period (due to isolation during the war and the occupation) and a greater ability to absorb technology. Denison and Chung found that people did achieve higher levels of education after the war (which ought to increase the ability to use foreign technology) but that better education contributed less to growth in Japan than in other countries. However, they may have missed part of the importance of education in their data. Better postwar educa-tion contributed less because changes after the war were less dramatic than in other countries. However, during the war Japan had built up a pool of workers, many of whom had acquired technical education and experience from their military service. This created a disequilibrium in the early postwar period; many well-educated and trained people were seriously underutilized, and they were ready to move into positions in which their skills could contribute much more.

While investment-driven growth provides a tidy explanation of Japan's experience that is consistent with growth-accounting evidence, other factors were also involved. First, the private sector generated high and rising savings to feed the strong investment demand. This was important because the government chose not to borrow heavily from abroad to finance domestic investment, a choice different from that made by most developing countries today. Had domestic savings been lower, investment would have been limited unless government changed its stance and allowed dependence on foreign capital inflow.

Second, Japan has been politically stable since the war, with a popularly supported, noncoercive government. The Liberal Democratic party has been in power for virtually all these years, but its success has been based on free elections and not military power or suppression of opposition groups. The experience of South Korea, where economic growth temporarily dropped below zero during the uncertainty generated by the transfer of power after the assassination of Park Chung Hee in 1979, demonstrates the impact of political instability on growth.

Third, the Japanese government provided supportive economic policies. At the macroeconomic level the government followed tight fiscal policies and expansionary monetary policies. It maintained a balanced budget until the mid-1960s, thereby avoiding competition with the private sector for use of domestic savings (foreign borrowing was largely prohibited). Furthermore, public works spending was skewed toward industrially useful investment rather than social amenities. The money supply was allowed to grow rapidly enough to meet the needs of economic expansion. Because Japan had a capital-scarce economy after the war, interest rates were not low by international standards, but the government managed to keep them low enough so that they did not seriously impede new investment.[4]

At the microeconomic level the government also adopted supportive policies, but experts question the importance of some of them.[5] It imposed high import barriers, supposedly to protect infant industries (and perhaps out of simple economic nationalism), behind which industries could grow without much competition from abroad. These barriers helped provide additional incentives for investment. At the industry level a variety of other aids were supplied, but many were minor and some were used in ways totally unrelated to goals for economic growth and development (some aids, such as support of the domestic coal industry in the 1950s in the face of cheap imported oil, even ran counter to stated goals). How much government macroeconomic and microeconomic policies together contributed to growth is impossible to quantify, but overall they seem to have been supportive.

Fourth, Japan faced a favorable world environment. Trade liberalization under the auspices of the newly created General Agreement on Tariffs and Trade, rapid economic growth worldwide, and an end to colonialism that enabled former colonies to diversify their trade patterns all helped Japan expand exports in the 1950s and 1960s. Raw material prices fell in the 1950s and then remained stable in the 1960s, allowing the country to improve its terms of trade (the ratio of the price of exports to the price of imports).[6] The favorable price movements in the terms of trade enhanced national welfare and may have increased the growth rate by improving Japan's balance-of-payments position. (As mentioned earlier, balance-of-payments problems periodically forced monetary authorities to slow the economy, but favorable movements in terms of trade meant that these problems were less severe than they would have been otherwise.)

Fifth, the Japanese have long valued education, hard work, and loyalty. These emphases found expression in an educated and dedicated labor force with the ability and willingness to accept rapid technological change. In addition, the destruction of the war forged a strong social commitment to economic growth as a national goal. People were willing to forgo leisure and social amenities in order to promote rapid industrial development. Other social features that probably contributed to growth in intangible ways include the relative homogeneity of society and language, the absence of debilitating regional disparities, and sufficient social mobility to prevent class conflict.

Sixth, labor-management relations evolved in a relatively nonconfrontational way. Although the union movement was militant in some industries and strikes were frequent in the early postwar years, by the late 1950s and early 1960s most of the radical unions had been crushed and replaced by more moderate ones. This was a divisive period for labor, but the fact that the radical unions could not command sufficient loyalty among workers to stay in power confirms the broad nature of the social consensus on rapid growth and hard work. Japanese workers accepted a system of enterprise-based unions with very weak national organizations, moderate strike activity (in which strikes are of limited, preannounced duration), transfers between jobs or factories within a company as technological change eliminated old functions, and moderation in wage demands when corporate profits fell. In general, unions have been flexible on wages and work rules.

Finally, the postwar occupation by the United States brought a number of political and economic reforms that may have been very important to economic growth. These included extensive land reform (essentially eliminating tenancy), legalization of labor unions, and dissolution of the powerful business conglomerates (*zaibatsu*) that had increasingly dominated Japanese industry before and during the war. The dissolution may have brought greater competition and thereby more aggressive investment activity in the corporate sector. The establishment of an antitrust law helped prevent a reemergence of the zaibatsu and some of the more egregious forms of anticompetitive behavior (even though antitrust enforcement was lax by American standards).[7]

The effects of most of these factors cannot be measured, but they must not be ignored in explaining why Japan grew. They created an atmosphere in which private business could realistically hold expectations of high rates of return on investment in plant and equipment. Thus they are essential to explaining Japan's rapid growth and the difference between its prewar and postwar experiences.

As a result of these years of growth, by the early 1970s Japan was transformed from an impoverished, war-devastated nation into a prosperous, industrialized country. As put succinctly in *Asia's New Giant*, "Japan's surge over the past quarter-century, seemingly from nowhere, to join the vanguard of the world's economies has been an unprecedented, exciting, and at times disruptive event. By any economic criteria Japan is now an immense, rich nation."[8]

Expectations in the Early 1970s

By the early 1970s the Japanese and the rest of the world were beginning to realize that Japan's prosperity was not just a temporary or fragile phenomenon. But analysts began to err in the direction of unbounded optimism, engaging in projections for the future that assumed endless growth. In *The Emerging Japanese Superstate*, a best-seller in Japan, Herman Kahn confessed that "the overriding reason for my interest in Japan is its spectacular past and expected future economic growth—better than 10 percent a year in the last two decades, and likely to be maintained at around that rate for at least the next two or three decades."[9] Such enthusiasm was not surprising considering the self-confidence and optimism many Japanese displayed. Students, for example, were using the phrase *Nippon ichiban* (Japan is number one) as an expression of where they saw their country headed.

The optimism spilled over into discussions of policy. In 1972, just before he became prime minister, Kakuei Tanaka published *Nihon Retto Kaizō Ron* (*Building a New Japan* was the English title) in which he proposed that high growth could be sustained and great improvements made by the government in roads, schools, hospitals, and other works for the welfare of the public. "The period of rapid growth," he wrote, "has given rise to such distortions as pollution, inflation, urban overcrowding, rural depopulation, and agricultural stagnation. To solve these problems and to provide a worthwhile life in a pleasant country, we must waste no time in improving social overhead capital and the social security standards."[10] A key feature of his proposals was to encourage redistribution of economic activity away from the Tokyo–Osaka industrial belt and toward more rural areas.

When Tanaka became prime minister in the summer of 1972, he quickly ordered the Economic Planning Agency (EPA) to draw up a long-term economic plan incorporating the basic philosophy of his book.[11] The Basic Economic and Social Plan for 1973–77, adopted in February 1973 just before the outbreak of problems that dramatically reduced growth rates, represented the last major policy statement of the high-growth era. Following the Tanaka script, the plan recognized the problems stemming from rapid growth and the concurrent need to redistribute resources. An awareness of the problems of pollution, old age care, inadequate social overhead capital, and others, it said, "once confined to a small portion of the population, has now emerged as broad national demands, partly because of the tardiness of policy response, and it is therefore necessary now that there be a policy switch that will make it possible to meet these demands."[12]

Projecting much the same confidence as Tanaka himself, the plan forecast about a 9 percent real GNP annual growth rate (in 1965 prices), down from the 11 percent rate that prevailed from 1961 to 1970. That was hardly a change at all. Helping to buoy the projected rate was the assumption that Tanaka's plan for redistributing economic activity more evenly around Japan would be implemented—that there would be improvements in regional transportation infrastructure, controls on further development in urban areas, inducements for industry to relocate away from urban areas, and financial assistance to regional cities to promote development.[13]

As a whole, the plan was a very liberal document, endorsing a wide range of social programs, including increased spending on housing, expanded public park lands, more resources for home care and community care of the elderly and seriously handicapped, increased spending on medical facilities, and the institution of a five-day workweek. The authors of the plan did acknowledge that to achieve these goals increased government deficits would be necessary. With a modest slowdown in private-sector investment, they predicted that government expenditures on social programs would cause a ¥6.0 trillion deficit by fiscal year 1977, or approximately $22 billion at average 1973 exchange rates. By way of comparison, the actual government deficit in fiscal 1977 was ¥9.6 trillion.[14]

The EPA plan also anticipated that continued expansion at home would hold the current-account surplus to a moderate $5.9 billion, with an equal outflow of long-term capital yielding a zero basic balance.[15] The actual current-account surplus for fiscal 1977 was $14 billion (1.5 percent of GNP), and most of the offsetting capital outflow was in short-term assets, so that the basic balance showed a surplus of $11.6 billion.

This optimistic forecast purported to show how Japan could continue to grow at very high real rates despite a moderate shift from private-sector investment to government spending in order to improve the quality of life. Continued rapid growth would allow the government to make these new or expanded expenditures without going too far into debt because tax revenues would rise rapidly. Finally, growth would absorb resources at home, keeping the current-account surplus under control so that Japan would not get into political trouble with its trading partners. None of these projections came true.

The EPA was not alone in its optimism. The Japan Economic Research Center, often at the upper end of private-sector Japanese forecasts, published an even rosier forecast early in 1974, just as pessimism was settling in elsewhere. It predicted 9.2 percent average annual growth for the 1970–85 period, but then in a bow to the uncertainty of the future said that a wider range of 7 to 9 percent would be realistic. The forecast assumed continued high investment levels with some moderate shift from plant and equipment toward housing and government investment. Plant and equipment investment was to drop from 20 percent to 15 percent of GNR, while housing investment would be up from 6.6 percent to 10 percent. Government investment would be up from 8.2 percent to 10.5 percent, a more moderate rise than anticipated in the EPA plan. All this investment would be supported by continued high savings rates. The research center also predicted domestic demand would rise rapidly enough that the current-account surplus would increase to only $9.4 billion, or 0.3 percent of GNP at expected exchange rates (compared to an actual surplus in 1985 of $49 billion, close to 4 percent of GNP).[16]

The research center's projection was so optimistic that it implied a GNP almost as big as that forecast for the United States in 1985, with Japan's per capita income 74 percent higher than that of the United States. Thus the center joined the school that thought Japan could continue to grow at extremely high rates and divert resources to improving social welfare for a number of years to come.[17]

Not everyone leaped on the high-growth bandwagon. In *How Japan's Economy Grew So Fast*, Denison and Chung concluded that Japan's growth rate would be 6.9 percent annually between 1974 and 1982.[18] Brookings scholars Philip Trezise and Edward Fried came to a similar conclusion. Using the same growth-accounting techniques, they forecast 6 percent annual growth from 1975 to 1985 because of slower labor, capital, and productivity growth.[19] Although both estimates turned out to be too high, they did focus on the central feature of Japanese economic growth: much of it was based on special, temporary factors that by the early 1970s were reaching the limit of their contribution. What happened to these influences explains why growth dropped so much after 1973.

While the conclusion that growth would not continue at an annual rate of 10 percent into the indefinite future may seem obvious in hindsight, predicting the future from straight-line projections of the recent past was an easy and satisfying exercise in the early 1970s. Rapid growth had become a way of life in Japan, and a sharp decline was almost inconceivable. When the break did come, it turned out to be much sharper and more traumatic than anyone anticipated.

THE 1973–74 WATERSHED

The disruption of oil supplies in late 1973 in combination with other domestic and foreign events marked the end of Japan's phenomenal economic growth. Abandoning the euphoric mood of the long-term economic plan approved early in 1973, EPA Director General Tsuneo Uchida announced before the Diet in January 1974 that "for both the international economy and the Japanese economy, one age is to pass, and a new age is to start."[20]

What happened to make these years so traumatic? Basically, Japan suffered from simultaneous high inflation and recession. Much of the inflation was caused by the sharp increases in world prices for raw materials (including but not confined to oil). Government macroeconomic policies designed to stimulate domestic demand also contributed because the potential for growth of supply was diminishing.[21] As inflation mounted, the country faced a temporary cut in oil supplies from the Middle East. This combination of events not only created Japan's first recession of the postwar period but also raised extreme fears about long-term dependence on basic resources, a dependence that seemed likely to limit the country's ability to grow in the future. Had these events not transpired, a softer, more gradual shift to slower growth rates could have taken place. With them, the transition from one era to another was much faster and more frightening.

The 1973 Shocks

At the opening of 1973 the Japanese economy was growing rapidly, part of a business recovery from a growth recession in 1971 that had been caused by the revaluation of the yen.[22] And yet by early in the year inflation was running at higher levels than expected, fed by excess demand and rising import prices. Table 2–2 illustrates what happened to prices. During the 1960s Japan had had a pattern of very stable wholesale and import prices with moderate consumer price inflation. This pattern continued in the early 1970s. But after falling by 0.8 percent in 1971 and rising only 0.8 percent in 1972, wholesale prices began to accelerate rapidly. In January they were running 7.6 percent above levels of a year earlier, and by March the rate had reached double digits. Import prices rose even more rapidly. After falling 4.3 percent in 1972, by January they were already 12.9 percent higher than a year earlier and by July were up 24 percent, reflecting world inflation trends that predated the oil shock. Consumer prices followed wholesale prices, with the rate of inflation rising continuously from 6.2 percent in January to 10.9 percent by May and 23.1 percent by January 1974.

Table 2–2. Inflation Rates, Selected Years and Periods, 1959–75

Percent change from same period in previous year

Year	Wholesale price index	Import price index	Consumer price index
1961–70 average[a]	1.3	0.6	5.9
1971	−0.8	0	6.1
1972	0.8	−4.3	4.5
1973	15.9	21.0	11.7
1974	31.3	66.3	24.5
1975	3.0	7.6	11.8
1973			
January	7.6	12.9	6.2
February	9.2	11.5	6.7
March	11.0	13.1	8.4
April	11.4	11.7	9.4
May	12.3	14.1	10.9
June	13.6	18.4	11.1
July	15.7	24.0	11.9
August	17.4	27.4	12.0
September	18.7	25.4	14.6
October	20.3	25.3	14.3
November	22.3	32.6	15.9
December	29.0	34.7	19.1
1974			
January	34.0	42.8	23.1
February	37.0	69.3	26.3
March	35.4	69.2	24.0
April	35.7	74.8	24.9
May	35.3	74.8	23.1
June	35.4	71.9	23.6
July	34.2	70.5	25.2
August	32.9	71.8	25.4
September	30.6	71.3	23.8
October	28.7	69.3	26.2
November	25.1	59.1	25.8
December	17.0	53.3	21.9
1975			
January	10.4	37.0	17.4

Sources: Bank of Japan, *Economic Statistics Monthly* (January 1973), pp. 139, 145, 147; (January 1974), pp. 145, 151, 153; (January 1975), pp. 145, 151, 153; (January 1976), p. 163; and Bank of Japan, *Economic Statistics Annual, 1970* (Tokyo: BOJ, 1970), p. 259; 1971, pp. 249, 262.

a. Figures for 1961–70 average are in 1965 base year. All others are in 1970 base year.

Inflation at the levels evident by the spring of 1973 was an unpleasant experience for Japan. From 1961 to 1970 the wholesale price index had risen at an average annual rate of only 1.3 percent, while the consumer price index had increased at a 5.9 percent rate. This pattern of stable wholesale prices, reflecting great strides in manufacturing productivity, and moderately high inflation in consumer prices, because imported technology did not apply to many labor-intensive services, is typical of newly industrializing countries. While consumer inflation in the 1960s was higher than that experienced in the United States, it was accepted by the Japanese as a minor price to pay for rapid economic growth.[23] But the experience of 1973 began to remind people of the hyperinflation of the late 1940s.

Besides rising inflation, 1973 was marked by other new concerns. At the beginning of the 1970s the Japanese were fiercely committed to the idea of fixed exchange rates; the stability of the Bretton Woods system was one of the rocks upon which postwar prosperity was built. The revaluation at the end of August 1971 had been an enormously difficult decision to make, and when the Smithsonian agreement on exchange rates was signed in December 1971, there was hope that stability would return at the new parities. But in March 1973 the agreement collapsed and currencies were allowed to float. Some Japanese firmly believed that the uncertainties generated by floating rates would be so severe that international trade would collapse. Therefore, it was with great trepidation (and a great deal of direct intervention in the exchange market) that Japan began the era of floating rates.

At the end of June 1973 the Japanese faced another surprise: the United States announced a complete embargo on exports of soybeans. Soybeans are an important element in Japanese cuisine (in both an esthetic and nutritional sense), but Japan had not protected domestic producers from import competition as it had producers of some other agricultural products, and as a result only 6 percent of the country's supply was produced domestically. The United States accounted for 88 percent of soybean imports in 1973 and 84 percent of total supply.[24] The embargo turned out to be very short-lived once the U.S. government realized the damage it implied for Japan, and no contracted shipments for the year were actually prevented. Nevertheless, that a valued ally could do such a thing added to Japanese feelings of vulnerability.

The soybean shock fed broader concerns about imports. An editorial on June 29 in the *Nihon Keizai Shimbun* noted:

> Because of a series of problems, including contaminated fish, the miserable drought in West Africa, frequent earthquakes, rising inflation, and the world shortage of grain since last year, people have become extremely anxious. We are now close to the point at which even a minor bit of bad news will be blown out of proportion and "anxiety will beget anxiety."[25]

Representative of these fears were Japanese press reports that Washington would restrict log and lumber exports to Japan or that it would limit wheat exports because of lobbying pressure from the All-American Bread Manufacturers Association, which wanted to keep

U.S. domestic prices down.[26] Such rumors led to panic among consumers, who feared restrictions would multiply and shortages would spread to other commodities. In the fall of 1973 came the famous toilet paper shortage, when new shipments disappeared from store shelves as soon as they arrived. Self-fulfilling prophecy then led to panic buying and hoarding of soy sauce, cooking oil, and other necessities, creating shortages when no real supply problem existed.

All these fears came to naught. In April 1974, with a possible drop in U.S. prices and overproduction already in the offing, Secretary of Agriculture Earl Butz visited Tokyo to reassure the Japanese government about exports of foodstuffs. He guaranteed Minister of Agriculture Tadao Ku-raishi stable supplies from the United States and recommended stockpiling as a way to ease problems in times of short supply.[27] These guarantees were followed in 1975 by the Butz-Abe agreement, an unusual bilateral document of "understanding" that set minimum annual quantities of wheat, feed grains, and soybeans the United States would supply to Japan in 1976–78.[28]

The possibility of embargoes and other disruptions of imports generated some calls for achieving self-sufficiency in food production, but no actions were taken. In fiscal year 1965, government measures showed 61 percent of the calories the Japanese consumed were produced domestically; by 1975 the figure had declined to 43 percent and by 1983 to 32 percent.[29] Thus, far from acting on the fears generated in 1973, Japan has actually followed the economically rational policy of decreasing dependence on uncompetitive domestic food producers (and could move much farther in that direction). Even for soybeans this was the case, despite calls for diversifying sources of supply after the 1973 shock. By 1984 the United States accounted for 86 percent of Japan's total soybean supply.[30]

Of all the events of 1973, the most dramatic was the October war in the Middle East and the accompanying oil market disruptions. On October 16 the Organization of Arab Petroleum Exporting Countries announced an increase in the price of oil from $3 a barrel to $5. The next day it announced a 5 percent cutback in oil shipments. On October 19 it imposed a total embargo on the United States and a 10 percent cutback for other countries. On November 4 the cuts were increased to 25 percent and were to be increased to 30 percent in December. On November 6 the restrictions were eased somewhat for the European countries but not for Japan, apparently out of a belief that Japan was still too closely tied to American diplomatic positions. On November 22 Japan finally issued a strong pro-Arab statement, and in December, Deputy Prime Minister Takeo Miki was dispatched to the Middle East. During his trip OAPEC eased the restrictions on Japan to a 15 percent cut, the same imposed on the European countries. On March 13, 1974, the restrictions were lifted entirely.[31]

Coming on top of rising general inflation, the soybean embargo, and the panic-driven shortages, the oil shock was a truly traumatic experience for the Japanese. Among other things, they worried that the international companies handling most of the actual supply of oil would not treat Japan equally with their home countries. As one major newspaper noted, "There is no doubt that the shortage of oil supply will concentrate, after all, in the consumer countries having no international oil capital."[32] Although such fears were groundless, they demonstrate the deep belief of the Japanese that they are not fully accepted in the international community and will be discriminated against when the economic chips are down, a fear no doubt reinforced by the soybean fiasco.

This disastrous combination of events created strong concerns that Japan would not be able to cope with the problems. An editorial in Sankei Shimbun speculated that "economic and social confusion will be beyond all imagination." *Tokyo Shimbun* expressed similar fears: "It will be presumed that such a scene, where social unrest will whirl around in the Japanese archipelago, will arise." The more cautious *Mainichi Shimbun* shied away from predicting social turmoil but noted that "people will be compelled to endure austerity, which has not been seen since immediately after the end of the war."[33] Such dire predictions may seem examples of journalistic excess, but they did represent the widespread public shock that more than two decades of unparalleled growth and prosperity could be so abruptly compromised.

By the beginning of November the Ministry of International Trade and Industry dared to suggest that in the worst-case scenario growth in the next fiscal year could be as low as zero. But most other government pronouncements in November and December said Japan would manage to pull through with a real GNP growth rate of 4 to 5 percent, which demonstrates how ingrained the high-growth mentality had become among government officials: even in adversity it was difficult to conceive of anything worse than the growth recessions of the 1960s.

The 1974 Recession

Despite official optimism 1974 was the first year since World War II that Japan suffered a real recession, and one combined with very high inflation. At the beginning of the year the government refused to accept this possibility. The Economic Planning Agency forecast for fiscal 1974 called for 2.5 percent real growth, with a 10.4 percent rise in the GNP deflator, a 14.6 percent rise in wholesale prices, and a very modest current-account deficit of $450 million. Even these figures represented a downward revision made between the time the forecast was discussed at a cabinet meeting at the beginning of the year and its announcement to the Diet at the end of January. The somewhat more cautious organization of big businesses, Keidanren, predicted 1.4 percent growth.[34] In fact, real GNP growth was –0.4 percent in fiscal 1974, the GNP deflator was up 18.9 percent, wholesale prices were up 23.5 percent, and the current account was in deficit by $2.3 billion. On a calendar year basis, GNP growth was –1.4 percent, wholesale price inflation was 31.4 percent (following a 15.8 percent jump in 1973), and consumer prices were up 24.5 percent.[35] For a country used to 10 percent growth this was a devastating blow.

Two decades of rapid economic growth had eliminated the large pool of underemployed labor in Japan, and in the tightened labor market conditions of the early 1970s, unions were determined not to lose economic ground when inflation heated up. Union wages in Japan are set by one-year contracts, and all unions negotiate their contracts in the spring, during a period known as the *shuntō* (spring offensive). The outcome, as measured by a government survey after the negotiations were over, was an average increase in wages of 32.9 percent, following a 20.1 percent rise in 1973. This figure is somewhat higher than the one shown by published wage data for all workers (in establishments of thirty or more employees) because only part of the work force is unionized. But even the data for all workers show a 27 percent increase in wages for 1974.[36] These high wage settlements became a mechanism for spreading the effects of inflation broadly through the economy.

Faced with simultaneous inflation and recession, public attitudes were gloomy. A survey at the beginning of January indicated 22 percent of those polled expected shortages of goods to last three years or more (including 9 percent who said shortages would last forever). Those who felt that they personally suffered from shortages were predictably more numerous among younger Japanese than among the older generations, who were used to living in more austere conditions.[37] Another poll found that 73 percent felt the Japanese economy was frail and worried about what would happen to it.[38]

While external factors—the oil shortage and price rise and the increases in the prices of other imported materials—can be blamed for much of the economic problem facing Japan, government policies may have made the situation worse. At the macroeconomic level the government made mistakes in both monetary policy and fiscal policy, supplying too much stimulus when inflation was rising. At the microeconomic level the government responded to inflation by controlling prices of some goods and services, thereby postponing needed price adjustments and distorting prices in the economy.

Both monetary and fiscal policies had been expansionary in 1971–72 to stimulate the economy following the shock of yen revaluation. Not only did such action help the economy, but it also took some of the upward pressure off the yen–dollar exchange rate by diverting goods from exports to domestic demand (at that time monetary authorities were still resisting appreciation of the yen, hoping to keep it at the new parity of 308 to the dollar set by the Smithsonian agreement of December 1971). According to EPA statistics, real GNP growth in 1971 (measured in 1980 prices) had been only 4.3 percent but had rebounded to 8.5 percent in 1972, partly because of these policies. Fiscal expansion was also related to implementation in 1973 of Prime Minister Tanaka's ideas for improving welfare in a high-growth environment.

Some prominent Japanese economists, especially the new breed of monetarists, have chosen to place the blame for inflation on monetary policy. They have argued that the government allowed the money supply to grow too fast in 1971–72 and that to some extent policy was out of control, since extensive unsterilized direct intervention in exchange markets had the side effect of increasing domestic money supply. According to a number of senior economists, including Yoshio Suzuki of the Bank of Japan, Ryūtarō Komiya of Tokyo University, and Seiji Shimpo of the EPA, the Keynesian economists in control of macroeconomic policy seriously underestimated the inflationary potential of excessive monetary growth.[39]

To evaluate the contention, table 2–3 presents data on the increase in money supply from 1972 to 1975. By the second quarter of 1972, both M1 and M2 were 20 percent higher than a year earlier; the measures peaked at thirty percent for M1 and twenty-five percent for M2 in the second quarter of 1973, then increases moderated for the rest of 1973 and all of 1974. By 1975 M1 was rising at less than ten percent and M2 at about eleven percent. Such rates of increase were not unusual—money supply growth exceeded twenty percent for several years in the 1960s. What was unusual in 1973 was that the economy responded with more inflation and less growth than in the earlier years. Monetary stimulus came at a time when the economy was operating close to capacity; the supply of additional goods and services could not meet the increased demand created by the increased supply of money.

Table 2–3. Money Supply Growth, Quarterly, 1972–75[a]

Percent increase from same quarter of previous year

Quarter	M1	M2
1972		
First	27.7	24.0
Second	19.9	22.8
Third	19.5	22.0
Fourth	24.7	24.7
1973		
First	27.4	25.1
Second	29.9	24.7
Third	27.0	22.9
Fourth	16.7	16.8
1974		
First	15.4	15.1
Second	15.7	13.4
Third	10.1	10.9
Fourth	11.5	11.5
1975		
First	9.8	11.3
Second	7.4	11.4
Third	9.8	13.2
Fourth	11.1	14.5

Sources: Bank of Japan, *Economic Statistics Monthly* (January 1973–75), p. 13; (January 1976), p. 15; and Bank of Japan, Economic Statistics Annual, 1971, p. 11.

a. Figures are based on money supply at end of the final month for each quarter.

The problem of inflation could be attributed to a timing error; governments should not stimulate their economies when they are at cyclical peaks. However, such a situation had not arisen in the previous two decades, when monetary stimulus had worked because the supply capacity of the economy had responded very flexibly. The mistake, then, was the failure to recognize that the era of extremely high potential real growth was coming to an end, so that stimulating demand would generate more inflation and less growth of economic supply than before. The neat and simple division of the world into profligate Keynesians and sensible monetarists (made by economists such as Shimpo) is hardly the point; the Japanese economy was changing, and very few people recognized that fact regardless of their theoretical stripes. When policies have worked well for twenty years, it is difficult to be critical of continuing to use them.

Authorities finally realized that inflation was becoming a problem and tightened monetary policy, but the action was slow in having any impact. The large current-account surplus and the previous period of monetary ease had increased liquidity so much that the corporate sector did not feel the bite for some time. In tightening monetary policy, the Bank of Japan relied primarily on two instruments: the discount rate at which it lends funds to the commercial banks and "window guidance," direct and forceful "advice" to commercial banks on the rate their lending activity should increase. From 4.25 percent at the beginning of 1973, the discount rate was raised in a series of steps between April and December to 9.0 percent. This in itself was an unusual move, since during the 1950s and 1960s the discount rate remained very steady while window guidance acted as the main monetary policy instrument.[40] Under the influence of tighter monetary policy, though, the rate of increase in money supply did not sink below 20 percent until the fourth quarter of 1973 (see table 2–3).

Once monetary stringency was implemented, the Bank of Japan was very slow to reverse policy. The discount rate stayed at 9.0 percent until April 1975 and was not back to 1973 levels until 1977. While this may seem an unduly long time to maintain brakes on the economy, it was intended to disrupt inflationary expectations.

As for fiscal policy, the budget for fiscal 1973 was intended to be expansionary, aided by the beginning of the greater welfare and social infrastructure expenditures pushed by Prime Minister Tanaka. By the time the budget was passed by the Diet at the end of March, though, Ministry of Finance authorities realized that the economy was overheating and expenditures should be scaled back or postponed. Actual expenditures for the fiscal year were 4.4 percent below budget, with the cutbacks concentrated mostly in public works spending, which were 14 percent below the budgeted level.[41]

The Tanaka plan may have contributed to inflation in another way as well. A key element of Tanaka's concept for maintaining high growth was to spread industrial investment more evenly around the country. When he became prime minister after propounding these ideas, land speculation intensified. Land prices in urban areas had been rising at 13 to 20 percent each year since 1968, followed by increases of 24 percent in 1973 and 23 percent in 1974. This bubble was then followed by falling prices—they did not return to 1974 levels until 1978. It may be incorrect to place the entire blame for the rapid inflation of land prices on the Tanaka plan, since high inflation predated his proposals by several years, but land speculation certainly fed the overall inflationary mood of the nation.

At the microeconomic level the government stepped in soon after the beginning of the oil crisis to control certain prices. The Diet passed two laws giving the government power to impose price controls, and under this authority, the Ministry of International Trade and Industry placed controls on petroleum products. During the winter of 1973–74, liquefied petroleum gas and kerosene prices were controlled, since they were important for home cooking and heating. Prices on these products were allowed to rise by 62 percent in March 1974, but those of certain other basic commodities and essential consumer goods were then brought under MITI administrative guidance.[42]

These measures came with expected theatrics. Corporation presidents were hauled before the Diet, where angry politicians accused them of price gouging, while the oil industry countered that the controls left them operating at a deficit as the OAPEC price increases on crude oil came into effect. Price controls finally came off in a series of steps between August and September 1974 as MITI decided supply conditions had eased enough that the danger of hyperinflation was over.

This effort to control prices was a serious (though short-lived) mistake by the government, since the policy created distortions in relative prices. It also provoked threats by some international oil companies to cut crude oil supplies to Japan if prices for refined products were not allowed to increase (a threat arising not out of the nationalism earlier assumed by the Japanese press but out of basic profit motives). Perhaps the most egregious episode of price control, though, involved the Japanese National Railways. A government-owned entity, the JNR was required to have its basic fares approved by the Diet. In 1972 the railroad submitted a request for fare increases to the Ministry of Transportation, which accepted it and passed it on to the Diet, where it was approved in 1973. But implementation of the increase was postponed because of the oil shock and the desire of the government to hold down any price over which it had control. Not until October 1974 was the increase allowed to go into effect. By then the 21 percent adjustment that had been approved was considerably below the more than 50 percent rise in wholesale and consumer prices that took place over the same period of time, leaving the railroad with an even worse deficit problem that subsequently proved to be nearly intractable.[43]

Summary

The events of 1973 and 1974 are important for understanding subsequent economic developments in Japan. These two years included a variety of symbolic and real events that heralded an era of lower economic growth.

First, the problems were far more extensive than just the oil crisis of October 1973: the economy was overheated and inflation was building early in 1973; prices for imports other than oil were also rising; government provided too much monetary stimulus; and consumers reacted hysterically to reports of shortages of some basic goods.

Second, the monetary and fiscal policy actions taken in 1971 and 1972 that helped feed the inflationary burst of 1973 and 1974 demonstrate the economy was already undergoing a long-term structural change. Unrecognized by most analysts, growth potential was declining. Thus the effort to sustain the high growth of demand generated high inflation. Rather than the smooth decline in growth foreseen by such analysts as Denison and Chung, the pattern was a bubble of inflation followed by recession.

Third, recognizing Japan's extreme anxiety over the future is important for understanding later policy actions. It seems puzzling that the Japanese would describe their large and successful economy as frail, but events like those of 1973–74 helped further ingrain that attitude. That a real recession could occur after more than twenty years of uninterrupted growth only convinced them they should not be overly swayed by current conditions in setting policy. In the private sector, decisions on business investments depend on expectations about the future, and the combination of the oil shock, problems with supplies of other imported raw materials, and recession punctured optimistic expectations. The end of the technology lag between Japan and other industrial nations was reducing the expected profits from plant and equipment investment anyway, but these events lowered expectations more quickly and dramatically. Government also became more cautious. Large current-account surpluses might seem to call for easing import restrictions, for example, but some officials still worried that the day could come when Japan could have trouble paying for imports.

Finally, the burst of inflation made a deep impression on government officials responsible for macroeconomic policy. Japan had experienced hyperinflation of 200 percent a year and higher just after the war, and the 1974 experience raised the specter of a repeat performance, which was enough to instill a considerable dose of fear and caution in government officials. This affected later Japanese policy, with greater weight given to controlling inflation and less to stimulating demand.

THE ERA OF SLOWER GROWTH

From 1974 to 1985 Japan suffered no more recessions, but growth was far slower than before. Average annual growth for the entire period was 4.3 percent (table 2–4), which was less than half the rate that prevailed in the previous twenty years. Still, Japan managed to outdistance all other OECD member countries, though by a smaller margin.

Since 1974 the share of growth due to the expansion of net exports of goods and services has often been high (see table 2–4). Despite the small share of GNP accounted for by exports and imports, net export expansion contributed 38 percent of all growth in the economy between 1980 and 1985.[44] Even in 1984, which the Japanese government tried to tout as a year in which domestic-led growth was returning, net exports accounted for nearly 40 percent of growth. Only when the yen rose strongly against the dollar in 1985 did net exports begin to decline in importance (to 21.2 percent of total growth). By 1986 the effect of yen appreciation became so strong that net exports began contracting, constituting a drag on the economy.

In Japanese the new era is labeled *antei seichō*, or stable growth. This is a highly inappropriate term in two senses. First, there was nothing unstable about the high-growth era; it was unusually high and would necessarily come to an end eventually, but it was not based on unpredictable or fragile factors. Second, "stable" could be taken to mean more steady, but growth between 1974 and 1984 was not particularly steady. Even if the exceptional recession of 1974 is excluded, GNP growth rates varied from 2.7 percent in 1975 to 5.3 percent in 1977 and 1979. From 1976 to 1979 growth was very steady (ranging only from 4.8 percent to 5.3 percent), but thereafter it declined continuously to 3.1 percent in 1982. Even in the late 1970s when the overall growth rate was steady, the relative contributions of the economy's components varied greatly. Exports were important to growth from 1975 through 1977 but acted as a net drag in 1978 and 1979.

When growth returned to the economy after 1974 and Japan continued to perform well compared with other industrial countries, government officials regained confidence. They pointed proudly to their ability to guide the economy through the oil shock of 1979 without double-digit inflation or a recession. This confidence is clearly evident in the comments of Yoshio Suzuki of the Bank of Japan: "We owe this success [in the second oil shock] very much to the transformation of the monetary policy during the recent five-year period."[45] The principal change was that controlling inflation was given a much higher priority. Tokyo eased monetary policy very slowly after inflation came under control in 1975 in order to wring inflationary expectations out of the economy. However, given the steady slide in GNP growth rates from 1979 to 1983 and the international frictions resulting from external surpluses, it is not clear that the government was as successful in responding to the 1979 oil shock as it originally thought. Nevertheless its confidence continued, and controlling inflation remained an important factor in policy.

Confidence returned in the private sector as well. Despite slower growth, lower profits, and greater uncertainty about the future, corporations in the export sector became increasingly certain of their international competitiveness. Put less politely, many corporate executives became arrogant and contemptuous of foreign competitors. To a certain extent this attitude was reflected by the public, who, for instance, expressed doubt that the United States had anything to export that they would want to buy. Even some academic economists espoused the ascendancy of Japan: Tsuneo Iida of Nagoya University argued that Japan was not unique in terms of the model that explains its economic performance, but that as an economy fitting the neoclassical model, Japan simply performed better than other countries. He saw the country as providing a more competitive environment in the private sector and exhibiting better internal information flows so that the economy could operate more efficiently and more smoothly than the economies of the United States or European countries.[46]

The newly recovered self-confidence did not lead to rising expectations about future growth. By the early 1980s long-term forecasts tended to converge upon 4 percent real GNP growth, a very reasonable figure. Once slower growth was fully accepted, even the optimists' predictions were not far above 4 percent. Considering the obvious disappointment in light of the expectations that prevailed before 1973, Japan managed this transition relatively well. Labor unions, for example, accepted without a great deal of strife the slowing of growth and its implications for smaller wage increases. Growing at less than half the rate of the earlier period but faster on average than other industrial countries, Japan could easily see its cup as either half full or half empty; it chose to see the cup as half full.

Table 2–4. GNP Growth, 1973–85

Year	Real GNP (trillions of 1980 yen)	GNP growth rate (percent)	Percentage points of GNP growth due to net exports[a]	Share of GNP growth due to net exports[b]
1973	185.9	7.9	−3.0	-27.5
1974	183.3	−1.4	1.2	...[c]
1975	188.2	2.7	1.9	71.1
1976	197.2	4.8	1.0	20.9
1977	207.7	5.3	0.9	16.9
1978	218.5	5.2	−0.9	−14.8
1979	230.1	5.3	−1.4	−20.9
1980	239.9	4.3	3.4	79.8
1981	248.7	3.7	1.5	40.9
1982	256.4	3.1	0.3	9.7
1983	264.7	3.2	1.5	46.3
1984	278.1	5.1	1.3	25.7
1985	291.2	4.7	1.0	21.2

Source: Economic Planning Agency, *Annual Report on National Accounts, 1987* (Tokyo: EPA, 1987), pp. 118–21.

a. Growth of exports and imports is weighted by their shares in GNP. Net exports is exports minus imports. The figures thus show the percentage points of growth due to expansion (or contraction) of net exports. For example, in 1984 net exports contributed 1.3 percentage points out of the total 5.1 percent real expansion of GNP in that year.

b. Percentage points of growth due to net exports divided by GNP growth rate. Thus the 1.3 percentage points due to net exports in 1984 was 25.7 percent of the 5.1 percent GNP growth rate.

c. Item is meaningless.

Causes of the Slowdown

Why has Japan grown so much more slowly than it did before 1974? Why has its performance relative to other industrial nations also dropped? The disruption and confusion of 1973–74 was so strong in Japan that it is tempting to blame the oil crisis for everything. But the country did not return to its former high rates of expansion even after the effects of the oil shock should have dissipated. Since oil again rose in price in 1979, one could argue that Japan suffered through a prolonged adjustment to both episodes, so that by the mid-1980s a renewal of higher growth rates would occur, especially when oil prices began dropping. Higher oil prices are clearly one element in explaining what happened, but they are only one element and not the most important one.

The key to understanding Japan's slower growth rate is that the process of catching up with other industrial nations ended, which meant that rapid leaps in productivity could no longer be generated by importing foreign technology, However, other elements were also involved. The growth-accounting framework provides a useful way to organize and look at these factors. This is the same framework used by Denison and Chung and Fried and Trezise in their estimates of future Japanese economic growth.

If certain simplifying assumptions are made about the nature of production in the economy (unitary returns to scale and disembodied technological change),[47] then the production relationship can be described as

(1) $$Y_t = C\, L_t^a\, K_t^b\, R_t; \quad a + b = 1,$$

where Y is economic output (GNP), C is a constant, L is labor input, K is capital input, R is a residual accounting for all sources of output not included in labor and capital, a is the share of labor in national income, b is the share of capital in national income, and t is the time period.

The change over time can then be expressed as

(2) $$\frac{Y_t}{Y_{t-1}} = \frac{C\, L_t^a\, K_t^b\, R_t}{C\, L_{t-1}^a\, L_{t-1}^b\, R_{t-1}} = \left(\frac{L_t}{L_{t-1}}\right)^a \left(\frac{K_t}{K_{t-1}}\right)^b \left(\frac{R_t}{R_{t-1}}\right).$$

Expressed in logarithms,

(3) $$\ln Y_t - \ln Y_{t-1} = a(\ln L_t - \ln L_{t-1}) + b(\ln K_t - \ln K_{t-1}) \\ + (\ln R_t - \ln R_{t-1}).$$

Letting $\Delta y = \ln Y_t - \ln Y_{t-1}$ and so forth yields

(4) $\Delta y = a\,(\Delta l) + b\,(\Delta k) + \Delta r.$

Essentially, equation 4 says that the growth in GNP (expressed in logarithms) must be equal to the growth in labor and capital, weighted by their shares in national income, plus a residual that captures increased productivity from technological change and other elements that do not show up as either labor or capital inputs.

Table 2–5. Growth of Private Fixed Nonresidential Capital Investment, Selected Periods, 1956–85

Percent

Period	Average annual real growth
1956–1960[a]	22.2
1961–1965[a]	10.8
1966–1970	21.7
1971–1973	4.7
1974–1978	−1.0
1979–1985	7.6
1956–1973	16.0
1974–1985	3.9

Sources: Economic Planning Agency, *Annual Report on National Accounts*, 1987, pp. 118–21; 1970, pp. 86–87; and Bank of Japan, *Economic Statistics Annual*, 1971 p. 289.

a. 1956–65 average annual real growth is in 1965 prices. Other periods are based on 1980 prices.

As mentioned earlier, Denison and Chung found that in the high-growth era all these factors grew more rapidly than in other countries. In the slower-growth era all factors grew more slowly than before. Growth of capital stock was affected by the end of the catch-up process, rising energy costs, diversification of social goals (redirecting investment to such "nonproductive" uses as pollution control or constructing sidewalks), and slower growth abroad. Of these, closing the technology gap appears most important. The change in labor input is a relatively straightforward and simple factor to measure and forecast, but slower growth of labor contributed relatively little to slower GNP growth. Finally, productivity change was affected by the end of the catch-up process, of gains from reallocating labor from agriculture, and of dramatic increases in economies of scale.

SLOWER CAPITAL FORMATION. From 1956 to 1973 real fixed nonresidential capital investment grew at a 16 percent real annual rate, though with some unevenness (table 2–5). From 1974 to 1985, however, investment growth dropped to only 3.9 percent annually. The reduction was heavily affected by average annual real declines of –1.0 percent from 1974 to 1978. This drop can be attributed to the one-time shock of the 1973 oil crisis and a temporary deceleration effect as the economy slowed: corporations had invested in expectations of continued high growth and now found they had more capacity than needed, so investment temporarily dropped while output caught up with installed capacity. After this temporary adjustment, investment grew at a 7.6 percent real annual rate, but even this was far below the growth before 1973.

END OF TECHNOLOGICAL CATCH-UP. The end of the technological gap between Japan and other developed countries was critical for the slower growth of both capital formation and productivity in Japan. The impact of technological equality on capital formation was straightforward: because rapid increases in productivity based on imported technology were no longer possible, corporations could no longer expect the high levels of profit from new investment to which they had become accustomed. With lower expectations, investment decelerated. What had once been a powerful incentive for investment quickly evaporated in the mid-1970s.[48]

The end of the catch-up process also meant the cost of acquiring new, more productive technology was higher. While importing technology is by no means inexpensive, research and development expenditures are far lower than when technology is entirely developed at home. The change in Japan's position is clear from increases in research and development expenditures. By 1982 these expenditures (exclusive of social science research) were 2.20 percent of GNP, up from 1.70 percent in 1973 and 1.27 percent in 1965 (U.S. expenditures were 2.61 percent of GNP in 1982).[49] Thus Japan's R&D expenditures provide further indirect evidence that it was moving to the world technological frontier.

By the mid-1980s Japan had become the acknowledged world technological leader in a number of fields (including iron and steel, dynamic random-access memory chips, and automobiles). But no matter how successful it is at generating its own technology (or even continuing to adapt advances from other countries), the profit incentive from investment incorporating these new technologies remains smaller than when it lagged behind and was catching up. With a smaller profit incentive, corporate investment grew at a slower pace). Reduced growth of investment as a result of closing the technology gap thus becomes important in explaining reduced productivity growth due to technological change and economies of scale because these are closely linked to capital formation.

Table 2–6. Impact of Changes in Cost of Imported Energy, 1970–85

Year	Import price index for energy (1980 = 100)[a]	Percent change from previous year	Percent change in GDP deflator from previous year	Terms of trade[b] (1980 = 100)
1970	12.4	0.8	7.7	224.5
1971	14.3	15.3	5.6	221.3
1972	13.8	-3.5	5.6	223.6
1973	14.9	8.0	12.9	203.3
1974	43.7	193.3	20.8	162.3
1975	52.3	19.7	7.7	145.1
1976	56.1	7.3	7.2	137.0
1977	53.9	-3.9	5.8	136.7
1978	43.7	-18.9	4.8	154.7
1979	57.8	32.3	3.0	133.3
1980	100.0	73.0	3.8	100.0
1981	109.7	9.7	3.2	99.6
1982	121.3	10.6	1.9	95.9
1983	107.0	-11.8	0.8	97.8
1984	101.8	-4.9	1.2	101.8
1985	102.1	0.3	1.5	102.9

Sources: Bank of Japan, *Economic Statistics Annual, 1985*, pp. 311–12; and Economic Planning Agency, *Annual Report on National Accounts, 1987*, pp. 166–69.

a. Includes imported petroleum, coal, and natural gas.

b. Ratio of the unit price of exports to the unit price of imports.

HIGHER ENERGY COSTS. By 1985 the wholesale price index for imported oil, coal, and natural gas was more than eight times higher than in 1970 (table 2–6). The big increases came in the oil shock years, with a 193 percent gain in 1974 and a 73 percent gain in 1980, although as in other countries, the trend in energy costs was uneven, with declines in some of the years after the oil shocks. These increases far exceeded the overall inflation rate in the economy represented by the GDP deflator. The changes were more important for Japan than most other industrialized countries since it depended on imports for such a large portion of its total energy needs (83 percent in 1984).

Among energy sources, Japan is most dependent on petroleum. In 1973 it relied on oil for 76 percent of its total energy needs; even as late as 1985 oil accounted for 57 percent of total needs (compared with 42 percent for the United States in 1984). And because Japan produces almost no crude oil itself, its import dependency is virtually 100 percent. It is especially dependent on Middle Eastern crude oil—in the early 1970s for more than 80 percent of its petroleum needs; in 1985, 69 percent.[50]

How did the rising price of oil affect the economy? First, like other oil-importing countries, Japan suffered a loss of income to the OPEC members. As table 2–6 shows, its terms of trade worsened (meaning that the unit price of imports rose relative to the price of exports) in the immediate aftermath of the 1973 and 1979 oil shocks. With 1980 as 100, the terms of trade deteriorated from 203.3 in 1973 to 137.0 in 1976 and from 133.3 in 1979 to 95.9 in 1982.

In the longer run, again like other oil-importing countries, Japan also faced adjustment costs in coping with the relatively higher price of oil, but its problems were more serious than theirs. Its petroleum, petrochemical, aluminum refining, synthetic textile, and other industries were dependent on petroleum or petroleum-derived inputs that became relatively more expensive than in other industrialized countries. And in some industries Japan relied on petroleum-based energy, whereas other countries did not. As a result, its petroleum-dependent industries lost their competitiveness. Government policy may have exacerbated these problems. Import barriers erected in the 1950s and 1960s encouraged investment in some industries that, even before the oil shocks, had little chance of becoming competitive.

The aluminum industry provides the outstanding example of this adjustment problem. Smelting aluminum requires a great deal of electric energy, and aluminum smelters are usually located near sources of cheap hydroelectric power. In Japan the industry depended on oil-fired electric power plants. Because of import protection and new plants incorporating state-of-the-art technology, investment was attracted to aluminum refining during the 1960s. By 1979, though, under the combined impact of the two oil-price hikes, the industry could no longer compete against imports. Despite efforts to smooth and slow the process of decline (a euphemism for providing protection from the cold winds of international competition), companies went out of business or shut down capacity at a very rapid rate, so that by 1984 imports accounted for 71 percent of domestic consumption of aluminum in Japan (compared with 7 percent in 1965).[51]

Higher energy costs, then, caused a significant loss of income and a severe reduction of capital formation in some industries. Productive resources had to be removed from the declining industries, and higher oil prices meant lower expected rates of return, slowing new investment in others. However, the implications of higher oil prices were complex, and where capital (such as added equipment for saving energy) could be substituted for energy, the oil shock may have actually stimulated capital formation.

DIVERSIFICATION OF SOCIAL GOALS. The late 1960s and early 1970s brought a surge of public protest over pollution, and outspoken demands for increased investment in better roads, better housing, and other amenities. In response, government and industry reallocated some capital investment from plant and equipment, which had been heavily emphasized since the war. These actions clearly improved the quality of life but at the risk of slowing the steady growth of the economy, since investment in factories expands an economy's capacity to increase the supply of goods and services, while investment in pollution control or other amenities adds nothing measurable to future productivity. Sidewalks separating pedestrians from busy roads make life more comfortable and safer, but only the initial construction cost shows up in GNP statistics. In addition, changed public attitudes can cause an unfavorable environment for investment. In the United States, for instance, the costs imposed by lengthy public protests have largely halted investment in nuclear power plants.

In Japan the shift in public attitudes did cause reallocations, but the overall climate for investment was not noticeably worsened. The changes were also ambiguous in their implications. In a strict growth-accounting sense, reallocation in investment slowed the growth of output per unit of capital investment. However, the shift came at a time when investment in plant and equipment was decelerating anyway. Thus the increased investment in social infrastructure helped keep total investment in the economy higher than it would otherwise have been, stimulating economic growth.

During the 1950s the Japanese shared a rather broad consensus on the desirability of rapid economic growth. People were willing to work long hours and endure a lack of investment in social amenities on the assumption that this represented the best road to future prosperity.[52] In fact, the belief that this was the only feasible route to follow was so strong that many Japanese do not see even in retrospect that any personal sacrifice was involved; there was no realistic choice except to work very hard and do without if the country—and the individual—were to prosper.

The disintegration of this broad public consensus in the late 1960s was most visible and dramatic on issues relating to pollution. Rapid industrialization had been accompanied by severe degradation of the environment that ultimately resulted in a series of incidents of pollution-induced illnesses. In Minamata, mercury from an industrial process that was routinely dumped in a river poisoned hundreds of people and deformed their offspring. In Yokkaichi, smoke and fumes from a new complex of petrochemical plants created an upsurge in asthma and other serious respiratory conditions. In various parts of the country, *itai-itai* episodes of severe cadmium poisoning were caused by dumping wastes from lead and zinc smelting operations into rivers. In addition to enduring these acute incidents, some of which led to protracted and highly publicized court struggles, a broad segment of the public was suffering from generally increased air and water pollution. By the early 1970s, police directing traffic in Tokyo were given special roadside booths where they could take turns breathing pure oxygen. Newspapers and evening television news programs carried stories of groups of schoolchildren suddenly afflicted with fits of coughing or difficulty in breathing as stray clouds of chemicals drifted over playgrounds. Children being rushed en masse to hospitals for treatment did not create a good public image for industry, and people severely criticized government policies that allowed industrialization to bring about such severe conditions.

As public pressure mounted, the government reacted with new legislation and administrative action. In 1970 the Diet passed pollution control legislation. From 1970 to 1973 the central government's pollution control budget more than tripled, and if investments in related organizations for pollution control are added, expenditures almost quadrupled to ¥430 billion ($1.6 billion at 1973 exchange rates). Regional and local government spending in these same years rose more than 2.5 times to ¥954 billion (more than $3.5 billion). Although by fiscal 1984 the central government's environmental spending (again including transfers to other organizations) was up to ¥1.15 trillion (approximately $4 billion), the enormous increases had reached their limit. Government budget deficits had forced reductions of 2.5 percent in environmental expenditures between fiscal 1983 and fiscal 1984.[53]

Increased government spending for pollution control was matched by rapid increases in expenditures by private industry. In the iron and steel industry, spending for pollution control as a ratio to total sales rose from 0.9 percent in 1970 to 1.8 percent in 1974. The paper and pulp industry ratio went from 1.1 percent to 3.0 percent, while in chemicals it rose from 0.4 percent to 1.3 percent. Total private-sector investment in pollution abatement was roughly double expenditures by the central government and almost equal to those of local governments.[54]

These increased expenditures brought about a significant and visible improvement in environmental quality. Daily warnings about air quality (issued when photochemical concentrations exceed certain limits for one hour) were down from a peak of 328 in 1973 to a low of about 60 in 1981, followed by a sharp increase to 131 in 1983.[55] The number of people officially recognized as suffering from the effects of photochemical air pollution dropped from 46,081 in 1975 to a low of 446 in 1982, followed by a modest increase to 1,721 in 1983. (The unwillingness of some people to be officially recognized or designated as suffering from pollution problems may have contributed to the decline.) Regardless of the accuracy of official statistics of this sort, though, even casual observation provides striking evidence of the changes: local news programs no longer show children being rushed to hospitals from school playgrounds, Mount Fuji is visible on more days of the year from downtown Tokyo than in the early 1970s, and the major cities look and feel cleaner.

While less dramatic than pollution issues, gaps in social amenities also received increased government attention in the 1970s—and improvements in social infrastructure and social welfare confirm that the politicians' speeches were backed up by substantial increases in public investment. The mileage of roads newly paved in 1980, for instance, exceeded that of roads paved in all of Japan through 1960. The distance of roads paralleled by sidewalks doubled between 1970 and 1975, and almost doubled again by 1981. Investment in paved roads and sidewalks represented a general improvement in quality and safety, contributing to a dramatic drop in traffic fatalities. From 13.3 traffic deaths per million vehicle-kilometers in 1970, fatalities dropped to 3.5 per million in 1980 (the comparable figure for the United States is 2.0 per million vehicle-kilometers).[56]

Traffic safety was far from the only improvement. In 1970 only 20 percent of the population of Japan lived in districts served by public sewage treatment systems, a figure that rose to 32.5 percent by 1984. The situation is better than it appears. As table 2–7 shows, 58 percent of Japanese dwellings had flush toilets in 1983, up from 9.3 percent in 1963, with much of the expansion taking place after the late 1960s. A significant share of the improvement during the 1970s came from private investment in septic tanks, since the percentage of dwellings equipped with flush toilets expanded so much faster than the percentage of population living in sewage treatment districts.[57] Nevertheless, one is left wondering whether it is the improvement over time or the continued high percentage of houses with primitive facilities that is the more striking. By 1983, 74.3 percent of U.S. dwelling units were connected to public sewer systems, and only 2.4 percent of occupied dwellings lacked some or all plumbing facilities.[58]

Table 2–7. Dwellings with Flush Toilets and Percentage of Population Living in Districts with Sewage Treatment Systems, Selected Years, 1963–83

Year	Total dwellings (millions)	Dwellings with lush toilets (millions)	Percent with toilets	Percent of population in districts with sewage treatment systems
1963	20.4	1.9	9.3	...
1968	24.2	4.1	16.9	...
1970	...	...	...	19.6
1973	28.7	9.0	31.4	...
1975	...	...	...	24.7
1978	32.2	14.8	46.0	...
1980	...	...	...	28.0
1982	...	...	...	30.0
1983	34.7	20.2	58.2	...
1984	...	...	...	32.5

Source: Management and Coordination Agency, *Japan Statistical Yearbook, 1986* (Tokyo: Statistics Bureau, 1986), pp. 24–25, 516–17, 619.

Quality of life improved in other ways. The total area of local parks doubled from 1970 to 1981. The percentage of households with telephone service between 1970 and 1980 tripled from 25 percent to 77 percent.[59] (Since Nippon Telegraph and Telephone was a government-owned corporation, this change was also closely related to government policy decisions, which had favored business phone installations in the 1950s).

Housing, too, showed some improvement. The European criticism that the Japanese lived in rabbit hutches became something of a cliché in the 1980s. The share of government funds in the Fiscal Investment and Loan Program (FILP) directed toward housing rose from 11 percent in 1965 to 25 percent by 1980, while the share of FILP funds for the Japan Development Bank and the Eximbank (both of which lend exclusively to the corporate sector) dropped from 19 percent to 8 percent. These figures nicely demonstrate the government's movement from promoting industrial growth to encouraging a broader improvement of living conditions. But the picture is ambiguous because although greater resources were channeled into housing in the 1970s, the average dwelling remained significantly smaller than in the United States in the 1980s.

The greater availability of public funds, rising income levels, and changing demographics (fewer people per household because of both fewer children and fewer three-generation households) gradually produced a rising amount of space per person in Japanese houses. From approximately 14.5 square meters per household member in 1958, the figure rose rather steadily to 25.6 square meters by 1983. There is no indication of any acceleration of change in the 1970s; in fact, the average annual growth in space per person was 2.6 percent from 1959 to 1968 and 2.1 percent in the 1970s. But if one focuses on the increase in dwelling size, the picture changes. The average size of newly constructed dwelling units increased 1.4 percent annually in the 1960s and 3.3 percent annually in the 1970s, despite slower growth of personal incomes in the latter period.[60] The contrast with the space-per-person data comes from a stabilization in the number of family members per dwelling. Still, the increase in living space left the Japanese with dwellings just over half the size of American ones. In 1982 the total amount of heated space (excluding basements and attics, amenities that do not exist in Japanese houses) per household member in the United States was 49.5 square meters, almost double the 25.6 square meter value for Japan in 1983.[61]

How should Japanese housing be evaluated? It increased markedly in size, and the living space of dwellings increased more rapidly in the 1970s than before. Any visitor can also readily see that the quality of housing underwent an astounding change from the 1960s to the 1980s. Houses are no longer flimsy, drafty, or poorly constructed. And although space remains tight compared with housing in the United States, even if income levels were equal to those of Americans, the Japanese would not choose to build houses of similar size because land is more expensive and less available, and people want to live in individual units close to major urban centers (and must therefore squeeze together).[62] But while the improvements have been significant and size parity with the United States is not to be expected, the stock of Japanese housing in the mid-1980s can be still further improved. One-quarter of the housing was constructed in 1960 or earlier, and much of it is inadequate by 1980s' standards for size and quality.

For a country where the common wisdom is that government policy tends to be heavily business-oriented, the strong position taken on pollution and social spending may seem surprising. Many reasons account for the policy shift, but two stand out: the deficiencies and problems were very obvious and serious, and the adoption of pollution and social welfare as issues by opposition parties (especially at the local level) called for a response from the central government.

The late 1960s were a time of serious student protests on a variety of other issues—the Vietnam War, rising tuition, government authority in general, and other fashionable causes. While much of this is not particularly relevant to the growth of the economy, a strong antigovernment, antibusiness, proenvironmental thread ran through it all, as when radical students joined with the local farmers to protest construction of a new Tokyo international airport in the middle of rice fields, a protest begun in the 1960s and still continuing. However, the movement peaked in the late 1960s, when some universities were shut down for months at a time, and largely evaporated by the mid-1970s except for the actions of a very few, very small, but very radical nuisance groups. As in other countries, though, the breadth of the movement in the late 1960s was sufficient to cause concern within the government that policies were out of touch with public needs or desires.

More to the point for the Liberal Democratic party than the student protests was its slipping majority in the lower house of the Diet. Had the LDP chosen not to respond to public desires, it could easily have lost political control by the late 1970s to some form of coalition of opposition parties. Table 2–8 shows the distribution of Diet seats among the political parties. After comfortable majorities ranging from forty-five to sixty-two seats in the 1950s and 1960s, the election of 1972 whittled the LDP majority to twenty-five seats. In 1976 and 1979, the party did not win a majority of the Diet seats, but retained its majority position because formerly independent candidates joined its ranks after the elections. And although the election of 1980 brought a majority of twenty-eight seats, the election of 1983 put the LDP back into a minority that it again made up through the acquisition of independents and a coalition with a small splinter group called the New Liberal Club. Not until 1986, when it once more achieved a large majority, did the party feel that it had returned to a strong position.

Table 2–8. Number of Seats in Lower House of the Diet, by Party, Election Years 1958–86

Party	1958	1960	1963	1967	1969	1972	1976	1979	1980	1983	1986
Liberal Democratic	287	296	283	277	288	271	249	248	284	250	300
Socialist	166	145	144	140	90	118	123	107	107	112	85
Democratic Socialist	...	17	23	30	31	19	29	35	32	38	26
Komeito	...	...	...	25	47	29	55	57	33	58	56
Communist	1	3	5	5	14	38	17	39	29	26	26
Other	1	0	0	0	0	2	17	6	15	11	10
Independents	12	6	12	9	6	14	21	19	11	16	9
Total	467	467	467	486	486	491	511	511	511	511	512
Liberal Democratic majority	53	62	49	34	45	25	−7[a]	−8[a]	28	−6[a]	44

Sources: Takayoshi Miyagawa, ed., *Seiji Handobukku*, 1985 (Political Handbook, 1985) (Tokyo: Seiji Kōhō Sentā), p. 210; 1980, p. 200; Hans H. Baerwald, *Party Politics in Japan* (Winchester Mass.: Allen and Unwin, 1986), pp. 42–43; and Michael W. Chinworth, "The Elections: Oh What a Feeling," *JEI Report*, no. 25B (July 11, 1986), p. 2.

a. Deficit in LDP seats was made up by independents joining the party after the election.

The political shift of the late 1960s and 1970s was also evident in the proliferation of opposition party victories in local elections. On some issues, it was these progressive local governments that took the lead in instituting new social programs, becoming another prod for central government action.[63] The Liberal Democratic party was astute enough that by "responding skillfully to the challenge posed by the progressive local governments, it succeeded in removing the uniqueness of the progressive camp's policies by improving environmental protection and welfare measures."[64]

The success of the opposition parties at the local level began to wane in the 1980s, and by 1985 ten of forty-seven prefectural governors were from the LDP and an additional twenty-three were independents supported by coalitions that included the LDP. Most of the remaining governors were independents with no party affiliations or coalitions. Only three were officially endorsed by progressive parties or by coalitions of progressive parties that excluded the LDP.[65]

These political trends suggest why the LDP shifted its policies away from a strictly progrowth, probusiness stance to one of greater support for social demands in the 1970s. And the resurgence of the party in the first half of the 1980s may explain (along with concerns about budget deficits) the leveling off or decline in such policies.

Both the Tanaka proposal for remaking Japan and the subsequent long-term economic plan put forth by the Economic Planning Agency demonstrated the recognition of these public concerns. EPA Director General Tsuneo Uchida portrayed the new thinking when he said in his opening Diet speech in January 1974 that under the slower growth imposed by the oil shock, government policy would have to change from support of "quantitative growth" to "qualitative growth" and from "production theory" to "distribution ethics."[66]

In summary, the changes in investment patterns represented movement away from the single-minded pursuit of economic growth. To the extent that this involved a real reallocation of resources, it reduced the measured rate of economic growth. However, much of the change did not represent such a reallocation. Because private-sector investment in new plant and equipment was decelerating, increased investment in social infrastructure did not compete with it. The alternative was not an equal amount of investment directed more toward plant and equipment (and business-oriented infrastructure) but simply less investment. Social investment thus lessened the imbalances between savings and investment and kept economic growth from diminishing even further.

A SLUGGISH WORLD ECONOMIC ENVIRONMENT. From 1975 to 1985 the volume index for Japanese exports rose at a 6.9 percent annual rate, compared with 17.9 percent from 1961 to 1970 and 12.7 percent from 1971 to 1974. However, as these export data indicate, rising external surpluses occurred in an environment of slower real export expansion.

Much of the slowdown in export growth can be attributed to slower economic growth in the rest of the world, but there is another dimension as well. When Japan was economically a small force in the 1950s, its exports could expand rapidly without making much difference in world markets. But by the 1970s its exporting industries were important enough to represent a significant factor in world markets. This success created two reasons for export growth to drop. In economic terms the rapid gains of exports could be limited either because of market saturation or because the significant size of Japanese penetration provoked more successful counter-strategies by foreign competitors. In political terms Japan's success meant that attempts to expand rapidly exports of particular products would engender threats of protection from trade partners or real protectionist actions.

A CHANGING LABOR MARKET. In the 1970s and 1980s labor input in the Japanese economy grew somewhat more slowly than before because of slower population growth, a decrease in hours worked, and fewer gains from increased education. Partially offsetting these factors was a modest reversal of the earlier downward trend in labor force participation rates for women.

Table 2–9. Labor Force Participation and Unemployment Rate, Selected Years, 1950–85

Millions of people unless otherwise specified

Year	Population aged 15 and older	Labor force	Labor force participation rate (percent)	Unemployment rate (percent)
1950	55.2	36.2	65.6	1.2
1955	59.3	41.9	70.8	2.5
1960	65.2	45.1	69.2	1.7
1965	72.9	47.9	65.7	1.2
1970	78.9	51.5	65.4	1.2
1973	82.1	53.0	64.6	1.3
1975	84.4	53.2	63.0	1.9
1980	89.3	56.5	63.3	2.0
1985	94.7	59.6	63.0	2.6

Sources: Management and Coordination Agency, *Japan Statistical Yearbook, 1986*, pp. 70–71; *1973–74*, p. 49; *1960*, p. 42.

During the very early postwar period Japan experienced a baby boom similar to that in the United States. Children born between 1947 and 1951 outnumbered the next younger five-year group (1952–56) by 37 percent and the next older five-year group (1942–46) by 23 percent.[67] Since the early 1950s the birthrate has almost continuously declined. Therefore, even if the boom is considered to have lasted until as late as 1955, that generation was in the labor force by 1975.

The slowdown since the early 1950s is clearly visible in both population and labor force data. The number of people aged fifteen years and older grew at an average annual rate of 1.8 percent from 1956 to 1973 but at only a 1.2 percent rate from 1974 to 1985. Labor force participation rates, the percentage of people fifteen years and older with jobs or actively seeking employment, declined steadily from 70.8 percent in 1955 to 64.6 percent in 1973, primarily because the shift of workers out of agriculture led to falling participation rates for women. However, from 1974 to 1985 participation rates stabilized; the rate was 63.0 percent in 1985, down only slightly from the 1973 level.[68]

Table 2–9 shows the effects of population growth and participation rates on the labor force. From 1951 to 1960 the annual growth rate of the labor force was a high 2.2 percent. From 1961 to 1973 the rate of increase slowed to 1.3 percent, and from 1974 to 1985 dropped a bit further to 1.2 percent. In addition, after unemployment had dropped from a peak of 2.5 percent in 1955 to a stable 1.2 to 1.4 percent in the 1960s, it rose again from 1.3 percent in 1973 to a new peak of 2.6 percent in 1985 (and was still rising).

The labor force continued to be characterized by increases in the number of years of education in the 1970s and 1980s, but this too was changing more slowly. From 1960 to 1970 the percentage of the population aged fifteen years and older that had graduated from high school increased from 22.2 percent to 30.1 percent; from 1970 to 1980 it increased to 38 percent. Thus the portion of adults with high school diplomas rose by 36 percent in the 1960s and 26 percent in the 1970s. People with diplomas from all forms of educational institutions beyond high school increased from 5.2 percent of the population fifteen years and older in 1960 to 8.4 percent in 1970 and 13.7 percent in 1980, roughly equal rates of growth in each decade.[69] In the 1980s the percentage of each age cohort completing high school appears to have stabilized at just over 50 percent, although the percentage continuing on to higher education was still rising. Therefore the data on the rising educational level of those fifteen years and older indicate primarily that the generations educated before the reforms initiated during the occupation were declining as a proportion of the total adult population.

These trends in education suggest that gains in the quality of the labor force continued during the 1970s, but contributed less to economic growth than they had before. Any precise estimate of the contribution of changes in education though, ought to be viewed with a certain amount of suspicion—years of education are only crudely related to workers' productivity.

Growth of labor input was also limited in the 1970s and 1980s by decreases in hours worked. The average monthly hours per worker in all industry declined from almost 203 in 1960 to 182 in 1973. For manufacturing only the decline was from 207 hours to 182, an almost identical change (table 2–10).[70] This slow drift downward became a sharp drop as demand fell in the recession following the oil shock. For all industry, hours dropped to 172 by 1975, and to 168 for manufacturing. One contributor to the decline may have been the so-called lifetime employment system in Japan. With a portion of the work force covered by an implicit job guarantee until the mandatory retirement age, corporations tend to rely on overtime work to put flexibility into their labor costs. Large corporations are more constrained than their American counterparts in reducing employment when a recession hits, but they can cut overtime work heavily.

Table 2–10. Average Monthly Hours Worked, Selected Years, 1960–85

Year	All industry	Manufacturing
1960	202.7	207.0
1965	192.9	191.8
1970	186.6	187.4
1973	182.0	182.0
1974	175.5	173.2
1975	172.0	167.8
1980	175.7	178.2
1985	175.8	179.7

Sources: Management and Coordination Agency, *Japan Statistical Yearbook, 1986*, p. 110; and Bank of Japan, *Economic Statistics Annual, 1977*, p. 281.

Once the recession-related drop was over, hours worked in manufacturing recovered to almost 180 a month by 1985, and more moderately to 176 for all industry. This difference is probably due to the limited opportunity for overtime in sectors other than manufacturing. As a result of these changes, shifts in hours worked were actually less important to labor input after 1973 than before. The average annual decline in hours worked in 1961–73 was 0.8 percent, while in 1974–85 it was only 0.3 percent (concentrated in the recession-related drop of 1974–75).

Somewhat offsetting the effect of the decline in hours worked on total labor input, more women entered the labor force in the 1970s and 1980s. For all women fifteen years and older participation rates dropped until 1975, then increased modestly to almost 49 percent by 1985 (table 2–11). Considered by age group, the data indicate some weakening of the traditional expectation that women should leave their jobs when they get married (or at the latest when they have their first child). This tradition did not apply to work on family farms or in small family enterprises, so that well over 40 percent of women beyond their mid-twenties had always remained in the labor force. Following the first oil shock, though, more women chose to stay on the job or to return to work outside the home more quickly after having children. For the group aged twenty-five to thirty-four participation rates rose from 43.2 percent in 1975 to 52.2 percent in 1985, and for those aged thirty-five to fourty-four (who have presumably finished having children) rates rose from 56.9 percent to 63.7 percent.

Table 2–11. Female Labor Force Participation, by Age Group, Selected Years, 1960–85

Percent

Year	Total	Age group						
		15–19	20–24	25–29[a]	30–39[b]	40–54[c]	55–64	65 and older
1960	54.5	49.0	70.8	54.5	57.8	59.0	46.4	25.6
1965	50.6	35.8	70.2	49.0	55.4	60.2	44.8	21.6
1970	49.9	33.6	70.6	45.5	52.9	61.8	44.4	17.9
1973	48.3	27.9	67.1	44.5	51.4	61.3	44.5	16.9
1975	45.7	21.7	66.2	43.2	56.9	59.8	43.7	15.3
1980	47.6	18.5	70.0	48.7	60.9	62.0	45.3	15.5
1984	48.9	18.5	72.4	52.1	63.7	64.1	45.0	15.9
1985	48.7	16.6	71.9	52.2	63.7	64.6	45.3	15.5

Sources: Management and Coordination Agency, *Japan Statistical Yearbook, 1986*, p. 71; *1978*, p. 49; *1973–74*, p. 49.

a. Includes ages 125–34 after 1973.

b. Includes ages 35–44 after 1973.

c. Includes ages 45–54, only, after 1973.

Although Japan benefited from having more women choosing either to stay in or to return to the labor force, in a growth-accounting framework, this had both a positive and a negative effect. Had women not chosen to work, the labor force would have grown even more slowly than it did. However, because women are paid less than men, a higher share of women in the work force implies less growth in the measured value of output attributable to labor. Males made up 62.7 percent of the labor force in 1975 but 60.3 percent by 1985.[71]

Taken together these factors imply that labor's contribution to the Japanese economy grew somewhat less rapidly after 1973 than before. As labor force growth decelerated, creating a tight labor market, the continued rapid economic expansion of the late 1960s and early 1970s enabled unions to negotiate the very large wage increases of 1973 and 1974 mentioned earlier. This wage pressure was even more significant than implied by the wage settlements, since the strong seniority element in Japanese wage structures combined with the aging of the labor force implied rising wages even without annual overall increases.[72] After the recession of 1974, though, the situation changed. Slower economic growth and the longer-term effort of corporations to replace labor with capital moved Japan away from the tight labor market conditions. Growth in employment, in fact, was so slow that the unemployment levels rose (see table 2–9).

Reductions in the growth of labor supply in Japan should not be considered a major cause of slower overall economic growth, however. First, slower labor expansion need not be a problem if capital or technological change can be substituted. Second, the slowdown in labor supply was relatively mild, accounting for less than 1 percentage point of the reduction of economic growth in the growth-accounting framework. Finally, the expansion of unemployment implies that the demographic changes slowing the expansion of the labor force were not a constraining factor in Japan's growth performance. Constraints lay instead in the slower growth of the capital stock and smaller increases in productivity.

SLOWER PRODUCTIVITY GROWTH. Endowed with the intellectual and social capacity to efficiently absorb and adapt foreign technology, Japan was able to achieve great leaps in productivity as the private sector continually discovered new investment opportunities using imported technologies in the 1950s and 1960s. But by the 1970s this situation was coming to its logical end. Productivity increases due to implementation of new technologies slowed because the changes in technology became more incremental.

Productivity change in the growth-accounting framework includes all sources of change, not just increases due to new technologies. Of these other sources, Denison and Chung found economies of scale to be important during the 1950s and 1960s. Virtually every Japanese industry was starting from a small production base, so that economies of scale were achieved easily as output grew and larger production facilities were constructed. This effect was compounded in new industries, including most consumer durables, because domestic demand for their products proved highly income-elastic. Further economies were available as industries reached productivity levels high enough to be competitive in world markets. But by the mid-1970s these gains were largely realized, and economies of scale could be no longer be expected to contribute more to growth than they did in other industrialized economies. In addition, the slower pace of investment in new plant and equipment reduced the speed with which new, larger, more efficient production facilities replaced older facilities. Therefore, even if economies of scale could be realized, they were being realized more slowly.

Finally, there were fewer gains to be realized from the transfer of labor from low-productivity agriculture to other, more productive employment. The movement of labor out of agriculture was an important source of productivity growth between 1955 and 1973 because the shift took place so quickly. As table 2–12 shows, the proportion of employment in agriculture, forestry, and fishing dropped from 51.6 percent in 1950 to only 13.4 percent in 1973. This represented an absolute drop of 11.4 million people engaged in the primary sector. However, from 1973 to 1985 only 1.9 million people moved out, bringing the sector's proportion of total employment down to 8.8 percent. While the movement of workers did not come to a complete halt, it slowed from an average of 496,000 a year in the earlier period to 162,000 a year in the more recent period. Part of this absolute drop may not represent a movement of workers to other sectors as much as it does retiring workers not offset by new entrants: the population engaged in agriculture is older on average than the total labor force and is aging more rapidly. Future migration may be further limited because few farmers are engaged full time in agriculture. At what point Japanese statistics move a worker from one sector to another is unclear, but only 14 percent of farm households in 1985 were considered to be engaged full time in farming, and nonagricultural income accounted for more than half of all farm household income.[73] Thus the migration of workers from agriculture, forestry, and fisheries probably brought slower productivity gains because so much farm household activity was already off the farm by the mid-1980s.

Table 2–12. Employment, by Sector, Selected Years, 1950–85

Percent of total unless otherwise specified

| Year | Total employment (millions) | Sector | | |
		Primary[a]	Secondary[b]	Tertiary[c]
1950	35.7	51.6	21.7	28.6
1955	40.9	37.6	24.4	38.1
1960	44.4	30.2	28.0	41.8
1965	47.3	23.5	31.9	44.6
1970	50.9	17.4	35.2	47.3
1973	52.3	13.4	36.6	49.8
1975	52.2	12.7	35.2	51.9
1980	55.4	10.4	34.8	54.5
1985	58.1	8.8	34.3	56.5

Sources: Management and Coordination Agency, *Japan Statistical Yearbook, 1986*, pp. 72–73; *1973–74*, pp. 50–51; *1960*, pp. 44–45.

a. Includes agriculture, forestry, and fishing.

b. Includes construction, mining, and manufacturing.

c. Includes services and government.

Prospects

Most of the changes responsible for slower growth were longer-term shifts that implied high economic growth would not return. This can be seen in each of the factors of production.

LABOR. The labor force in Japan will continue to grow slowly. Official estimates of the population fifteen years of age and older in the year 2000 imply an annual growth of 0.84 percent after 1980, compared with 1.83 percent from 1956 to 1973.[74] How this will translate into labor force growth will depend on participation rates, of which the most uncertain aspect will be the participation of women. Will the modest upturn of the early 1980s continue as more women choose either to remain in the labor force or to return to it after marriage and children? This is impossible to predict, but the biggest part of the shift could be over. Certainly any straight-line extrapolation from the very recent past is suspect.

Demographics will also affect participation. An increasing proportion of the population will be aged sixty-five and older, at which point labor force participation drops quickly. In 1985, for example, only 37.0 percent of males and 15.5 percent of women sixty-five and older were still in the labor force.[75] Unless senior citizens increasingly decide to keep working or return to work, overall participation rates will fall, so that the labor force will grow more slowly than the 0.84 percent projected annual growth in population.

There is certainly no reason to expect increased output from any substantial increase in hours worked: by the late 1970s overtime work stabilized at between thirteen and fourteen hours a month.[76] The more likely possibility would be a small and slow decrease in hours worked as industrial structure continues to shift away from manufacturing to services. Some downward influence could also occur as observance of a two-day weekend continues to spread among corporations, but this trend will also be very slow. Although the two-day weekend has been part of official Japanese government pronouncements since the early 1970s, even by the mid-1980s very few corporations actually gave their employees Saturday off every week.

CAPITAL. There is no reason to expect capital stock to grow quickly either. A recent study by the Japan Economic Research Center predicted a 6.34 percent annual real increase in capital inputs for 1980–90, slightly slower than the actual increase for 1975–80.[77] This estimate appears reasonable, with capital investment continuing a moderate expansion after the one-time downward adjustment immediately after the 1973 oil shock. Now that Japan is no longer catching up in technology, there is no reason why investment should return to its earlier high levels. Without the large jumps in productivity available from imported technology, expected profits on new investment will remain lower than during the high-growth era.

Some optimists believe rates of investment will increase because of the wave of new technologies beginning to become important by the mid-1980s—personal computers, factory automation, new materials, biotechnology. Advances in high-technology industries will certainly have important repercussions for all societies, but their impact on investment rates is unlikely to be very great because while investment in these industries may continue at levels significantly higher than in other industries, they are a small part of total industrial capital stock. Other industries will, of course, also be affected, since some of these new products are intermediate inputs or capital goods (such as industrial robots), but this impact, too, is unlikely to be strong enough to make much difference in total investment.

Growth in export markets could also make a difference in capital investment. If the United States were to continue to grow and pull in Japanese exports as it did in 1983–85, profits and investment in exporting industries would rise. However, this growth was an unusual cyclical development (based on a low value of the yen against the dollar as well as an upturn in U.S. economic growth) that did not last. The rapid appreciation of the yen in 1985 and 1986 cut export-sector profits and resulted in sharp cutbacks in investment spending.

Finally, Japan is unlikely to reassemble that consensus on industrial growth that was a significant cause of the rapid gains of the 1950s and 1960s. For government, a return to tax and expenditure policies that heavily favored business would be difficult even if other conditions suggest such a redirection would raise investment levels. For labor, concern with the quality of life implies that a return to longer hours of work is unlikely. Recent attitudes could also result in a decline in dedication to the corporation, bringing slower productivity increases, though no major trend in that direction appears at all likely.

PRODUCTIVITY. Although Japan's productivity might improve because of new industries such as biotechnology, for the reasons discussed above any such gain will probably be moderate. A technological revolution may also have less impact than some anticipate because of the declining importance of manufacturing in the economy.

GROWTH ESTIMATES. Forecasts in Japan converged on an average 4 percent annual GNP growth in the mid-1980s, which is not unreasonable. Denison and Chung suggested in 1976 that growth would slowly decelerate from 5.7 percent in the 1980s to 4.6 percent in the 1990s to 3.2 percent by the year 2000. That scenario was overly optimistic because the oil shocks and recession of the 1970s kept actual growth below the potential. However, the basic point was valid: the factors producing very high growth were temporary, and growth rates will fall.

As of 1984 a Japanese government estimate for 1981–2000 placed annual real GNP growth at 4.0 to 4.4 percent, depending on assumptions about inputs.[78] A survey of public opinion done for the study came up with a weighted average of 4.36 percent, but in the text the authors stepped back from endorsing any precise figure. It is worth noting that this forecast was based on a rather optimistic 4.4 percent average annual increase in real final consumption spending, a level considerably higher than in the decade from 1974 to 1983. The long-term economic plan for fiscal years 1983 to 1990 also anticipated 4 percent growth and also avoided being very precise.[79]

Private-sector estimates converged at this 4 percent level as well. A forecast made in 1984 by the Nomura Research Institute predicted 3.9 percent growth for 1983–94 (identical to the 1973–83 average), but it was based on higher labor force growth than in the previous decade (a 1.2 percent annual increase instead of 1.0 percent) because of more working women—an assumption that could easily be challenged. Optimism on labor force growth was, however, combined with pessimism about employment, with a predicted increase in unemployment to 5.3 percent by 1994.[80]

The Japan Economic Research Center produces forecasts that are the product of different teams of researchers working with separate models, so that its forecasts are not entirely consistent. A five-year forecast for 1984–88 prepared in May 1984 estimated 4.2 percent annual growth in real GNP, but a year earlier a report predicted that growth from 1980 to 1990 would be 5.0 percent, while a report on Japan in the year 2000 called for 4.47 percent growth from 1980 to 1991 and 4.14 percent from 1991 to 2000.[81] This last forecast attributed the slowdown between the two decades primarily to a drop in hours worked; it anticipated approximately constant growth in capital stock and a modest rise in productivity growth. But the report went on to note that actual as opposed to potential growth would be about 4 percent because of slow expansion in the government sector (both current and investment expenditures by government) that would not be offset by higher growth in the private sector.

These government and private-sector estimates had several important features. First, they were not very far apart. Almost all were about 4 percent, with the Japan Economic Research Center somewhat more optimistic. Second, most of them anticipated U.S. growth to be about 2.5 percent and Europe's somewhat lower, so that Japan would continue to outperform other industrial nations. Third, all the estimates depended critically on assumptions about productivity change. The 5 percent annual growth anticipated in the 1980s by the Japan Economic Research Center assumed labor and capital would contribute only 1.74 percentage points; the remaining 3.26 points would come from growth in productivity. Lower estimates of growth produced by other organizations assumed roughly the same contribution from labor and capital but were more cautious about productivity growth.

A final point about all forecasts is that actual growth could be below the potential, depending on the handling of macroeconomic policy. All the figures cited are for potential growth (based on expansion of supply capacity), and at least the one Japan Economic Research Center forecast anticipated that actual growth (based on demand) would be slower because of government's failure to pursue full-employment policies.

SUMMARY

Japan experienced unprecedented rapid economic expansion for two and a half decades, raising it from an impoverished, war-devastated nation to an advanced industrial giant. That extraordinary period was gradually coming to an end in the early 1970s, and the traumatic events of 1973 and 1974 hastened the transition. From 1974 through the first half of the 1980s, annual growth was less than one-half the earlier level, averaging just over 4 percent. Although Japan's economic performance continued to be better than that of other industrial nations, it was by a smaller margin. None of this was entirely unexpected; some economists had been predicting in the early 1970s that Japan's miracle would have to come to an end. But the actual performance has been below the expectations of even the pessimists.

Why did these changes take place? The starting point for any explanation must be the end of the process of technological catch-up. By the 1970s the technological gap was largely closed, reducing the productivity gains that could be realized by importing foreign technology, thus decreasing the expected profits from investment in new plant and equipment and causing investment to decelerate. Lower rates of investment also slowed the productivity gains realized from economies of scale. This primary cause of slower economic growth was supplemented to a lesser extent by other factors: slower expansion of labor inputs because of slower population growth, a decline in labor force participation, and a decline in hours worked; rising energy costs that brought both a one-time loss of income and longer-run costs from shifting resources out of labor-intensive industries; less favorable world market conditions for exports; and a shift in priorities away from economic growth per se to a broader set of social goals. This final element may have inhibited productivity change by reallocating investment to programs with less connection to increased output (such as pollution control or building hospitals) but helped to keep investment levels higher than they would have been otherwise.

Because these represented long-term structural changes for the Japanese economy, rapid growth of the sort that characterized the earlier postwar period is unlikely to return. If growth does not rise to earlier levels, then the changes in macroeconomic structure of the economy that form the topic of the next chapter will remain for some time.

These statements may seem incongruous. How can the reality of slower growth be resolved with the impression of Japan as a vigorous, hardworking exporter of superior manufactured goods? If Japan is such a successful manufacturer, why are not investment rates and economic growth higher? The answer is that exports represent only a small share of total economic activity—especially since they are concentrated in relatively few product categories. Continued international success of these products does not represent the state of quality, innovation, competitiveness, profits, or investment levels in other sectors of the economy. Japan is doing relatively well, but it is no longer a high-growth country.

NOTES

1. Edward F. Denison and William K. Chung, "Economic Growth and Its Sources," in Hugh Patrick and Henry Rosovsky, eds., *Asia's New Giant: How the Japanese Economy Works* (Brookings, 1976), pp. 63–151.

2. Kazushi Ohkawa and Henry Rosovsky, *Japanese Economic Growth: Trend Acceleration in the Twentieth Century* (Oxford University Press and Stanford University Press, 1973), esp. pp. 39–43.

3. These relations can be expressed more formally. Let π = profit, K = capital stock, L = labor, W = wages, and O = output. Profits are the difference between output and the cost of labor: $\pi = O - W \times L$. The rate of return on capital can thus be expressed as $\pi/K = (O - W \times L)/K = O/K - W(L/K)$. An investment spurt eventually leads to a decline in profitability (π/K) because the additional amount of output from investment falls as the most productive investment opportunities are used up (declining marginal productivity of investment). This means that O/K falls. In addition, rapid investment may put pressure on labor markets, driving up wages (although this effect may be offset if the amount of capital per worker increases, that is, if L/K declines). Japan avoided a large drop in profitability in the 1950s and 1960s because the increases in productivity possible with imported technology meant that O/K was actually rising and because $W \times (L/K)$ did not rise faster than O/K. Wages rose rather rapidly, but

L/K fell as corporations substituted capital for labor. For more detail and data see Ohkawa and Rosovsky, *Japanese Economic Growth,* esp. pp. 147–53.

4. Rates on loans were controlled, but evidence suggests that financial institutions had a variety of means to circumvent those controls (such as requiring borrowers to hold some part of a loan as a savings deposit). See, for example, Akiyoshi Horiuchi, "Economic Growth and Financial Allocation in Postwar Japan," Discussion Papers in International Economics (Brookings, August 1984). pp. 16–20.

5. For a review of that debate, see Edward J. Lincoln, *Japan's Industrial Policies: What Are They, Do They Matter, and Are They Different from Those in the United States?* (Washington, D.C.: Japan Economic Institute of America, 1984).

6. Lawrence B. Krause and Sueo Sekiguchi, "Japan and the World Economy," in Patrick and Rosovsky, eds., *Asia's New Giant,* esp. p. 403.

7. After the war, firms that had been part of the zaibatsu reformed into loose groups called *keiretsu.* These groups look similar to the zaibatsu, but what ties there are (mainly through mutual stockholding and loans from the group bank) are weak enough that they have not suppressed competition in any measurable way. See Eleanor M. Hadley, *Antitrust in Japan* (Princeton University Press, 1970), esp. chaps. 11, 12.

8. Hugh Patrick and Henry Rosovsky, "Japan's Economic Performance: An Overview," in Patrick and Rosovsky, eds., *Asia's New Giant,* p. 3.

9. Herman Kahn, *The Emerging Japanese Superstate: Challenge and Response* (Prentice-Hall, 1970), p. 3.

10. Kakuei Tanaka, *Building a New Japan: A Plan for Remodeling the Japanese Archipelago* (Tokyo: Simul Press, 1973), p. 68. One can easily be cynical about Tanaka's motivation in offering this plan. His own background was in the construction industry in rural Niigata Prefecture, and the primary bastion of support for the Liberal Democratic party was in rural areas, so that the plan could easily be dismissed as an exercise in building political support. Furthermore, Tanaka was known as a master of pork barrel politics, making him enormously popular with his constituents. However, the book was more than a self-serving political piece, and Tanaka deserves at least some credit for a genuine desire to make Japan a significantly better place to live and a supremely confident belief that this could be done painlessly.

11. Japan has seen a series of these macroeconomic plans, which are a combination of forecast and hope about where the economy is heading, since the 1950s. However, they often do little to influence policy, so that they are far from plans in any real sense. When a new prime minister enters office, it is customary for the EPA to formulate a new plan, and Tanaka was certainly no exception.

12. Economic Planning Agency, *Basic Economic and Social Plan: Toward a Vigorous Welfare Society, 1973–1977* (Tokyo: EPA, 1973), p. 5.

13. Ibid., pp. 20–21, 29–30.

14. Ibid., p. 108. The ¥6.0 trillion is in current prices (that is, not adjusted for expected inflation). Exchange rates based on yen-per-dollar period averages are from International Monetary Fund, *International Financial Statistics Yearbook, 1986* (Washington, D.C.: IMF); and Bank of Japan, *Economic Statistics Annual, 1980* (Tokyo: BOJ), p. 211.

15. Economic Planning Agency, *Basic Economic and Social Plan,* p. 124. The term "basic balance" includes the current account plus long-term capital (investments in assets with a maturity greater than one year). This balance has no particular theoretical meaning, but it was popular with Japanese officials, who felt long-term capital was less volatile and therefore better than short-term capital in some undefined sense. The balance-of-payments accounting framework is considered in greater detail in chapter 5.

16. Japan Economic Research Center, *The Structure of a Three-Trillion Dollar Economy: The Japanese Economy in 1985* (Tokyo: JERC, 1974), pp. 3–5, 9, 24; Bank of Japan, *Balance of Payments Monthly,* (December 1985), p. 1; and Economic Planning Agency, *Annual Report on National Income Accounts, 1987* (Tokyo: EPA, 1957), p. 7.

17. Japan Economic Research Center, *The Structure of a Three-Trillion Dollar Economy,* p. 25. In all fairness, by 1975 in the aftermath of the first oil shock, the research center had lowered its sights to 7 percent growth. See *The Future of World Economy and Japan* (Tokyo: JERC, 1975), p. 3.

18. Edward F. Denison and William K. Chung, *How Japan's Economy Grew So Fast: The Sources of Postwar Expansion* (Brookings, 1976), p. 126.

19. Edward R. Fried and Philip H. Trezise, "Japan's Future Position in the World Economy," paper prepared for U.S. Department of State, 1974, p. 74.

20. *Nihon Keizai Shimbun* (Tokyo) Evening Edition, January 21, 1974. U.S. embassy translation.

21. When looking at economic growth, economists often make a distinction between potential and actual growth. The potential (or full-employment) growth rate is an estimate of how much the supply of goods and services would expand if all factors of production were fully utilized. Actual growth measures the demand for goods and services, and demand may be less than the potential supply, leaving some factors underused. This situation may result from external events or from the failure of government to follow economic policies to maintain full employment. Attempts to follow policies that push actual growth beyond potential levels, however, may result in inflation (as a means of restricting the level of demand to potential supply).

22. In August 1971 the fixed exchange rate of 360 yen to the dollar came to an end after the United States stopped convertibility of the dollar into gold. An agreement to fix exchange rates at a new set of parities was signed in December, establishing a ratio of 308 yen to the dollar, a 16.5 percent appreciation of the yen. While small compared to later exchange rate swings, this initial shift was a greater surprise to Japanese exporters.

As a result, real GNP growth dropped to only 4.3 percent in 1971 (from 9.5 percent in 1970). Economic Planning Agency, *Annual Report on National Accounts, 1987*, p. 123.

23. Average annual consumer price inflation in the United States from 1960 to 1970 was 2.3 percent, under half the rate in Japan. Bureau of the Census, *Statistical Abstract of the United States, 1987* (GPO, 1986), p. 463.

24. Management and Coordination Agency, *Japan Statistical Yearbook, 1978* (Tokyo: Statistics Bureau, 1978), pp. 113–14; Ministry of Finance, *Summary Report: Trade of Japan, 1974* (Tokyo: Japan Tariff Assoc., 1975), p. 84; and MOF, *Japan Exports and Imports: Commodity by Country, 1973* (Tokyo: Japan Tariff Assoc., 1974), p. 58.

25. *Nihon Keizai Shimbun*, June 29, 1973. U.S. embassy translation.

26. *Nihon Keizai Shimbun*, February 13, 1974; and *Nihon Keizai Shimbun*, January 15, 1974. U.S. embassy translations.

27. *Yomiuri Shimbun* (Tokyo), April 21,1974. U.S. embassy translation.

28. Emery N. Castle and Kenzo Hemmi, eds., *U.S.–Japanese Agricultural Trade Relations* (Johns Hopkins University Press for Resources for the Future, 1982), p. 80.

29. *Japan Economic Journal*, January 1, 1985. When measured in value terms, the share of imports is smaller. In 1984 the gross value of agricultural output was almost ¥12 trillion and foodstuff imports just under ¥4 trillion, making imports 32 percent of total supplies. But this was a large increase from the 20 percent reported in 1970. See Management and Coordination Agency, *Japan Statistical Yearbook, 1986*, pp. 172, 343.

30. Management and Coordination Agency, *Japan Statistical Yearbook, 1986*, p. 160; Ministry of Finance, *Summary Report: Trade of Japan, 1985*, p. 84; and Ministry of Finance, *Japan Exports and Imports: Commodity by Country, 1984*, p. 59.

31. Valerie Yorke, "Oil, the Middle East and Japan's Search for Security," in Nobutoshi Akao, *Japan's Economic Security* (St. Martin's Press, 1983), pp. 52–53; and *Sankei Shimbun* (Tokyo), December 27, 1973, and *Yomiuri Shimbun*, Evening Edition, March 14, 1974. U.S. embassy translations.

32. *Sankei Shimbun*, October 19, 1973. U.S. embassy translation.

33. *Sankei Shimbun*, November 12, 1973; *Tokyo Shimbun*, November 14, 1973; and *Mainichi Shimbun* (Tokyo), November 16, 1973. U.S. embassy translations.

34. *Nihon Keizai Shimbun*, January 20, 1974; February 27, 1974.

35. Economic Planning Agency, *Annual Report on National Accounts, 1987*, pp. 49, 61, 123; and Bank of Japan, *Economic Statistics Annual, 1977*, pp. 227, 285, 299.

36. Hajime Ohta, "As Economy Slows, Wage Increases Decline," *Council Report*, no. 27 (July 1980), table 2; and Management and Coordination Agency, *Japan Statistical Yearbook, 1980*, p. 399.

37. *Mainichi Shimbun*, January 1, 1974.

38. *Sankei Shimbun*, January 4, 1974.

39. Seiji Shimpo, *Gendai Nihon Keizai no Kaimei: Sutagufurēshon no Kenkyu* (The Contemporary Japanese Economy: A Study of Stagflation) (Tokyo: Toyo Keizai Shimposha, 1979), pp. 28–36.

40. Although the rise in the discount rate was sizable and unusual, real interest rates (nominal interest rates minus the rate of inflation) were below zero, as they were in other countries. Therefore the quantitive restraints on lending through window guidance remained a principal policy tool. Although real interest rates were negative, the discount rate is taken here to be a reasonable proxy for the overall stance of monetary policy.

41. Budget Bureau, *Zaisei Tokei, 1986* (Fiscal Statistics, 1986) (Tokyo: MOF, 1986), p. 225.

42. Organization for Economic Cooperation and Development, *OECD Economic Surveys: Japan, 1974* (Paris: OECD, 1975), pp. 35–36.

43. Edward J. Lincoln, "Regulation of Rates on the Japanese National Railways," in Kenneth D. Boyer and William G. Shepherd, eds. *Economic Regulation: Essays in Honor of James R. Nelson,* MSU Public Utility Papers Series (Michigan State University Press, 1981), p. 143; and Japanese National Railways, *Tetsudb Ybran, 1980* (Railways Handbook, 1980) (Tokyo: JNR, 1980), p. 65.

44. In 1984, for example, net exports of goods and services expanded by 59.3 percent in real terms. The impact of that large increase, however, was muted by the small size of net exports—2.8 percent of GNP. Growth for the whole period is calculated by weighing export and import growths by their respective weights in GNP. These weights are an average of their shares of GNP in 1979 and 1985.

45. "Why Is the Performance of the Japanese Economy So Much Better?" *Journal of Japanese Studies,* vol. 7 (Summer 1981), p. 412.

46. Hajime Ohta, "New Views of Competition in the Japanese Economy," *Council Report,* no. 17 (May 2, 1980), pp. 1–5.

47. Unitary returns to scale means that if all factors of production are doubled, then output will be doubled. In mathematical terms, if $Y = f(L,K)$, then $aY = f(aL,aK)$, where Y is output, L is labor, and K is capital. Disembodied technical change means that technical change can be measured as a separate factor of production rather than being entwined with either labor or capital. In mathematical terms, if T is technical change, then $Y = f(L,K,T)$ and $T \neq f(L,K)$.

48. Dale W. Jorgenson and Mieko Nishimizu found from their very detailed sectoral growth-accounting model that differences in technological level between Japan and the United States disappeared by the mid-1970s, with the remaining difference in output per worker in various industries in the two countries attributable to the differing levels of capital per worker. See "U.S. and Japanese Economic Growth, 1852–1973: An International Comparison," Discussion Paper 566 (Harvard Institute of Economic Research, August 1977).

49. Science and Technology Agency, *Kagaku Gijutsu Hakusho, 1984: 21 Seiki: no Arata na Gijutsu no Sōshutsu o Mezashite* (Science and Technology White Paper, 1984: Aiming

for New Technological Development in the 21st Century) (Tokyo: MOF, 1984), pp. 336–37, 339.

50. Keizai Koho Center, *Japan 1986: An International Comparison* (Tokyo: KKC. 1986), pp. 64, 67; Jon Choy, "Japan's Energy Policy: 1986 Update," *J EI Report,* no. 3A (January 1987), p. 7; Bureau of the Census, *Statistical Abstract of the United States, 1987,* p. 544; and Organization for Economic Cooperation and Development, *Energy Balances of OECD Countries, 1973–75* (Paris: OECD, 1977), p. 48.

51. Managment and Coordination Agency, *Japan Statistical Yearbook, 1986,* p. 228.

52. The existence of radical unions in the early postwar years, discussed earlier, implies that the consensus was not universal, but the failure of these unions in the 1950s indicates the direction of social attitudes. Given the poverty, poor housing, and generally harsh life after the war, it is easy to imagine that a different society could have generated a strong, radical union system with an agenda of reallocating resources to improve social welfare at the expense of investment in plant and equipment.

53. Environmental Agency, *Kankyō Hakusho, 1976: Shiren to Sentaku no Kankyō Gyōsei* (Environmental White Paper, 1976: Environmental Administration's Ordeals and Options) (Tokyo: MOF, 1976), p. 515; and Environmental Agency, *Kankyō Hakusho, 1984: Seijukukasuru Shakai ni Okeru Kankyō Mondai e no Arata na Taio* (Environmental White Paper, 1984: New Opposition to Environmental Issues in a Mature Society) (Tokyo: MOF, 1984), pp. 117, 479.

54. Environmental Agency, *Kankyō Hakusho, 1976,* pp. 402–03, 513–15. Comparison of private and government spending may involve some double-counting because the private-sector figures do not provide sources of funding (some of which was from government).

55. Environmental Agency, *Kankyō Hakusho, 1984,* pp. 6–7.

56. Edward J. Lincoln, "Infrastructural Deficiencies, Budget Policy, and Capital Flows," in Michèle Schmiegelow, ed., *Japan's Response to Crisis and Change in the World Economy* (Armonk, N.Y.: M.E. Sharpe, 1986), p. 171.

57. Even in suburban areas where sewage treatment plants have not been built and a septic tank or cesspool is not feasible, the Japanese are allowed to install special treatment tanks that hold and chemically process sewage and then periodically pump it into city storm sewers.

58. Bureau of the Census, *Statistical Abstract of the United States, 1987,* p. 710.

59. Lincoln, "Infrastructural Deficiencies," pp. 159–61.

60. Management and Coordination Agency, *Japan Statistical Yearbook, 1985,* pp. 268, 514–5, 518. The average size of new dwellings was 59.1 square meters in 1960, 68.1 square meters in 1970, and 93.9 square meters in 1980. Thereafter, size dropped modestly to 84.4 square meters by 1984. Because these data refer to new dwellings, the impact of increased size on the total stock of dwellings was more muted.

61. U.S. data are from Bureau of the Census, *Statistical Abstract of the United States, 1984,* pp. 47, 756.

62. Historically, the Japanese have lived in crowded villages surrounded by their farm fields, rather than in the middle of their individual properties.

63. John C. Campbell, "The Old People Boom and Japanese Policy Making," *Journal of Japanese Studies,* vol. 5 (Summer 1979), pp. 321–57, for instance, details the impact of local progressive government initiatives (especially in Tokyo) in establishing free medical care for the elderly.

64. Seizaburo Sato, "The Shifting Political Spectrum," *Japan Echo,* vol. 11 (Summer 1984), p. 30. Translated from "Kakushin Yato ni Nokosareta Saigo no Michi," *Chub Kbron* (March 1984), pp. 62–72.

65. Takayoshi Miyagawa, ed., *Seiji Handobukku, 1985* (Political Handbook, 1985) (Tokyo: Seiji Koho Senta, 1985), pp. 297–304.

66. *Nihon Keizai Shimbun,* Evening Edition, January 21, 1974. U.S. embassy translation.

67. Management and Coordination Agency, *Japan Statistical Yearbook, 1986,* p. 24.

68. Ibid., p. 70; and *Japan Statistical Yearbook, 1973–74,* p. 49.

69. Management and Coordination Agency, *Japan Statistical Yearbook, 1986,* p. 44. Data on population by educational level are available only for census years (the first year of each decade).

70. Japanese data display some inconsistency between average monthly hours and average weekly hours. According to the data series for weekly hours, employees—excluding self-employed and family workers—averaged 47.5 hours a week in 1986. Adjusting that figure to a monthly basis yields almost 206 hours a month. The weekly figures show that even in the 1980s the Japanese worked considerably more hours than their American counterparts. Average weekly hours in U.S. manufacturing fluctuated close to 40 in the first half of the 1980s; for Japan the figure remained close to 47 hours—almost a full day more a week. Bureau of the Census, *Statistical Abstract of the United States, 1987,* p. 394; and Management and Coordination Agency, *Monthly Statistics of Japan* (March 1987), p. 19.

71. Management and Coordination Agency, *Japan Statistical Yearbook, 1986,* p. 70.

72. When economic growth was high, corporations hired large numbers of young employees, which helped keep the age and seniority structure of the work force biased toward the young, inexpensive end of the scale. In the adjustment to slower economic growth in the years just after 1973, though, firms hired fewer workers with an implicit lifetime employment commitment. This in effect increased average pay per worker as existing employees moved up the seniority ladder. Among large firms, the average seniority of male employees rose from 11.7 years in 1970 to 15.4 years by 1984. Management and Coordination Agency, *Japan Statistical Yearbook, 1986,* p. 97.

73. Ibid., pp. 149, 171.

74. Ibid., p. 25; and *Japan Statistical Yearbook, 1973–74,* p. 49.

75. These participation rates are much lower than for workers younger than 65. Approximately 97 percent of males are in the labor force between ages 25 and 54, with a drop to 83 percent for ages 55–64; see Management and Coordination Agency, *Japan Statistical Yearbook, 1986,* p. 71. Data for women, showing lower participation rates (but still much higher than for women aged 65 and older) are presented in table 2–11. However, labor force participation rates for both men and women aged 65 and older are much higher than is the case in the United States. For men the rate in the United States in 1985 was only 15.8 percent and for women 7.3 percent; Bureau of the Census, *Statistical Abstract of the United States, 1987,* p. 376.

76. Bank of Japan, *Economic Statistics Annual, 1985,* p. 305.

77. Hisao Kanamori and others, *Japanese Economy in 1990 in a Global Context: Revitalization of World Economy and Japan's Choice* (Tokyo: Japan Economic Research Center, 1983), p. 34.

78. Economic Planning Agency, *Japan in the Year 2000: Preparing Japan for an Age of Internationalization, the Aging Society and Maturity* (Tokyo: Japan Times, 1983), pp. 60–64.

79. Economic Planning Agency, *Outlook and Guidelines for the Economy and Society in the 1980s* (EPA, 1983), p. 17.

80. Nomura Research Institute, "A Long-Term Outlook for the Japanese Economy (Fiscal 1984 to 1993)," unpublished document (August 1984), pp. 2, 4.

81. Nobuyoshi Namiki and others, *Five-Year Economic Forecast, 1984–1988* (Tokyo: Japan Economic Research Center, 1984), pp. 26–27; Kanamori, *Japanese Economy in 1990,* p. 36; and Japan Economic Research Center, *2000-Nen no Shōhi Shakai: Shin Gijutsu Kakumei no Inpakuto* (Consumer Society in the Year 2000: The Impact of the New Technological Revolution) (Tokyo: JERC, 1984), p. 5.

Chapter 3: Employment Relations

By Panos Mourdoukoutas

There is no secret ingredient or hidden formula responsible for the success of the Japanese companies. No theory or plan or government policy will make a business a success; that can only be done by people. The most important mission for a Japanese manager is to develop a healthy relationship with his employees, to create a family-like feeling within the corporation, a feeling that employees and managers share the same fate.

—Akio Morita

Corporate organizations cannot compete effectively unless management enjoys harmonious relations with labor, especially in the face of growing international competition and rapid diffusion of new technology that dictate flexible labor deployment.

Japan's corporations are fortunate enough to enjoy employment relations that allow for flexible labor deployment to the needs of a changing market environment, an important factor for Japan's success in dealing with the two oil shocks and the yen shock. Arguing this hypothesis, this chapter is a comprehensive review of Japan's employment relations and the ways those relations accommodate adjustments to external shocks.

Aside from self-employment, employment relations in modern Japanese corporations may be classified in two categories: (1) Noncontractual employment founded on an implicit understanding between labor and management, an informal contract regarding job security, labor remuneration, and matters of labor deployment, and (2) Contractual employment founded on an explicit understanding between labor and management, a formal contract which specifies the term of employment, the labor remuneration, and the terms of labor deployment, if any. Both employment sectors have their own distinctive characteristics, but each depends on the other in various ways.

As the Japanese government does not publish statistics on noncontractual and contractual employment, quantitative assessments of the size of the two sectors are quite difficult. If one, however, begins with the official statistics which currently estimate self-employment at 14 percent of the labor force, the remaining 86 percent of the labor force is employed in the noncontractual and contractual sectors. This labor force is, in turn, allocated about forty percent to the noncontractual sector and 46 percent to the contractual sector (see studies below).

This chapter includes three sections. The first section is a discussion of the characteristics of the noncontractual sector. The second section is a discussion of the characteristics of the contractual sector, and the third section is a discussion of the relationships between the two sectors.

3.1 THE NONCONTRACTUAL SECTOR

Employment relations in the noncontractual sector are often identified with the three "sacred treasuries" of Japanese management: (1) lifetime employment, a mutual labor-management commitment that lasts until workers retire, (2) seniority wages, a labor remuneration system that emphasizes tenure with the company as a major factor for wage increases and a significant factor for promotion, and (3) enterprise unionism, a form of worker organization by enterprise rather than by trade.

In addition, in order to preserve the three sacred treasuries, workers have accommodated the development of an internal labor market and the application of measures, such as training, retraining, work reassignments, and labor transfers which allow firms to adjust labor input to varying economic conditions. But let us examine the facets of noncontractual employment in more detail.

Lifetime Employment

The term "lifetime employment" describes an employment system under which a worker starts employment with a particular company that is expected to last until retirement. Though most known and most praised, lifetime employment is, perhaps, the least understood Japanese institution that deserves several clarifications before any meaningful conclusion is drawn from it. First, lifetime employment is an agreement without contract, a mutual implicit understanding between labor and management (inshin-denshin). Second, Japanese workers do not always start and end their working careers with the same employer.

Job shifting and job search may occur, and "voluntary" quits and early retirement may follow a "lifetime" employment commitment.

Bearing these two clarifications in mind, long-term employment, an institution existing in all industrial countries, may be a more appropriate term to characterize employment in the noncontractual sector. Third, long-term employment applies to less than 50 percent of the Japanese labor force. Specifically, an early estimate by Van Helvoort (1979) finds that long-term employment accounts for 40 percent of the Japanese labor force, while a more recent OECD (1986) estimate brings that figure down to 39.1 percent. The same estimate also finds that long-term employment is not a unique Japanese institution but exists in all other major industrialized counties. It accounts for 37.7 percent of the labor force in Germany, 36.7 percent in Italy, and 35.8 percent in Belgium (see exhibit 3.1). Fourth, as Japanese society expects women to quit work upon marriage, long-term employment is primarily confined to men. Hashimoto (1979) and Hashimoto and Raisin (1985) find that long-term employment extends to 36.4 percent of the male labor force in Japan as compared to 30 percent in the U.S. Fourth, while long-term employment (ten years or longer) extends throughout enterprise of all sizes, it prevails only in large enterprises. In Japan, it ranges from 44.2 percent in tiny firms to 60.9 percent in large firms. In the U.S. it ranges from 22 percent in tiny firms to 42.6 percent in large firms (see the cumulative figures in brackets 10 to 20+ of exhibit 3.2).

It should be emphasized that cross-country comparisons of long-term employment are sensitive to the definition (number of years with the same company) and the reference period adopted. As Koike (1983) observes, long-term employment was more prevalent in the U.S. in the sixties, but the trend was reversed in the seventies. Between the years 1966 and 1978, the proportion of employees with long-term employment (fifteen years and over) dropped from 22.2 percent to 19 percent in the U.S. Between 1962 and 1979, the proportion in Japan increased from 17.7 percent to 33.1 percent (see exhibit 3.3).

As with any other long-term relationship, employers and employees must search thoroughly and think carefully before they find one another and commit themselves. Employer-employee selection is a complex process. Screening includes two stages: the first stage, school selection, starts with elementary education and continues with high school and university education. Students must struggle to enter and graduate from reputable institutions. The second stage, recruitment, takes place upon graduation in the spring of every year. It is no wonder that child education has become the full time occupation of Japanese mothers that make sure that children get the right preparation and enter top schools.

Exhibit 3.1

Country	Year	Under 2 years	of which under 1 year	2–9 years	10 years or more	of which 20 years or more	Total	Average length in years
Australia[a]	1985	35.6	22.9	44.5	19.9	..	100	6.6
Canada[a]	1985	35.1	25.4	37.1	27.8	9.6	100	7.8
United States[a]	1983	38.5	27.3	34.2	27.3	10.0	100	7.2
Japan	1982 (a)	21.2	9.8	30.8	48.0	21.9	100	11.7
	1982 (b)	27.5	10.2	33.4	39.1	13.2	100	9.4
Belgium[b]	1978	17.6	..	46.6	35.8	13.4	100	9.6
Denmark[b]	1978	27.1	..	46.1	26.8	9.1	100	7.7
Finland[c]	1984	28.2	17.7	37.9	33.9	9.5	100	8.3
France[b]	1978	17.8	..	47.0	35.2	13.2	100	9.5
Germany[b]	1978	18.6	..	43.7	37.7	15.1	100	10.0
Ireland[b]	1979	21.9	..	45.5	32.6	12.9	100	8.9
Italy[b]	1978	12.9	..	50.4	36.7	9.1	100	9.4
Luxembourg[b]	1978	18.9	..	46.1	35.0	17.2	100	9.8
Netherlands[b]	1979	27.6	..	41.6	30.8	11.9	100	8.4
United Kingdom[a]	1984	27.5	18.5	43.1	29.4	10.0	100	8.5

Distribution and Average Length of Current Job Tenures

a) Household surveys

b) Establishment surveys

c) Administrative data

Source: *Flexibility in the Labor Market, OECD*, Paris, p.51, 1986.

Exhibit 3.2

Percent of Employed Males by Tenure and Firm Size: Japan and the U.S.

Tenure	Japan (1979)					US (1979)				
	All (1)	Tiny (2)	Small (3)	Medium (4)	Large (5)	All (1)	Tiny (2)	Small (3)	Medium (4)	Large (5)
Less than 1yr.	7.9	10.4	9.7	7.7	3.8	19.4	29.7	22.3	16.0	11.2
1–4	21.5	24.8	22.2	21.6	13.5	30.6	37.7	37.1	32.2	24.4
5–9	22.2	20.4	22.4	23.9	21.8	19.4	16.0	18.5	21.3	21.7
10–14	17.7	16.4	16.6	18.9	19.1	11.7	7.6	8.9	12.6	15.4
15–19	11.9	9.1	10.0	12.3	16.2	6.5	3.9	5.2	7.3	8.4
20+	18.8	18.7	16.0	15.7	25.6	12.4	5.0	7.9	10.5	18.8
Median (years)	8.2	8.0	8.0	8.1	12.0	4	2	3	5	7
Eventual tenure years	25.0	23.6	22.4	23.6	30.8	15.6	9.6	12.2	15.4	20.6

Notes: Employed males in private industries.

Tiny means 1–9 for Japan and 1–25 for the United States, small means 10–99 for Japan and 26–99 for United States, Medium means 100–999, and Large means 1,000+ for both countries. Eventual tenure is calculated as twice the mean tenure.

Source: Hashimoto and Raisian (1985), p.726.

Exhibit 3.3 Composition by length of service in Japan and the U.S. Male non-agricultural employees)

	USA			Unit: % Japan			
	1966	1973	1978	1962	1974	1977	1979
Total (years)	100	100	100	100	100	100	100
Less than							
1	23.2	22.4	25.2	9.1	8.4	7.2	7.5
1	8.5	10.5	10.4	10.5	6.5	2.7	2.7
2	6.4	7.4	7.1	10.0	6.9	6.4	6.6
3–4	9.7	13.0	11.9	14.9	13.2	12.3	11.1
5–9	15.2	16.8	16.9	21.4	21.5	22.8	21.7
10–14	11.6	9.6	9.6	16.9	16.6	16.9	17.3
15 and over	22.2	20.5	19.0	17.7	26.8	31.3	33.1

Sources: 1. U.S. Department of Labor. Bureau of Labor Statistics. Job Tenure Survey.

2. Japan, Rodosho (Ministry of Labour). Shugyo Kozo Kohon Chosa (Survey on Employment Structure). The table was kindly provided by professor Koike.

Although graduating from a prestigious university is, perhaps, an important step for a successful job placement in any corner of the world, it is of particular importance in Japan, where university professors act not only as teachers but as labor market brokers, too. During the spring of every year in what is called *teiki* sayo, professors submit their student recommendations to major corporations which approach them for this purpose. Followed by job interviews, such recommendations almost guarantee employment. It should be emphasized, however, that before employees become Toshiba or Hitachi members for "life," they must undergo extensive orientation on the philosophy and the demands of the company. Such emphasis is reflected in the expenses that Japanese companies assume for this purpose. Comparing Japanese and American hiring practices, professor Higuchi (1987) finds that Japanese companies spend on recruitment an average of 759 dollars per employee compared to 411 dollars spent by U.S. companies.

The origins of lifetime employment are a very controversial issue. Institutionalists trace lifetime employment in the vestiges of feudalism, the religious influence of Confucianism, and the egalitarian spirit of the Occupation (Labor Standards Act). They claim that lifetime employment rewards and reinforces company loyalty as well as job and income security in line with social justice.[2]

Neoclassicists, on the other hand, trace the origins of lifetime employment to the rational behavior of employers and employees under conditions of imperfect information and uncertainty. In one set of models which emphasize the asymmetric risk behavior of employers and employees over the business cycle, lifetime employment is a form of an employment insurance policy that firms underwrite to employees that guarantees employment in periods of a business decline in exchange for wage restraints in periods of business expansion. In another set of models which emphasize labor transaction costs, lifetime employment minimizes labor turnover and the high transaction costs associated with it in the face of higher labor transaction costs. In a third set of models, which emphasize company-specific human capital over general human capital, employers and employees have too much to loose in human capital in case of a separation. The longer employees stay with the same company, the more they invest in human skills specific to that company, and the less likely they are to quit.

While the reasons for staying with the same company are well understood, two interesting questions can be raised at this point: if workers are comfortable that the company will not lay them off, why should they work hard? What imposes work discipline? The answer is that team production effort does. Workers are divided into numerous teams that make production decisions and coordinate and bear the responsibility for the production outcome. Through frequent training, job rotation, and interdepartmental transfers, workers have a good knowledge of the whole production process. From product development to production planning and operation, production on the shop floor and off the shop floor is the outcome of team effort. The team, not the individual, is credited with any success and debited for any failures. Thus, the hard working members have good reasons to discipline the members working not so hard. Regular team meetings and after-hours meetings provide the forum for dealing with discipline problems without the need for management intervention.

Despite the appealing features and promises, lifetime employment could not stand alone without reinforcement from the second "sacred treasury," the seniority wage system.

Seniority Wages

Seniority is an important factor for wage increases in Japan. In 1987 the seniority factor accounted for 46 percent of wage increases, with ability accounting for the remaining (see exhibit 3.4). Ability is reflected in rank; the higher the rank the higher the wage. In 1989, for instance, branch managers were earning close to 700 thousand yen monthly, more than double the earnings of the ordinary staff (see exhibit 3.5).

Exhibit 3.4 Relative Contributions of Seniority and Merit Factors to Pay Raises

	Seniority	Ability (Merit)
1978	57.9%	42.1%
1983	54.4	45.6
1984	49.0	51.0
1987	46.0	54.0

Source: Mroczkowski T. and Hanaoka, M., 46.

In the conventional economic wisdom, the term "seniority wages" is used to describe the direct relationship between on-the-job experience and wage growth, a hypothesis well tested with data from several counties.

When applied to the Japanese economy, the term has a slightly different meaning: first, company-specific experience exerts a higher impact on wage increments than general experience. Higuchi (1986) estimates that a year of general experience of male workers in Japan contributes 0.6 percent to wage increases as compared to a corresponding 0.9 percent in the U.S., while a year of experience within the company in Japan contributes 3.1 percent to wage increases as compared to a corresponding 1.2 percent in the U.S. Second, wages in Japan are primarily assigned to workers not to jobs. Such factors facilitate labor deployment, a practice we will discuss later on.

As with long-term employment, institutionalists trace the origins of the seniority wage system back to the Occupation and even to feudalism. This system is a vehicle that rewards and reinforces worker loyalty to the company; it also promotes wage equity across occupations. Workers identify themselves with the company and promote the interests of the company as family members promote the interests of the family.

Neoclassicists argue that seniority wages are consistent with the rational behavior of employers and employees under certain constraints. In one set of models that emphasize labor transaction costs (recruitment and layoff costs), seniority wages discourage quitting and therefore minimize such costs. In another set of models which emphasize company-specific investments in human capital, seniority wages represent the labor share in the rents generated through joint labor-management investments in human capital. In a third set of models, which emphasize the cost of shirking and supervision, the seniority wage system is a device that discourages shirking and therefore minimizes supervision costs.

Irrespective of which model is the most appropriate explanation for seniority wages in Japan, surveys have shown that seniority wages reinforce worker loyalty and commitment to corporate objectives. Lincoln (1989) studying the employment attitudes states:

> Our survey found, as previous studies had, that age and seniority are strong predictors of company commitment and job satisfaction. Moreover, we found pervasive evidence that these and other working attitudes were more age-dependent in Japan. Part of the reason, it appears, is that rewards and opportunities are more likely to be explicitly tied to age and seniority than in the American workplace. Another reason has less to do with age or seniority per se than with differences among generations. Given Japan's rapid postwar social change, older Japanese are apt to have the scarcity-and-production mentality typical of populations in the early stages of economic development. Younger Japanese are much more likely to share American-style values of leisure, consumption, and affluence.[3]

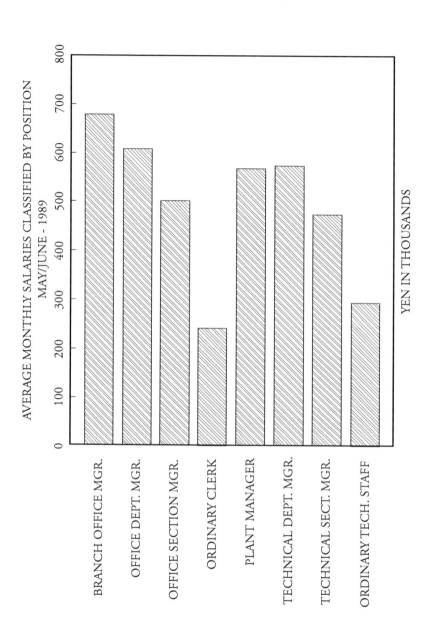

Exhibit 3.5

Both long-term employment and seniority wages could not have survived without the support of and reinforcement from organized labor, the third "sacred treasury," enterprise unionism.

Exhibit 3.6 Unionization Rate* in Selected Countries (1988)

	U.K.	Germany, F.R	Japan	U.S.
No. of Labor Union Members (1,000)	10,593	9,344	12,227	16,913
Unionization Rate (%)	48.9	41.2	29.8	17.0

* The U.K. figures include the union members of branch offices outside U.K. The U.S. unionization rate is the ratio of union members to the number of non-agricultural laborers.

Source: *Labor Statistics Handbook*, Japanese Ministry of Labor, 1989.

Enterprise Unionism

In contrast to what one might expect, unionization is extensive in Japan, the Japanese unionization rate is below the European rates but ahead of the U.S. rate. In 1988, close to 30 percent of Japanese labor was unionized, compared to 41 percent in the former West Germany, 48.9 percent in the U.K. and 17 percent in the U.S. (see exhibit 3.6).

The union system in Japan is quite complex. Central unionization is quite weak and confined to annual wage negotiations. By contrast, company unionization or enterprise unionism is quite strong.

Enterprise unionism is a form of workers' organization where workers band together within a firm rather than across a craft or profession, as it is the case in the U.S. According to Shirai (1983), enterprise unions display four general characteristics: (1) membership is limited to the regular employees of the company, i.e., employees who enjoy long-term employment; (2) membership includes both blue-collar and white-collar workers; (3) while in office, union officials retain employee status, but they are paid by the union; and (4) a large proportion of enterprise unions, about 72 percent, are connected to corresponding national federations without loss of independence. To these characteristics, we must add that as with long-term employment, enterprise unionism is mostly found in large Japanese enterprises (see exhibit 3.7).

The enterprise union performs a dual function, as a workers' representative and as a member of the enterprise team. As a workers' organization, the union bargains collectively in a manner similar to the way U.S. unions bargain. Collective bargaining sessions are held several times a year, during the "spring offensive," to resolve wage matters, during

Exhibit 3.7 Union Membership by Firm Size (1984)

No of Employees	Percent
–29	0.75
39–99	5.1
100–299	11.6
300–999	16.0
1000–	56.5

Source: *Bank of Japan: Comparative International Statistics*

the fall to resolve fringe benefits matters, and as needed for lump-sum allowances. As a member of the enterprise team, the union is involved in joint consultations, a "firm relationship" of mutual trust and understanding, like coodetermination arrangements in West Germany, Switzerland, and other European countries. The Japanese system, however, differs markedly from the system of coodetermination in Western Europe: coodetermination in Western Europe is compulsory and mandated by law; Japanese "coodetermination" is voluntary and therefore likely to be more efficient than that of Western Europe.

Japanese and Western scholars have offered a variety of explanations for the rise of enterprise unionism. Komatsu (1971) traces the origins of enterprise unionism to the emergence of industrial conglomerates and state enterprises in the 1920s. Kawada (1973) argues that enterprise unionism is the result of the early postwar communist strife influenced by the World Federation of Trade Unions declaration "one single union in one plant." Shimada (1982) argues that enterprise unions emerged after the splitting of the labor movement following a period of labor unrest in the late 1940s and the early 1950s. Specifically, after a long period of strikes in major enterprises, workers were divided into two groups, those adopting a radical strategy of confrontation and those adopting a conservative, pro-management strategy, with the latter ultimately dominating most enterprises.

The three "sacred treasuries" provide stability for noncontractual employment relations and reinforce loyalty and harmony. This does not mean that Japanese workers never strike. On the contrary, strikes are frequent in Japan, but labor disputes are settled relatively quickly in negotiations between the enterprise union and management. A comparative survey of working days lost due to labor disputes between 1978 and 1988 shows that Japan lost well below five thousand days annually and the U.S. and the U.K. well above ten thousand days each year for most of the period (see exhibit 3.8).

While broadly known and broadly praised, the three "sacred treasuries" do not reveal the whole story of the labor-management relations in the noncontractual sector. Another important tale is the way the noncontractual sector adjusts employment to varying business conditions: it does so through the workings of the internal labor market.

Internal Market

Separated from the external market, employment relations in the noncontractual sector have been conducive to the development of the internal market, a mechanism that adjusts labor compensation and input to varying business conditions.

Labor compensation in the noncontractual sector is fairly complex. Remuneration consists of basic wages, fringe benefits, bonuses, and overtime payments. Fringe benefits are extensive and include housing, dormitories for singles, and housing loans; medical and

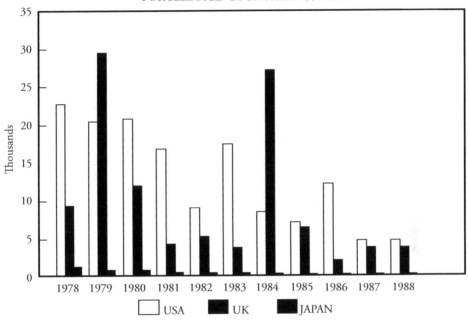

DAYS LOST IN LABOR DISPUTES
FOR SELECTED COUNTRIES: 1978-1988

Exhibit 3.8

health care; living support (nurseries and shopping and canteen facilities); mutual-aid credit facilities; cultural, sports, and recreational facilities (libraries, gymnasiums, seaside and mountain lodges, ski resorts); and such "additional benefits" as employee share-holdings and supplementary labor compensation insurance. For example, the 1976 Statistics of the Japanese Iron and Steel Federation indicate a high proportion of non-statutory expenses (housing, family insurance, pension, and unemployment insurance). These amount for 53.3 percent and 46.7 percent of wage and salary payments, respectively (Tanaka, 1981).

While basic wages are set at relatively low levels, actual remuneration is augmented by sizable bonuses. Labor bonuses, paid twice a year, amount on average, to 1.5 to 2 times monthly salaries (see exhibit 3.9). Bonuses rise with company size, from 1.5 times monthly salary in companies with less than 100 employees to 2.5 times in companies with more than 500 employees. Bonuses are reduced or not given in times of recession. Therefore, even in bad years, firms can adjust the amount of bonuses and other allowances and thereby adapt to the firm's profit position while leaving the number of employees fairly unaltered. Overtime is extensive in Japan, currently accounting for 8 percent of the hours actually worked. But overtime premiums account for 25 percent of pay half as much as in the U.S. This feature is in striking contrast to American labor compensation practices and contributes to flexibility of labor compensation and employment adjustment in Japan.

BONUS PAYMENTS

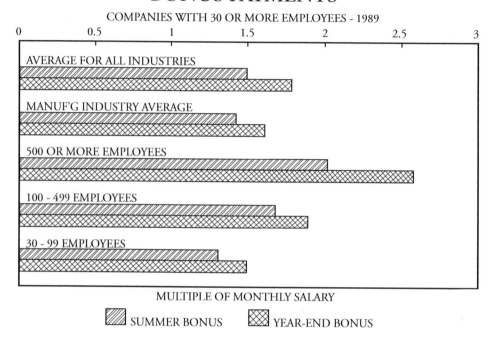

COMPANIES WITH 30 OR MORE EMPLOYEES - 1989

MULTIPLE OF MONTHLY SALARY

SUMMER BONUS   YEAR-END BONUS

Exhibit 3.9

SOURCE: MINISTRY OF LABOR

In addition to labor compensation flexibility, employment adjustments in the noncontractual sector are aided by labor deployment, i.e., labor hoarding, training and retraining, labor rotation, labor transfers. For example, the Toyota labor agreement states that "the philosophy inherent in labor-management relations in Japan is that the healthy growth of a company is essential in improving the living conditions of its employees."[4]

Labor hoarding is a practice that allows firms to stand up to the promise of long-term employment in the face of adverse economic conditions. Firms opt not to lay off workers but rather to keep them on payroll, reducing the hours of work.

Freed from the fear of losing workers to other firms, management in the noncontractual sector emphasizes labor training and retraining. In a recent survey comparing labor practices in Japanese and U.S. factories, Professor Higuchi finds that 24 percent of workers in Japanese companies received training in the preceding twelve months compared to 13.48 percent of workers in American companies. In dollar terms, Japanese spending on training amounts to $550.7 per worker compared to $392.4 per worker spent by U.S. counterparts.

Training and retraining are enhanced by job rotation and labor transfers. Toyota rotates employees as frequently as once every three years. Canon sets a three-department rotation as prerequisite for promotion eligibility, and Honda has a plan of extensive job rotation.

"An electrical engineer may go from circuit design to fabrication to assembly; a technician may work on a different machine or in a different division every few years; and all managers will rotate through all areas of business."[5] A typical worker who reaches age 65 in Japan has changed jobs five times while his U.S. counterpart has changed jobs eleven times (Hashimoto and Raisin, 1985). A typical steel worker in the U.S. works in about a dozen of different jobs within the steel plant by retirement, whereas as a similar worker in Japan works in about three dozen jobs.[6]

Labor transfers can be classified as regular and emergency. Regular labor transfers are another part of the Japanese training and promotion system. Before promotion, workers who hold managerial positions are transferred to domestic or foreign subsidiaries. For instance, in 1986, Toyota transferred about 600 employees to foreign subsidiaries for a three-year period. Unlike regular transfers that are considered promising to a worker's career, emergency transfers are considered as an alternative to layoffs.

Transfers of this sort involve assignments to new jobs that may be less satisfying, inducing workers to quit. For instance, some steel companies have gone so far as to transfer steel workers to a newly developed business of eel aquariums.[7] In addition, as some emergency transfers are from the automated divisions to the non-automated ones, they result in productivity and wage gaps that have prompted the opposition of unions: "personnel transfers should be confined to within the establishment, wage conditions should not deteriorate as a result of the labor transfer, and proper training should be given to employees.[8]

To summarize, contrary to what one might think, employment relations in the noncontractual sector are fairly flexible. They are facilitated by the internal labor market, an in-firm mechanism that continuously adjusts labor input and compensation to business fluctuations. It should be remembered, however, that the noncontractual sector and the internal market which lubricates its wheels include only one segment of the labor force employed in the Japanese enterprises, the rest being employed in the noncontractual sector.

3.2 THE CONTRACTUAL SECTOR

Employment relations in the contractual sector are defined by explicit contracts between labor and management. Contracts specify the duration of employment, the amount and the terms of labor remuneration, and the ways, if any, by which labor can be deployed in different tasks.

As this sector is residual to the contractual sector, it includes all workers who could not or would not find employment in the noncontractual sector. Unlike the contractual sector, where the typical worker profile is well defined, there is more than one profile of contractual workers. It includes those young workers who are searching for the right noncontractual job, married females, and early retirees.

Economists theorize how contractual employment works in various ways. Contractual employment is consistent with the conventional wisdom of general equilibrium under the conditions of perfect information and certainty, low transaction costs, and a homogeneous labor pool (for each job category). In this abstract setting, it is efficient for both employers and employees to form a short-term affiliation with one another, based purely on relative wage remuneration.

Unlike in the noncontractual sector where adjustment is in the form of labor quality, in the contractual sector adjustment it is in form of labor quantity. Firms can lay off workers and then appeal to the market to hire new ones. Workers can quit their jobs and search for new ones (inter-firm mobility).

3.3 INTERACTION BETWEEN NONCONTRACTUAL AND CONTRACTUAL SECTORS

Despite the significant differences that are summarized in exhibit 3.10, contractual and noncontractual employment should not be seen as two isolated sectors but rather as integral parts of the Japanese economy. Both employment sectors extend throughout all Japanese enterprises with noncontractual employment prevailing in large enterprises and contractual employment prevailing in small enterprises. And any change in one sector affects the other. For instance, a hiring freeze or early retirement measures taken in the noncontractual sector releases more workers into the pull of the contractual sector.

By tying one part of their labor force to the noncontractual sector and the internal labor market associated with it, and another portion to the contractual sector and the external market, Japanese fims can maximize functional flexibility. While external labor markets allow firms to appeal outside their own organization and adjust labor requirements (lay off or hire new labor), internal labor markets allow firms to appeal to their own internal networks and adjust to new labor requirements through labor deployment measures. Thus, each mechanism is both rigid and flexible in its own way. The external mechanism is rigid in terms of occupational tasks and compensation but flexible with regard to the required size of the labor force; the internal market is rigid in terms of the size of the labor force but flexible in terms of labor deployment. And the coexistence of the two sectors within the same enterprise provides the firm with the mechanisms which adjust labor to the spread of microelectronics.

Exhibit 3.10 Characteristics of the Noncontractual and Contractual Sector

Parameters	Noncontractual Sector	Contractual Sector
Employment Duration	Long-term	Short-term
Enterprise union	Yes	No
Seniority wages	Yes	No
Labor Deployment	Yes	No
Layoffs	No	Yes
Compensation	Flexible	Fixed

SUMMARY AND CONCLUSIONS

This chapter scrutinizes another institution that has contributed to Japan's productivity, growth, and international competitiveness, facilitating labor market adjustment to the needs of new technology, the world market, and employment relations.

Our two-sector employment model classifies employment in Japanese enterprises into two sectors, noncontractual and contractual. Employment in the noncontractual sector is characterized by an implicit understanding between labor and management regarding employment duration, labor remuneration, and labor deployment; such an implicit contract is overseen by an enterprise union. In contradiction to the popular belief, noncontractual employment is not the prevailing norm of employment in Japan. It accounts for about 40 percent of Japanese employment, while contractual employment accounts for 46 percent.

Employment in the contractual sector is described by an explicit contract regarding duration, labor enumeration, and labor deployment, if any. Both employment sectors slice through Japanese enterprises of all sizes with the ratio of noncontractual to contractual employment rising with enterprise size.

The dual structure of the Japanese employment system provides Japanese corporations with the mechanism to assimilate new technology with little labor friction.

NOTES

1. Kazuo Koike, "Workers in Small Firms and Women in Industry," Keizai Kagaku, vol. 27, 1, 1980.
2. The institutionalist view, also known as "the uniqueness hypothesis," emerged in the sixties as an explanation of the phenomenal Japanese growth. For a survey of the relevant literature, see Haruo Shimada, "Perception and the Realty of Japanese Industrial relations: Role in Japan's Industrial Success," *Keio Economic Studies*, Fall 1982.
3. James R. Lincoln, "Emploee Work Attitudes and Management Practice in the U.S. and Japan: Evidence from a Large Comparative Survey," *California Management Review*, Fall 1989, 93.
4. *Outline of Toyota*, Toyota Motor Company, Japan, 1987, 17.
5. Ouchi, 1981.
6. Koike, 1983.
7. Mourdoukoutas, 1988
8. *Japan Institute of Labor*, 9.

Chapter 4: Revisiting the Japanese Economic Model

By T. J. Pempel

Why revisit the Japanese economic model? Have events not proven it to be intellectually flawed as well as politically and economically irrelevant? During the late 1980s and early 1990s, airport bookstalls bulged with countless titles breathlessly promising to disclose "the secrets behind the Japanese economic miracle" or predicting that the twenty-first century would belong to Japan (or Asia). Policy-makers across Europe and North America trembled nervously in anticipation of an inevitable "Japanese takeover." Then suddenly, Japan was mired in the swampy after-effects of a classic asset bubble, which, after it burst in 1991, left the country mired in over a decade of unprecedented slump: gross national product (GNP) growth was the lowest in the OECD; the yen was 50 percent below its 1995 high; the financial sector faced non-performing loans four to six times greater than those that confronted the United States during its savings and loan crisis of the 1980s; unemployment catapulted to the highest levels since the years immediately following World War II; and public sector debt as a percentage of GNP was the highest in the industrial world while the Nikkei index hit a sixteen-year low. Asia's former behemoth had become a limping Lilliputian.

Meanwhile, as the editors to this volume stress in the first chapter, liberalization gained prominence as the prevailing economic ideology across wide stretches of the world. This was a result, among other things, of the resurgence of the U.S. economy, the growing power of venture capital and information technology, the political decline of the left in Europe, the rapid economic development of China following the at least partial embrace of neo-liberal criteria for foreign direct investment, as well as the ability of the United

States and the International Monetary Fund (IMF) to impose neo-liberal conditionality on much of developing Asia during the regional crisis of 1997–98. At the turn of the century it was the People's Republic of China (PRC), far more than Japan, that was attracting the attention of policy-makers, business leaders, and investors worldwide. Under such conditions, why devote serious attention to a Japanese "model" that seems obviously to have been a limited, if not disastrous, prescription for economic improvement?

This chapter suggests that there is still a need to assess and understand the Japanese economic model. It argues that, despite the subsequent difficulties faced by the national economy of Japan, the developmental state model that was generated to explain its earlier successes (as well as those of South Korea and Taiwan at a minimum) is worthy of retention, albeit with some reassessment. Indeed, as will be argued below, many of Japan's current economic problems arise from the difficulties associated with disestablishing the institutions and policies created under the earlier model of developmentalism and which have become problematic in a world dominated by economic liberalization. Only by examining the Japanese economy in both its blooming and its fallow periods can the complexity of factors critical to both phases become clear. Any useful model of Japanese development must be able to identify not only the causes of rapid growth, but also those of subsequent slowdown.

Two additional reasons for such an investigation stand out. First, despite any subsequent economic problems that arose, the Japanese success story remains marked by vastly more sophisticated engines of production, and its citizens benefit from immensely higher standards of living, than is the case in countries to which Japan was comparable three or four decades earlier. Whether it does so successfully, strategically, or unwillingly, as discussed in the other Japan chapters to this volume, the fact is that Japan at the beginning of the twenty-first century is far better poised economically to deal with the new-world paradigm of liberalization than it was in the 1950s or 1970s. Nor should one discount the importance of Japanese economic success for the rest of Asia, many of whose governments explicitly sought to emulate Japanese developmental patterns. During the last quarter-century, among all the world's major regions, only Asia has achieved a substantial increase in the share of world GNP and world incomes enjoyed by its populations. Current downturns should not obscure the longer-term economic restructurings that took place across Asia during the 1980s and 1990s and the permanent gains these generated, nor the enhanced abilities of economies across the rest of Asia to adjust to new-world conditions from positions of economic strength.

Second, despite the recent triumphalism of neo-liberal economists, the economic problems faced by Japan and other parts of Northeast Asia provide little convincing evidence of any inherent flaws in their approaches to growth. Japanese troubles do not, as is too often contended, provide incontrovertible evidence that certain allegedly underlying principles of "market economics" transcend geography and admit of no long-lasting exceptions. Neither Japan nor Asia generally should serve as a warning to others about the dangers of trying to flout Adam Smith and of interfering with "free markets" in capital flows and the production of goods. If Japan, like other countries of the world, must now adjust to the prevailing economic paradigm of liberalization, it is highly unlikely to adjust through blind emulation. Rather, again as the individual chapters by Pekkanen, Solis, Katada, and Anchordoguy show, the adaptation of Japan's future economic mix is almost certain to involve residues of "developmentalism" onto which will come new graftings of neo-liberalism. Just as earlier decades of Japanese success were not easily explained through neo-classical economics, so too the recent problems by themselves say little about the relative strengths or weaknesses of the discipline of economics or of the inevitability of worldwide liberalization. Rather, the mix of Japan's successes plus downturns sheds valuable light not only on the limitations endemic to early theorizing about the sources of Japanese growth but on that model's inherent promises as well. And many of the pluses endemic in developmentalism are likely to survive any onslaught of liberalization.

This chapter is organized into three main sections. The first recapitulates what I see as the major components of the various Japanese developmental models. The second then examines how several of these components contributed to subsequent economic problems faced by Japan, as well as many of the other East Asian national economies. Finally, a third section suggests lessons that might be culled from the combination of successes and limitations of the models of Japanese development, especially as calls for liberalization continue unabated worldwide.

KEY COMPONENTS OF JAPANESE DEVELOPMENT MODELS

One of the great puzzles of comparative political economy concerns how nation-states can improve both their relative and their absolute well-being. How do national economies that are relatively underdeveloped at one point in time "catch up" to those that are more advanced? For the most part, they have not. Since the 1960s, for example, the relative share of world GNP held by the richest 20 percent of the world's population has increased dramatically while that accounted for by the bottom 20 percent has shrunk. The ratio was 30:1 in 1960, 45:1 in 1985, and more than 60:1 by the turn of the century (Frieden and Lake 1995: 417).

A host of rather pessimistic scholarship has developed around world systems theory and dependency theory, arguing to varying degrees that the relative international pecking order remains essentially fixed over time. Yet, Asia carried out a striking collective break-out from that pattern. In 1960, Japan and the rest of Asia accounted for about 5 percent of world GNP compared with 37 percent for North America. By the early 1990s, they accounted for roughly 30 percent of world GNP, about the same share as North America and Western Europe. The early leaders of Asia's development were Japan, South Korea, and Taiwan, followed later by several successes in Southeast Asia and eventually Greater China. Collectively, Asian development makes it clear that one need not accept as permanent any relative division of economic power. Not only is catch-up possible in the abstract, it has been demonstrated across Asia as a historical reality.

Over the post-war period the national economies of Japan, and then later South Korea and Taiwan, using similar models of development, moved substantially ahead of those in countries that initially enjoyed higher GNPs and better standards of living. Japan's GNP grew at rates double those of the other OECD countries from the early 1950s until the beginning of the 1990s. Its share of world exports quadrupled, and it went from the twentieth to the second largest economy in the world. For fully four decades Taiwan's GNP grew at an average of 8.7 percent per year; exports expanded at 20 percent per year; and the industrial share of production increased from 25 percent to 45 percent (T.J. Cheng 1989). Korea's growth was slower to start, but over the approximately thirty-year period 1961–91 it rose by 8.4 percent per year. By 1997, as noted, it ranked ninth in world GNP and had been welcomed into the OECD as a member of the industrialized bloc. Both countries roared past others that were once their economic peers. To be sure, all three countries provided excellent examples that any division of world economic power is more variable than constant. A country "down" at one point in time could look to the countries of Northeast Asia during the post-war period and see proof that moving "up" was not impossible.

Virtually all studies of Japan agree that economic development is possible, both absolutely and relatively. Yet not all agree on the causes or the replicability of the Japanese model. Individual studies differ on the particular contribution of Asian culture or values, for example, to macroeconomic growth and industrial transformation.[1] Yet regardless of specifics, studies of Japanese (and Asian) development long provided a broadly optimistic picture for countries facing the arduous uphill trek of economic development. The Japanese developmental experience appeared to offer a welcome example of successful climbs.

A second important commonality—though not always as vigorously stressed—is the extent to which Japanese (and Northeast Asian) growth was achieved in tandem with relatively high levels of social equality. This commitment to social equality came about despite the fact that none of the East Asian success stories had left of center or socialist governments, elements typically associated with low levels of social inequality. Thus, Japan long enjoyed a Gini Index similar to that of Sweden or Norway, rather than to more conservative countries such as Canada, the UK, the United States, or West Germany.[2] And, in contrast to Latin American countries such as Brazil and Argentina with Gini Index figures around 0.60, Taiwan's was always low and falling, with a figure of just below 0.30. South Korea's has generally been in the range of 0.33–0.35 since the mid-1960s.[3] In addition to having relatively small gaps between rich and poor in terms of wealth and life expectancy, the nation-states of East Asia also provided relatively equal access to health care and education. Furthermore, although far from gender neutral, they were far more equal than many parts of the world in the provision of educational and health care opportunities to females. Such a commitment built up broad support from a variety of diverse constituencies and created commitments to broad segments of society in ways that the harsher versions of liberalization and market capitalism did not. This is especially critical in the period characterized as late liberalization by the editors. As a consequence, electoral politics was rarely fought over sweeping class and distributional issues such as prevailed in North America or most of Western Europe, but more frequently over the particular compensations paid out to a wide range of diverse and segmented constituencies.

In this regard, too, the comparative picture for students of development is far more sanguine than that proposed by world systems theorists or dependencistas. East Asia appeared to offer a mixture of high growth with social equality, thus undercutting any claims that the two were incompatible. East Asia, developmentalists argued, demonstrated, quite to the contrary, that the two not only were mutually achievable, but might indeed be mutually interdependent.

Two major models have dominated discussions of Japanese development. These represent the classic dichotomy between "states" and "markets." The first is highly political; the second is economic. They share the view that nations can achieve significant improvements in their economies without the wide disparities between rich and poor found in so many developing countries. Despite such agreement, however, the two models identify quite different causes for Japanese advances, reflecting the very different approaches to political economy taken by political scientists and economists.

The first model concentrates primarily on the steering role played by a highly meritocratic national bureaucracy. By far the best known of these is that of Chalmers Johnson, articulated first in his 1982 volume, *MITI and the Japanese Miracle*. Johnson's argument centers on the concept of the "developmental state," and his notion is reflected in many other studies.[4] Japan and the other Northeast Asian states, such studies typically argue, have been successful because governments there work consistently on behalf of catch-up economic growth. In contrast to so many other parts of the world, political institutions in Japan, it is argued, particularly the national bureaucracy, acquired control over a variety of tools presumed critical to economic success: they can extract capital, generate and implement national economic plans, manipulate private access to scarce resources, coordinate the efforts of individual businesses, target specific industrial projects using specific criteria for selection, resist political pressures from popular forces such as consumers and organized labor, insulate their domestic economies from extensive foreign capital penetration, and, most especially, carry through a sustained project of ever-improving productivity, technological sophistication and increasing world market shares. Initially and most forcefully articulated with specific reference to Japan, the developmental state model has also been widely applied to South Korea and Taiwan.

This state-centric political model concentrates attention on several valuable elements, which again need to be center stage in debates over late liberalization. First, authors stressing one or another variant of the "developmental state" typically give primacy to the importance of political choice in the setting of economic priorities and in creating economic institutions. Markets, such authors assume, operate neither in political vacuums nor as "invisible hands." Rather, they function within specific boundaries set for them by the politically powerful. State officials, in particular senior bureaucrats, are seen to be critical to the structuring of political choices and public policies conducive to growth. As such, these models start with a presumption that the key to understanding economic development is a national government exercising state power, rather than an unstructured mass of economic maximizers. Indeed, in one of the most explicitly anti-market aphorisms to emerge from the developmental state literature, Alice Amsden (1989) argues that the South Korean economy did so well precisely because government officials "deliberately got prices wrong."

In addition, state-centric models focus heavily on the importance of government-directed industrial policies that transfer resources to increasingly higher value-added sectors of the economy. Thus, investments and production move from bicycles to motorcycles to cars, and from radios to televisions to computers. Even more importantly, such industrial policies are explicitly linked to the production of internationally competitive goods, making for a development strategy based on export-led growth rather than import substitution.

A final element that demands attention is openness or closedness to the outside world, which is critical for debates over liberalization. While individual studies differ on specifics, most developmental state research underscores the extent to which development operates as a zero-sum, us-against-them, national project of "catch-up." Governments act to enhance their interpretation of the "national interest," defined almost invariably as rapid growth in the interests of domestic, rather than foreign, owners and producers. Governments and domestic businesses are presumably closely enmeshed with one another during their quest for national economic improvement. The common interests of these two are presumed to outweigh any specific disagreements they might have. Most typically, the domestic economy is kept insulated from penetration by foreign capital, products, and managers. Relatedly, while national consumers may not be ignored in the pursuit of national economic improvement, their specific interests as consumers are unquestionably secondary to those of producers. Hence, if cheaper prices for consumers require the opening of the national economy to foreign imports or products, then truly free trade and investment must be kept secondary to mercantilist protectionism. In this regard, developmental statists are frequently associated with glib clichés about "Japan, Inc." or "Korea, Inc."

In all of these ways, the developmental state model concentrates its explanatory power on how governments shape economics in ways designed to enhance the long-term national well-being of key national corporations and industries at the relative expense of other nation-states. In these ways, the developmental state is explicitly antithetical to liberalization and, given its centrality in Japan, cannot be ignored in debates over liberalization. Not surprisingly, economic models lay stresses elsewhere.

A limited number of economists studying Japanese development have put forward claims that nothing about its development need be examined beyond the standard principles of economics (e.g., Saxonhouse 1983). More frequent, however, is the argument that particular government policies contributed an important, but largely environmental, climate for the true engines of growth, namely the private sector. One of the earliest economic approaches to understanding Japan's rapid growth was the 1976 study edited by Patrick and Rosovsky entitled *Asia's New Giant: How the Japanese Economy Works* (Patrick and Rosovsky 1976: esp. 47). As a summary of their position, they stated: "Our view is that, while the [Japanese] government has certainly provided a favorable environment, the main impetus to growth has been private—business investment demand, private saving, and industrious and skilled labor operating in a market-oriented environment of relative prices." An even more recent market-focused study was the 1993 study of the World Bank entitled *The East Asian Miracle* (World Bank 1993; esp. 5 ,192–6, 265–73). This book, prompted by the Japanese government as a way to encourage greater understanding among economists of the ways in which Japan and other countries in Asia had developed, actually took an approach dramatically different from that of the developmental statists. While sensitive to the possible contributions of government policies to growth, it concluded that "In large measure the HPAEs [high-performing Asian economies] achieved high growth by getting the basics right. Private domestic investment and rapidly growing human capital were the principal engines of growth."

In this context, most economic models are quick to acknowledge that directed credit may have contributed to Japan's and Asia's improvements, but largely insofar as financial markets were deepened through economic growth. Similarly, in the case of the correlation between high economic growth and such things as improved education, better health care, low population growth, and lower gender discrimination, most economic models argue or imply that the causal arrows run from the former to the latter rather than in reverse. An educated populace is thus seen less as a contributor to high growth and more as its consequence; policies designed to shape the character of the labor market are, as the World Bank puts it, given less weight in growth than are policies whereby governments "let markets work."

The two camps' claims mirror the perennial disputes between the two disciplines from which they emerge: When and how do political structures and policies shape economic choices? When and how are they instead the outgrowth of underlying economic logic? This question is as relevant to the past of Japan's economic model as it is to the future of Japan's liberalization efforts. Hindsight suggests that each set of claims contributed significant, but partial, insights into why the economy of Japan grew as quickly and with the particular character that it did. Clearly, Japan's political institutions and its prevailing policy profile set conditions under which it was possible for Japanese-owned companies to develop and thrive at home. They also encouraged rapid improvements in productivity and in the technological sophistication of products. And with domestic markets well protected and often with domestic consumers undergirding profit margins, a number of Japan's most internationally oriented companies were able to export their increasingly competitive products to global markets. It is impossible to imagine that these companies at the micro level and the Japanese economy at the macro level could have achieved the successes they did without the political structures and policies that prevailed in Japan from the early 1950s until the 1990s. At the same time, only by exploiting global market opportunities through price and product quality could so many of Japan's global companies gain market shares as rapidly as they did. Not at all incidentally, however, by guaranteeing domestic protection to potentially declining sectors, the developmental state created a constituency for economic development and reduced the potential political opposition from slow-moving or domestically based firms and sectors to the broader agenda of rapid industrialization. With a strong state commitment to giving them semiguaranteed slices of the domestic market, such constituencies had little incentive to resist the global market orientations of other government policies.

Yet, missing from most treatments of both models, yet equally important to understanding Japan's development, is the fact that many of the policies pursued in Japan were strongly "anti-market" at home, insulating numerous sectors from international competition and protecting an increasing number of global noncompetitive firms at high costs to domestic consumers. The model that led to success also built in many important but less than fully examined elements that subsequently led to its eventual stagnation, and that continue to be important elements in concerns over Japan's late liberalization. Furthermore, periods of rapid growth obscured some of these more vital components of past economic successes. Particularly after recent economic difficulties in Japan and much of the rest of Asia, it is thus critical to explore the limitations that were built into the Japanese development models and to re-examine these models from the more contemporary vantage point of liberalization.

LIMITATIONS ON THE JAPANESE ECONOMIC DEVELOPMENT MODEL

As the bloom faded from the rose of Japanese economic growth, it became increasingly clear that the various development models did little to predict the subsequent Japanese fizzle. Nevertheless, post-developmental problems in Japan and across Asia should encourage us not to discard the models completely, but rather to search for those of their elements that were undertheorized, and to examine how these in turn contributed to later economic problems.

Both of the models advanced to explain Japanese development, in my view, paid inadequate attention to two vital factors. Through time's rearview mirror, it is possible to see how certain elements rarely emphasized were in fact critical to its development during the boom years—and equally central to subsequent slowdowns and problems.

First, the models were constructed predominantly to stress domestic, rather than international, conditions. To the extent that they devoted much attention to international conditions, the presumption was that these provided arenas within which domestic national economies competed with one another for relative improvement in national well-being. Alternatively, the international context was presumed to be inherently benign or else was taken to be far less relevant than domestic actions. Without question, international conditions for the first forty years or so after the end of World War II were largely conducive to Japanese growth. However, such benevolent conditions were far from irrelevant to the successes achieved during those years. And when these conditions changed in several critical ways by the middle of the 1980s, their influence moved from benignly supportive of growth to malignly interruptive. The emphasis on the international, as the editors have suggested, has now become critical as Japan faces an external environment with overwhelming pressures for wholesale liberalization.

Second, the models, particularly as they applied to Japan, were preponderantly static. A host of demographically generated advantages were presumed to be ongoing, rather than temporary. Furthermore, domestic power balances and socioeconomic conditions were taken largely as a given and presumed to be positive contributors to economic growth. As a result, the models failed adequately to address issues of change, flexibility, and institutional stickiness. Nor did they address the ways in which demographic and economic conditions endemic to the model were almost guaranteed to change in ways that would reverse their earlier consequences (but see Evans 1995: Haggard 1990). For both reasons, factors that contributed to rapid Japanese growth at earlier times were often the sources of problems and deterioration at subsequent stages.

Consider first the international conditions. Few if any of the developmental models focused on Japan give explicit attention to the indispensable contribution made by positive international conditions to Japanese and Northeast Asian economic development. This is highly ironic since one of the fundamental goals shared by Japan, South Korea, and Taiwan was the improvement of their economic conditions *relative to other states*. As a consequence, all three had to act with sensitivity to regional and international power balances and the opportunities these provided. Yet such external conditions are constantly in flux, at some times offering far greater opportunities for marginal or industrializing countries than at others. Economic options are highly contingent on the broader external arena, such as the pro-liberalization one today, within which any industrializing nation's leaders must operate. For all three countries during the highpoints of their post-war development, benign international conditions contributed greatly to their successes, just as the international ones today constrain their options.

Most basically, Japan, but Korea and Taiwan as well, were important components of the U.S. strategic nexus. For most of the post-war period, the United States gave primacy to maintaining positive security and defense relations with all three as a part of America's bipolar confrontation with the Soviet Union and its allies. This necessitated a variety of actions to ensure the continued stationing of U.S. troops in Japan, and South Korea, access to ports and air facilities across the Asia-Pacific, coordination of strategy with the military forces of all three countries, and guarantees that each would remain a close U.S.

ally and avoid either becoming politically neutral in the Cold War or, even worse, falling into alignment with the camp dominated by the major communist powers—China and the Soviet Union.

During the first three to four decades following World War II, the United States treated improved economic conditions within all three countries as not only congruent with, but also critical to, the achievement of U.S. strategic goals. To the extent that these countries did well economically, their domestic conditions would be less conducive to non-capitalist economic alternatives at home and anything other than alliance with the United States abroad. Moreover, national economic successes by these countries would provide positive alternative development models to those put forward by the communist camp.

Foreign aid was an early part of U.S. economic assistance to all three countries. Thus, South Korea received some US$13 billion in American assistance; Taiwan received about US$5.6 billion (US$600 per capita in the Republic of Korea, US$425 per capita in Taiwan) (Cumings 1984). More than two-thirds of Japan's imports in 1947 were covered by U.S. aid. Subsequently Japan's corporations benefited tremendously from military procurements during the Korean and Vietnam Wars; indeed, both were undeniable catalysts to Japan's subsequent and uninterrupted growth (e.g., Nakamura 1981; Kosai and Ogino 1984). In addition, U.S. troops were used in the early post-war years in both Japan and South Korea to suppress anti-government protests and to provide armed support for pro-United States governments. Secret payments from the Central Intelligence Agency (CIA) and other U.S. agencies were also liberally spread among U.S. supporters and pro-United States institutions in all three countries.

The strategic sustenance given to all three regimes by the U.S. military was of great importance to their continuation and economic well-being. Military objectives insured that America would be the external patron for regime success in Northeast Asia; America's strategic policies opened up space for these three countries to pursue their own economic policies. Japan's overall international muscle allowed it substantial measures of independence from the United States from early on but, as late as the early 1980s, South Korea and Taiwan could probably not have remained in existence without the international support provided by both the markets and the military of the United States.

Equally important, and of greater weight as the immediate threats of foreign invasion or domestic subversion waned, for the bulk of the post-war period, the United States opened its domestic markets to exports from Japan, as well as from South Korea and Taiwan, on terms that were exceedingly generous and devoid of demands for reciprocal access. All three countries exported heavily to the United States while maintaining largely closed markets at home. This ability to export goods to the United States and the other advanced industrialized countries combined with the ability to nurture protected manufacturing and capital markets at home was vital to their economic successes. Domestic transformations in all three countries rested heavily on this imbalanced approach to trade and investment. Yet, in most models of Japanese (and Northeast Asian) economic development, U.S. strategic contributions to economic growth are accorded little, if any, attention.[5]

A second set of international conditions was also important: that is, the relatively complementary nature of national economies across Asia. In the first few decades following World War II, Japan benefited greatly from the import of relatively inexpensive raw materials from elsewhere in Asia. As South Korea and Taiwan accelerated their industrial projects, they could often rely on more sophisticated Japanese technologies and business models. All three economies subsequently benefited from the growing markets for their exported goods across the rest of Asia. The region's national economies demonstrated a complementary mixture of strengths and weaknesses that came to be mutually beneficial across Asia.

A third condition was also critical to early Japanese and Northeast Asian success, namely the conditions of international finance. For most of the post-war period state bureaucracies in all three countries buffered their domestic economies from international financial and capital markets. As a result, even as late as the mid-1980s all three countries were able to retain high degrees of domestic control over monetary policy and exchange rates. This left them relatively free of the threat of leveraged buyouts, hostile takeovers, and the loss of national control over key industrial sectors. Mercantilist policies in trade were augmented by domestic insulation from potentially threatening international capital flows. In effect, all three could function primarily as domestically driven economies, with domestic savers cut off from access to internationally competitive rates of return and with national savings recirculated back to domestic users of capital at below market rates. Profits generated by nationally owned companies remained largely within national markets.

In addition to the shift to an international context far more favorable to market-oriented economics, all three of these conditions changed substantially by the mid- to late-1980s in ways that had profound affects on continued developmental possibilities in Northeast Asia. When the United States emerged from World War II, its domestic GNP was roughly six times larger than the world's second largest economy, Britain. Meanwhile, Japan, South Korea, and Taiwan were all very much weaker than they were by the 1980s. As a consequence, the United States could cheaply and easily afford to be economically generous to all three, at little cost to its own domestic well-being. Certain individual U.S. firms or sectors did suffer as a consequence of the growth in export competitiveness among Asian firms. But U.S. policy-makers were typically tolerant of such seemingly normal market shifts in the broader interest of keeping close security relations with Asia.

For roughly a hundred years until the early 1970s, the United States had enjoyed a favorable balance of trade with the rest of the world. This balance swung to unfavorable with increasing speed from the Nixon administration onward. Contributing most heavily to this shift was the increasing import penetration of domestic American markets by Japanese and, later, Korean and Taiwanese products. As a result, U.S. policy-makers came under ever-intensifying pressure to "do something" to protect American industries and jobs and to rectify the growing trade gap. The result, particularly with Japan, was a variety of so-called "voluntary export agreements," sector-specific targets for market openings and efforts to remove structural impediments to investments. Subsequently, the United States shifted to monetary agreements, including the Plaza and Louvre Accords of 1985 and 1987 respectively. These currency realignments among the major powers, including Japan, were designed to reconfigure each country's incentives for exports and imports. More recently, the United States applied a host of pressures to open up the domestic markets of all three to U.S. investment and exports.

Such changes in U.S. behavior made it increasingly problematic for old patterns of East Asian insularity to continue, requiring states to adapt to new realities. Ever more holes were punched in Asia's hothouses, exposing domestic manufacturers in the cozily insulated home markets to the chilling winds of foreign competition. Of particular importance was the fact that the currency realignments of Plaza and Louvre affected not only the value of the Japanese yen but also, through ripple effects, the values of both the won and the new Taiwan dollar.

All three Asian currencies jumped vis-à-vis the U.S. dollar, thus undercutting the price competitiveness of exports from these countries. Moreover, stronger currency values also led to waves of outgoing investment by companies headquartered in all three countries, as overseas prices of land, labor, and production became irresistibly cheaper (see, *inter alia*, Naughton 1997; Pempel 1999c). Companies that were once largely domestic producers subject to national monetary and capital allocation policies became far more regional or international in their production, and far less subject to national capital controls. As many of these companies set up operations abroad, sharp divisions between companies and sectors that were truly internationally competitive and those whose businesses survived largely as a result of a closed domestic economy and government assistance were exposed.

In this context, even as governments continued to mediate the processes of liberalization, Asian regional successes contained certain seeds of destruction. As industrialization spread across the Asian region, more and more companies began to adopt the export-led model of growth. The result, in sectors such as steel, textiles, electronics, personal computers, semiconductors, and shipbuilding, was the proliferation of international competition and in many cases the glutting of world markets with an oversupply of goods. The development model successfully pioneered by Japan and adopted with variations by South Korea and Taiwan eventually had its adherents in Malaysia, Thailand, Singapore, and even the PRC. As the Asian region flourished, its very success created region-wide conditions that made it ever more difficult to sustain on a permanent basis. This became particularly clear in the 1997–98 currency crises, when many Asian economies found themselves in a competitive race with one another to expand their share of world markets through production based on cheap labor. Competition with each other was inherently problematic; once the PRC, with its virtually infinite supply of cheap labor and tight national controls over capital, began aggressively pursuing the same goals, what had once been a race between a few Asian countries and the rest of the world was transformed into an intra-Asian bloodletting that left many of the participants as devastated as the American rust belt had been decades earlier (Pempel 1999a).

The focus on national economic success, and particularly the extent to which that success was achieved with high levels of social equality, had long made it easy to conclude that all of Japan (or all of Taiwan) was moving along a common trajectory. There is an old adage about the man who had his head in the oven and his feet in ice, but *on average*, should have been quite comfortable. Similarly, the models of Japanese development too easily obscured the extent to which overall growth and success in that country was the product of highly disparate and uneven performances in different sectors of the economy. By the early 1990s in Japan (and the late 1990s in South Korea and Taiwan) it had become clear that national economic success had long masked relatively large swaths of unadaptive and sclerotic private sector firms. The cumulative drag of so many inward-looking sectors and firms became an increasingly important proportion of the total national economies, particularly in Japan but later in South Korea as well.

This leads us to the second major flaw in the Japanese development models, namely their inherently static quality, which became apparent as they confronted the forces of liberalization. Many facets to this could be explored at greater length. The broad point can be captured, however, with several clarifying examples. As one example, consider the structural changes that take place as economies become more sophisticated. The models do little to account for the fact that relatively small and underdeveloped economies face quite different choices and constraints than do larger and more sophisticated ones. Countries (and private sector companies) anxious to "catch up" face many difficulties, but they do have the advantage of earlier examples of development that leave them with clear signposts as to the technologies and industries they should be targeting. Once they have caught up, however, the path ahead becomes much murkier. During catch-up, industrial development can effectively proceed by relying on techniques such as copying, reverse engineering, and product refinement. Continued success after achieving greater sophistication in the economy, however, typically requires much heavier investments in research and development, more original design, attention to creating, rather than invading, markets, and the like. This is not to suggest that Japan, Korea, and Taiwan are inherently lacking such abilities, but national leaders and many individual companies within all three have had to confront such adjustments through rapid shock under present conditions in the world economy, and many found the transition less than simple.

Consider also the demographic changes that accompany rapid economic development. At base, the national population profiles of all three countries in 1990–2000 were substantially different than those in the early post-war years. Improved health care and birth control led to smaller families and longer lives. All three countries had benefited from expanding, young, and low-cost labor forces during the early years of their development. As industrialization moved forward, farms closed down and younger workers moved into cities to provide a large, reliable and low-cost workforce. Similarly, state expenditures for social welfare, public health, and retirement could be kept relatively low with a young population. By the 1990s, however, all three countries had aged considerably, creating corresponding increases in the costs of labor along with rising demands for welfare, health care, leisure, and retirement allowances. This was most especially true in Japan. Government on the cheap was less easy to sustain, as were ever-ready and cheap sources of private sector labor.

Finally, it is worthwhile examining the ways in which power, once institutionalized to provide a strong engine for growth, can become ossified and focused on self-perpetuation rather than its original mission of economic development. Long-term rule by the Liberal Democratic Party (LDP) in Japan, the Kuomintang (KMT) in Taiwan, and a succession of generals in South Korea, combined with well-entrenched national bureaucracies in all three, fostered political structures with explicitly privileged constituencies and guaranteed compensations. The result was that these constituencies became ever more focused on self-preservation and less on adjustment to changing domestic and international conditions that could undermine their holds on power—a factor that was and is critical to debates over liberalization. This problem became particularly acute in Japan, with the LDP increasingly concentrating its policy efforts on its least internationally competitive long-standing constituents, notably construction, agriculture, distribution, and, subsequently, banking and financial services. The results were devastating to the national economy.

Ironically, political democratization and changes in the rulers in both Taiwan, and South Korea broke some long-existing hammerlocks on power in the late 1980s in ways that the Japanese system avoided. Still, failure to reform Korea's *chaebol* structures contributed greatly to the liquidity problems of 1997–98. KMT ownership of many of Taiwan's largest oligopolies created similar rigidities there. In addition, the long-standing commitments to anti-communism in both countries have made it politically difficult for them to work toward more normalized, and presumably potentially highly profitable, economic relations with North Korea and the PRC.

The examples could be multiplied but the major point should be clear. Most models of Japanese development failed to account adequately for the inherent ways in which instruments and characteristics critical to success at one point in time might themselves become impediments to continued growth once initial developmental goals had been achieved. It is this difficulty of adaptation that continues to hamper the political and economic reorientation of Japan to a world in which economic liberalization has become the predominant paradigm. Japan has made certain moves to deregulate various sectors of its economy and to open up more of its state structures to popular input and electoral competition (see, for example, S. Vogel 1996; Gibney 1998; and the other Japan chapters in this volume). Individual corporations have also engaged in restructurings designed to adjust to more liberal market conditions in the domestic market. In many instances, however, these have resulted in more rules to ensure continued compensation for potentially injured constituents. To date, the country and its companies have been slow to break with the developmentalist past and to embrace a future based on liberalization.

CONCLUSION

The above analysis has made clear that, in light of recent downturns across Asia, there is far more merit to re-examining the Japanese developmental model than in discarding it as a simple byproduct of an earlier and more optimistic era. Such a re-examination, with an eye to both successes and stumbles, allows a better appreciation of both the contributions and the flaws in the model itself, as well as making us aware of how and in what ways it may adapt to the ongoing forces of liberalization.

For many, current economic problems provide proof that the alleged Asian miracle had been no more than a mirage. However, as was noted above, two major blind spots within the model contributed to the relentlessly optimistic views taken by both academics and policy-makers toward Japanese economic success for most of the last two decades. Most models took too little account of changing international conditions and of the ways in which domestic political, economic, and social conditions once conducive to growth could inhibit its continuation. Appreciation of these two blind spots allows one to return with some appreciation to the positive contributions that can still be applauded in the (admittedly now more limited) East Asian development model that, contrary to the new wisdom, is still of great relevance in understanding the moves toward and against liberalization taken by Japan and other countries in the region.

At least four of these remain worthy of underscoring, regardless of whether the models retain their full credibility. Most notably, models of Japanese (and Northeast Asian) development drew attention to the ways in which economic growth could be successfully pursued as a catch-up strategy. Even after the economic crisis of 1997–98, the comparative economic infrastructures of Japan, South Korea, and Taiwan (as well as of Malaysia, Singapore, Thailand, Hong Kong, and even Indonesia) were vastly superior to those of countries counted as their equals only a decade or two earlier. Second, the development models demonstrated with unmistakable clarity that economic growth could advance along more than one path—indeed, more specifically, they reinforced the more general argument that there was more than one way to organize a capitalist economy.[6] This serves as a reminder that there is also more than one path to liberalization. Third, the models drew new attention to the importance of public policy choice and the design and potency of political institutions, even when these were accorded less overt endorsements of causal primacy, as was the case in most economic models. The models advanced to explain the experiences of success were all compelled to recognize the inherent economic power of political choice. Fourth, virtually all of the models stressed to a greater or lesser extent the importance in any national economy of mutually reinforcing linkages between the state apparatus and private market actors, which also continues its relevance in debates over liberalization. If "state" and "market"' were in competition elsewhere in the world, in Japan, and much of Northeast Asia, they were far more frequently in collaboration.

All of these features deserve recognition. The Japanese development model did a great deal to bring them front and center in comparative analysis as well as in the thinking of policy-makers charged with advancing national economic development. At the same time, the current economic problems in Japan, traced as they have been to shifts in international political power balances and particularly to a reconfiguration of international finance, make it clear that economic development strategies can no longer be nurtured in nationally insulated vacuums. The prevailing orthodoxy of economics has become liberalization, and national leaders anxious to achieve success today must be wary of assuming that they can emulate the experiences of Asia's success stories too directly. The United States is surely far less likely to tolerate, let alone embrace, mercantilist approaches today than it was during the heights of the Cold War. Success may well depend too on compatible and supportive economic conditions throughout its regional neighborhood. And new conditions of global capital will make purely domestic control of capital investments highly problematic.

In addition, developmentalists should learn from Japan and Northeast Asia the value of flexibility and the dangers of entrenched power, twin elements of added importance in the contemporary pro-liberalization context. Unshakable commitments and compensations to constituents unable to contribute to economic growth, while perhaps socially stabilizing, can become impediments to rapid adjustment to changing economic needs. Development, as Joseph Schumpeter (1970) made clear decades ago, involves not only the ability to generate the new, but also the ability to destroy the old. "Creative destruction" is as critical an ingredient of growth in the current century favoring liberalization as it was in the last favoring development.

NOTES

1. Classic examples of such an approach are Pye (1985) and Tai (1989).
2. This point is explored at length in Pempel (1989). See also Sawyer (1976) and Verba *et al.* (1987).
3. A useful comparative table summarizing finding on Gini Indexes for several major NICs is presented in Haggard (1990: 226). See also Koo (1984) Evans (1987), and Schwartz (1989: 266).
4. Among the other relevant studies, see Pempel (1976, 1999b), Amsden (1989), Wade (1990), and Pekkanen (2003).
5. A particularly important exception in the case of South Korea is Woo (1991).
6. Among the more prominent works in this field see Albert (1993), Hollingsworth *et al.* (1994), Pempel (1998), and P. A. Hall and Soskice (2001).

Chapter 5: The Bubble Economy

By Carl Mosk

A JAPANESE SYSTEM?

During the 1970s and early 1980s the nature of Japan's economic success loomed larger and larger on the international stage. In one sense this simply reflected the fact that Japan's national income had reached gigantic size. Japanese goods showed up everywhere. Even with a low ratio of imports and exports to GDP, the sheer volume of Japanese goods sold abroad, and the sheer volume of Japanese purchases of raw materials—of coal, iron ore, nickel, zinc, petroleum, potash, timber, and rubber—grew by leaps and bounds during miracle growth, reaching massive levels by the early 1970s.

Consider automobiles. New Japanese cars made huge inroads in North American and European markets, in part because they were fuel efficient and small, in part because they embodied quality in their components, their excellent repair records garnering praise in consumer magazines. Used Japanese cars—sold by Japanese drivers wishing to avoid the *shaken*—appeared all over Southeast Asia, even in New Zealand. Taxi cab drivers in Bangkok were churning the streets with Toyotas and Hondas.

There was a second reason why the subject of Japan's economy became a matter of burgeoning interest to Americans and Europeans: trade deficits. In the United States in particular the bilateral trade imbalance between itself and Japan became an increasingly potent political topic. Since the 1960s the American government establishment responsible for trade negotiations (the office of the United States Trade Representative office, Congressional committees appointed to look into trade related matters) tends to focus on that country enjoying the largest bilateral trade surplus with the United States. Spurred on by political demands on the part of industries that felt besieged by imports from Japan—the American iron and steel industry pressed for a trigger-price mechanism designed to drive up prices of imports of Japanese steel on the American market, the American automobile industry lobbied for the negotiation of voluntary export restrictions that would restrict the volume of cars brought in from Japan. Congress appointed a committee of American economists with expertise on Japan to better learn about Japanese exporting companies, to better understand how American companies could make inroads into the Japanese consumer market.

In the case of the United States some of the concern was about global leadership, both technological and economic. In the late 19th century the United States supplanted England as the global technological leader. After World War II it emerged as the political leader committed to promoting, international trade through its support for multilateral organizations like the General Agreement on Tariffs and Trade, the World Bank, the United Nations. In addition it underwrote international currency markets with the Bretton Woods system. Some of the concern in the United States about Japan's rapid growth and its gargantuan economic size reflected anxiety that Japan was now taking over global leadership from the United States. Linear projections suggesting that Japan's economy would soon become the biggest in the world bolstered the view that Japan was rapidly becoming an economic "superstate," a cornucopia for commercial and industrial innovations, the world's largest capital market to boot.

Interest in Japan's successful development also blossomed in the developing world. In many ways South Korea and Taiwan, two of Japan's former colonial possessions, seemed to imitate Japanese economic policy making and Japanese economic performance. Industrial policy and *zaibatsu-style* combines (called *chaebol* in Korean) were especially important in South Korea's remarkable economic growth between the mid-1960s and the late 1980s. To policy makers in the nations of Southeast Asia, to Latin American regimes struggling with the problem of moving from import substitution to export promotion—along the lines of the flying geese model of trade—it seemed that Japan offered a better model of development than did the more market driven model associated with United States economic advance. Of course drawing this conclusion required that one buy into a particular theory of Japanese economic development, one in which political constraints and/or norms and values played an important role along with invisible hand market forces.

In short, Japan's remarkable success forced intellectuals and policy makers in both the advanced industrial world and in the developing world to ask a set of probing questions. What can be learned from the Japanese experience? Are there aspects of the Japanese economy that are transferable to other economies? How do foreign leaders cope with, negotiate with, Japan? Can they, should they, shape and change Japanese practices? How did Japan get to where it was in the early 1980s? How is it likely to change in the not so distant future?

To many foreign students of the Japanese the problem of Japan's global leadership posed disturbing thoughts itself. One concern was political corruption as exemplified in the political rise of Tanaka Kakuei, prime minister of Japan and author of a prominent treatise, a vision statement, about how Japan should revamp itself in the future. Tanaka's volume—published in English 1972—entitled *Remodeling of the Japanese Archipelago* seemed to be a direct extension of the pork barrel logic he had used in rising to national power. A second concern was Japan's closed nature. The growing popularity of *nihonjinron* books in Japan exemplified an attitude of Japan as different—unique—impossible to imitate or really learn from.

A third concern was that Japan's economy was part of a system in which politics and policies, economic behavior, and social norms and values interacted.

TANAKA KAKUEI, MASTER OF PORK, AND THE "REMODELING OF THE JAPANESE ARCHIPELAGO"

There is no better illustration of the importance of the three adages of politics in a democracy—"money is the mother's milk of politics," "all politics are local," and "power corrupts; absolute power corrupts absolutely"—than the career of Tanaka Kakuei, prime minister of Japan between 1971 and 1974.

Perfecting the art of pork barrel politics that had permitted him to consolidate his hold over the politics of rural Niigata prefecture, Tanaka Kakuei mastered the art of the shady real estate deal, adroitly using his money and his personal connections to build a powerful faction in the Liberal Democratic Party. Eventually grasping the reins of power with the prime minister's post. Tanaka accepted bribes amounting to $1.8 million from the Lockheed Corporation in exchange for his directing Japan's national airlines to purchase the Lockheed L–1011 aircraft. Arrested in 1976 for accepting the bribes, Tanaka was convicted in 1983 and sentenced to four years in prison. He died in 1993 with his appeal of the conviction lingering on the docket of Japan's Supreme Court.

Tanaka built his power base through the sponsorship of a group known as the Etsuzankai (the "Niigata Mountain Association"). The function of the group was to review local applications for government, funded pork barrel projects, choosing a select group to promote in the Diet—like the Tadami River hydroelectric power project, the New Shimizu bullet train Shinkansen line that snaked its way out to Niigata—in exchange for contributions to the Etsuzankai. During the 1950s Tanaka would bring Etsuzankai members to Tokyo, sponsoring tours of the Diet and the Imperial Palace, wooing most on an individual basis in one-on-one meetings.

Through these dealings Tanaka became known as the godfather of Japanese politics, earning a shady gangster like reputation that his dabbling in shady land deals did nothing to dispel. Slated to become secretary general of the Liberal Democratic Party, when Satō

Eisaku became prime minister in 1965, Tanaka was forced to surender his bid for the powerful position when the Black Mist scandal that centered upon Tanaka's dealings in the Tokyo land market broke.

Despite his compromised image for corruption, Tanaka's base in the Etsuzankai made him a formidable rival to Fukuda Takeo, who was Tanaka's chief rival for becoming the heir to Satō's faction in the Liberal Democratic Parry. Testimony to Tanaka's staying power in the "Kaku-Fuku war" within the party, prime minister Satō appointed Tanaka minister of international trade and industry in 1967, turning the most powerful economic ministry during the miracle growth era over to the Niigata politician, signaling his appreciation for Tanaka's political skills by rewarding him with one of the chief posts in the cabinet.

Flaunting his influence over Japanese industrial policy Tanaka gained considerable leverage over American negotiators attempting to secure quotas, limits, on Japanese exports of certain products, meeting with many of them on an ongoing basis. Exploiting these connections with the American diplomatic corps posted to Tokyo, Tanaka played a major role in negotiating the reversion of Okinawa from American to Japanese rule, enhancing his image as a no-nonsense politician capable of dealing with American political pressure.

Assuming the position of prime minister in 1971, Tanaka sought to enunciate a vision for Japan, one that would provide direction for his government, one that would constitute his political legacy. In 1972 he published "Rettō kaizb rōn" subsequently translated into English as "Building a New Japan: A Plan for Remodeling the Japanese Archipelago." In the volume Tanaka advocated setting up a central administrative body to handle land development, including the building of new Shinkansen bullet train lines designed to knit the nations land markets closer together. He proposed construction of new high-rise danchi apartment buildings housing higher-quality units than those commonly built during the 1950s and 1960s. He also pushed for the promotion of key nodal cities that would serve as growth poles for regional economic expansion, thereby raising the income per capita levels in rural regions to those characteristic of the great metropolitan centers. He emisioned a new zoning approach, facilitating the conversion of the agricultural land that continued to pockmark urban landscapes to non-agricultural purposes, freeing up real estate for infrastructure construction. Finally Tanaka's fifth proposal was to tap the high level of national savings so that this thoroughgoing, radical, remodeling of Japan could be achieved.

Sadly for his legacy, Tanaka was unable to muster the political muscle or governmental access to the financial resources needed to realize his grand scheme. Instead of leaving a legacy graced by credit for the redirecting of regional Japanese economic development, Tanaka's legacy was dominated by scandal, influence trading and pork barrel politicking, his restless striving for power and money overcoming his patriotic love for Japan and for the welfare of the common Japanese citizen.

Note: Tanaka's volume was translated into English, published as Tanaka (1972).

There was a System, the Japanese System. The chief advocate for this view was von Wolferen (1989). He argued that holding and achieving power was paramount in Japan. For this very reason it was widely diffused: bureaucrats, political elites, corporate managers, and union federation leaders, all having some power. With power came responsibility. To blunt the efforts of those enjoying less power to make claims on the powerful, to keep at bay attacks on one's power from other power seeking quarters, those with power attempted to hide, disguise, their prowess. The result was a System without a core. No one was in charge. No one holder of power could easily impact the behavior of other power centers. The Japanese state was doughnut-like, lacking a true center, power diffused around the ring.

This view suggested three disturbing conclusions. It would be difficult to negotiate with Japan because it would be impossible to find someone who was truly in charge. It would be difficult to learn from Japan since behavior in any one sector of the society was connected to behavior in every other sector, the System being in some kind of equilibrium. How could you pluck out one practice, one lesson, when everything was intertwined? It would be difficult to change the economic and political behavior of the System since it was in some kind of long-standing equilibrium. Indeed von Wolferen (1989) went as far as to argue that Japan had been this way since the 8th or 9th century. He did not rule out change. But he thought it would be difficult.

An equally provocative account of Japan's disturbing place in the world was Schmiegelow and Schmiegelow (1989). The focus of their volume was on how Japan's performance challenged the very conceptual bases of Western social science. No Western models were up to the task of understanding how and why Japan performed as well as it did. Japan fit into every theoretical competing category in at least some ways, hence in none. It could not be pigeonholed. The key to their interpretation was that Japan was Schumpeterian in a novel way: policy making was innovative, emphasizing strategic pragmatism. Key Japanese innovations were administrative guidance, the promotion of implicit contracts linking public actors and corporations, negotiating potential conflicts between policy outcomes by establishing clear hierarchical ranking of policies, and the managing of markets in danger of being disrupted for instance by gluts of production or excessive growth.

Most social scientists were not willing to go this far. For instance Vogel (1979) argued that there were very specific aspects of Japan's society, polity, and economy that could and should be emulated or at least learned from. From the economist's viewpoint, however, the most concerted attempt to argue that Japanese economic behavior was explicable in terms of Western social science concepts and transferable abroad was due to Aoki (1988). Aoki's key points concern the different ways hierarchies and information flows are managed in typical Japanese and in typical American companies (he calls the former the J-firm, the latter the A-firm). Armed with these arguments, Aoki concludes that a hybrid form is emerging, one that combines features of the two extreme opposite models of market oriented enterprises.

"JAPAN AS NUMBER ONE"

During its heyday in the 1950s and 1960s, there was a decided tendency, in the literature on modernization, especially in that penned by American scholars, to assume that societies successfully achieving economic development were increasingly likely to mimic the society that was considered to be economically most advanced, namely the United States.

There is a target for modernization. The target is the United States. Modernization is basically a linear process, less developed nations all moving toward the same target.

Analogous is the interpretation of income per capita convergence in terms of sigma convergence: countries with income per capita levels falling short of the United States (assumed to be the technological and market leader) are assumed to grow until they catch up with the leader. By contrast beta convergence involves a shrinking of variance between nations. Some might converge downward, actually experiencing a fall off in income per capita; some might converge upward, their income per head expanding; Unlike sigma convergence, beta convergence does not assume that there is a leader, a target, toward which other nations are moving.

By the early 1970s, the emergence of Japan as a world beating economic dynamo was calling into question the simple linear development hypothesis implicit in much of the modernization doctrine. Particularly impressive was the growth rate of the Japanese economy, linear extrapolation suggesting that Japan's per capita income would surpass that of the United States within a matter of decades. For instance, during the period: 1956–60 the relative level of Japanese income per capita compared to the United States set at a value of 100 was 29.9; by 1971–75 it was 66.1; and during the late 1970s it was 68.5. That Japanese politics and society seemed so radically different from that of the United States and yet Japan seemed to be on a growth trajectory to pass by the United States in economic affairs, called into question the very foundations of modernization theory.

This is the background for the publication of "Japan as Number One: Lessons for America" by Harvard University sociologist Ezra Vogel in 1979. In this volume Vogel turned his back on modernization theory, arguing that there are different flavors of democracy, different flavors for the welfare state, different flavors for industrial competitiveness, different flavors for learning, different flavors for governing. Even between two countries where the level of per capita income is similar, where the technologies applied in manufacturing are relatively identical there can be profound differences in social customs and political: practices.

Vogel pinpointed seven features of Japanese society and polity that he believed made Japan radically different from the United States: group-oriented, as opposed to individual-oriented learning, reaching consensus being a salient feature of the Japanese landscape; meritocracy in a bureaucracy that exercises far greater leverage over policy than it does in the United States; multi-purposed group democracy, villages, firms and professional organizations in Japan being strongly held together by group solidarity and a commitment to everyone getting a "fair share" of the economic pie; "bottom up," as opposed to "top down," decision making in Japanese enterprises; the use of competitive examinations coupled with uniform national standards in shaping basic education in Japan; enterprise as opposed to state based, welfare; and a high level of professionalism amongst Japanese police officers and public cooperation in identifying potential criminal behavior resulting in low crime rates per capita.

Taken as a whole, Vogel believed that these seven features of the Japanese environment made the Japanese formidable competitors to the United States, not only in economic matters, but also in developing technology and in providing global leadership to market oriented economies. Thus his title "Japan as Number One." He chose a deliberately provocative title as a wake up call to Americans.

In making his case for Japan as number one, Vogel was not only intent on wakening up Americans to the Japanese challenge to American leadership. He was also using his argument to encourage change within the United States, to force Americans to borrow from Japan, to become more like the Japanese. In effect he was saying that beta type convergence rather than sigma type convergence should be the rule of the day. Japan might become more like the United States and at the same time the United States might become should become more like Japan.

While the audience Vogel seemed to address was American, the irony is that the book became a best seller in Japan. For a country obsessed with ranking, the fact that a Harvard professor—Harvard commonly considered the top ranked university in the world in the Japanese media—had proclaimed Japan to be number one was an event to be much celebrated. But this was in the late 1970s, when many Japanese were feeling immense confidence, even arrogance, over the performance of their economy. In the aftermath of the bursting of the bubble economy, in the wake of scandal after scandal among bureaucrats and politicians, in the aftermath of growth in antisocial behavior among teenagers, matters look quite different than they once did. Indeed, returning to income per capita as an admittedly imperfect indicator of performance, we see that Japan's relative level compared to the United States, 88.1 in 1991–95, had dropped to a level of 81.6 in 1996–2000. That Japan is no longer perceived as number one in the United States or in Japan seems to be widely accepted at the end of the twentieth century. More important is the possibility that there are no targets toward which societies are or perhaps should move. To put the matter somewhat differently: is conceptualizing national economic; and social development in terms of a ranking scheme for nations desirable? Can we not argue that no society is number one, that particular societies enjoy impressive strengths in some areas and at the same time glaring weaknesses in other dimensions?

Note: Vogel's book was published in hardback by Harvard University Press and in a paperback edition as Vogel (1979).

Aoki (1988) rests his analysis on theoretical arguments made about why firms exist anywhere and on empirical studies of job rotation in Japanese work groups notably the observation field work of Koike (1984). The basic argument is that when transactions costs are sufficiently expensive, firms—by definition organizations in which hierarchical command and control modes of behavior are normal—dominate over invisible hand market solutions. For instance, we have seen how putting-out gave way to factory production with the introduction of steam power and the orientation of manufacturers toward wide ranging mass markets. Specifically organizing production in firms provides the following benefits: by centralizing information about material requirements to meet production objectives, a hierarchy can economize on inventories stockpiled, on how materials are most efficiently utilized on the shop floor; by encouraging specialization and division of labor and repetition of tasks, firms drive down labor input costs per unit of output; by centralizing information, hierarchies can respond to changing demand for the output that they generate.

As Aoki (1988) notes, these arguments are typically used to justify the existence of the A-firm. In the typical A-firm, a small group of managers and engineers establish plans for production, laying out tasks to be performed on the shop floor, giving orders about how many components of a product are to manufactured in a given period, how many are stockpiled. Production decisions are highly centralized. By contrast in a typical A-firm evaluation of workers and assignment of wages is done in a decentralized manner. Shop stewards and union representatives work with detailed scales set through collective bargaining or at least posted by management for all to see.

The J-firm is the mirror opposite. Personnel decisions—wage determination—are highly centralized. They are made in the company personnel division that enjoys a wealth of information about each and every worker. But the production plan is implemented in a decentralized, non-hierarchical manner. Job rotation is common, workers changing work assignments on an ongoing basis, flexibly adjusting to changing market demand conditions, filling in for one another when someone is ill or disabled due to accident or injury.

In short, a duality principle applies. In the A-firm, personnel decisions are decentralized, production decisions centralized and hierarchically applied. In the J-firm, personnel decisions are centralized and hierarchically applied, production decisions decentralized. There are two distinct models of how information flows and hierarchies are established in capitalist firms.

Aoki (1988) argues that the J-firm type model is transferable. Indeed, steps taken in some American firms during the 1980s to reduce the number of distinct occupational codes—from hundreds to five or six—seemed to bear out his prediction. In advancing this line of analysis he criticizes the view of social theorists like Nakane who believe Japanese are prone to form small groups, frames into which they fit. He notes that keeping the small work group from spiraling off on its own, losing its connection to the rest of the factory, would be a real problem in the J-firm if Japanese workers were simply committed to working in small work teams.

What about negotiating with Japan? There is ample evidence that the political leaderships of the two nations could and did work together in an effort to correct the trade imbalance between the two countries that was generating waves of concern in Washington. Getting agreement between the central banks of the two nations was key to negotiating the Plaza accord that led to dramatic appreciation of the yen relative to the United States dollar. When this policy of manipulating relative prices failed to correct the trade imbalance, the two governments worked together to hammer out agreements on structural issues that they believed would help address not only the trade imbalance but also other sources of political friction in the two countries associated with the trade imbalance. In the Strategic Impediment Initiative negotiations and talks that took place in the late 1980s, both countries demanded more open access to one another's markets. The United States was keen to break up the hold that the vertical *keiretsu* in the distribution system seemed to have, relaxing of the restrictions on department store square footage specified in the Large-Scale Retail Store Law, and speeding up of import clearance procedures. Japan was equally keen to see the United States clarify its anti-dumping measures, making them more transparent; end language based discrimination in the way the United States adhered to international patent agreements (involving a requirement that the patent be expressed in the English language); and encourage reform of product liability laws. In short, recognizing that their combined national incomes were almost 40 percent of world GDP, recognizing the growing capital market integration of the two economies, encouraged the governments of both Japan and the United States to reach cooperative agreements in the economic field.

THE PLAZA ACCORD

The political friction over Japan's continuing ability to rack up bilateral trade surpluses with the United States became an ongoing drone, a rhythmic drumbeat, for American diplomacy with its great Pacific economic rival. It played a role in the negotiations over Okinawa's repatriation, in Nixon's decision to impose quotas on selected Japanese products, and it threatened to stabilize the mutual security treaty binding the militaries of the two countries together.

At the same time it roiled multilateral trade negotiations and the stability of the international exchange rate system. It would not be correct to attribute the decision of the executive branch in the United States to end the Bretton Woods system in 1971 by severing the connection between the United States dollar and gold solely to Japan's current account surpluses with its most important export market. Problems with the Bretton Woods system had developed earlier with the Western European countries, especially with Germany and France. Still, the decision to let the American dollar devalue in 1971 did have the effect of pushing the yen up from its Dodge Line value of 360 yen to a dollar.

The theory that adjustment in exchange rates will lead to adjustments in trade surpluses and trade deficits has been discussed earlier in this volume. If one's products become cheaper on international markets one expects to export more; if one's products become more expensive one exports to export less. Complicating this simple story are some important details that bear rehashing here.

First, inflation rates in countries trading with one another may be different. In this case the real exchange rate may not mimic movements in the nominal exchange rate. Second, the J-curve holds, at least in the short run. When the currency of an exporting nation is pushed upward, the financial aspects of all import/export agreements already entered into change, but the quantities do not necessarily change. Suppose a Toyota dealer in San Francisco has already placed an order for one hundred Toyota trucks. If the yen appreciates before the vehicles are shipped the order still goes through but the dollar cost of completing the order actually goes up, making the bilateral trade deficit between the United States and Japan temporarily worse when it is denominated in dollars (in yen terms there is no change as long as the dealer sticks to its commitment to take the one hundred trucks). In the long run the dealership is likely to cut back on the volume of Toyota trucks that it brings in, thereby making the adjustment envisioned by the exchange rate theory of trade.

There is a third problem, peculiar to the country whose currency serves as the main linchpin of the global monetary system, most goods shipped internationally—crude oil, wheat, coal, zinc, and coffee beans—being priced out in units of its money supply (the United Kingdom in the period 1870 to 1914; the United States after 1945). In the post-1945 period, when the currency of a country appreciates relative to the United States dollar, the cost of importing raw materials falls in terms of its own currency. This was the situation that Japan found itself in as the yen began to appreciate upward relative to the dollar: the price of raw materials fell, counteracting to some extent the rise in its export prices attributable to yen appreciation. The price of a Japanese automobile reflects both production costs in Japan (labor, land, capital) and the costs of the imported raw materials used in its production. Thus yen appreciation was a two-edged sword.

A fourth factor involves restrictions on imports from other countries, either in the form of tariffs, or quotas, or other non-tariff barriers like those established by a regulatory agency in a country that sets product standards that apply to both domestic production and to imported items.

This was the background for the Plaza Accord of September 1985—signed onto the central banks of France, West Germany Japan, the United States and the United Kingdom—in New York. The goal of the accord was to devalue the dollar against the yen (then trading at 235 yen to the dollar) and the German Deutsche Mark by intervening in currency markets, selling dollars, buying yen and marks. The intervention was deemed successful in the sense that it did not produce panic in world financial markets, although speculation against the dollar did *drive it below the level planned by the central banks. It was also deemed successful in reducing the United States trade deficit with Western Europe. However it did not appreciably impact Japan's bilateral trade surplus, at least as denominated in United States dollars, for the four reasons suggested above.*

In part because the Plaza Intervention did not correct the bilateral trade imbalance between the United States and Japan, and in part because the American position was based on a two-pronged theory of why the imbalance existed—the yen was undervalued; and domestic aggregate demand growth in Japan was too lackluster—American and Japanese negotiators continued to meet, trying to work out solutions to the bilateral problem. In 1986, the Baker–Miyazawa agreement was hammered-out, Japan committing itself to stimulating its economy through a variety of means, thereby presumably increasing its demand for American goods and services. Again, in 1987, in the Louvre accord, negotiators for Japan agreed to "follow monetary and fiscal policies which will help it to expand domestic demand and thereby contribute to reducing the external surplus."

If the response of the trade imbalance between the two countries to the Plaza Accord seemed to be paradoxical, even more unexpected was the response to the Baker–Miyazawa and Louvre accords. By agreeing to expand its money supply (see table A.4, concentrating on the figures for 1986–90), the Bank of Japan intervened in its domestic financial market, driving interest rates down in order to stimulate investment. In increasing the volume of yen outstanding it cheapened the value of the yen on international markets, thereby counteracting the impact of the Plaza Accord to some extent. In increasing the domestic money supply it also gave an additional upward kick to asset prices that were moving upward with the changing terms of trade, and hence with the United States dollar/yen exchange rate, for reasons discussed in the text of this chapter.

Interestingly enough, as Alexander (2002) shows, negotiations designed to mitigate trade friction between the two economies went on a completely separate track from negotiations over other bilateral issues, military security for instance. Both countries avoided linking their economic negotiations to geopolitical issues. As important as correcting the bilateral trade imbalance was to the United States, it was not important enough to endanger strategic military arrangements that mutually benefited both nations, perhaps East Asia more generally.

THE YEN/DOLLAR EXCHANGE RATE

The upward drift in the yen turned into a gallop after the Plaza Accord. This is apparent from table A.4 and from figure 5.1. More important, the Plaza Accord marked a fundamental change in the terms of trade (the price of exports relative to import prices). As figure 5.1

shows there is a tendency for movements in the yen/dollar exchange rate to be associated with, to be mirrored by, parallel movements in the terms of trade. When the yen goes up, the relative price of exports improves. However, prior to the mid-1980s, export prices tended to fall faster than import prices, regardless of whether the yen was appreciating or depreciating relative to the dollar. Prior to the mid-1980s import prices tended to go up even though each yen was buying more raw materials, more natural gas, more petroleum, more iron ore, most of these commodities denominated in United States dollars. To some extent this was the result of the price hikes for petroleum that roiled the global economy during the 1970s.

From the mid-1980s Plaza Accord until the mid-1990s, appreciation in the yen went hand in hand with positive movements in the terms of trade. Import prices fell more than export prices. Japanese firms were paying less and less for the raw materials that they were bringing in. The tendency of import prices to fall—because the international purchasing power of the yen was going up—kept export prices from rising as much as they would have risen in the absence of yen appreciation. This was one reason why the dramatic appreciation in the yen (known as *endaka* in Japanese) after 1985 did not correct the bilateral United States/Japan trade imbalance, at least as it was calibrated in United States dollars. A number of other factors operating in the medium run kept the bilateral balance computed in dollars from closing. First under the agreements reached in the *shuntō* that mainly dealt with extending the retirement age, the union federations agreed to modify their wage demands so that exporting firms could continue to export even under *endaka*. This kept a lid on inflationary pressures in the Japanese economy. As can be seen from panel A of table A.4, the consumer price index hardly increased during the late 1980s or 1990s. Cost-push due to upward movement in nominal wages was muted under the collective bargaining umbrella. Because inflationary pressures were less in Japan than in the United States, the real exchange between the yen and the dollar did not increase as much as the nominal exchange rate. This worked to keep Japanese goods competitive in the American marketplace.

Alexander (2002) shows the yen/dollar nominal exchange rate did tend to diverge from the real exchange rate after 1985, the yen growing stronger than would be expected taking into account inflation rates in the two economies. Why? The answer lies in the discrepancy between movements in prices for goods and services only produced and consumed in Japan—wholesale and retail, rent on land, infrastructure—the so-called non-tradable sector, and movements in prices of tradable exports and imports. As you can see from table A.4 tradable goods and services fell in price (export prices continued to decline throughout the period 1980–2000) while overall goods and services, tradable and non-tradable, rose somewhat in price over the same period. The export oriented sector was far more efficient—enjoyed more rapid productivity growth—than did the non-export oriented sector. The result is that the nominal yen/dollar exchange that mainly reflects the flow of traded goods and capital movements moved up more vigorously than the real exchange rate.

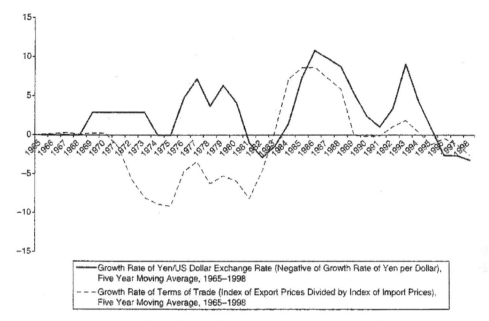

Figure 5.1. Growth rate of yen/U.S. dollar exchange rate (negative of growth in number of yen per U.S. dollar) and growth rate of terms of trade (index of export prices divided by index of import prices), five year moving averages, Japan, 1965–1998.

Second, the total cost of consumer durables includes the discounted costs of maintenance and repair. Once a Japanese automobile is purchased in the United States and used there, maintenance costs are expressed in United States dollars and are unaffected by any further changes in the yen/dollar exchange rate. The reputation for building quality into cars that Japanese manufacturers enjoyed allowed them to hold onto market share in the United States despite *endaka*.

In the short term there are two factors that always help explain why the bilateral trade balance at least measured from the American side, in United States dollars, did not vanish. The J-curve is one factor. Once orders are placed by wholesalers and retailers in the United States for Japanese goods, the dealer must absorb any depreciation in the dollar relative to the yen occurring between the date the order is placed and the date shipment takes place, paying out more dollars than the dealer originally expected to spend. This J-curve effect weakens the bilateral trade imbalance calibrated in United States dollars. Adding to these concerns is currency speculation. Acting on expectations about future movements in the yen/dollar exchange rate, speculators can drive the exchange rate at least in the very short run. In the medium term, fundamentals shape exchange rates. But in the short run speculation can drive it.

In one sense, in terms of actual volumes of goods traded, the bilateral trade imbalance between the two countries did shrink as the yen appreciated relative to the dollar. Indeed, calibrated in yen the bilateral imbalance actually shrunk. Negotiators for Japan could and did point this out to their American counterparts. Unfortunately for the American side what counted was the bilateral trade imbalance computed in American dollars. It was cold comfort that the Japanese side was observing shrinkage when it carried out its computations in yen.

THE BUBBLE

From the mid-1980s until it began bursting in December 1989, Japan was caught up in talk of twin bubbles in land prices and in stock prices. Is this description an accurate reflection of the facts on the ground?

The figures in table A.4 and the graphical evidence presented in Figure 5.2 suggest that talk of a bubble was exaggerated. The inflation in land and stock market prices was greater during the 1970s than it was during the late 1980s. Indeed in the first two decades of the twentieth century, when the intercity railroad lines were being built and bedroom suburbs were proliferating, the upward thrust in land prices was probably equal to that of the 1970s. Is this surprising? When rapid urbanization is occurring, dabbling in land speculation is a natural thing to do. Buy cultivated fields and unused land when it is still cheap; sell it when it becomes dear. Moreover, investing in housing that appreciates in value is a good way to make more money on asset holding than by putting your funds into a bank account, particularly with a shaky financial institution that might go under.

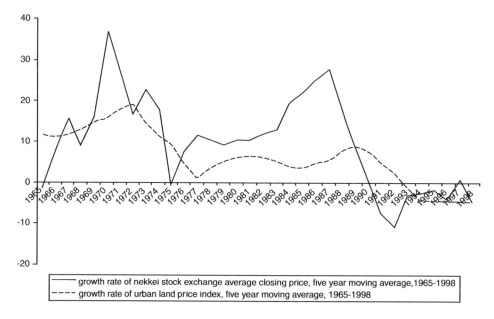

Figure 5.2. *Growth rate of Nikkei stock exchange average closing price and growth rate of urban land price index, five year moving averages, Japan, 1965–1998.*

The only way to make sense of the talk of a bubble economy is to relate the upward thrust in land and stock prices to *endaka*. Once one does this talk of a bubble makes sense. Calibrated in American dollars land and stock in Japan became incredibly expensive. It is the linkage between the yen/dollar exchange rate and domestic land prices that makes the idea of a bubble occurring during the late 1980s reasonable.

A PRICE TAG FOR THE IMPERIAL PALACE AND ITS IMMEDIATE ENVIRONS

The upward surge in asset prices—for real estate prices and for stocks and bonds bought and sold on the Nikkei exchange—characterizing Japan's so-called bubble economy is evident in the cold hard growth rate estimates for the period 1986–90 appearing in table A.4. But grasping the sheer dramatic extent of the inflation in Japanese assets is difficult to do through a simple perusal of these figures. A better vehicle for communicating the extremity of Japan's asset inflation is to consider the price, of the Imperial Palace and its immediate surroundings, namely the price tag for several hundred acres of downtown Tokyo. At the height of the bubble in 1989 the value of this small piece of real estate had the same value as all of the land in Canada, the same value as all of the land in California!

There is no doubt that the upward spike in Japanese real estate values was especially pronounced in Tokyo, especially in the commercial properties of downtown Tokyo for which prices more than doubled between 1986 and 1990. But residential prices in Tokyo also soared, roaring up by almost 70 percent during 1988 alone, a year that saw Tokyo commercial real estate values jump by almost 89 percent. And what was true in Tokyo was true elsewhere in urban Japan, in great metropolitan centers like: Osaka and Nagoya, and in relatively remote cities like Sendai in-northeastern Honshu and Sapporo in Hokkaidō.

If we are using the value of the Tokyo real estate as a barometer for Japan's bubble, it is fair to use its value as a barometer for the bursting of that very same bubble. By 2001 the highest priced real estate in Tokyo was trading at about a quarter of its value at the peak of the bubble. What went up like a rocket came down like sledgehammer, reminiscent of the crash in tulip prices in early 1637 in Amsterdam and the sharp fall off in closing stock prices on the New York exchange in 1929 as the American economy lurched its way into the Great Depression of the 1930s. In Japan the bursting of the bubble seemed to mimic the dismal American experience, ushering in the lost decade of the 1990s.

Why did land and stock prices escalate during the late 1980s? In the literature on the subject we can distinguish three major lines of argument: those that mainly focus on domestic circumstances; those that take into account globalization, Japanese companies increasingly financing their activities abroad, foreign financial institutions moving into the

Japanese market, the range of tradable services being extended to finance and banking; and those that directly link movements in the yen/dollar exchange rate and the terms of trade to the inflation in land and stock prices.

We begin with arguments centering upon domestic circumstances. Consider expectations. What counts in a stock or bond market is what other people do. One forms expectations based on what you think other people expect. In this way, expectations can drive expectations. This may explain some of the most famous bubbles in history. Underlining these arguments is deregulation of the stock and bond market. Had the volume of securities traded on the Nikkei exchange not exploded as fast as it did the bubble would not have gathered the force it did. As Lincoln (1988) points out the Japanese government had no choice but to deregulate the equity market during the early 1970s since it was increasingly engaging in deficit financing—bond issue—in order to raise funds to cover its outlays.

THE TULIP MANIA AND THE SOUTH SEA BUBBLE

Asset price bubbles are not necessarily typical of market economies, but they do occur with some frequency. Two of the earliest well documented bubbles occurred in seventeenth- and eighteenth-century Europe. In both cases expectations about future asset prices seemed to drive the run-up and then collapse of the markets. In both cases the specific institutional rules underlying the operation of the financial markets played a role in generating expectation driven buying of the assets.

The tulip mania was largely confined to Holland in the 1630s. The tulip bulb, considered an especially exotic and attractive flower, cannot be rapidly multiplied, thus opening up the possibility of demand outstripping supply, generating a rise in tulip prices relative to other prices. Complicating matters was the fact that a tiny fraction of the tulips in seventeenth-century Holland were infected. Attacked by a mosaic virus, the infected tulip generated petals of contrasting colors, flamed as it were. These were especially rare and hence commanding of exceptionally inflated prices.

Further contributing to the bubble in tulips was the existence of a futures market in Holland. Purchasers could pay for the flowers well in advance, obtaining delivery of them during the ensuing spring. During 1636–37, the market for tulips spread rapidly in taverns, the prices for all bulbs—but especially for the flamed bulbs—rising dramatically. The market broke in February 1637, prices dropping drastically thereafter. Future contracts were not enforceable, leading to the bankruptcy of many speculators in the market.

The term South Sea bubble actually refers to two bubbles, both taking place in 1720, one occurring in England and the other in France. At the heart of the bubbles was the fact that the state governments in both countries had allowed for the establishment of joint-stock companies that issued shares on the stock market in exchange for taking on the public debt of the governments. The particular joint-stock companies involved invested in other activities, but at their financial heart was management of the public debt.

As a result of the government support for, and dependence on, joint-stock activity for handling debt, speculation in the shares of the companies spread from London and Paris to Amsterdam and Hamburg. Expectations for further increases in share prices tended to bid up share prices. Benefiting from the surge of interest in joint-stock issue, shares in the South Seas Company surged upward in the summer of 1720. When confidence in the company collapsed, financial panic ensued, exacerbated by rumors of insider trading, directors of the company issuing new stock to the public while selling off their own shares at the same time. As a result of the fiasco the British government decided to prevent any new joint-stock companies from being formed, issuing the Bubble Act that stayed on the books until the 1850s.

Other famous bubble collapses include the panic of 1837 in the United States involving speculation in land, the panic of 1847 in Europe that centered around investments in mining and railroads, and the panic of 1873 in the United States that followed upon the foundering of the banking firm of Jay Cooke that had lavished funds on the building of the Northern Pacific Railroad. The most famous of the collapses occurred in the twentieth century however: the stock market collapse of 1929 in the United States. Fueled by the growth of investment trusts that used funds that they acquired from the public to purchase stocks and bonds, operating under the claim that the experts in the investment trusts were wiser than the public in the ways of the market, the stock market mania of the 1920s was driven by investment trusts buying shares in investment trusts, and by margin buying, a purchaser of a stock or bond only putting down a portion of the purchase price at the time the purchaser acquired the asset. Once the industrial conditions underlying the stock mania of the 1920s turned sour, once the threat of trade wars in retaliation for American protectionism as the high tariff Smoot-Hawley bill made its way through the halls of Congress became a real possibility, the mania broke, the stock market diving during the fall of 1929. From the United States the ensuing downturn in investment and production spread to a broad range of countries worldwide.

Note: This discussion draws heavily upon O'Donnell (2003).

An alternative view, also domestic in its orientation, has to do with the rate of return on capital in the industrial sector. As we have seen the capital/output ratio in Japan surpassed the American level during the late 1980s. Other things equal this should drive down the marginal product of capital. Investing in corporations became increasingly unattractive. Seeking higher returns on alternatives to industrial loans, banks turned to funding real estate developers who put up land as collateral. As the value of the collateral held by real estate developers escalated so did the attractiveness of continuing to lend to them. Compounding the bubble like potential of this type of market activity was the linkage of stock market prices to land prices (cf. figure 5.2). Banks lent to individuals wishing to speculate in stocks on the basis of collateral, in particular on the assessed value of the land assets that they held. As land prices jumped so did stock and bond prices. The headlong upward drive of the market became self-fulfilling, expectations feeding on expectations.

Moral hazard is usually invoked in stories that emphasize bad banking practices. As long as banks think that they will be bailed out—under the convoy system by other banks, the scenario played out under Ministry of Finance administrative guidance or by the Bank of Japan or by the taxpayer—they have little incentive to be cautious in their decisions. As long as a market is on an upward spiral, as long as the downside risk of failure is negligible, why not jump in, riding upward with the rest of the market? This is a basic theorem of financial economics. Allen (2001) provides a good treatment of the logic underlying this theorem.

Financial globalization may help account for the bubble. In 1980 the Japanese government revised the Foreign Exchange Control Law, allowing Japanese firms to freely issue unsecured foreign bonds. Attracted by the less regulated atmosphere in overseas markets, major Japanese firms entered the Euromarket, floating bonds and stocks, raising funds that they could use to liquidate their obligations to Japanese banks. In effect globalization encouraged Japanese companies to switch from indirect financing of their debt using banks to direct equity issue, issuing stocks, bonds and debentures on both domestic and foreign markets. Banks had no choice but to switch away from loaning to export oriented prestigious companies to loaning to real estate developers, construction companies and more risky domestic manufacturing ventures. In this version of the story the emphasis is on deregulation rather than on the declining marginal productivity of capital. But the two arguments are not inconsistent with one another.

Foreign pressure to open up the Japanese capital market to non-Japanese banks and investment houses increased competition in the financial market, applying further pressure on Japanese banks. Many bankers felt that Japanese banks had to consolidate through wholesale mergers before Western banks were allowed relatively free entry into the Japanese market. Foreign banks were far more knowledgeable about financial opportunities than Japanese banks that had relied almost exclusively on industrial loans to make returns on their capital. Not coincidentally Western banks tended to crowd into the heart of the Tokyo financial district, adding fuel to the flames of land inflation in the center of Japan's capital.

A third line of analysis links movements in terms of trade to the movements in the stock market, hence to the land market. Consider figure 5.3. As you can see the terms of trade and the Nikkei stock exchange index tend to move together from the mid-1970s until the bubble had fully burst in the early 1990s (the terms of trade did not start moving as long as Japan was adhering to the Dodge Line with a fixed exchange rate of 360 yen to a dollar). The key to a possible linkage between the two variables lies in expectations about the fortunes of the major exporters, of the top ten "name brand" companies in particular. As the terms of trade improved so did the expectations about future profits in the exporting sector. This drove up stock prices in the tradable goods sector. Stock—like land—could be used as collateral. In this version of the story trade becomes crucial to the bubble.

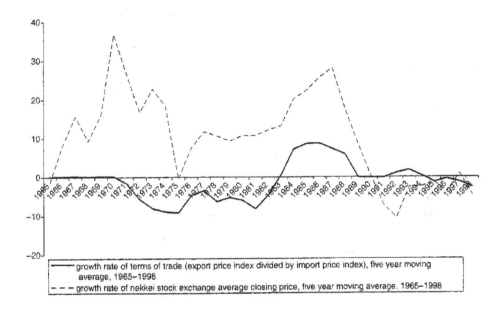

Figure 5.3. Growth rate of terms of trade (index of export prices divided by index of import prices) and growth rate of Nikkei stock exchange average closing price, five year moving averages, Japan, 1965–1998.

Regardless of which story one finds the most convincing one thing is certain. Any convincing story about the bubble economy must include a discussion of *endaka*. In that sense the bubble economy was an outgrowth of the process by which a once tightly shut system was being integrated into the international economic order, an international economic order in which the menu of tradable goods was being steadfastly enriched. Globalization and the bubble economy went hand in hand.

JAPAN'S TRANSFORMATION

Chapter 6: Stagnation and Reform

By Carl Mosk

DECELERATION WITH A VENGEANCE

In the wake of the initial bursting of the bubble in late 1989, Japan's growth rate slowed to a crawl. During the bubble phase and even during the first five years after the bubble began to burst Japan's per capita income continued to converge towards American levels. However during the next five-year period—between 1996 and 2000—it diverged.

Whether this divergence will persist is unclear. Projections for Japan's growth of income have a high level of variance. There are a number of reasons why the variability of the estimates is considerable: national income is estimated imperfectly at best; and nailing down statistical models of an economy that can be usefully employed in forecasting is treacherous, highly controversial at best. Compounding difficulties are ongoing technical disputes about whether the national income accounting schemes employed by the governmental agencies in charge of national income estimation are used to confuse and mislead rather than inform the citizen about the underlying reality. After all, politicians do not like figures showing anemic growth in national income. Why not cook the books?

This said, most estimates suggest that the Japanese per capita income has grown over the post-1990 period and will continue to grow in a range between 1 percent and 2 percent per year (extreme optimists put the figure higher at 3 percent but this is less likely). While the difference between the two rates appears to be small, the difference does matter significantly in the long run: if the economy grows at 2 percent per annum in per capita terms, real income per capita doubles in thirty-five years; if it grows at 1 percent per annum income per capita doubles in 70 years.

Growing from 1–2 percent per annum is respectable. Indeed in a Swann-Solow model in which the capital/labor ratio is high, the marginal product of capital low, and there is relatively slow growth in technological progress achieving growth in this range is completely expected. Growing at rates in the 1–2 percent range puts Japan's growth squarely within the economic territory occupied by other advanced industrial countries. However, in terms of Japan's historical record—growing faster than the other advanced industrial economies over the last half century—the possibility that Japan has once and for all entered a new era of dramatic deceleration is a very sobering thought indeed. To bureaucrats and politicians accustomed to growing far faster than other advanced industrial economies the slowdown to so-called normal growth seemed to be a chastening experience.

Does the bursting of the bubble represent a fundamental watershed in Japan's economic development, a sharp structural break with the past? In a provocative book Teranishi (2005) argues that it has. Reasoning that a capitalist economy has three major subsystems—the division of labor between private sector and government, the institutions of the private sector, and the interface of government and private sector—Teranishi argues that fundamental system change takes place when three conditions characterizing a political economic system occur. The economic costs of maintaining it are too costly; the political costs of keeping it going are too high; and the rules governing the operation of the system become incompatible with social norms and values. When these conditions are met, the prevailing system becomes dysfunctional. Evolution takes place. A new system emerges out of the ashes of the old structure being discarded.

Using this framework, Teranishi argues that post-1870 Japan has passed through two systems: the Meiji-Taishô system and the high (miracle) growth era system. In the Meiji-Taishô system the private sector dominated the economy, government playing a relatively minor role. The main interface between government and the private sector was local, the *meibôka* elite lobbying for infrastructure in their districts in return for drumming up votes for the two major political parties. Local pork barrel politics dictated what the bureaucrats in the national ministries could and did accomplish. Eventually, during the 1920s and 1930s this system became dysfunctional. Extension of the franchise empowered tenant farmers; agriculture's share in national product fell, weakening a fiscal system mainly dependent upon the land tax; small rural banks became increasingly fragile; and many companies that had carved out niches during the World War I boom when imports were largely cut off became shaky, bringing down banks with them in some cases.

Out of this system emerged—during the late 1930s, World War II and the American Occupation—the institutions of the high-speed growth era. These included internalization of labor, extensive intervention of national government ministries in the private economy, industrial policy emerging as the key interface between the private and public sectors. This was the system that generated miracle growth.

Eventually it too became dysfunctional. Rising political costs of carrying out industrial policy were one problem. Increasingly, ministries were at cross purposes in implementing industrial policy, declining sectors competing for attention, each demanding intervention, cutting into the interests of other sectors when they managed to get protection from imports or subsidies that propped them up at least temporarily. The economic costs of maintaining the system soared as the yen appreciated. Consumers clamored for the benefits of a strong yen, becoming increasingly restive over high prices that they attributed to excessive regulation. In addition consumerism affected social values. The younger generation became oriented towards consumption of material goods, less inclined to derive satisfaction from being a member of a prestigious "name brand" corporation. The bubble economy marked the last gasp of the high-speed growth system. A new system began emerging during the 1990s.

Is there evidence bearing out the notion of a system change? There are at least four quantitative indicators that suggest that a new era has dawned: a substantial drop in the investment and savings rates; a rise in unemployment rates, especially for young individuals, from the extremely low unemployment levels of the miracle growth period; a worsening of the income distribution; and consolidation and restructuring of the financial sector.

Consider investment and savings. As Table A.6 demonstrates investment demand has been falling off: particularly striking is the sharp drop in the contribution that investment demand growth makes to aggregate demand growth during 1991–2000 (see Panel B of the table). Even more striking is the decline in measured household savings rates. Estimates suggest that the rates have steadily declined over the 1990s—from around 10.8 percent in 1990 to 6.4 percent in 2000, tumbling further to around 2.4 percent in 2004. Moreover, credit card usage has spiraled upward during the same period. Estimates for 1980 showed Japan with a ratio of consumer credit to disposable income of around 10 percent (about half of the level in the United States). During the 1990s Japan's rate was actually greater than the American rate, dropping back to around 20 percent during the early years of the twenty-first century. During miracle growth most households in Japan had to save in order to purchase consumer durables. No more.

Showing that a structural break has occurred in savings behavior can be justified by considering the impact of factors that probably shaped savings in the past: income per capita growth, the level of assets relative to income, and aging. True, the Japanese population continues to age, thereby depressing savings. But the drop in savings in the 1990s and early 2000s is far too dramatic to be explained away in terms of aging. True assets have fallen relative to income in the aftermath of the bursting of the bubble. But savings rates were dropping even as asset prices were being driven up during the 1980s. Finally income per capita growth—embarrassingly low by miracle growth standards perhaps—has tended to be positive, albeit low, beginning in the early 1990s.

The labor market has also been transformed. From Table A.3 it is apparent that the rate began to creep up after the era of miracle growth had largely come to a close, accelerating in the late 1990s. Particularly striking is the growth of unemployment amongst the young aged 15–19. The growth of young adult unemployment has gone hand in hand with the proliferation of "freeters." The term "freeter" is an amalgamation of the German word "frei" (or the English word "free") with the German word "Arbeiter" (worker). It describes a person who is either unemployed or underemployed (moving in and out of employment) or working as a freelance worker, perhaps for a company that dispatches temporary workers to employers seeking an employee who works on a short-term basis. Examples of "freeter" employment are convenience store workers, supermarket checkout employees, fast food employees, and waiters in restaurants. Estimates of the number "freeters" in Japan varies depends on which ministry is doing the counting. The Japanese Ministry of Labor began publishing estimates of the number of NEET (not in education, employment, or training), a definition that approximates the freeter definition, in 2000. A White Paper on National Life in 2003 estimated the number of freeters at over 4.1 million (an alternative official estimate was about half that number).

What motivates an individual to choose a freeter work style? The Japan Institute of Labor classifies freeters into two categories. One describes those who reject the values that the adult generation of the miracle growth era held regarding working for a large prestigious company. To some degree these individuals may be reacting to the way the implicit contracts of internalized market were revamped in the aftermath of miracle growth: the struggle for promotions was intensified, the possibility of forced transfer becoming a disquieting reality. A second type is the individual who has no alternative, who has no chance of securing employment in a good salaried position.

The social consequences of the freeter life style are important. Earnings being low most freeters cannot afford to marry and start a family. Female freeters tend to marry late or not marry at all. Often they end up living with their parents, joining the ranks of the so-called "parasite singles." As more Japanese embrace the freeter life-style, it is likely the gross reproduction rate will continue to fall.

Does low fertility encourage even further drops of fertility in post-1990 Japan? One can argue that parents are willing to tolerate housing freeters precisely because the number of children that they raised is small.

Another sign of changing labor market institutions is the growth of demand for mid-career hires. Rather than relying on fresh school graduates more and more companies are recruiting workers who have experience working elsewhere. Is this due to the increasing presence of foreign managed companies and subsidiaries in the Japanese market? Or is it the result of an increasing disintegration of the internal labor market model? Is Japan's labor market converging toward an American style market in which ten-year job retention rates are relatively low, especially for adults in their twenties and thirties?

Has the natural rate property of the Japanese economy changed? Has the Japanese economy shifted from one where the non-inflationary rate of unemployment, the so-called natural rate of unemployment, is over 4 percent, as opposed to the rates ranging between 1 and 1.5 percent characteristic of miracle growth?

One of the miracles in miracle growth was the fact that high-speed growth was achieved with equity. This surprised many economists. One of the assumptions made by most mainstream economists is that there is a tradeoff between growth and equity. At a low level of income per capita when agriculture predominates income is assumed to be distributed fairly equally. With industrialization and rapid accumulation of capital this changes. For instance when dualism emerged in Japan during the early twentieth century, income inequality did worsen. But during miracle growth income inequality seems to have been muted, partly because agriculture was subsidized with the government's rice procurement program, partly because of the way the *shuntô* operated. Using estimates of the Gini coefficient (the lower the level of the Gini coefficient the more equal is income distribution) for Japan in 1968 (0.350) and in 1979 (0.336), we see that income distribution in miracle growth Japan and its immediate aftermath was relatively equal. However during the 1990s this changed: the Gini coefficient seems appears to have shot upward, from around 0.4 to around 0.433 (estimates of the Gini coefficient vary a bit depending on the nature of the households surveyed). There is little doubt that this trend mirrors the increasing presence of freeters and unemployed in the labor force.

Another quantitative indicator of structural change is the shakeup in the banking sector. Some banks were allowed to fail. As van Rixtel (2002: 250) shows, between 1990 and 1998 three city banks disappeared, eight second-tier regional banks vanished, 109 credit cooperatives closed their doors, and most dramatically over 2,000 agricultural and forestry cooperatives folded. Has Japan entered an era when unconditional moral hazard—every bank is bailed out no matter how badly managed it is, no matter how bad its loan program is—has given way to conditional moral hazard? Under conditional moral hazard government stands prepared to salvage responsible banks, not those managed irresponsibly. True, fear of foreign takeovers of Japanese banks limits the willingness of the Ministry of Finance and the political leadership to carry out a consistent conditional moral hazard approach. But the existence of bank failures suggests that the days of unconditional moral hazard are over.

Hyogo Bank goes under

From the theory of moral hazard, we have learned that an insuring agent—a central bank, a private insurance broker selling automobile premiums—can provide too much insurance, encouraging profligate and irresponsible behavior. For this reason there are limits to a central bank's willingness to bailout private banks whose managers may have made badly conceived non-performing loans, to fledging startup companies in industries going nowhere, to real estate speculators building structures that no one is likely to purchase, let alone occupy.

As we have seen there are two practices, peculiar to but not unique to Japan, that created an atmosphere of moral hazard in Japanese financial circles: the over loan policy of the Bank of Japan and the convoy system managed by the Ministry of Finance. Under the logic of the convoy system, groups of banks insured each other against the possibility of bankruptcy. In the event of a commercial bank failure government regulators would move in, arranging a merger of the embattled financial institution facing insolvency with a solvent bank. What was the incentive for the healthy bank to acquire a bad business? Dangled in its face by the regulators was the acquisition of the acquired bank's branching rights (allocated by the regulators), potentially very valuable for future growth in depositors, especially in the big six cities. In addition, an acquiring bank might expect to be especially well treated by the Ministry of Finance, perhaps securing preferential treatment.

In August 1995 Hyogo Bank announced that it was failing. The regulators had finally decided to draw a line in the sand. Giving up on their effort to arrange assistance for beleaguered Hyogo with a package involving a group of strong banks, regulators let a very big Bank—the Hyogo Bank was the thirty-eighth largest bank in Japan—that had made too many non-performing loans, had lost too much money in the Nikkei and land market rundowns of the early 1990s as the bubble economy came crashing to a dismal close—go under.

To some degree the willingness of the regulators to allow a major bank to fail was the result of the "big bang" reforms of the 1980s, substituting ex post inspection of banking practices for advance guidance by the regulators. But it was also a signal that the Ministry of Finance was only willing to go so far in cleaning up messes attributable to poor commercial calculation, bad luck, or a combination thereof.

This said it is clear that the regulators were not willing to jettison bailouts as a general rule. For instance in March 1998 the government pumped around 1.8 trillion yen into twenty-one banks perched on the edge of ruin, and another 7.46 trillion yen into fifteen large banks in March of the following year. When deemed necessary, the regulators were prepared to use funds taxed away from the public to shore up a shaky profit oriented banking system.

The willingness of the government to abandon its blanket bailout policy impacted international financial markets. Letting a major commercial bank like the Hyogo Bank fail triggered the emergence of the "Japan premium," a term describing the extra interest charged to Japanese banks by foreign lenders based in other countries. Unlike a Japanese bank's domestic depositors whose accounts are almost certain to be partially guaranteed in the event of a bank's failure, offshore lending to the bank is unlikely to creditors following an unexpected failure.

Studies show that the Japan premium emerged in the wake of the Hyogo Bank's collapse, declined in 1996, remaining low through until late 1997 when a fresh rash of bank failures occurred, including the collapse of a "city bank," Hokkaidō Takushoku. Since late 1997 the amount of the premium has fluctuated, the market responding to informed opinion and rumors about the stability of particular banks and the willingness of the regulators to carry out thoroughgoing bailouts in the aftermath of the bubble economy collapse.

In addition to quantitative indicators of system change there are a number of qualitative indicators suggesting that Japan was undergoing substantial and wrenching change in the aftermath of the bursting of the bubble. International surveys of happiness carried out in the early twenty-first century ranks Japan very low; suicide rates for middle aged men terminated from their jobs appear to have been increasing during the 1990s and early 2000s; a Japanese television series about "Project X" highlights quality defects in Japanese manufacturing. Egregious examples cited in the television series include Sony's recall of over 300,000 batteries and a upward surge in the number of recalls carried out by Toyota, that latter committing itself to hiring thousands of engineers in an effort to reverse criticism of its deteriorating quality. To a growing number of Japanese consumers it appeared that South Korea, Taiwan, and China were producing higher-quality goods than Japanese manufacturers were.

Teranishi's theory of sweeping structural transformation aside, economists and political scientists have weighed in with an abundance of theories about why growth in Japan has slowed down as much as it has. The idea here is that interest rates had been driven to such a low level during the 1990s by Bank of Japan policy that further use of expansionary monetary policy was impossible. In one variant of this hypothesis emphasis is put on expectations about the yen/dollar exchange rate. To encourage investors to purchase American securities in the face of a possible depreciation of the dollar relative to the yen, Japanese interest rates dropped to a low level. True, nominal interest rates in Japan declined to extremely low levels during the 1990s. But as we can see from Table A.4 inflation rates were also very low during the late 1990s and the dollar actually appreciated against the yen during this period. Still, if Japan was in a liquidity trap during the 1990s, monetary policy became useless, sharply limiting the number of stabilization policy options.

A second line of argument focuses on facilitating/coordinating policy, especially industrial policy in manufacturing and Ministry of Finance administrative guidance in the case of banking. Anchordoguy (2000) argues that Japan's system of "catch-up" capitalism in which the Ministry of International Trade and Industry promoted models for acquiring foreign technology from international industry leaders began to sour during the post-miracle growth era. Using the software industry as an example, Anchordoguy argues that the Japanese computer companies became obsessed with using IBM style methods under administrative guidance from the Ministry of International Trade and Industry, employing reverse engineering wherever possible. In 1982, Mitsubishi and Hitachi were caught stealing IBM technology, ultimately being forced to fork over massive annual fees to IBM for the use of the technology. Reacting to the "IBM industrial spy incident" the Japanese government sponsored a series of research and development projects designed to lead the industry away from the IBM standard, the most ambitious being the TRON project aimed at creating a Japan-specific operating system. While this project had some limited success within Japan itself, outside of the country it had little appeal. Internationally, IBM mainframe and personal computer software had a dominant position that TRON could not assail. Japan had locked itself out of international markets in the mainstream software sector.

Japan's computer game sector offers an interesting contrast according to Anchordoguy (2000). Largely left alone by the Ministry of International Trade and Industry it has flourished, enjoying strong demand in both domestic and international markets. The lesson is clear: industrial policy may be a good way to speed the process of "catch-up" growth. But it is a bad strategy for creating industries that flourish on their own innovative drive in a post-"catch-up" environment.

The critique by Van Rixtel (2002) of Ministry of Finance administrative guidance in the financial sector emphasizes other problems in the facilitating/coordinating model of policy-making, policy arising partly out of the regulated industry itself. Van Rixtel argues that Ministry of Finance accommodation of the wishes of the banks helped fuel the bubble itself, whose bursting undercut the viability of many of the banks. In effect he argues that administrative guidance in the financial field spawned moral hazard problems that would not have occurred had a different type of regulatory regime been in place. The problem was not regulation *per se*. The problem was the type of regulation.

The plight of the banks is often cited in explaining Japan's slow growth during the 1990s and early 2000s. It is said that they did not lend enough—or rather that they were not willing to lend to potentially innovative entrepreneurs—that they became overly cautious, that they refused to terminate non-performing loans. The fact that land prices continued to fall throughout the 1990s (see Table A.4) certainly made their fiscal lives difficult. As long as the value of their collateral kept following they were reluctant to terminate non-performing loans, continuing to extend credit to bad borrowers.

As is pointed out in the introduction to Blomström, Gangnes, and La Croix (2001) the fact that Japanese banks were viewed as increasingly shaky and ill advised in their lending policies created growing distrust of Tokyo as a world-class financial center. Stung by this evaluation—maintaining the prestige Japan had garnered during the late 1970s and 1980s cannot be discounted as a motivation—the government further deregulated the industry with the Big Bang reforms of 2003. Despite these reforms many foreign financial institutions remain skeptical of the Japanese government's commitment to a responsible regulatory regime, in large part because of Ministry of Finance use of administrative guidance as opposed to clear and transparent rules.

For many students of the Japanese economy, however, it is not the banks, not aggregate stabilization policy, not administrative guidance and industrial policy, which is at the roots of Japan's current economic woes. Rather according to Katz (2003) the problem is total factor productivity. As long as sectors are protected from imports and thus shielded from the sting of global price reduction stemming from technological change in leading countries (whether the leader in a particular sector be the United States as in information technology and general purpose software, or Germany in the case of automobiles) productivity growth in Japan is likely to lag behind that of other countries. Exacerbating this problem is the fact that the most successful exporting companies, Toyota and Honda for instance, are increasingly carrying on their manufacturing outside of Japan. Another factor cited in discussing Japan's productivity problem: a decline in the skills acquired by youthful engineers, perhaps fueled by a failure of the Japanese educational system to keep up with trends in schooling initiated elsewhere. Is the long-standing emphasis on rote memorization in examinations catching up with the Japanese educational system? Or is the shop floor—once stimulating, indeed exciting to work in—becoming boring as workers are replaced with robots and digitally controlled machines?

True productivity can grow from sources other than total factor productivity. Accumulation—an increase in the capital/labor ratio—can fuel it. But as we know from Table A.1, Japan's capital/output ratio is already extremely high. So this is not a likely source for growth, at least for quite a while. Again, productivity growth can come from shifting resources like labor out of low productivity areas of a sector into higher productivity areas of the same sector. Moving workers from "mom and pop" retail outlets to convenience stores is one example of a possible productivity spur. How much productivity gain can be squeezed out of this type of change is questionable however. Unlike the sweeping gains during miracle growth in which agricultural employment gave way to manufacturing employment (one sector giving way to another), the type of structural change envisioned here involves change within a sector, less likely to boost the productivity figures at the aggregate level.

THE POLITICAL RESPONSE

The fact that the bubble economy and the retardation afterward coincided with a growing number of scandals involving high level bureaucrats and politicians did not go unnoticed by the Japanese voter. Not surprisingly the Liberal Democratic Party's political support continued to erode. Still a fragmented opposition was having difficulty capitalizing on the disenchantment with the party that had ruled the country for so long. Growing dissatisfaction with this state of affairs was the political backdrop for the jettisoning of the system of voting for lower house representatives that had been put into place during the American Occupation, the multi-member medium sized district system being abandoned in favor of a system that mixed proportional representation with a single member district scheme.

As Reed (2003) points out there has been ongoing debate among students of democracy over the merits of single member "winner takes all" versus proportional representation systems. Those who think that it is important to have a majority in government—one that can actually pass legislation, one that can be held accountable in a future election for its deeds—favor "winner take all" systems in which one candidate from an electoral district emerges triumphant. This approach is known as majoritarian. The alternative view is that obtaining discussion, dialogue and consensus is the proper goal of democracy. Each voice should be heard. Parties should be represented in the legislature in proportion to their relative vote getting power in elections.

Between 1993 and 1996 Japan changed its system, moving away from the multi-member district system in which a voter cast one non-transferable vote, to a mixed system in which a voter cast one vote for a single candidate in a single member district and a second vote for the party of his or her choice, the proportional representation component of the election system. That Japan took this radical step—relatively few democracies have tinkered with their electoral systems in the post-World War II period (New Zealand has taken similar steps)—suggests that the Diet was concerned about growing discontent with the political status quo. Less convincing as a theory of the why the political system was willing to gamble on a radical change in the electoral system is the much vaunted theory that the Japanese people seek consensus. If this were true, why was proportional representation not adopted earlier?

Indeed, in the 1993 election the Liberal Democratic Party did not actually garner a majority of seats in the Diet. Thirty-nine members of the party precipitated the 1993 election by voting to support a no-confidence motion aimed at bringing down the party's cabinet. In bolting from the ranks of the Liberal Democratic Party they formed several new parties, including the Renewal Party and the Japan New Party. A combination of Liberal Democratic Party defections and the possibility of voting for fresh new parties ended almost four decades of Liberal Democratic Party rule. Ironically introducing the new voting system actually helped the Liberal Democratic Party. No longer were its candidates pitted against one another in districts. Now individual Liberal Democratic Party candidates could draw upon party funds, rather than upon individually managed local fundraising bases, in standing for election. Rather than minority/coalition governments emerging from the new voting system, the Liberal Democratic Party's fortunes were revitalized.

While Liberal Democratic Party hegemony over the national political scene soon resumed it occurred in an environment in which the demand for economic and political reform continued. As a result the party itself split into reformist and non-reformist wings, in effect one wing of the party engaging in all out political warfare with the other wing. The result was the dramatic election of 2005 in which Prime Minister Koizumi Junichiro triumphed over the opposition of his own Liberal Democratic Party colleagues. At the heart of his campaign was a drive to weaken the faction within the party committed to the Tanaka Kakuei pork barrel approach to policy making.

Postal reform as political theater

In a parliamentary democracy the astute prime minister must master the art of strategically picking clearly etched battles. Focusing on one or two symbolic issues designed to rally political allies and flesh out political enemies is one key. Another is timing. Knowing when to dissolve parliament and call an election; knowing how to frame the dissolution decision; knowing how to carry the battle to the electorate. In Japan post-bubble economy Koizumi Junichiro has proven to be a master of the art.

Making reform of Japan Post symbolic of his drive to transform Japan's political economy, Koizumi turned the lower house elections on 11 September 2005, into political theater of the highest order. Returned to power in 2003 with a diminished majority for his Liberal Democratic Party facing an apparently increasingly popular Democratic Party of Japan, Koizumi had watched the fortunes of his party falter, mired as it was in a reputation for corruption, tarnished as it was for creating the regulatory politics of the 1960s and 1970s whose apparent legacy was the bubble economy.

Securing lower house passage of the postal reform in July 2005, by a vote of 233–228, dividing his own party in the process, Koizumi's commitment to postal reform ran into concerted opposition in the upper house which voted down the measure by a 125–108 vote. Unable to muster enough votes in the lower house to override the upper house vote, Koizumi dissolved the lower house, calling for a September election to decide the fate of his proposed reform package. In the September election, Koizumi was triumphant, securing a landside, winning a commanding 296 seats in the 480-seat lower house, forcing the twenty-two members of the Liberal Democratic Party in the upper house who had voted against the reform to reconsider their positions.

To understand why the September 2005 election represents one of the most important examples of post-1950 political theater in Japan, an understanding of what Japan Post is and what privatization of the system (specifically splitting the banking and insurance services of the system off from mail delivery in 2007 and selling the banking and insurance services a decade later) may accomplish, is essential. In doing so it is important to consider economic aspects of the privatization scheme separately from political aspects although they are both ultimately intertwined.

The economic reform drive centers upon reducing the role of government in the Japanese economy, increasing the returns on pensions (which will he a growing political issue as Japan ages), and making the financial sector more competitive. Japan Post is one of the most powerful financial institutions in the country, managing around a quarter of Japan's personal assets, around 85 percent of Japanese having savings accounts or other deposit accounts in the system. In 2006 it employed over 250,000 workers in about 25,000 post offices around the nation, far exceeding the 2,600 branches of the seven major banks.

Privatizing the financial wing of the system creates a major player in the private financial sector one that can muster clout in going head to head with commercial banks. In theory privatizing the system, making it more competitive and market oriented, should increase the returns that investors in the system earn, bolstering pensions built up within it. From an economic viewpoint, postal reform is tantamount to making the Japanese economy more market oriented.

As important as the symbolic breakup of Japan Post is for the economy, as crucial as it may be to making a break with an overly regulated economic past, it is in the political arena that Koizumi's postal reform victory of September 2005 seems to be especially path breaking. In rural areas the post office has been intertwined with politics, used as a vote-generating machine by powerful politicians bent on keeping their Diet seats, used as a funding vehicle for pork barrel projects dear to the local rural district. Liberal Democratic Party politicians based in rural areas naturally wanted to keep this system functioning, protecting the jobs of postal workers who had assisted them in past campaigns, therefore breaking with their own party leader over the reform proposal.

Having gone to the polls with a clear intent of defeating this rural based old guard of the Liberal Democratic Party, Koizumi has effectively transformed the image of the party, making it more urban in its orientation, making it less dependent on the rural political machine wing that tended to prioritize the interests of farmers and rural pork masquerading as infrastructure needed for assisting remote villagers.

One can argue that Koizumi was completing a process initiated by the administrative reform movement of the late 1970s and early 1980s. In that movement the bureaucracy was under attack, but not the Tanaka style model of dispensing pork for votes. Koizumi carried the logic of the attack one step further. After all, Koizumi had progressed through his political career during the heyday of the administrative reform movement. His thinking was shaped by the debates going on about the spectrum of reforms that should be packaged into the rinchō program.

One of the main tenets of the administrative reform movement, however, was reining in government spending. Koizumi adhered to the logic of this position, thereby discouraging the use of expansionary fiscal policy as a tool for stimulating growth and reducing unemployment. In this sense, his commitment to political reform may have hampered his willingness to counteract Japan's economic doldrums through bold stabilization measures. Concerns about inefficient uses of public funds in pork barrel projects, concerns about controlling the bureaucracy, concerns about the impact of aging on the viability—in short structural concerns—dominated the Koizumi agenda.

The question whether this approach to reform will continue to dominate Japan's politics remains to be answered. What is clear is that Liberal Democratic Party rule in the early twentieth century (if it continues) is likely to look very different than it did in the miracle growth period and its immediate aftermath.

PATHS WALKED, PATHS TAKEN

Path dependence is a strong concept. Whatever happens in the future depends at least partly on what has gone before.

Many social scientists think the idea is absurd. Consider Japan's economic transformation over the period 1886–2000 as captured in the snapshots that are tables in the Appendix. By all accounts Japan is so different in the early twenty-first century from how it was in the late nineteenth century—in terms of per capita income, in terms of life expectancy and fertility, in terms of structure of output and labor force, in terms of the structure of aggregate demand, in terms of the anthropometric measures of height and weight—that talk of continuity over time is seemingly ridiculous.

Still continuity abounds. Indeed one can argue that the greatest continuity is in the very drive to innovate what became apparent when entrepreneurs built the first steam driven integrated spinning and weaving mills in Osaka in the 1880s. Even during the bubble and its problematic aftermath Japanese companies continue to be innovative, continue to take risks, continue to push into new ventures. In so innovating, they embody a past that they project into the future.

Sharp gambles on liquid crystal display technology

In the Schumpeterian model of invention, innovation, imitation, and creative destruction corporate survival depends upon taking risks, gambling on new products, jettisoning old product lines. In the course of an industry's evolution, companies come and go, those wedded to the ways of the past disappearing, new startups taking their place.

The company that manages to remain in the marketplace for a long time—for a half century or more—goes through a parallel evolution, its product line and its target base continually changing as the industry it is associated with twists and turns through the forces of innovation and creative destruction. In this process of transformation, an externally imposed crisis can play a positive role, forcing management to think anew about the company's focus, necessity being the mother of invention as it were.

Sharp is an old company. Originally established in 1912, the company was founded by Hayakawa Tokuji to manufacture mechanical pencils, "ever sharp" pencils, hence taking on the name Sharp. From pencils Sharp shifted its manufacturing focus to vacuum tube radios, exporting them throughout Asia during the 1930s. After the American occupation ended, Sharp moved into television set production, following other Japanese consumer electronics companies into making air conditioners and appliances for the rapidly growing domestic market of the miracle growth era.

In the early 1970s Sharp began to shift out of labor intensive manufacturing of consumer durables into the new technology intensive sector developing around the manufacture of semiconductors and especially electronic calculators. Through the 1960s and the 1970s Sharp research laboratories churned out impressive inventions in the calculator field—the world's first all transistor-diode electronic calculator in 1964, the first electronic calculator with solar cells in 1976, the world's first 1.6 millimeter thin electronic calculator in 1979—putting Sharp in the forefront of the industry, focusing on the younger generation of consumers in Japan and abroad with "life products" exemplified by clever designs and aesthetics attuned to persons in their twenties. In pursuing this strategy, Sharp's management put strong emphasis on selling abroad, exports accounting for almost 60 percent of sales in the early 1980s. Then came the violent upward movement of the yen. rapid appreciation following the 1985 Plaza Accord.

In the wake of yen appreciation, sales of calculators dropped precipitously. Avoiding layoffs at all costs, Sharp focused on introducing emergency measures, cutting costs on all fronts and establishing new lower prices for exported products. More important, Sharp decided to initiate a shift away from labor-intensive consumer electronics exemplified by its calculators and semiconductors to knowledge intensive products, exemplified by its research and development in the liquid crystal business. Continuing to manufacture, calculators while it built up its liquid crystal technological base, Sharp gambled on a technologically oriented strategy, risky because research and development takes time, often proceeding down blind alleys.

That Sharp was willing to enthusiastically embrace the new and risky and downplay the old and well worn was partly due to the relatively youthful structure of its management and its rank and file employee base. Of course the association between the youthfulness of a company and its innovation capacity is tricky; Innovative companies tend to grow fast, taking on young recruits at a higher rate than less innovative competitors, ending up younger.

Despite its attempts at restructuring initiated in 1986 in the wake of the Plaza Accord, Sharp continued to struggle through the late 1980s and early 1990s as weak sales of its calculators resulting from growing competition: from manufacturers elsewhere in Asia imitating Sharp's products cut into its profits. By 1998 when Machida Katsuhiko took over the reins of the enterprise, the company was mired in a serious financial crisis.

Once again, Sharp's management responded to crisis by playing the card of technology, of innovation. Machida decided that Sharp needed to give up completely on semiconductors, computer monitors and tube televisions, products that had become increasingly cheap as global production and global imitation drove down profit margins for already established producers. Instead, Machida argued that the company needed to focus completely on its knowledge intensive product lines, especially those exploiting its own research advances in liquid crystal display that Sharp management had invested in aggressively on the heels of the rapid yen appreciation of the mid-1980s.

Focusing on flat-panel televisions that took advantage of the liquid crystal display technology that it originally developed in the 1970s for calculators and had improved upon in its laboratories during the 1980s and 1990s, Sharp's management turned the fortunes of the enterprise around, bolstering its formerly embattled profit margins in the early 2000s. Root and branch restructuring paid off. Still the restructuring of the late 1990s and early 2000s would have been far harder to carry out, perhaps impossible to achieve, had an earlier management team not committed itself to intense research and development in liquid crystal display technology during the crisis of the 1980s brought on by rapid yen appreciation. In this sense necessity, pounding on the door of Sharp several times, was the mother of Sharp's newest revival as it pushed into its ninth decade of continuous operation.

True, much of the innovation in Japan involves hybridization, the adapting of foreign technology to the Japanese economic, social, and political environment. But this is true everywhere. Indeed the same charge was leveled against the American innovating entrepreneurs during the 19th century. One of the greatest examples of Japanese innovation is in facilitating/coordinating policy making, an area that may be proving to be as much a barrier as a fillip to future economic advance in Japan. But as we have seen administrative guidance is itself undergoing change, unconditional moral hazard giving way to conditional moral hazard in the financial field.

It is easy to dismiss Japan's long-run growth potential in light of the struggle its economy has been enduring in the wake of the bursting of the bubble economy. That would be a mistake. When the Western powers broke Japan open in the 1850s they set in motion one of the greatest locomotives of economic growth the world has ever witnessed. Once unbound from its shackles, this locomotive of growth—powered by innovation—has continued on its dramatic journey for over a century.

It will continue on that journey, perhaps gaining speed at times, perhaps slowing down at times, for centuries to come. The strongest continuity in Japan's modern history is change itself. Whether we view Japan through the lens of markets, or norms and values, or political constraints, the continuity of change is the one overriding reality, the one bedrock proposition that we should never ignore. Emerging out of Japan's long and tumultuous history, wedding traditional norms and values to Western institutions and technology, the Japanese company is a formidable innovator, a formidable competitor, adapting to changing market conditions, to changing political realities, to changing social norms. That is the most important implication to draw from this account of Japan's remarkable long-run economic development.

Table A.6 Gross domestic expenditure

Panel A *Composition of gross domestic expenditure (GDE) in terms of percentages. Percentage attributable to consumer demand (C%), gross domestic fixed-capital formation (I%), government consumption expenditure (G%), exports of goods and services (EX%), imports of goods and services (IM%) and net imports (NX% = EX%-IM%): 1886–2000*

Years	Percentage of gross domestic expenditure[a]					
	C	I	G	EX	IM	NX
1886–1890	85.2	9.0	6.9	3.2	4.2	−0.9
1890–1895	84.0	9.4	7.9	3.7	5.1	−1.4
1896–1900	85.4	12.1	7.5	4.9	9.9	−5.0
1901–1905	80.2	10.6	14.3	6.5	11.7	−5.2
1906–1910	79.6	13.5	11.3	8.0	12.4	−4.4
1911–1915	79.0	15.6	9.1	10.7	14.4	−3.7
1916–1920	74.9	17.9	8.1	13.8	14.6	−0.8
1921–1925	82.3	18.8	9.0	10.4	20.4	−10.1
1926–1930	79.8	17.8	10.3	14.5	22.3	−7.8
1931–1935	74.0	16.5	12.7	19.3	22.5	−3.2
1936–1940	63.8	25.7	12.9	21.2	23.4	−2.3
1941–1945						
1946–1950	62.2	21.1	9.9	4.1	6.8	−2.6
1951–1955	61.9	17.8	14.8	8.3	6.9	1.4
1956–1960	61.6	22.8	11.9	8.8	8.0	0.8
1961–1965	56.8	30.5	9.6	9.5	9.7	−0.2
1966–1970	55.5	34.3	7.8	12.1	11.1	1.0
1971–1975	53.8	36.3	8.6			0.9
1976–1980	57.3	31.7	10.5			0.5
1981–1985	55.1	29.3	13.8			1.9
1986–1990	53.8	30.6	13.3			2.3
1991–1995	54.5	29.8	13.8			1.9
1996–2000	55.9	27.4	15.5			1.3

Panel B *Growth in real gross domestic expenditure. Absolute magnitude of changes in GDE over 5 year periods (ΔGDE), and percentage contributions that absolute increments to consumption (ΔC), absolute increments to gross domestic fixed capital formation (ΔI), absolute increments to government consumption expenditure (ΔG), and absolute increments to net exports (ΔNX) make to the changes in GDE: 1886/90–1996/2000*

Five year period	ΔGDE	Percentage contribution to ΔGDE[b]			
		ΔC	ΔI	ΔG	ΔNX
1886/1890	525	100.2	18.3	−2.3	−21.9
1891/1895	792	56.7	12.6	45.3	−14.7
1896/1900	389	75.6	9.8	20.3	−5.7
1901/1905	363	−40.5	40.2	267.5	−167.2
1906/1910	1,147	99.0	24.4	−37.0	13.5
1911/1915	564	103.4	−37.8	−12.4	47.9
1916/1920	2,118	64.8	57.6	13.9	−36.3
1921/1925	729	156.2	−58.2	−5.4	7.3
1926/1930	1,521	38.7	6.1	26.1	29.2
1931/1935	4,118	31.8	27.7	6.2	33.5
1936/1940	4,303	11.1	81.6	28.9	−21.6

Five year period	ΔGDE	Percentage contribution to ΔGDE^b			
		ΔC	ΔI	ΔG	ΔNX
1941/1945					
1946/1950	7,556	55.8	5.1	11.9	11.4
1951/1955	2,353	73.8	20.2	2.6	−2.3
1956/1960	5,811	52.9	41.8	4.5	−0.6
1961/1965	9,125	58.7	33.6	7.9	7.0
1966/1970	21,259	39.3	47.3	4.1	0.5
1971/1975	11,528	94.0	7.6	25.0	−14.7
1976/1980	20,377	44.9	35.3	27.0	−7.2
1981/1985	13,920	57.4	7.8	12.8	22.1
1986/1990	25,804	48.5	53.4	10.4	−12.3
1991/1995	1,204	397.8	−486.8	213.1	−24.1
1996/2000	4,666	65.3	−66.0	69.0	31.6

Sources: Ohkawa and Shinohara with Meissner (1979: pp. 256–60) and *Japan. Statistical Yearbook 2006* published by Japan. Ministry of Internal Affairs and Communications. Statistics Bureau (2005: 2).

Notes

A blank cell indicates that there is no estimate available. In a few cases, the averages are for three or four years rather than for five years.

a The estimates for components of gross domestic expenditure in both Panels A and B are based on estimates in constant prices (in 1934–6 prices for the pre-1941 period and in 1965 prices for the post-1945 period).

b Due to the method of calculation and to rounding error, the percentages do not necessarily add to 100.

Table A.3 Labor force

Panel A *Labor force participation rate (lfpr – percentage of the population aged 15 and over in the labor force), unemployment rate (ur) ,unemployment rate for persons aged 15–19 (yur%), monthly hours worked by regular workers in the non-service sector in firms of 30 workers or over (mhw), and percentages of primary, secondary and tertiary sectors who are self-employed or family workers (sefw%)*[a]: *1920–2000*

Year(s)	Unemployment rates				Self-employed or family workers		
	lfpr	ur	Yur	mhr	Primary	Secondary	Tertiary
1920	72.8						
1930	69.8						
1940	71.1						
1947	55.9	1.9					
1950	65.4	2.0		195			
1951–1955	67.3	1.9		193	93.3	24.5	40.8
1956–1960	67.4	0.8		200	92.3	18.9	36.8
1961–1965	66.0	1.4		197	92.6	14.9	30.4
1966–1970	67.1	1.1	2.0	191	94.0	16.8	26.9
1971–1975	64.2	1.4	2.8	180	93.6	17.4	24.3
1976–1980	64.0	2.1	4.3	176	92.5	17.9	22.9
1981–1985	63.5	2.5	6.2	177	91.5	17.7	21.2
1986–1990	63.1	2.5	7.2		90.7	16.4	19.4
1991–1995	63.6	2.6	7.2		88.8	13.4	16.0
1996–2000	61.1	4.1	10.6		87.8	11.8	14.2

Panel B *Relative labor productivity of the three major sectors of the labor force*[a]: *1951–2000 (P = Primary; S = Secondary; T = Tertiary)*

Years	Percentage of labor force in sector:			Percentage of GDP in sector:			Relative labor productivity in sector:		
	P	S	T	P	S	T	P	S	T
1951–1955	38.5	24.5	37.0	18.4	34.6	46.9	47.9	141.3	126.8
1956–1960	32.9	26.7	40.4	14.9	37.9	47.3	45.2	142.0	117.0
1961–1965	26.2	30.9	42.9	10.6	41.0	48.4	40.5	132.6	112.9
1966–1970	19.8	33.8	46.3	7.8	41.1	51.1	39.1	121.4	110.5
1971–1975	13.9	35.9	50.0	5.4	41.5	53.2	38.9	115.6	106.4
1976–1980	11.5	34.7	53.6	4.5	38.0	57.6	38.7	109.5	107.4
1981–1985	9.3	34.3	56.1	3.2	36.8	60.0	34.8	107.1	107.0
1986–1990	7.9	33.6	58.0	2.6	35.9	61.5	33.2	106.6	106.0
1991–1995	6.1	33.6	59.9	2.0	32.6	65.3	32.8	97.1	109.1
1996–2000	5.3	31.7	62.5	1.5	29.1	69.3	28.4	91.7	111.0

Sources: Japan Statistical Association (1987), *Historical Statistics of Japan. Volume 1:* various tables; and various tables at the www.stat.go.jp/english/data/chouki website (downloaded in April, 2006).

Notes
A blank cell indicates that there is no estimate available. In a few cases, the averages are for three or four years rather than for five years.
a The primary sector consists of agriculture, forestry and fishing; and the secondary sector of mining, construction and manufacturing. The tertiary sector consists of electricity, gas, heat supply and water; transport and communication; wholesale and retail trade; eating and drinking places; financing and insurance; real estate; services; and government (including not elsewhere classified).

Table A.4 Prices and money supply

Panel A *Percentage growth in domestic prices (overall prewar price index, pwi; consumer price index, cpi; land price index for all cities, ulpi; land price index for six big cities, b6clpi) and money supply (Bank of Japan notes, BOJ; currency, cur; and money stock, ms): 1901–2000*

Years	Overall prices		Land prices[a]		Money[b]		
	pwi	cpi	ulpi	b6clpi	BOJ	cur	ms
1901–1905	5.0				8.7		
1906–1910	0.8				5.3		
1911–1915	1.3				1.5		
1916–1920	22.0				28.8		
1921–1925	−4.4				2.7		
1926–1930	−7.2				−2.3		
1931–1935	2.9				4.4		
1936–1940	10.7				22.4		
1941–1945	17.5				74.7	71.4	
1946–1950	161.5				56.8	56.2	
1951–1955	7.8				10.0	10.5	
1956–1960	0.6		23.0	24.2	13.0	13.4	
1961–1965	0.4		22.8	31.4	15.8	15.8	
1966–1970	2.2		12.8	9.5	16.8	17.0	17.1
1971–1975	10.0	11.5	14.6	14.1	18.0	17.9	18.9
1976–1980	5.9	6.7	3.8	5.4	9.0	8.9	11.9
1981–1985	−0.1	2.8	5.3	6.5	5.7	5.9	8.3
1986–1990		1.4	8.0	24.5	9.4	9.8	10.4
1991–1995		1.4	−1.0	−11.1	3.1	3.1	2.1
1996–2000		0.3	−4.5	−7.9	6.7	6.4	3.3

Panel B *Percentage growth in price indices for trade and the Nikkei stock exchange closing price*

Years	Trade			Yen/US dollar exchange rate[d]	Closing average price for the Nikkei stock exchange
	Export price index	Import price Index	Index for Terms of Trade[c]		
1961–1965	−0.8	−0.1	0.3	0.0	0.7
1966–1970	1.4	1.4	0.1	0.0	9.2
1971–1975	7.1	18.4	−8.0	2.9	22.8
1976–1980	1.5	11.3	−6.3	3.7	10.6
1981–1985	−0.4	−0.8	0.6	−1.4	13.2
1986–1990	−3.2	−6.5	5.9	8.7	17.6
1991–1995	−4.4	−6.1	1.9	9.1	−2.6
1996–2000	−1.4	1.5	−2.6	−3.2	−4.7

Sources: Various tables at the www.stat.go.jp/english/data/chouki website (downloaded in April, 2006) and *Japan. Statistical Yearbook 2006* published by Japan. Ministry of Internal Affairs and Communications. Statistics Bureau (2005: p. 7).

Notes

A blank cell indicates that there is no estimate available. In a few cases, the averages are for three or four years rather than for five years.

a The six big cities are Tokyo, Yokohama, Nagoya, Kyoto, Osaka and Kobe.

b Money stock (ms) includes "near-money" (e.g. certificates of deposits).

c The terms of trade are the ratio of export prices to import prices. Growth rates in the terms of trade in this table were computed by computing the growth rate for the ratio of the index of export prices divided by the index of import prices (both indices based at the year 2000 with an index value of 100).

d Growth rate in the yen/US dollar exchange rate was defined as the negative of the growth rate in the number of yen equaling one US dollar at the official exchange rate.

Table A.1 Income per capital and the capital/output ratio: Japan and the United States (Maddison's estimates)

Years	Income per capita for Japan[a]			Capital/output ratios[b]	
	y	$G(y)$	$R(y)$	Japan	U. S.
1886–1890	907	0.97%	27.1%		
1891–1895	1,004	2.08	28.5		
1896–1900	1,094	3.13	28.5		
1901–1905	1,130	1.66	25.1		
1906–1910	1,259	0.90	25.5		
1911–1915	1,324	3.95	26.3		
1916–1920	1,633	2.87	29.6		
1921–1925	1,775	0.15	30.1		
1926–1930	1,849	−0.25	28.1		
1931–1935	1,951	4.14	37.8		
1936–1940	2,443	5.19	37.7		
1941–1945	2,408	−9.93	23.4		
1946–1950	1,627	8.36	17.8		
1951–1955	2,393	6.74	22.5	1.44	2.28
1956–1960	3,291	8.51	29.9	1.23	2.35
1961–1965	5,046	8.01	41.1	1.28	2.23
1966–1970	7,822	9.03	53.5	1.44	2.09
1971–1975	10,579	3.11	66.1	1.81	2.20
1976–1980	12,218	3.58	68.5	2.23	2.25
1981–1985	14,247	2.89	75.2	2.55	2.36
1986–1990	16,995	4.36	79.9	2.72	2.32
1991–1995	19,451	1.15	88.1		
1996–2000	20,554	0.66	81.6		

Sources: Various tables in Maddison (1995, 2000).

Notes
A blank cell indicates that there is no estimate available.
a y stands for income per capita for Japan; $G(y)$ for the growth rate of income per capita for Japan; and $R(y)$ stands for the income per capita of Japan relative to that of the USA 5 100.
b Both national income (GDP) and capital (non-residential structures plus machinery and equipment) are measured in 1990 Geary-Khamis dollars.

Chapter 7: Japan's Back

By Daniel Citrin and Alexander Wolfson

AFTER ITS LOST DECADE, JAPAN'S ECONOMY IS SET ON A RECOVERY PATH

J APAN is on the move again, and it seems for real this time. Over the past year or so, much has been written about the revival of the Japanese economy and its emergence from the ashes of the lost decade that began in the early 1990s. But for those who missed it, here is the news: the Japanese economy is heading for its longest expansion in the postwar period—one that has already lasted more than four years. In 2005, Japan grew by almost 3 percent and, over the course of the year, was the fastest-growing of the Group of Seven economies (on a fourth-quarter on fourth-quarter basis). And, although the recovery initially was driven mainly by exports, the latest phase has been led by buoyant domestic private spending, for both consumption and investment (see Chart 1).

What happened? To answer this question, consider what the Japanese economy was like ten years ago. During Japan's deepest and longest postwar recession, private spending and economic activity were beset by structural problems in the banking and corporate sectors. In the aftermath of the bursting of the land and equity price bubbles in the early 1990s, persistently high nonperforming loans and a declining value of banks' equity portfolios constrained bank credit and sapped household and business confidence. And the corporate sector was burdened by the three excesses from the bubble period: debt, capacity, and labor. These imbalances combined to hold down both investment demand and household income (and thereby consumer spending). The depth of the problems and the gradual approach to dealing with them, along with certain unforeseen external shocks, led to the vicious circle of falling demand and falling prices that persisted for so long.

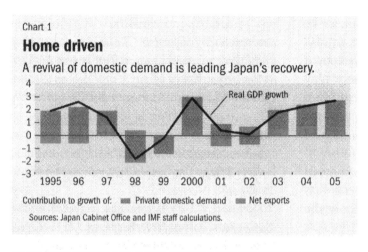

Chart 1

Home driven

A revival of domestic demand is leading Japan's recovery.

Contribution to growth of: ■ Private domestic demand ■ Net exports

Sources: Japan Cabinet Office and IMF staff calculations.

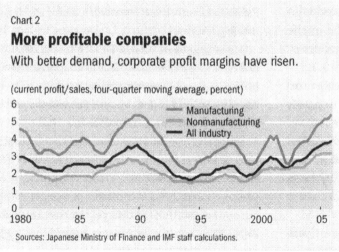

Chart 2

More profitable companies

With better demand, corporate profit margins have risen.

(current profit/sales, four-quarter moving average, percent)

Sources: Japanese Ministry of Finance and IMF staff calculations.

Ten years on

The Japanese economy of today stands in sharp contrast with that of ten years ago, especially in the banking and corporate sectors.

Healthier banks. By end-September 2005, the ratio of nonperforming loans at major banks had fallen to below 2.5 percent from a peak of 8½ percent in early 2002; the situation at regional banks improved as well, although more modestly. With banks having less need to make provisions against impaired assets and bad loans, their profitability also recovered, although it still remains low by international standards. On the whole, Japan's banks are now less vulnerable to shocks and better able to support economic activity. Whereas corporate restructuring and the economic recovery helped reduce the overhang of bad debts, heightened government efforts in supervision and other areas played a vital role in restoring the banking system to health.

Stronger companies. Firms have largely succeeded in tackling the excesses of the 1990s by trimming costs, reducing unused capacity, and using increased profits to reduce their indebtedness. The focus has been on the following issues:

- *Improved profits.* With persistent efforts to cut labor and other costs, the exit of inefficient producers and suppliers, and stronger demand, firms of all sizes have enjoyed a surge in profitability. Indeed, the ratio of current profits to sales stands at the peak levels of the late 1980s for both the manufacturing and nonmanufacturing sectors (see Chart 2).
- *Improved balance sheets.* Strenuous efforts to reduce debt burdens have paid off, particularly for medium and large firms. The nominal value of corporate debt has been slashed by ¥125 trillion since 1996, and debt-sales ratios are back down to historical pre-bubble averages in manufacturing, with steep declines in the rest of the economy as well (see Chart 3). As a result, firms' cash flows have been freed to upgrade physical and human capital and to reward both employees and shareholders with higher bonuses and dividend payouts.
- *Elimination of capacity overhang.* Along with repaying debt, corporate restructuring efforts since the mid-1990s have involved slashing new investments to deal with excess capacity. As a result, the fixed capital overhang was eliminated; by 2005, capacity utilization had returned to its 1980–89 average range (see Chart 4).
- *Completion of adjustment in labor costs.* Company efforts to shed surplus labor also appear to have borne fruit. After initially relying on more conventional strategies, such as cutting back on new hires and overtime work, firms have shifted to a more aggressive approach—laying off workers and beginning to replace full-time workers with part-time ones or workers on fixed-term contracts. But with sales declining in nominal terms in a deflationary environment, unit labor costs continued to rise through 1999. The labor cost burden declined thereafter, however, and by 2005 had returned to early 1990s

levels. Although some further adjustment may be forthcoming, just as the success in reducing excess capacity has been supporting investment since 2003, the improved labor cost position has supported employment and wage growth since early 2005. Job-offer ratios are at an all-time high, and full-time jobs are now growing faster than part-time jobs.

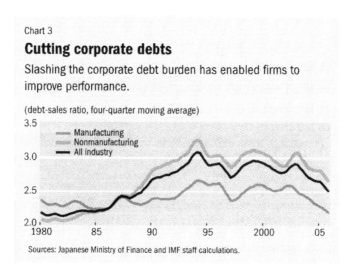

Chart 3

Cutting corporate debts

Slashing the corporate debt burden has enabled firms to improve performance.

(debt-sales ratio, four-quarter moving average)

Sources: Japanese Ministry of Finance and IMF staff calculations.

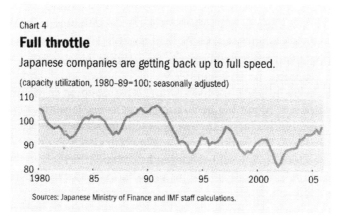

Chart 4

Full throttle

Japanese companies are getting back up to full speed.

(capacity utilization, 1980-89=100; seasonally adjusted)

Sources: Japanese Ministry of Finance and IMF staff calculations.

These positive developments have become increasingly evident and are being recognized by both the Japanese public and international investors. Stock prices have more than doubled from their 2003 low, land prices have bottomed out and begun to rise, and consumer confidence is buoyant. And, although price deflation has proved stubbornly persistent, consumer price inflation finally turned slightly positive in late 2005. In a move symbolic of the strength of the recovery and the end of a long and painful period, the Bank of Japan in early March exited from its extraordinary policy of "quantitative easing," which featured a massive provision of liquidity to banks in the midst of Japan's financial system crisis and deflation problem.

The near-term economic outlook is indeed very favorable, with the IMF now forecasting real GDP growth of close to 3 percent in 2006 and above 2 percent in 2007. But does the brighter outlook reflect the fruits of reform or just the predictable rebound, after enough time, from a cyclical trough?

"JAPAN'S MAIN CHALLENGE IS TO ENSURE STRONG SELF-SUSTAINING GROWTH IN THE FACE OF MOUNTING DEMOGRAPHIC PRESSURES."

Although it is difficult to give a definitive answer, it is striking that Japan's turnaround followed stepped-up regulatory pressure on banks to clean up their balance sheets. The improvement in financial sector health, in turn, helped support corporate sector revitalization (and vice versa). At the same time, a decline in the importance of cross-shareholdings between banks and insurance companies on the one hand and *keiretsu* companies on the other has promoted a more efficient resource allocation because managers are now better able to make decisions on the basis of price and quality. In general, Japan's improved economic performance has coincided with a gradual shift away from the insular business and government practices of the past. Still, lingering structural rigidities hold back growth. The process of removing labor and product market distortions, cutting overbearing regulation, and strengthening the antitrust framework is only now under way.

The next 10 years

What remains to be done? The agenda is long and includes steps to improve labor utilization, enhance competition in product markets, liberalize the agricultural sector, and encourage foreign direct investment. At the same time, the high public debt (a legacy of the post-bubble years) needs to be brought down. Although it is generally agreed that such reforms are needed—the most recent elections in September 2005 were seen as a public endorsement of further reform—implementing them may be tough, given staunch opposition from entrenched interests and the beneficiaries of the status quo.

With near-term economic prospects looking good, Japan's main challenge is to ensure strong self-sustaining growth in the face of mounting demographic pressures. Japan is aging rapidly, with a birth rate well below the population's replacement rate. The working-age population has been contracting since 2000, and the elderly dependency ratio (the share in the working-age population of people at least 65 years old) is the highest among industrial countries. Although it is true that a shrinking population requires a lower overall growth rate to maintain current living standards, strong per capita income growth is needed to meet the rising pension and health care costs associated with a graying society.

With a declining labor force, per capita growth will depend on higher productivity achieved by using resources more efficiently and by taking advantage of technological advances. A recent government-sponsored report, "Japan's 21st Century Vision," sets out the importance of raising productivity and reaping the benefits of globalization to avoid deteriorating living standards, for example by encouraging foreign direct investment, liberalizing agricultural trade, and easing labor supply constraints by relaxing both labor regulations and immigration policy.

Can the government and the private sector work together to transform the economy and create this "new Japan"? Early signs are encouraging. Japan's economy seems poised to enter a new phase, the hallmark of which will be a move to more normal financial conditions, a smaller government, and a more efficient private sector.

Normalized financial conditions. With deflation coming to an end, households and firms will need to deal with a return of real interest rates to more normal levels. Even as financial conditions normalize, monetary policy is expected to remain accommodative. In the first stage, the removal of surplus liquidity from the banking system will be implemented gradually over several months, during which the key interest rate will stay at zero. Beyond this period, interest rate rises are likely to be gradual, given the expected path of prices.

A smaller government. After years of large deficits, fiscal consolidation is under way to arrest the rise in public debt and create room for the spending needs associated with an aging population. With net debt of the public sector approaching 100 percent of GDP, the precarious fiscal position could act as a drag on recovery prospects. Progress is being made toward the official goal of achieving a primary surplus (excluding social security) by early in the 2010s, with the primary deficit falling to some 3 percent of GDP in FY2005 from 5.5 percent in FY2003 (see Chart 5).

So far, the emphasis has been geared toward expenditure restraint, notably through cuts in wasteful infrastructure spending. But revenue measures will need to play an increasing role in coming years, including a likely increase in the consumption tax (which in Japan is at the lowest rate among all industrial countries with a similar tax). In addition, a mixture of benefit cuts and premium increases will be needed to address the sharp projected rise in social security and medical care expenditures (on current trends, and despite recent pension reforms, spending on social security will rise to 20 percent of GDP in FY2025 from 16 percent of GDP in FY2005, with medical care expenditures doubling).

The government is also expected to continue to reduce its role in the economy by scaling back the activities of its financial institutions. Loans at such institutions other than Japan Post have already dropped by 20 percent since 2000, and deposits at Japan Post—which largely fund suboptimal public investments—are also down 20 percent.

The privatization of Japan Post, the world's largest deposit taker, will remove a source of unequal competition for the private banking system. Privatization will take a long time, but the benefits from a more efficient use of Japanese savings could be sizable.

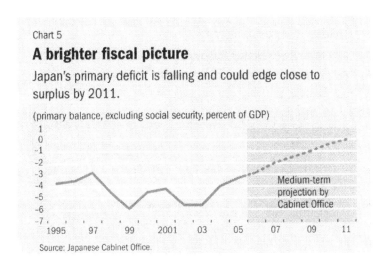

Chart 5

A brighter fiscal picture

Japan's primary deficit is falling and could edge close to surplus by 2011.

(primary balance, excluding social security, percent of GDP)

Medium-term projection by Cabinet Office

Source: Japanese Cabinet Office.

A stronger banking sector. There has been significant consolidation among Japanese city banks, which now comprise three large banking groups that have earned sizable profits in recent years. Better profitability will allow banks to repay public capital injections and shore up their capital bases. In the near term, rising interest rates should bolster profits by raising net interest margins, but the key to sustaining financial sector strength and avoiding future problems will be to continue moving toward better loan pricing (based on forward-looking risk assessments of loans) and away from excessive collateral-based lending. This will be particularly important as the improvement in corporate health supports revived demand for bank lending. (Indeed, in February 2006, credit growth finally turned positive after eight years of uninterrupted decline.)

A more efficient corporate sector. To a large extent, Japan's economic prospects depend on whether companies are able to productively use their restored balance sheets and not repeat past errors (that is, by keeping debt ratios at healthy levels, responding to price signals, and focusing on profits). The corporate sector's focus is shifting from paying down debt toward expanding operations. Large Japanese manufacturers are well placed to face the challenges of globalization and have rationalized operations and intensified global integration, notably by establishing production facilities in China and Southeast Asia. The latest survey of overseas operations of Japanese manufacturers suggests that the ratio of overseas production to total output may reach 34 percent over the medium term from 28 percent in FY2004. In addition, firms have increased spending on research and development and have begun raising investment to replace an aging capital stock (see Chart 6). The adjustment in labor costs will help sustain firms' demand for full-time workers, which bodes well for income and consumption growth.

Chart 6

Investing for the future

Japan's research and development spending is higher than competitors.

(research and development spending, percent of GDP)

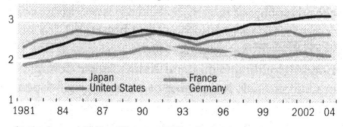

Sources: Japanese Ministry of Finance and IMF staff calculations.

The quality of corporate governance will play a key role in ensuring that Japanese companies make the most of their strong current position. Already, there are signs that the environment for corporate governance is improving as the tight links with the banks (exemplified by large cross-shareholdings) continue to weaken and accountability to shareholders increases. Despite some recent high-profile scandals, the competition for corporate control seems to be intensifying: merger activity is at an all-time high, and cash-rich firms are under increased pressure to raise dividend payouts. New rules to ease corporate acquisitions and clarify takeover defenses could accelerate this process, although much will depend on implementation (the proposal to allow foreign firms to use their shares to acquire Japanese firms has already been delayed).

Turning point for Japan

Japan truly seems at a crossroads. With the improvements described above, and facing a generally supportive external environment, it should achieve much higher growth over the coming decade. Indeed, several academic observers and market analysts now believe that Japan's trend productivity growth has accelerated and that overall GDP growth could reach 2–2½ percent on a sustained basis even with a declining population. Achieving growth at such a pace would demonstrate the benefits of past reforms and could help create a virtuous circle to support the next set of structural reforms needed to safeguard the strong expansion.

Self-sustained growth in Japan would have significant global benefits. Growth in Japan, the world's second-largest economy, would have knock-on effects throughout Asia and the global economy and contribute to a more balanced pattern of global growth. This would also help to reduce global current account imbalances. The road has been long, but Japan is now well placed to contribute to a stable and vibrant world economy.

Daniel Citrin is Deputy Director of the IMF's Asia and Pacific Department (APD). Alexander Wolfson, currently a Director at Citigroup Inc. within Global Country Risk Management, was an Economist in APD during 2001–05.

REFERENCES

International Monetary Fund, 2005a, Japan: *Staff Report for the 2005 Article IV Consultation* (Washington).

———, *2005b,* "Recovery of Japanese Firms," in *Japan: Selected Issues* (*Washington*), pp. 28–39.

Koll, Jesper, 2005, "Japan Is back, for Real This Time," *Far Eastern Economic Review*, Vol. 168 (October), pp. 11–15.

Chapter 8: Deregulation and Competition

By Panos Mourdoukoutas

The most important task is to increase the purchasing power of consumers by adopting a policy aimed at bringing about lower prices. Cutting prices as much as possible would increase the purchasing power of consumers, accelerate the distribution of goods, support firm economic growth, and subsequently help reduce the trade imbalance by boosting imports.

My contention is that we cannot expect traditional medicine to cure the current illness of Japan's slumping economy and lowering external surplus. Admittedly a dose of public investment will generate some new demand. But the record shows that even repeated doses of such stimulus have failed to revive the economy, and the reason is to be found in the nature of the Japanese economic system.[1]

Change has always been difficult and costly in every society. Sometimes, change comes slowly, a step at a time. At other times, change comes abruptly, in leaps and bounds. In either case, change stems from pressures from within or without the system that bury the old system like a tidal wave, replacing it with a new one.

In Japan's case, the transformation from the Old to the New Economy came from both external and internal pressures, the twin frictions that prompted many prominent Japanese businessmen and western scholars, such as those quoted above and below, to question Japan's early economic policies and to call for a shift in economic priorities:

> Japan must cast off its growth-first obsession, shifting its attention from the sellers to the buyers. Pricing systems and other business practices must be reformed to provide consumer satisfaction in an era of multidimensional values.[2]

Starting with the Nagasone government and intensifying under the Hosokawa government in 1982, economic policy priorities have shifted away from production into consumption, and many import barriers and regulations of domestic industry have been lifted. Like previous developed countries, Japan is being transformed from an emerging, developing economy growing against her trade partners and citizens to a "normal," mature economy growing with her trade partners and citizens.

The shift from a producer- to a consumer-oriented economy has been a lengthy and painful process that has taken the Japanese economy on a roller-coaster ride known as the Bubble and its Burst. The sharp upturn and prolonged expansion in the 1980s was followed by a sharp down turn and prolonged contraction in the 1990s, which pulled the country into a financial crisis and deflation that lasted well into the early 2000s.

Addressing Japan's transition from the Old to the New Economy, this chapter is divided into three sections. The first section discusses Japan's shifting of priorities, the second section describes the growth of the Bubble Economy and its subsequent Burst, and the third section reveals how Japanese governments have coped with the lingering banking crisis.

SHIFTING ECONOMIC PRIORITIES

Shifting economic priorities and promoting completion are two difficult tasks in every society, especially in Japan where bureaucrats and *keiretsu* groups commanded enormous powers over economic policy.[3] Yet, in response to growing consumer dissatisfaction and mounting foreign pressure, Japanese governments revised their economic priorities, trying to become a "normal society."[4] Goals, such as "contributing to the international community and promoting internal reforms" and "improving the quality of Japanese life," jumped ahead of economic growth on the priority list of MITI visions for the 1990s:[5]

> Over the medium to long-term, we must put in place economic structures that are primarily based on domestic consumption and ensure that domestic social capital is provided to create a rich, vibrant society and economy in anticipation of the onset of an aging society.[6]

Starting in the late 1980s, Japanese governments took a number of measures to put in place economic structures that promoted domestic consumption: working hours were reduced, domestic demand was expanded, the yen began appreciating in value, tariffs were slashed, and domestic markets were opened to competition.

Reduction in Working Hours

In Japan's Old Economy, people worked long hours, on average 15–20 percent more than their industrial counterparts, and that did not include "offing time," or the time workers spent in the company in after-hour meetings without getting paid, as explained in this JETRO report: "In most sectors, career-track employees, particularly in administrative, creative, and high-tech positions, are unlikely to record all, if any, overtime hours. Although in many cases they may have two or three hours of paid overtime allotted by the company per day, these categories of employee generally are expected to work beyond these allotted hours at no extra pay."[7]

In Japan's New Economy, people do not work as much as they once did. Working hours have fallen from 2,100 in 1988 to 1,750 in 2002, closer to those of her industrial counterparts, particularly the U.S. Saturday working hours dropped from 4.59 hours in 1996 to 4.19 in 2002, while Sunday working hours dropped from 2.24 hours to 2.19 hours.

Expansion of Domestic Demand

Following the 1985 Plaza Accord, Japan launched an expansionary monetary and fiscal policy. Between 1985 and 1989, the Bank of Japan cut the official discount rate five times, from 5.5 to 2.5 percent. In the meantime, the Japanese government boosted domestic spending several times, especially spending on infrastructure. In February 1994, for instance, Hosokawa's coalition launched a stimulus package of $140 billion. But even before the Hosokawa government, domestic demand was expanding at respectable rates. Between 1985 and 1990, domestic demand expanded at 3.7 percent in 1985, 6.8 percent in 1988, and 4.6 in 1990. During the period of 1993–1999, the Japanese government launched seven stimulus packages, ranging from 6.2 percent of GDP (September 1993) to 23.9 percent of GDP (November 1998).[8] And while Japan boosted domestic spending, the yen gained in value against the dollar, making imports less expensive to Japanese consumers.

A Stronger Yen

In early 2005, the Japanese currency was trading at 105 yen to the dollar! That's hard to believe, given that ten years earlier, the Japanese currency was trading at 150 yen to the dollar, and that twenty years earlier it was trading at 300 yen to the dollar. But the persistence of Japan's trade surplus and the expansion of domestic demand finally took their toll on the Japanese currency, which had a pervasive effect on the Japanese economy. On the one side, as export prices rose, the export sector found it more difficult to compete in world markets. On the other side, as import prices declined, the domestic sector found it more difficult to fend off foreign competitors. Under these pressures, government deregulation and business restructuring were accelerated.

With the rise in export prices, for instance, Japanese companies were compelled to cut costs and to allocate production overseas, an issue to be further addressed in the next chapter.

In short, after years of seeding and growth, harvest time had arrived in Japan in the late 1980s. Consumption and leisure began to replace savings and work. Stabilization policies had to be supplemented by structural measures that promoted competition by eliminating the long-standing protectionism and regulation that limit domestic and foreign competition and fueled external and internal imbalances.

Promotion of Competition

As is the case with everything else in Japanese life, the promotion of competition has been a lengthy and slow process. It includes measures to remove protectionism and to deregulate the noncompetitive sector.

Lifting Protectionism

Whether the country is Japan, South Korea, China, Germany, or the U.S., identifying and comparing tariff and quota barriers with other countries is fairly easy. Nontariff barriers, such as product standards and certification systems, distribution networks, and government regulation and government procurement, however, are more difficult to identify and compare. After all, every market has its own peculiarities and specificity as determined by economic and noneconomic barriers.

A developing country in the '50s and '60s, Japan had high tariff and non-tariff barriers to protect her infant and inefficient industries. Different product standards and certification systems for electric products and extensive government regulation of the retail, transportation, and financial industries formed a formidable web that kept foreign products out of these markets. But as Japan joined the developed countries in the '70s and '80s, and many of her infant industries grew up and even exceeded their western peers, many tariff and nontariff barriers were lifted.

For instance, Japan eliminated tariffs for most of the industrial products for which she enjoyed a competitive advantage over her trade counterparts. She also adjusted some product standards and certification systems to those of other industrial countries, and simplified customs clearance procedures. Yet Japan maintains tariffs and quotas for food and beverage products, textiles, chemical products, and machinery products, as well as regulation for retailing, construction, and financial services. According to some estimates from the Institute for International Economics in Washington, nontariff barriers doubled the cost of many imported products to Japanese consumers. In 1989, for instance, trade barriers cost Japanese consumers 10–15 trillion yen, which translates to between 2.6 percent and 3.8 percent.[9]

Lifting Tariffs

In an attempt to protect inefficient industries, Japan's tariffs and quotas were quite high in the '50s and '60s, well above its industrial trade partners. But as many of those industries became efficient by the '70s and '80s, tariffs were slashed across the board to levels below those of her major trade partners. With the exception of some agricultural products and alcoholic beverages, Japan's tariffs have been in line with those of the U.S. and the European Union. In 2000, for instance, Japan's average tariff was slightly above 5 percent, while those of the U.S. and E.U. were slightly below 5 percent (see Exhibit 8.1).[10]

Exhibit 8.1 Average Tariff Rates for Selected Countries

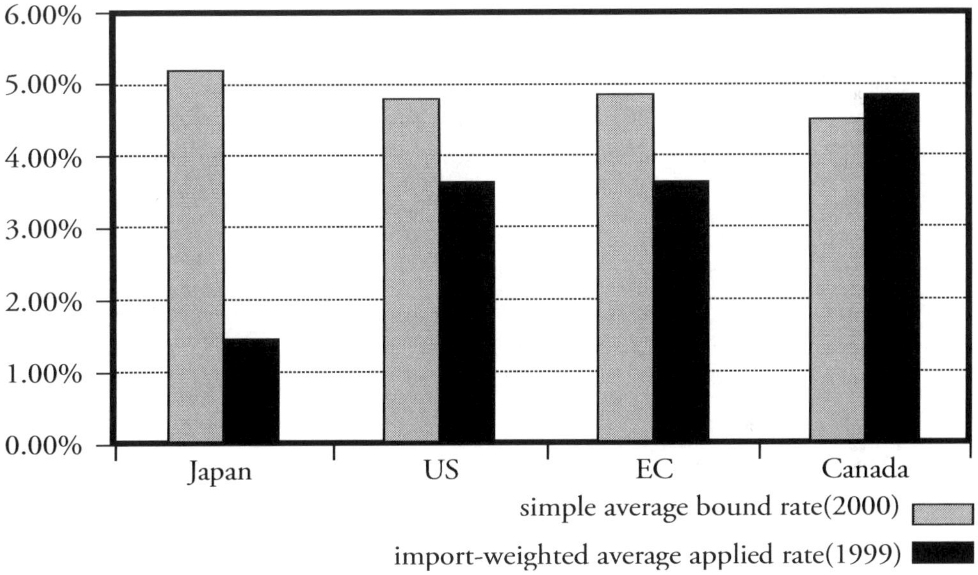

simple average bound rate(2000)

import-weighted average applied rate(1999)

Lifting Nontariff Trade Barriers (NTB)

Less visible and harder to identify and monitor, nontariff trade barriers are often far more formidable to international trade than tariffs. Nontariff trade barriers, such as customs procedures, product standards and certification, government procurement and subsidies, and a backward distribution system, have been blamed for slowing or even limiting access to Japan's market. From electrical appliances to transportation, nutrition, and pharmaceuticals, Japan had its own strict product standards and certification system. Concerns over natural disasters, limited space, an obsession for quality, and the protection of special interests are some of the factors that could explain Japan's adoption of such standards. Yet these standards limited foreign competition, yielding much higher prices for Japanese consumers.

According to an IMF (International Monetary Fund) report, the proportion of Japan's imports protected by NTBs in 1986 was about 43 percent, compared to 45 percent for the

U.S. and 54.1 percent for the EU.[11] Japan's progress in lifting product standards as a trade barrier at this point was confirmed in a survey by McKinney that found that 11.8 percent of the respondents thought that product standards had remained the same in 1986, as compared to 12.5 percent in 1979, and 18.1 said that changing product standards was frequently the case in 1986, as compared to 23.9 in 1979.[12]

As of August 2002, the Japanese government implemented a host of measures to bring product specification in line with those of her major trade partners. The Electrical Appliances and Material Control Law, for instance, simplified certification for foreign appliances and electric products. The Measurement Law simplified the procedure for the importation of measurement devices.

Lifting Barriers in Other Sectors

Progress was even made in such highly protected sectors as agricultural products, insurance products, automobiles, and automobile parts. In 1987, under pressure from Japan's two main beef exporters (Australia and the U.S.), Japan reached an agreement that provided for a two-stage liberalization of beef imports. In the first stage, from 1988 to 1990, import quotas were raised from 274,000 metric tons to 394,000 metric tons, maintaining a 25 percent tariff. In the second stage, from 1991 to 1998, quotas were raised from 472,000 metric tons to 680,832 metric tons and tariffs were raised to 50 percent. Additionally, in 1993, under a severe rice shortage and pressure from the U.S., Japan opened her market to that highly protected product.[13]

In 1988, Japan made concessions in another disputed, yet lucrative, area for foreign firms: insurance products. Between 1988 and 1989, 49 companies received approval to sell cultural artifacts fire insurance, 22 companies received approval for savings installment plans, and many more received clearance for various types of accident and indemnity insurance policies. In 1995, Japan acceded to the U.S. demand to monitor the progress made on new insurance policies underwritten on a year-to-year basis.

Between 1992 and 2001, progress was made in another disputed area, automobiles and automobile parts. During President's Bush trip to Japan in 1992, Japanese automobile companies promised to raise imports to specified targets: Toyota promised to import 5,000 GM cars and $5.28 billion worth of auto parts; Nissan promised to import 3,000 Ford cars and $3.7 billion worth of auto parts; and Honda promised to buy 1,200 Chrysler and $4.94 billion worth of auto parts. The Japanese kept their promises. In 1994, imports of Ford cars reached 14,321 (180.2 percent over the previous year), imports of Chrysler reached 13,601 (+138.7 percent), and General Motors 8,696 (+2.0 percent).[14] Yet ten years later, in 1994, foreign-brand car imports remained at 20,823 units.

Deregulation

Japan's Old Economy consisted of a modern, export-oriented sector and a backward, domestically oriented sector. While the modern sector was open to domestic and foreign competitors, the backward sector was not. A host of government regulations, such as licensing and product standards and certification systems, kept industries in this sector sheltered from competition. Some industries, such as railroads, telecommunications, and tobacco, were still governmentally owned monopolies that cost Japanese consumers dearly. To elevate the Japanese standard of living to those of other industrialized countries, the government lifted many of those regulations in answer to the call of such Japanese economists as Ozawa, in the *Blue Print for a New Japan:*

> The excessive number of anachronistic regulations constrains the lives of people on every front. ... Meaningless regulations tie up our lives in issues related to transport, finance, distribution, and land use. They distort our lives. To build a truly liberal society, and to make our lives more pleasant, we must immediately commence deregulation.[15]

Nothing happens immediately in the Japanese society, however. Japan is have too much power to relinquish and too much vanity to adopt foreign institutions. This was particularly true under the political environment of weak coalition governments of the mid–1990s, when the sagging economy and financial markets made things even worse. The precipitous decline in the Tokyo stock market, for instance, made it difficult for the government to pursue its privatization plan that started in the late '80s.[16] But let us review some of the measures taken so far, and the ways they have impacted the economy.

Distribution System/Retailing

Though an advanced, developed country in many respects, Japan's distribution system was still backward and outdated into the 1990s. Layers of wholesalers and a large number of small retailers formed a wedge between consumers and producers that kept prices high and sales low. Because of this, Japan's distribution system was the focus of the Structural Impediments Initiative. Japan's trade partners, especially the U.S., claimed that *keiretsu* relations and large numbers of small retail stores formed a formidable barrier between foreign products and Japanese consumers in two several ways.

Not only did *keiretsu* groups push local stores to discriminate against foreign products, they exercised market control by promoting consumer loyalty to domestic product brands. Such loyalty was not limited to inter-group purchases; it extended to individual purchases. Industrial companies that belonged to the Mitsubishi group, for instance, gave their banking, insurance, real estate, and trade business to other Mitsubishi subsidiaries or affiliates, as explained in this 1990 U.S. Congressional report:

Mitsubishi companies pay their wages through Mitsubishi Bank, rent their head offices from Mitsubishi Real Estate, and their storage space from Mitsubishi Warehouse. By choice, they use air-conditioning units made by Mitsubishi Electric, machinery made by Mitsubishi Heavy Industries, trucks made by Mitsubishi Motor and fuel supplied by Mitsubishi Oil. Their factories are insured by Tokyo Marine and Fire, the group insurance company, and their forget-the-year parties are supplied by Kirin, the group brewer.[17]

By maintaining monopoly power, the distribution system was in a position to profit from any yen appreciation rather than passing the savings on to consumers. In fact, between 1985 and 1990 import prices fell by 40 percent, but domestic prices fell by only 5 percent. A substantial decline in the import price of bicycles, leather shoes, and VCRs failed to stimulate the import volume of these products.[18]

Between the looming recession and deregulation, promising developments were soon underway in Japan's distribution system. First, as more independent retail stores opened, the power of the *keiretsu* system began to erode. In fact, in 1990, the share of the big six groups' current income dropped to 13.3 percent, and their share in the work force dropped to 4 percent, compared to the corresponding shares of 16.92 percent and 4 percent in 1985. But the biggest blow to the distribution system came from the recession, which pushed more and more consumers toward discount stores, mail orders, and many other nontraditional distribution systems.[19]

Second, under pressure from the U.S., the Japanese government revised its retail store laws, and practically abolished them by 2001. In 1978, a new law allowed the establishment of 300 square meter stores. In 1990, MITI introduced an 18-month time limit for the social approval of large-store applications. In May 1994, MITI exempted supermarkets of less than 1,200 square yards from the bureaucratic licensing process required of larger stores. In 1998, the Large-Scale Retail Store Law was repealed, and the Large-Scale Retail Store Location Law was enacted in 2000. Recently, discount supermarket chains, such as Daiei, began streamlining their operations and introduced state-of-the-art logistic systems to bring value to consumers.[20]

Financial System

For many developed countries, the era in which the government owned savings institutions and set interest rates on deposit is long gone, even forgotten, as is the era of regulated commissions for brokers. Yet, for Japan, this era only recently came to an end. In fact, it was not until the second part of the 1980s that the Japanese government lifted many restrictions on deposits and allowed the introduction of new financial products. And as of the early 2000s, the Japanese government still controlled the Post Office, which competes with banks for deposits.

In the meantime, the Japanese government took a number of measures to create an open, fair, and global financial system, comparable with those of New York and London:[21]

- March 1985: Money market certificates became available
- April 1985: Yen bankers' acceptance market inaugurated; decision made to allow foreign banks to enter trust banking business

NOTES

1. Kazuo, "A Dose of Deregulation to Buoy Business," 23.
2. Tajima, "Catering to the Needs of a Diversifying Market."
3. Sanger, "Japan's Bureaucracy."
4. Ozawa, *Blueprint for a New Japan*, 196.
5. "MITI's Vision for the 1990s (cover story)."
6. Ryutaro, "Directions for the Future of the Japanese Economy."
7. JETRO, *Meeting the Challenge*, 44.
8. IMF, *Japan, Economic and Policy Developments*.
9. Holloway, "Soul of Inefficiency," 26.
10. OECD, *The Sources of Growth in OECD Countries*.
11. International Monetary Fund, *World Economic Outlook*.
12. McKinney, "Degree of Access," 54.
13. Ozawa, *Blueprint for a New Japan*, 12.
14. Toga, "94 Auto Imports Raced to Record High."
15. Ozawa, *Blueprint for a New Japan*, 198.
16. Sapsford, "Tokyo Hits a Wall with Economic Plans," A1.
17. U.S. Congress Joint Committee, *Hearings on The Japanese Market—How Open is It?*, 48.
18. Japanese Ministry of Finance, "Export and Import Statistics."
19. Thornton, *Japan's Struggle to Restructure*, 36.
20. JETRO, *TRADESCOPE*.
21. Arayama and Mourdoukoutas, *The Rise and Fall of Abacus Banking in Japan and China*, Chapter 2.

Chapter 9: Business and Political Restructuring

By Panos Mourdoukoutas

CHANGING CORPORATE OBJECTIVES

In the Old Economy, corporate governance favored management and labor at the expense of stockholders. Management focused more on long-term objectives, such as sales growth and market shares, that served its own interests and the interests of enterprise union members, while overlooking short-term objectives, such as quarter-to-quarter profits and dividends that served the interests of stockholders. Institutional investors passively followed management, rarely participating in stockholder meetings and voting only on such important matters as election of directors, management compensation, and share repurchase. Management softened external shocks with savings in energy and raw materials, labor compensation cuts, labor deployment, and new product development rather than layoffs. Banks provided low-cost financing, while foreign loan demand made it up for the slack of domestic demand.

In the New Economy, corporate governance favors stockholders over management and labor. Companies have shifted their focus from sales and market share growth to profits and dividend growth. A 1993 JETRO report stated:

> Urgent measures are now in progress across the board in the manufacturing sector. Focus has turned sharply away from market share at all costs and towards making a profit, with the aim of survival and maintenance of at least a basic business health. Corporate departments increasingly are being held responsible

for cost cutting and contributing to profitability. Restructuring is under way to streamline operations.

Some companies have pursued stock repurchasing plans to boost shareholder value. Sony Corp., for instance, has initiated a 650 billion yen stock repurchasing plan, Hitachi 300 billion yen, and Nomura Holdings Inc. 221 billion yen.[1] A 2003 Nihon Keizai Shimbun survey found that 314 out of 1,838 surveyed companies planned to raise their dividend payout, close to 50 percent higher than a year earlier. Dividend hikes were particularly popular in the automobile sector, where more than 50 percent of the surveyed companies planned a dividend hike.[2]

Companies have been further slashing the size of corporate boards. Marubeni Corporation and Mazda Motor Co., for instance, slashed their board size by one-third.[3] At the same time, institutional investors have become more active in electing and monitoring corporate boards. According to the Pension Fund Association, in 2002, pension funds voted in a total of 970 motions—138 concerning election of directors; six concerning director remuneration; 124 concerning election of auditors; 161 concerning distribution of profits; 133 concerning bonuses to retiring directors; and 95 concerning the repurchasing of shares.[4]

The shift from a pro–management–labor organization to a pro-stockholder organization was fueled by a number of factors shaping Japan's New Economy. First, the Japanese government adopted a number of amendments to commercial and corporate governance laws, most notably a law that went into effect in April 2003, giving stockholders the power to control management. Specifically, the law:

- Makes corporate auditing mandatory.
- Increases the number of external auditors.
- Makes it easier for stockholders to file class action lawsuits.
- Requires that large corporations appoint additional in-house independent auditors.
- Lowers the size of shareholding needed to access company records to 3 percent from 10 percent.
- Lifts restrictions on the size of bonds issued by large companies.

Second, the loosening up of *keiretsu* relations and the uproar over "American-style" hostile takeovers, eliminated inefficient and ineffective management, enhancing shareholder value. Jason Singer, writing for *The Wall Street Journal,* reported:

> The uproar signals the arrival in Japan of American-style capitalism and the loud voice it gives to shareholders. As in the U.S. in the 1980s when hostile takeovers and corporate raiders thrived, a lot of executives are decrying the development as a destabilizing force, fearing it puts too much power in the hands of financiers,

looking for a short-term pay-day. On the other hand, as in the U.S., it could spur companies to be more efficient and accountable.[5]

Third, strategic alliances between Japanese corporations with American and European companies have multiplied—Mazda with Ford, Nissan with Renault, and Mitsubishi Motors with DaimlerChrysler, to name but a few. In some cases, these alliances have taken the form of equity stakes. General Motors, for instance, took equity stakes in Isuzu Motors, Suzuki Motors, and Fuji Heavy Industries; Roche Group took a 50.1 stake in Chugai Pharmaceutical Co.; and Wal-Mart took a 6 percent stake in Seiyu. In his book *Globalization and Growth: Case Studies in National Economic Strategies*, Richard H. K. Vietor stated:

> More and more American firms operate inside the castle, with or without Japanese partners, employing large numbers of Japanese workers, who are increasingly participating directly in the Japanese policy process. American firms thus can become part of the domestic *niatsu* (inside pressure) process for change.[6]

Several of these alliances have resulted in a new synthesis, or "cross-fertilization," of cultures that turns problems into opportunities, as is the case with the Nissan-Renault alliance, reported by *Strategic Direction* magazine:

> In the case of the Nissan-Renault alliance, the cultural differences were a source of strength and cross-fertilization rather than problems. The Nissan management understood the severity of the difficulties they faced and saw the arrival of Renault as an opportunity. The revival plan had very strong, clear objectives and left no room for worrying about cultural conflicts. Instead, the emphasis was on seeing the different approaches that each company could bring to the joint objectives.[7]

Fourth, the swapping of debt financing in favor of equity financing gave stockholders a louder voice in management than creditors.[*]

In some cases, the shift from a pro-stakeholder organization to a pro-stockholder organization has already produced the right results. Corporate profitability (current ratio) has increased from 3.3 percent in 1999 to 4.6 percent in 2003. Excess capacity has declined from around 20 percent in 1994 to around 9 percent in 2004.[8] To give some specific examples, Honda's operating revenue has increased from 6,000 billion yen in 1999 to 10,000 billion in 2003. Toyota's operating margin increased from roughly 3 percent in

---

* Interest-bearing debt has fallen from close to 200 trillion yen in 1999 to 175 by 2003.

1993 to 8 percent in 2003, while its net income increased from roughly 10 billion yen in 1999 to 22 billion yen by 2003.[9]

In short, as Japan shifted from the Old to the New Economy, its corporations became more stockholder- rather stakeholder-oriented, emphasizing profits over sales and making it easier for stockholders to monitor management performance.

HOLLOWING OUT

"Hollowing out" refers to the offshore relocation of traditional manufacturing operations, a strategy that mature, industrialized countries often apply to cope with the strengthening of their currency. Great Britain and the U.S. experienced this process, and certainly Japan couldn't escape it. The precipitous rise in the yen made it difficult for Japanese companies, especially consumer electronics companies, to compete effectively in world markets without shifting production to overseas plants in the U.S., E.U., and especially Asia, as noted in a number of international business periodicals:

> In the past two years, Japanese consumer electronics makers have all but given up production of audio equipment in Japan. Production of ordinary color television sets, once a symbol of Japan's export juggernaut, will be shifted completely to other Asian countries within a few years. The number of people employed by Japanese companies overseas is soaring. And after four years of recession-induced decline, corporate Japan's direct investment overseas rose 5.5 percent in fiscal 1993 to $36 billion, due to the shift to offshore production.[10]
>
> Already, almost 70 percent of the color televisions made by Japanese companies are made overseas. For VCRs, the figure is about 30 percent. There are even a few Japanese companies, like Uniden, the cordless telephone maker, that do all their manufacturing outside Japan.[11]

Every industry that makes less sophisticated, low value-added products has been shifting production to Southeast Asian and China, transforming them into backyard assembly factories. An April 2001 JETRO survey entitled *Competitiveness of Chinese Products in the Japanese Market* found that close to 58 percent of Japanese companies imported products from China. Of these companies, 60.2 percent imported finished products, 29.6 percent semi-finished products, and 35 percent parts and materials. Additionally, 37.6 percent owned a plant in China, and 42.2 percent had plans to shift production to China.[12]

Increasingly, products made in Japanese transplants in Asia reach western markets. A confirmation of this trend is the reduction in Japan's surplus with the U.S. and an increase in China's and Southeast Asia's surpluses with the U.S., plus the decline of China's surplus with Japan. In 2003, for instance, China's trade surplus with the U.S. soared by 20 percent, while its surplus with Japan dropped by 24 percent.[13]

The rush to Southeast Asia is not universal, however. Industries that make highly sophisticated, high value-added products like flat-panel displays and lithography equipment stay home, as noted in *The New York Times:*

> Much of the assembly of low value-added consumer products, like television sets, has already moved out of Japan. Much of what is left of Japan's exports are high-value components and machinery and products in which the Japanese face little competition, like flat-panel display for computer screens, some types of lithography equipment for making computer chips, and laser-printer mechanisms.[14]

Some Japanese corporations have devised a variety of strategies to counter hollowing out, such as the development of new products, the pioneering of another field, the changing of product lines, and the expansion in the domestic market. One survey of 219 responding manufacturers found that 42.7 percent of materials and processing industries applied product development as a strategy to deal with hollowing out.[15] This strategy continues in the early 2000s. Canon, for instance, makes its conventional digital cameras in China, but retains its endoscopes in Japan. Canon and Sony have also been shifting the manufacturing of their conventional, modular-type products to China, while retaining manufacturing of integral architecture products in Japan.[16]

As Southeast Asian countries and China begin to develop their own technologies and catch up with Japanese manufacturing, Japanese companies must re-evaluate their strategies. Japanese managers, who have found comfort in the thought that manufacturing is everything, must either come up with novel products and processes or shift to services, reaching outside the company and the country for new talents to develop the new products, processes, or services. Managers must develop a whole new corporate culture, a global rather than a Japanese culture. But can Japan afford to develop a whole new management culture without undermining, or even abandoning, the institutions that gave them flexibility and strength in the first place?

AN END TO TRADITIONAL BUSINESS PRACTICES?

Business practices and business models have their place in history, meaning that they work in some historical instances, but not in all. And this seems to be the case with the three sacred treasures of the Japanese management system: lifetime employment, seniority wages, and enterprise unions. They worked well in the high-growth environment of the Old Economy of the 1950s and 1960s, but not in the prolonged stagnation of the 1990s, as explained by Ono, in a 2001 *Wall Street Journal* article.

Young people are no longer offered lifetime employment. Instead of battling for scarce full-time positions, many young people are drifting from one part-time job to another in today's only growth industries: flipping burgers, delivering pizzas, selling soda in convenience stores. The media have dubbed these serial part-timers "freeters"—a Japanese neologism combining the English word "free" and "arbeiter," the German word for worker. It means anyone who chooses to make a living by juggling part-time work.[17]

The lifetime employment system has become less popular among the country's corporations. According to a survey conducted by the Prime Minister's Office, the percentage of companies abandoning the lifetime employment system increased from 36.4 percent in 1990 to 45.3 percent in 1999. This trend is more evident among smaller companies of 30–99 employees (see Exhibit 9.1). Over the same period, the share of female part-time workers to the country's overall employment increased from 33.2 percent to 39 percent, well above the corresponding OECD figures of 23.6 and 24 percent respectively (see Exhibit 9.2).

Exhibit 9.1 Declining Share of Companies with Lifetime Employment

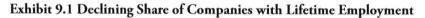

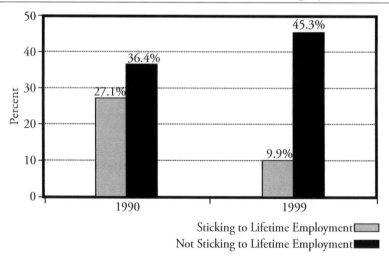

Do these statistics mean an end to lifetime employment? British sociologist Ronald Dore argues that Japanese companies will find it difficult to abandon such a popular institution. Instead, he expects companies to find ways to expand the employment opportunities for people who lack the skills and the ability to adjust to the demands of new technology.[18]

Exhibit 9.2 Rising Share of Part-time Female Workers in Japan

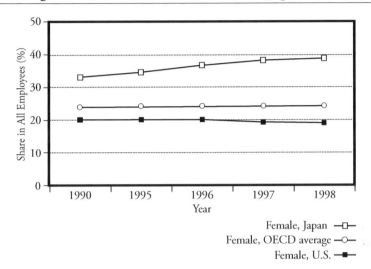

Source: OECD Employment Outlook, OECD, Paris, 1999

Compounding the problem of economic stagnation, the aging labor force and growing business complexity have made the seniority-based system both expensive and incompatible with the demands of the workplace, as explained by Sebastian Moffett in *The Wall Street Journal.*

> Many companies, meanwhile, are being sapped by the effects of corporate traditions such as Japan's seniority-based wage system, where pay rises according to age. The average age at electronics behemoth Matsushita Electric Industrial rose to 41 in 2002 from 31 in 1980. The aging trend imposes a swelling wage burden, straining companies' bottom lines.[19]

Some companies have shifted from a seniority-based system to a merit-based system, as reported in *Focus Japan* magazine and in JETRO studies:

> In the past, new workers were given on-the-job training and reassigned every few years to give them broad experience.
> Many of Japan's large companies are introducing a form of performance-based salary system, or *nenpo-seido,* at least on a trial basis. The new systems vary according to company, but they usually include a base salary (which may need to be negotiated by the individual employee periodically), and usually apply only to manager-level employees.[20]

According to a survey conducted by the Prime Minister's Office, the percentage of companies favoring merit over seniority increased from 37.8 percent in 1993 to 49.5 percent in 1999; while the percentage of employees favoring merit increased from 52.4 in 1978 to 63 percent in 1995. This trend is more evident among younger workers (see Exhibit 9.3).[21]

Some companies have been adopting even more revolutionary labor remuneration policies. Following the revision of the Commercial Code in 1997, 983 (30 percent of all listed) companies have introduced stock option packages.[22] In 2002, 983 or about 30 percent of Japanese firms offered stock option packages.[23] Does the gain in popularity of the merit system mean an end to the seniority-based system?

TDK President Ken Aoshima believes in the emergence of a mixed merit-seniority system to address the employment needs of less qualified workers, the handicapped and the elderly:

> Sometimes in some business magazines or newspapers there are articles about corporations with very drastic merit-based compensation systems that succeeded. But if you look at them from the other side, it is because the system was an exception that could become an article, not a case that could become a general feature of all corporations. If compensation is purely merit-based, then there would not be many older people or handicapped people working. This could be possible as an exception, but not all companies can do this. We live in a society with senior people who need to work. I think there should be some social or business system to guarantee this social aspect.[24]

Exhibit 9.3 Share of Companies Offering Merit System

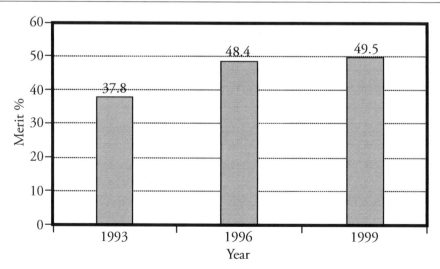

Source: Prime Minister's Office

The layoff of lifetime employees, the crafting of fictitious positions, and the hollowing out phenomenon have undermined the third tenet of the traditional Japanese labor market—enterprise unions——making them obsolete and irrelevant. In a personal interview with me, one Japanese worker reported:

> The Japanese people no longer think that unions are capable of solving the major problems in Japanese business today. Union activities are focused only on small, domestic problems, not on the far-reaching problem of overseas competition.
>
> In brief, Japan's transformation from an emerging to a mature, capitalist economy, and the business restructuring that accompanied it, have shaken up traditional institutions but not completely eliminated them, as is the case with the country's political system.

POLITICAL RESTRUCTURING

The Burst of the Bubble has taken its toll on Japan's political system, creating mutations and permutations in the ruling LDP party, giving rise to coalition governments. In the early 1990s, for instance, rivalry among LDP factions led to a rift between conservatives and reformers, which in turn led to the 1993 creation of the Japan Renewal Party by 44 LDP members.

The splitting of the LDP party and the elections that followed in July 1993 put an end to one-party rule, opening up a period of sweeping change under coalition governments led by Hosokawa, Hata, Murayama, and Hashimoto. The splitting of the LDP further allowed the passage of electoral reforms that put an end to the policy that allowed four or five members to be elected by a single constituency, creating a whole new Japanese political system. As Neville de Silva reported in *Hong Kong Standard,* in 1996, "Japan's political culture has changed. The days of the old faction leaders, controlling politicians and powerful and rich political patrons buying votes seem to be dying, although it is far from dead."[25]

Far from dead, indeed! In July 1996, the LDP refused to support measures that would limit the powers of the legendary Ministry of Finance and clean up the banking mess. Instead, it proceeded with public works projects that boosted the bottom line of the construction industry, but failed to stimulate the ailing economy. In December of the same year, the newly formed LDP government failed to proceed with aggressive measures that would have limited the influence of the powerful Ministry of Finance on the Bank of Japan.[26] And the drafting of the 1997 government budget reincarnated the *zoku giin* the "tribes of the Diet"—members who pursued the old agenda of special interests rather than the modern agenda calling for deregulation and the weakening of bureaucracy.[27]

In the 1996 elections, the low voter turnout and the regaining of ground by LDP reflected both the disenchantment and the confusion of the Japanese people with the political system and the parties that represented it. The election result further reflected the clash between the old Japan, where politicians reigned and special interests ruled, and the modern Japan, where politicians reign and people rule.

The clash between the old and the new Japan continued with the 2001 elections, which led to the popular Koizumi government. Koizumi, for instance, departed from traditional Keynesian stimulus policies by adopting pro-growth monetarist policies, creating new institutions, privatizing govern-mentally owned companies, cutting taxes, limiting the power of special interests, and creating a smaller, more efficient government. It reduced the number of government ministries and agencies from 24 to 14 (see Exhibit 9.4).

Exhibit 9.4 The Koizumi Agenda

Creation of New Institutions	Council on Economic and Fiscal Policy; create enterprise zones.
Administrative Reform	Consolidate the management and coordination agency with the Ministry of Home Affairs and the Ministry of Posts and Telecommunications; consolidate the Ministry of Transportation with the Ministry of Construction, the Hokkaido Development Agency, and the National Land Agency; consolidate the Prime Minister's Office, the Okinawa Development Agency, and the Economic Development Agency into the Cabinet Office; consolidate the Financial Reconstruction Commission and the Financial Supervisory Agency with the Ministry of Finance; consolidate the Science and Technology Agency with the Ministry of Education.
Stabilization	Cut public-works allocation in 2002 budget by 10 percent; introduce government subsidized programs.
Privatization/Deregulation	Privatize Narita and Haneda airports, Japan Highway Public Corp., Japan Oil Corp., The Urban Development Corp., the Housing and Loan Corp., and the postal services; introduce employee-pension scheme.
Banking Reforms	Require banks to write off nonperforming loans over three years.
Tax Policy	Cut taxes for business and stock investors; create tax incentives for equity investing.
Local Subsidies	Cut subsidies to local governments for infrastructure projects (an attempt to limit the power of construction company interests).
Social Welfare	Strengthen welfare and insurance, making people feel more secure; launch Medical Services Efficiency Program.

MITI's failure to provide for industrial direction in the 1970s; the strengthening of corporations; pressure from trade partners after the first oil shock; the political and financial scandals that shook the Nagasone, Takeshita, and Kaifu governments; and the failure of the Ministry of Finance to avert the banking crisis all weakened the earlier cozy relations between the two parties. With the weakening of the business/government ties, MITI's powers drifted away, and by the mid-1990s, industrial policy gradually transformed from active to passive, in line with policies of other industrialized countries, as these Japanese economists explained:

MITI was once one of the most powerful institutions in Kasumigaseki—Japan's Whitehall—orchestrating the country's industrial policy in close cooperation with the business sector. However, now that Japan has achieved economic success and the role of industrial policy in economic development has diminished, the ministry has been marginalized among even clannish bureaucrats.[28]

> In comparison to the high-growth era, the government, by which I mean the ministry or agency that was responsible for policy, became much more passive. In other words, during the high-growth period, the government was on the one hand seeking to bring about rapid growth through industrialization and a strengthening of international competitiveness, while on the other hand it was preparing for the transition to an open economy required by Japan's status under GATT and the goal of membership in the OECD. Positive activist policies were central. After the oil crisis, however, negative and passive policies became central.[29]

Passiveness weakened the ties between government and business to the extent that the two sides could no longer deal effectively with crises. In 1992, efforts by the Bank of Japan and the Ministry of Finance to convince brokerage firms to step into the market to support equity prices failed again, and the Nikkei average could not find a bottom heading to the 16,000 mark. Even worse, the same institutions failed to avert the banking crisis that caused the prolonged stagnation of the Japanese economy during that period.

To sum up, striving to survive and adjust to the new competitive and technological regime, Japanese companies took sweeping restructuring measures, including relocating production facilities overseas, shifting their priorities away from sales and market shares to profits, and reconsidering their stance towards the traditional institutions of lifetime employment. Restructuring was not confined to Japanese corporations; it extended into political institutions that modernized in line with other countries, opening the Japanese economy to world business. The decision making soon shifted from bureaucrats to elected politicians.

NOTES

1. Ono, "Buy-back Plan Lifts Hitachi, Backfires on Sony," 12.
2. "Profits Net Shareholders Dividends," 4.
3. Marubeni Corporation, Corporate Annual Report; Mazda Motor Co., Corporate Annual Report.
4. Pension Fund Association, "The Behavior of Domestic Investors," 10.
5. Singer, "Hostile Treatment: With '80s Tactics, U.S. Fund Shakes Japan's Cozy Capitalism."
6. Ibid., 16.
7. Anonymous, "The Turnaround at Nissan Motors," 25.
8. OECD, *Economic Outlook*, 25.
9. Toyota, 2003 *Annual Report*.
10. Hirose, "Hollowing Out: Can New Growth Replace Japan's Pruned Industries?"
11. Pollack, "Japan's Companies Moving Production Overseas."
12. *JETRO, White Paper on International Trade 2001*.
13. Moffett and Dvorak, "Asian Fusion: As Japan Recovers, an Unlikely Source Gets Credit: China," Al, A12.
14. "Shellshocked by the Yen, Japanese Companies Still Find Ways to Cope."
15. Look *Japan*, 7.
16. Takahiro, "A Twenty-first Century Strategy for Japanese Manufacturing."
17. Ono, "Buy-back Plan Lifts Hitachi, Backfires on Sony," Al and A10.
18. Dore, "Japan in Recession," 6.
19. Moffett, "Going Gray: For Ailing Japan, Longevity Begins to Take Its Toll," A12.
20. JETRO, *Japanese Market Report*.
21. Prime Minister's Office, *White Paper on National Lifestyle*, 2000.
22. Hiroy, "Re-examining Corporate Governance in Japan," 1.
23. Ibid.
24. Ibid.
25. De Silva, "Hashimoto Faces Mammoth Task," 11.
26. Sapsford, "Japan's Bureaucrats Balk at Curbing Clout," A7.
27. Neff, "Why Hashimoto Has to Hang Tough."
28. Terazono, "Success Has Whittled Away MITI's Powers."
29. Komiya, Okuno, and Suzumura, *Industrial Policy of Japan*, 95.

THE NIE MODEL

Chapter 10: The New Asian Capitalists

By Mark Borthwick

OVERVIEW

When the U.S.S.R. and East European communist governments collapsed in 1989–1991, self-congratulatory comments could be heard throughout the West about the "victory of capitalism." It seemed only a matter of time before the struggling command economies in Asia (e.g., China, North Korea, Vietnam) would succumb to similar forces of change. For reasons connected with their successful revolutionary histories, however, Asian communist states are likely to come to terms with capitalism differently and more slowly than those in Europe. Government planning continues to play a major role in these communist societies.

The capitalist governments of Asia, too, have intervened heavily in the management of their economies—far more so than most of their counterparts in the West. Classic economic theory suggests that a high degree of governmental interference in making excessive "choices" for the private sector is doomed to failure, and there have been such failures in Asian capitalist states. Yet as Japan's early record of growth illustrates, forceful intervention can also have positive results (leading some observers to suggest jokingly that, for a time at least, it was "the only communist system that worked"). The success of government intervention in Asia has become the subject of much debate inasmuch as it challenges traditional free market assumptions. It is a complex issue and the results of government intervention must be measured over many years. In the previous chapter, we examined Japan's success in the post-war era and the extent to which early strategies of success may

Mark Borthwick, "The New Asian Capitalists," from *Pacific Century: The Emergence of Modern Pacific Asia*, 2nd Ed., pp. 271–287. Published by Westview Press. Copyright © 1998 by Perseus Books. Permission to reprint granted by the rights holder.

have undermined later dynamism and growth. Here, we undertake a similar review of the successes, crises, and failures of other capitalist states in Pacific Asia.

All capitalist systems generally share the characteristics of private ownership of property and the means of production and they encourage private initiative to respond to market (supply and demand) forces, but there is considerable variation world-wide among them in the nature and degree of state intervention. A major difference with the "command economies" has been that the capitalist economies allow true price mechanisms to operate: markets are the primary determinants of product values.

Japan dominates Pacific Asian capitalism, both in size and example. Its largest businesses, which form interlocking networks in the *keiretsu* system, tend to make their strategic priority the control or domination of markets—often with the support of the Japanese government. The alternative "free trade" emphasis reverses the order of priority: Markets should be allowed to develop without being manipulated by governments and companies are expected to fend for themselves. In fact, the two approaches have mutually influenced one another over the years. On the one hand, Asian governments have sheltered or controlled their key business sectors, with Korea going even further than Japan in controlling the behavior of its businesses. More recently, however, a counter-trend has begun in which many governments are privatizing state-owned or controlled entities and cautiously deregulating their business environments. This has been prompted not only by the need for investment capital but by the demonstrable need to maintain globally competitive industries.

In the early postwar era, Pacific Asian economies were major beneficiaries of the lower tariff barriers that resulted from global trade liberalization under the aegis of a new institution, the Geneva-based General Agreement on Tariffs and Trade (GATT). Amid a steady expansion of world trade, they turned toward export-driven economic strategies and saw their national revenues soar. The scope and scale of their dramatic post-war economic growth owed much in particular to the vastness and relative openness of the American market.

Besides Japan, the high-growth economies of East Asia (South Korea, Taiwan, Hong Kong, and Singapore) have led the regional growth trend, but other countries have begun to move up rapidly. Historically, their economies shared several characteristics. First, their governments participated in strategic planning and cooperated with the private sector to promote specific national industries. Second, all shared a commitment to export-oriented growth. This implied an acceptance, in the manufacturing sector, of the principle that both quality and fair price are to be measured by international standards and that wages will be tied to productivity. Third, all shared high levels of savings and investment. Most have exceeded a savings and investment rate of 20 percent or more of GNP which is widely held to be a level at which development becomes self-sustaining.

This chapter will examine the economic expansion of these economies, using South Korea to illustrate the range of factors and choices confronting a "late developer." In examining Korea, and in the final section, we ask what role, if any, Confucian traditions may play in promoting economic development.

Complexities of the Economic Boom

The strategies and circumstances of the growth policies pursued by Pacific Asia's capitalist economies have varied considerably from one country to the next in terms of timing, sequence, and prioritization. They are summarized in the accompanying table by William Overholt. All such strategies have not been pursued in each country, nor has there been an ironclad formula for economic success in the region generally. Amid the turmoil that followed the Pacific War, economic setbacks and political crises were the norm in the early stages. The Philippines stumbled badly in the course of its economic development and in spite of rapid growth rates, poverty is still a massive problem in several other Asian economies. Moreover, economic development has given rise to a host of new social and environmental problems which will be taken up in later chapters. For now, however, we will concentrate on the success stories.

DEVELOPING ECONOMIES OF THE ASIA-PACIFIC REGION

—East–west Center

Since 1960 the market economies of Pacific Asia, with few exceptions, have been growing at average annual rates of 6 percent or more. Growth rates in China and some Southeast Asian countries have been only slightly lower over the same period. This level of economic performance is far higher than that of any other world region. If present and foreseeable trends continue, by the end of the century the western Pacific rim countries will have an aggregate economy comparable in size to those of Western Europe or North America.

Japan is the premier developed economy in the Asia Pacific region. In 1960 it accounted for approximately 20 percent of the region's income and 3 percent of that of the world. In 1975 these figures stood at approximately 50 percent and 9 percent, respectively. In the intervening years Japan graduated from the status of a developing country to that of a developed country. A century-long process of catching up with the advanced developed nations had come to a close. Once Japan was at the forefront, the country's growth rate dropped, from approximately 10 percent annually in the 1950s and 1960s to about 5 percent or less after the oil shock of 1974. It will continue to grow at rates below those of its East Asian and Southeast Asian neighbors. Nevertheless, by the year 2000 Japan will still account for over 40 percent of the value of goods and services produced in Asia and the Pacific.

PACIFIC ASIAN STRATEGIES FOR ECONOMIC DEVELOPMENT

- Stimulate a sense of nationhood, if necessary by antagonism toward the developed powers.
- Clean up institutions:
  - Purge corrupt timeservers, and incompetents.
  - Install Western-trained technocrats.

- Crack down on crime, political strikes, and disorder.
- Repress pressure groups that cause patronage, corruption, and inflation.
- Come to terms with the advanced industrial countries in order to share their capital, markets, and technology.
- Keep military budgets small, development budgets high.
- Shift to export-led growth.
- Reform income distribution:
  - Land reform.
  - Labor-intensive industry (cheap labor, textiles, agriculture, and consumer electronics).
  - Huge investment in education.

- Coopt the Left with egalitarian reforms, the Right with growth: Give the masses a stake in society.
- Create large, modern firms to enhance trade.
- Acquire technology, capital, and trading from multinational corporations and international banks.
  - Use technocrats and nationalistic leadership to maximize benefits for the country.

- Move up a ladder that starts with labor-intensive sectors:
  - Agriculture and raw materials.
  - Textiles, shoes.
  - Light industry, especially consumer electronics.
  - Heavy industry.
  - High technology.

- Use authoritarian means, if necessary, to accomplish the above.

—William Overholt

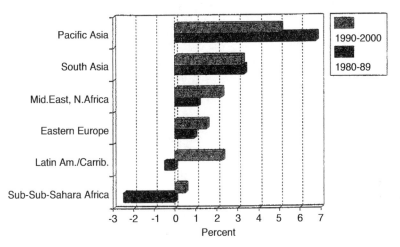

Real Per Capita Growth
Developing Nations, 1980s & Forecast

Graph 10.1

With the possible exceptions of Hong Kong, and Singapore, no other Asian and Pacific developing economies can be expected to follow Japan into the ranks of the fully developed economies before the end of the century. Nevertheless, since the mid-1970s the new cutting edge of economic growth in the region has moved west and south to: (1) South Korea, Taiwan, Hong Kong, and Singapore; (2) the resource-rich countries in Southeast Asia (Malaysia, Thailand, Indonesia and, since 1992, the Philippines); and (3) the People's Republic of China.

Neither theoreticians or practitioners of development have been able to agree on a definitive set of answers to the question of how economic growth occurs. Clearly, however, there must be substantial investment in public and private infrastructure, and this requires a high rate of savings and effective means of channeling savings into productive investment. The labor force must be better educated and trained. Technology must be upgraded and foreign exchange receipts increased to buy needed raw materials and technology from abroad. The government must provide a stable political climate and a relatively predictable policy environment to encourage economic activities.

No countries have met these challenges more successfully than Japan and the newly industrialized economies (NIEs) of East Asian and Southeast Asia—Hong Kong, Singapore, South Korea, and Taiwan. Why have these economies been so spectacularly successful? There may be disagreement on the weight that should be placed on different factors, but there is consensus on some main elements in the East Asian and Southeast Asian economic success stories.

First, the international orientation of the economies of Japan and the NIEs allowed them to exploit opportunities in a generally favorable world economic environment and to overcome limitations in the domestic market. Exports have been encouraged through favorable tax and credit treatment, the monitoring of export opportunities, and realistic foreign exchange rates.

Second, the East Asian economies had a substantial start on economic modernization during the prewar period. This is obviously true of Japan, which by the 1930s had an industrial base sufficient to fight a major war. Much of this was destroyed in the war, but considerable progress had already been made in developing a modern industrial infrastructure, acquiring managerial and technical expertise, and training the labor force. In South Korea and Taiwan the colonial experience, for all its repugnant aspects, did result in the development of rural infrastructure including roads, irrigation works, electrification, and farm organizations, all of which bolstered agricultural production and laid the groundwork for decentralized industrialization. Hong Kong, and Singapore, as colonial entrepôt centers, also had benefited from the early development of commercial and educational infrastructure.

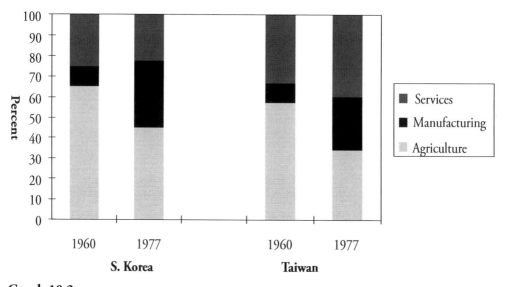

Structural Change: Korea and Taiwan
Percentage Labor Force in Sectors

Graph 10.2

A third factor has been political consensus on economic development as an overriding national objective, which except in the case of Hong Kong justified a strong governmental role in charting and guiding economic growth. In Japan, catching up with the West had long been a national goal both before and after the war, and it was only in the late 1960s, when this task was essentially completed, that other values such as environmental protection and leisure time became more important. In South Korea and Taiwan economic growth was seen as an aid in achieving political goals of strengthening and legitimizing the government. The Singapore government also placed great emphasis on the need for economic modernization as a key in Singapore's struggle for national "survival."

It has frequently been noted that the developmental orientation of Japan and the NIEs was facilitated by a combination of sociopolitical characteristics unusual in developing economies: (1) the absence of wealthy landowning classes, which are often biased against industrialization and may siphon, off surpluses derived from increased agricultural productivity; (2) relatively weak labor movements; and (3) strong economic bureaucracies with considerable independence in shaping policies. Except in Hong Kong, the government's role was particularly prominent in the early stages of industrial development. Close government-business relations, protection of infant industries (that is, start-up industries that are not yet able to stand up to large, international competitors), vigorous promotion of exports, government guidance in directing credits and foreign exchange to favored industries, and the establishment of public sector enterprises are characteristic of most East Asian economies.

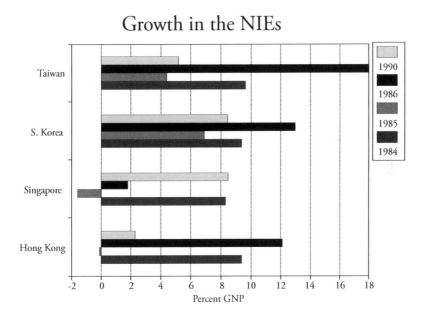

Growth in the NIEs

Graph 10.3 Economic slumps in the mid-1980s illustrate the difficulties of upgrading small economies like Singapore and Hong Kong.

Fourth, there has been a high degree of political stability: all of the independent East Asian and Southeast Asian high-growth economies have been ruled by centrist or conservative political forces that have favored close alignment with Western countries. There has been strong authoritarian control in some cases. This stability has meant predictability and consistency in government policy, which encourages private savings and long-term investment. Profits have remained to be invested at home. Uncertainty about the political order, as in South Korea after the assassination of Park Chung Hee or in Hong Kong just prior to the Sino-British agreement of 1984 on the colony's future, have been associated with economic recessions.

Perhaps the most elusive factor is the cultural one. Japan and the newly industrialized economies are said to share Confucian values, which emphasize hard work, savings, discipline, secularism, entrepreneurship, and educational attainment. Such values do not automatically lead to economic development in the absence of other necessary conditions and policies, but they may encourage an orientation that is conducive to the formulation of policies at the public level and modes of behavior in the private sector that promote economic growth. The "Confucian factor" is taken up later in this chapter.

The Newly Industrialized Economies (NIEs)

The economies of South Korea and Taiwan have undergone profound structural change in the past three decades. These economies are today so thoroughly identified with exports of industrial goods that it is difficult to recall that as recently as 1960 both could be described as natural resource-based economies. In 1960 the agricultural sector provided 37 percent of South Korea's domestically derived production (gross domestic product, or GDP) and 33 percent of Taiwan's. Primary products, mostly farm goods, accounted for 86 percent of South Korea's exports and 73 percent of Taiwan's. By 1983, however, agriculture's share of GDP had dropped to 14 percent in South Korea and 9 percent in Taiwan. Industry's share in South Korea had increased in 1960 from 20 percent to 40 percent of GDP, and in Taiwan from 25 percent to 44 percent. Industrial goods now account for more than 90 percent of the exports of both economies. No other developing countries have experienced such a remarkable shift of economic structure over such a short period of time.

This economic transformation owed its initial impetus to increased agricultural productivity, which provided surplus labor for the manufacturing sector and generated savings that were turned into productive investments. In the early 1960s both South Korea and Taiwan had adopted import-substitution, industrial developmental strategies, encouraging the growth of domestic manufacturing through import protection or subsidies. However, these policies gave way at a rather early stage to policies designed to encourage outward-oriented, export-based industries founded on the comparative advantages in labor. This did not mean that previous import-substitution programs were dismantled, but that policies discriminating against exports were eliminated or altered. Exporters were given subsidized credits and were exempted from duties on imported capital goods and raw materials. Exchange controls and multiple exchange rates were abolished, and many quantitative restrictions on imports were lifted.

TAIWAN

Japan's first overseas possession, Taiwan was intensively developed and rigorously administered by the Japanese colonial bureaucracy. Japanese colonial policies were in large part shaped by the needs and interests of the home islands rather than those of the Taiwanese, who were permitted little voice in the management of the Colony. This colonial relationship was reflected in the Japanese policy slogan "Agricultural Taiwan-Industrial Japan." Nevertheless, Japanese colonialism yielded substantial benefits to the Taiwanese. Under Kodama Gentaro, the fourth governor-general, and his energetic and talented civil administrator, Goto Shimpei, a series of administrative and economic reforms were carried out in the early 1900s, marking the initial stage of the remarkable modernization and economic growth that the island enjoyed under Japanese rule over the next forty years.

Through the 1920s Taiwan played an important role in satisfying Japan's growing demands for agricultural products and raw materials. In the 1930s, as Japan began to prepare for war, Taiwan was intensively developed as an industrial base. Early in the Pacific War the island was a staging area for Japanese offensives into Southeast Asia, but by 1944 Taiwan came under heavy American aerial attack. On 25 October 1945 Japan surrendered Taiwan to the government of China in accordance with the Cairo Declaration of 1943. Misrule and oppression by rapacious Chinese troops resulted in the bloody Taiwanese uprising of 1947 and the brief formation of an autonomous republic. This was quickly suppressed by Chinese troops.

In 1949, as the Chinese Communists took power on the mainland, the Nationalist regime of Chiang Kai-shek and the remnants of his army escaped to Taiwan. Initially, the U.S. government refused to provide military protection, but two days after the outbreak of the Korean War on 27 June 1950, President Truman ordered the Seventh Fleet to protect Taiwan from Communist attack. This presidential directive prevented the Communists from uniting Taiwan with the mainland. As a result, the governments in both Beijing and Taipei (Taibei) continue to claim to be the legitimate authority for all of China.

Retreating from the Communist victory on the mainland in 1949, Chiang Kai-shek established the seat of government of the Republic of China (ROC) in Taipei. As president, he was responsible for perpetuating the policy of mainland recovery and rejecting all compromises with the People's Republic of China (PRC). In maintaining his claim to represent all of China, Chiang reorganized the government to place more control in the hands of the mainlanders. This policy created tensions between the mainlander refugees (about two million) and the Taiwanese (about nine million). Security controls were increased and martial law was employed against both Communist and Taiwanese "rebels." Since Chiang concentrated on military and political preparations for retaking the Chinese mainland, he delegated the economic policies to a pragmatic group of technocrats. As military reconquest became an improbable dream and Chiang aged, he withdrew into an austere and ascetic life. He died on 5 April 1975 at the age of eighty-seven. His body is temporarily interred near Taipei, awaiting a final resting place in China.

Following Chiang Kai-shek's death, power was turned over to his son Chiang Ching-kuo. He [did] not abandon his father's ultimate goal of mainland recovery, but actively concentrated on economic reforms, reindustrialization, and modernization. Under Chiang Ching-kuo, Taiwan became more than just a province of China supporting a hostile competitor to Beijing. Reelected in 1984 to another six-year term, Chiang Ching-kuo chose the Taiwanese-born technocrat Lee Deng-hui to be vice president. The "taiwanization" of the political regime is a major issue for the leaders of the Republic of China.

Economically, the island has shown spectacular growth. Success has been made possible by the strong Japanese legacy, substantial U.S. aid, an energetic land reform program, state intervention, and a growing class of technocrats.

—Richard C. Kagan , *EAH*

SINGAPORE

Singapore and Penang were the staging areas for British economic penetration of the Malay Peninsula. Chinese miners and planters, moving in from the Straits Settlements, pioneered the economic development of the peninsula. In the 1870s, when conflicts between different groups of miners arose, the British government intervened and extended its political hegemony over the Malay states of the peninsula.

By the beginning of the twentieth century, Singapore had been displaced by Kuala Lumpur as the administrative center of the British colonies in the federated and unfederated Malay states. But as the terminus for the Malay railroad system and as the banking and commercial center of the region, Singapore retained its primary role as the economic capital of the British empire in the Malay world.

The ease with which Singapore was taken by the Japanese in 1942 demonstrated the uselessness of trying to maintain such a colony if the state did not already control the surrounding air and sea routes. Following the war, the British began the process of decolonization. With its overwhelming Chinese population, Singapore was seen as incompatible with the political aspirations of the Malays. Thus, the Federation of Malaya remained administratively separate from Singapore, and each began to develop its own political structure. The 1950s were marked by outbreaks of communal violence between Malays and Chinese as well as by British moves to destroy communist or socialist movements in both Singapore and the Federation of Malaya.

As Singapore moved toward independence in the 1950s, a number of political parties emerged, among them the Socialist Front (Barisan Sosalis) and the People's Action Party (PAP). The latter was led by Lee Kuan Yew, a London-trained lawyer who by the early

1960s had emerged as the clear victor in the power struggle to dominate the new state. Following a one-year attempt to rejoin Singapore to the rest of former British Malaya in the Federation of Malaysia, Lee led Singapore to full independence in 1965. The PAP and Lee then dominated Singapore into the 1980s. During these years the island republic made the transition from entrepôt to an export-oriented manufacturing center and attained an impressive degree of economic progress.

—Carl A. Trocki. *EAH*

The export-oriented industrial strategies of the NIEs helped them overcome the limitations of their relatively small domestic markets, but also placed them among the world's most highly trade-dependent economies. Lacking the basic raw materials for industry, the NIEs carved out a special place in the world economy as manufacturing centers, making full use of their comparative advantage in relatively abundant and disciplined labor. Later, as population growth began to fall and surplus labor from the agricultural sector diminished, labor-intensive manufacturing industries began to lose their advantage to more capital and technology-intensive industries.

The critical economic challenges the two economies now face derive from their heavy dependence on external trade and from the uncertainties inherent in their current transition away from labor-intensive industries. Because the growth sectors in their economies

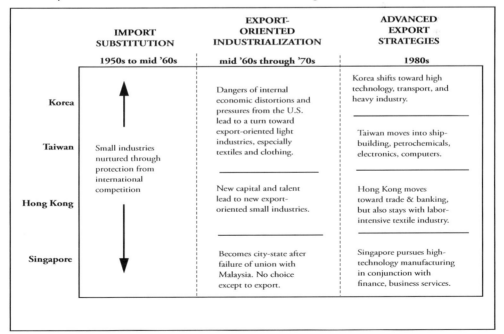

	IMPORT SUBSTITUTION	EXPORT-ORIENTED INDUSTRIALIZATION	ADVANCED EXPORT STRATEGIES
	1950s to mid '60s	mid '60s through '70s	1980s
Korea	Small industries nurtured through protection from international competition	Dangers of internal economic distortions and pressures from the U.S. lead to a turn toward export-oriented light industries, especially textiles and clothing.	Korea shifts toward high technology, transport, and heavy industry.
Taiwan			Taiwan moves into ship-building, petrochemicals, electronics, computers.
Hong Kong		New capital and talent lead to new export-oriented small industries.	Hong Kong moves toward trade & banking, but also stays with labor-intensive textile industry.
Singapore		Becomes city-state after failure of union with Malaysia. No choice except to export.	Singapore pursues high-technology manufacturing in conjunction with finance, business services.

Graph 10.4 Changing economic strategies of the NIES.

are so dominated by exports of manufactured goods and so dependent on raw materials and fuels from abroad, the NIEs have become highly vulnerable to international economic conditions. Access to supplies at favorable prices was threatened by the two oil shocks in the 1970s, but despite short-term economic difficulties both economies were able to compensate by increasing exports. A more difficult adjustment was required by the recession in the early 1980s, which affected demand in export markets. By the mid-1980s, as exports boomed again, both economies had weathered this crisis, but the boom increased their dependence on the U.S. market.

Uncertainty about exports has augmented longer term problems associated with upgrading industries. The economic authorities in both countries believe the development of more capital and technology-intensive industries is needed to compensate for the decline of the NIEs' labor advantages. In Taiwan, however, business caution about the viability of new industries and concern about the greater initial investments required to develop new product lines in competition with producers in Japan and other developed countries have discouraged investment.

South Korea probably faces more serious adjustments. Its home industries have received more protection and subsidies than those of Taiwan. Moreover, South Korea more explicitly sought to follow the Japanese path, emphasizing heavy industries such as steel, shipbuilding, and automobile manufacturing, which entail heavy investments. The small business and agricultural sectors have been relatively less developed, and the large-scale industries accounting for more than a quarter of South Korean income are controlled by a small and rich new business elite. Unlike Taiwan, South Korea had a low rate of domestic savings at the beginning of its industrialization process. Although domestic savings had increased from 1 percent of GDP in 1960 to 26 percent by 1983, investment has exceeded savings, requiring substantial borrowing from abroad. Some economic projects, including harbor improvements and hydroelectric and nuclear power projects, have been delayed to avoid incurring new debts.

The two smaller NIEs, Hong Kong, and Singapore, are city-states whose per capita incomes (US$ 21,650 and US$ 23,360 respectively, in 1994 using the World Bank Atlas method) have increased so quickly that they are the only economies in the developing world to have effectively closed the absolute gap between their income levels and those of the industrialized nations of the north. Both cities play a prominent role as regional centers for financial and other services. Their developmental strategies, however, have differed considerably. Hong Kong has been a free trade economy whose colonial government has believed in a minimum of government regulation of the economy. Singapore experimented briefly with an import-substitution strategy of industrialization in the mid-1960s but subsequently abandoned it in favor of export growth. Its government has been much more actively involved in economic development, establishing state corporations and playing a crucial role in setting wage rates. Whereas investment in Hong Kong has been led by domestic capital, Singapore's industrialization has relied more heavily on foreign investment.

Both economies have experienced economic difficulties in recent years, a result of the general recession in the early 1980s and other special factors. In Hong Kong uncertainty over the outcome of Sino-British negotiations on the colony's future affected investor confidence and has led to some capital flight. Singapore benefited to some extent from Hong Kong's difficulties in the early 1980s, but by 1985 the Singaporean economy was seriously troubled. Its petrochemical and petroleum-refining industries were depressed by a worldwide glut in supplies. Singapore's role as a refining center, the world's third largest, was undercut by new competitive facilities in the oil-producing countries of the Middle East, Indonesia, and Malaysia until the Gulf War in early 1991 led to a boom in Singapore refining. Electronics, another growth industry in Singapore, consisted mainly of subsidiaries of Western companies and was depressed in the mid-1980s as the U.S. industry began undergoing a major restructuring. Shipbuilding and repairing has been adversely affected by excess capacity.

Although Singapore's mid-1980s economic slump was short-lived, it illustrates the difficulties of upgrading a small economy. In the late 1970s the Singapore government encouraged large across-the-board wage increases to give priority to more capital and technology-intensive activities; this policy is now thought by some to have priced Singaporean labor too high.

The Resource-rich Economies of Southeast Asia

The members of ASEAN (the Association of Southeast Asian Nations) comprise Brunei, Burma, Indonesia, Laos, Malaysia, the Philippines, Singapore, Thailand, and Vietnam. The smallest, Brunei, is an oil-rich sultanate with a per capita income that had already reached approximately US$ 20,000 annually by the mid-1980s. Another, Singapore, has been described as a rapidly growing, newly industrialized economy. The remaining four ASEAN countries (known as ASEAN-4)—Indonesia, Malaysia, the Philippines, and Thailand—are middle-income countries (using the World Bank classification) with 1994 per capita annual average incomes ranging from US$ 880 for Indonesia to US$ 3,520 for Malaysia. All are comparatively rich in terms of primary products. Agricultural and mineral products, such as petroleum (for Indonesia and Malaysia), tin, rubber, palm oil, coconut products, rice, sugar, and tapioca have been the mainstays of their economies.

The ASEAN-4 economies have had high rates of growth and have undergone structural transformation, although the degree of change has been less rapid than for the NIEs. Thailand has had the best overall growth performance, with average annual real per capita income increasing by 4.2 percent between 1965 and 1989. Malaysia at 4.0 percent and Indonesia at 4.4 percent have also done well, Indonesia having leapt ahead after a slow start before 1966. The Philippines has the poorest record among these countries, with per capita income increasing by an average annual 1.6 percent between 1965 and 1989.

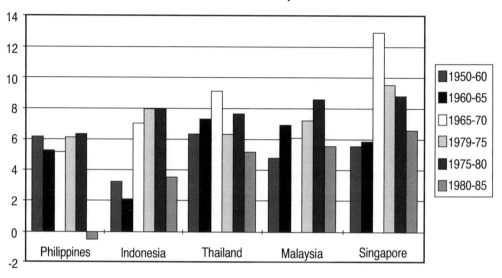

Average Annual GDP Growth of ASEAN In Constant Prices, 1950-85

Legend:
- 1950-60
- 1960-65
- 1965-70
- 1979-75
- 1975-80
- 1980-85

Graph 10.5

This would be a respectable performance in any other region, but it is less satisfactory in comparison to its neighbors and was tarnished by a serious economic in the 1980s.

The share of national income contributed by agriculture has declined over the past quarter century in all of the ASEAN-4 economies and now is in the 20 percent to 25 percent range, although half or more of the labor force is working in agriculture. During the same period agricultural production has expanded more rapidly than population growth in all four countries, although only one (Thailand) is self-sufficient in food. The growth of Malaysia's food production, about 50 percent per capita during the 1970s, reflects the introduction of high-yielding plants, a doubling in the application of fertilizers, and high government priority on programs to help the rural sector, whose predominantly Malay population has considerable political power. Thailand has succeeded in diversifying its agricultural sector from rice into higher-value crops, such as tapioca, maize, pineapples, and sugar, and into fish farming. Increased food production in Thailand, however, has depended heavily on the expansion of arable land—now reaching its limits—and the yields for some staples have been lower than in other Southeast Asian countries. Thailand has begun to shift to an agricultural strategy emphasizing increased productivity on available land.

Indonesia's achievement of rice self-sufficiency in the 1980s has been one of the most impressive agricultural performances in the Asia-Pacific region. During the 1970s and 1980s, rice output increased by nearly 5 percent annually, and yields now exceed the Southeast Asian and South Asian average. This is a consequence of the availability of fast-maturing seeds, incentives for increased fertilizer use, and multiple cropping made possible by expanded irrigation. The Philippines also concentrated on achieving self-sufficiency in rice, reaching this goal in the 1970s. However, its agricultural sector suffered setbacks along with the rest of its economy until the mid-1990s, necessitating periodic rice imports.

Economic growth in rural areas is essential, both to provide employment opportunities for a still rapidly expanding labor force and to increase demand for the expanding manufacturing sector. The manufacturing sector has become more important in exports, already accounting for 62 percent of the value of the Philippines' exports by 1989 (compared with 6 percent in 1965), 54 percent of Thailand's (from 3 percent in 1965), 44 percent of Malaysia's (from 6 percent in 1965), and 32 percent of Indonesia's (from 4 percent in 1965). The Philippines was the first ASEAN country to develop import-substitution industries in the 1950s and 1960s, protecting them through high tariffs, exchange controls, and an overvalued exchange rate. Although deregulation began in the 1960s and a period of relatively rapid growth occurred in the 1970s, the lagging rural economy acted as a drag, failing to create sufficient income or savings to sustain overall growth. As the limits of the domestic market were reached, industrial expansion lost momentum. Recognizing this at the beginning of the 1980s, the Philippine government sought to promote manufactured exports, but the industrial sector remained biased toward production of capital-intensive and final-stage consumer goods, a legacy of the earlier period. The protectionism surrounding these inefficient domestic-based industries is being reduced.

In the early 1980s, the Philippine economy was buffeted by declining terms of trade for primary product exports, such as copper, sugar, and coconut products, and by high inflation and a heavy external debt. A massive capital outflow and the near collapse of the banking system following the assassination of Benigno Aquino in August 1983 propelled the country into a full-scale economic crisis. In 1984 a financial rescue package was negotiated with the International Monetary Fund requiring a number of politically difficult reforms. The Philippines permitted the peso to fall, adopted an austerity budget, reduced trade restrictions, and disbanded some monopoly arrangements in the agricultural sector but then failed to implement these reforms effectively. Unlike that in the NIEs, the economic bureaucracy in the Philippines has been weak. Broader development goals frequently have been subordinated to the self-interest of those with political influence, but reforms enacted after 1992 have reduced the protection afforded local industries and have stimulated new foreign investment.

In contrast to the Philippines, Indonesia's economy was buoyed in the 1970s by the rising price of petroleum, by far its principal export. The post-1966 Suharto government brought political stability and macroeconomic reforms, such as the freeing of foreign exchange markets and the imposition of budgetary discipline. The industrial sector grew at an average annual rate of 11 percent between 1970 and 1982, although this was more a product of the oil boom than of the planning process. Support was provided through import restrictions and the heavy subsidization of public enterprises and large-scale, capital-intensive projects, such as the Asahan aluminum project in Sumatra and the Cilegon cold-rolling steel mill. Heavy bureaucratic controls, a legacy dating from Dutch colonialism, remained characteristic of the Indonesian economy.

This approach did little to improve the competitiveness of Indonesian manufacturing, which remains oriented toward the protected domestic market. Indonesia's capital-intensive industries have limited ability to provide employment for the growing labor force or to generate related economic activities. Petroleum exports had contradictory economic effects, providing the foreign exchange needed for development projects but also helping to maintain a high value for the rupia, thus undermining the competitiveness of Indonesia's other exports and its manufactured goods in their home markets.

When oil revenues began to decline sharply in the 1980s Indonesia devalued its currency, canceled some large-scale projects, cut subsidies for consumer goods, such as domestic fuel and rice, and initiated reforms of its banking and financial institutions, its tax system, and the management of its customs, tariffs, and harbors. Efforts to diversify exports have had some success; textile and plywood exports have grown rapidly. The abundance of natural resources and low-cost labor are definite assets. How these physical and human resources are used will determine the pace and direction of growth. In the aftermath of the oil bonanza Indonesia has demonstrated considerable ability to carry through new policy directions in a less favorable economic environment.

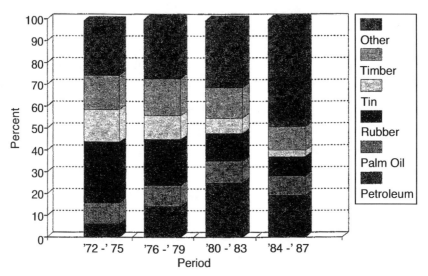

Malaysia's Changing Export Structure
by Commodity Classification

Graph 10.6 The changing structure of Malaysia's export economy indicates its transition toward a stronger industrial base that promises to place the nation, along with Thailand, in the category of a NIE within a few years.

THE NEW NIEs

Japan is fond of employing the metaphor of a flock of geese flying in a "V" formation to describe the way it would like to see East Asia's economy develop. Japan is out there in the lead, followed at a respectful distance by the NIEs—South Korea, Taiwan, Hong Kong, and Singapore. The poorer members of ASEAN (Indonesia, Thailand, Malaysia, and the Philippines) take up the rear. The metaphor appeals to the Japanese sense of harmony, but these particular geese are a bit more unruly than the image suggests. Some of the laggards are catching up on the leaders.

… The growth of GDP in Malaysia, and Thailand is expected to exceed that of the NIEs. Even the economy of lumbering Indonesia will probably expand [at about] the same rate as those of Singapore and South Korea. As a result, the "V" formation is flattening slightly and there are at least three good reasons to think that its shape is changing permanently.

The first is that the economies of Malaysia, and Thailand have "taken off in the sense that industrialization is accelerating at a rate comparable with the speed at which South Korea and Taiwan built up their manufacturing bases in the early 1970s. In Thailand, manufacturing output has grown at an annual rate of more than 16 percent a year since 1988 and at an even faster pace in Malaysia.

The second factor is demographic: the population of the proto-NIEs is younger than that of the "old" NIEs. Their labor forces are growing faster as a result. Malaysia's pool of labor is expected to expand by 2.9 percent a year in the 1990s, five times faster than Singapore's. The NIEs, therefore, have to produce more goods and services per worker than countries like Thailand simply to grow at the same rate.

Third, foreign investment has been pouring into Malaysia, Thailand and Indonesia over the past five years or so. It has provided a much bigger impetus to growth in these three countries than in Taiwan and South Korea, but not as much as in Singapore, 80 percent of whose manufacturing investment comes from abroad.

The NIEs themselves are slowing down for similar reasons to those that caused the rate of Japanese economic expansion to halve after the first oil shock of 1973. One reason is that services are growing as a proportion of their economies and annual productivity gains have therefore halved.

Can Malaysia, Thailand and Indonesia keep it up? Many people say "no," because their inadequate infrastructure is expected eventually to strangle economic growth. In actual fact, however, this kind of bottleneck tends to cap the rate of expansion rather than to cut it drastically.

As for the three factors mentioned earlier, the first, industrialization, tends to take on a momentum of its own. Once economies become less dependent on the production of raw materials, opportunities for trade and specialization tend to grow exponentially.

Demographics—the second factor—looks set to support rapid economic growth well into the next century.

Foreign investment seems more problematical. On the face of it, the capital flow from Japan and the NIEs depends on the vagaries of exchange rates. But it will probably continue to infuse Malaysia, Thailand and Indonesia for the foreseeable future. The savings surplus is dwindling rapidly in Japan and Taiwan, and has disappeared in South Korea, but capital from all three of these countries will continue to look for cheaper homes in the rest of Asia.

If this admittedly rosy prospect is correct, East Asian economic integration is about to enter a new phase. The first was the supply of raw materials to Japan by the poor countries of the region. The second phase, now nearing its end, is the supply of components to Japan. The next stage is the export of finished goods, not just from the NIEs, but from countries like Thailand and Malaysia, too. The geese are still flying Japan's way.

—Nigel Holloway, *Far Eastern Economic Review*

In both Thailand and Malaysia there has been relatively steady industrial growth. Manufacturing was initially related to processing primary products, such as vegetable oils, finished wood products, and rubber products. More recently, new, mostly light industries, such as electronics and textiles, have appeared, which use few local materials but exploit the two countries' competitive advantages in labor. In Malaysia, in particular, there has been a heavy emphasis on manufacturing for export from free-trade zones. The business communities of both countries have continued to be dominated more by traders than by industrialists. Partly for this reason import protection has been relatively mild, with some exceptions.

Today, the Malaysian and Thai governments stress larger-scale industrial projects, such as Malaysia's ambitious scheme to become an automobile manufacturer and Thailand's plan to develop an industrial center along its eastern seaboard (adjacent to new gas fields) as an alternative to Bangkok. The hope is that these new ventures will complement rather than displace light industries and the incentive policies that enabled them to flourish. These ventures are locally controversial, some opponents arguing that too rapid a leap into more capital-intensive production—relying on imported materials, equipment, technology, and management—may run counter to comparative advantage and soon come up against the kinds of constraints and needs for adjustments experienced by South Korea (described later in this chapter).

**DOES RAPID ECONOMIC GROWTH IN ASIA THREATEN THE
PROSPERITY OF DEVELOPED COUNTRIES?**

There has been ambivalence in the Western advanced countries about the rapid growth and industrialization of the Asia-Pacific region. Some fear the continuing strong Asian economic and export performance threatens the prosperity of their own countries. This fear frequently underlies the protectionist sentiments growing in some Western economies. There are good reasons to be wary of protectionist thinking, however.

- The Asia-Pacific region has become a center of dynamic economic development; therefore, countries that adopted protectionist policies would partly isolate themselves from the benefits of increased economic efficiency, reduced prices, and expanded consumer choice that become available with freer trade.
- As economic growth continues in the Asia-Pacific region, its economies become increasingly important markets for the exports of other countries. Because of the growth of incomes in the region, for example, the share of U.S. exports purchased by Asian developing countries has increased significantly. The share and amount of U.S. products purchased by Japan has also been growing.
- Opportunities for high return on direct investments expand with dynamic growth in Asia-Pacific economies. These investments provide incomes and may help expand markets for investors while providing recipient countries with the capital and technology needed for continued growth.
- Economic growth in Asia and the Pacific has improved the political and security environment there to the benefit of the entire world. Countries in the region contribute positively to maintaining the security of their region, reducing the burden on outside powers. As they have developed economically, foreign aid provided to these countries on political, security, and humanitarian grounds has decreased.

Imports from Asia-Pacific countries have hurt specific industries in the United States and Western Europe and are beginning to affect some industries in Japan, but they are helpful and not harmful to the national prosperity of these countries when they are based on comparative advantage as determined by market forces. Most economic studies show that more jobs are gained than lost as a result of freer trade and that protectionism results in reduced economic momentum and income growth.

The ASEAN-4 countries have had remarkable success on many other fronts related to economic development. They have reduced population growth, improved their educational systems, and strengthened the quality of other public services. Some measures of social welfare, including access to safe water, availability of medical care, and increased food supply, have shown remarkable improvement. On the other hand, the benefits of economic growth have not been shared as equitably as in the East Asian countries. Measurements of income distribution from the late 1980s cited by the World Bank show that the poorest 20 percent of the population received only 4.6 percent of household income in Malaysia, 6.5 percent in the Philippines, 6.1 percent in Thailand, and 8.7 percent in Indonesia. Rapid aggregate growth may increase the absolute incomes of the poor, but less directly and not as much as those in middle- and higher-income categories, thus increasing internal income gaps. This, however, is a problem the region's policy-makers recognize and are trying to address.

The ASEAN-4, with the exception of Malaysia, have potentially large internal markets. Savings are slightly higher than the average for countries at a similar socioeconomic level and investment rates are even higher. Except for the Philippines, most have financed this gap prudently by borrowing cautiously in international markets. In general, their governments have consciously sought to improve their economic performances.

Income Inequality and the Growth of GDP in Developing Economies

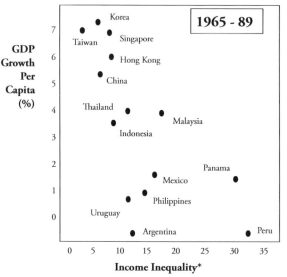

* Income inequality is the ratio of the income shares of the richest 20 percent and poorest 20 percent of the population. Data on income distribution are from surveys conducted mainly in the 1960s and early 1970s.

Graph 10.7

The somewhat slower aggregate growth performances among the ASEAN-4, compared with the NIEs, can be partly attributed to their larger agricultural sectors in which expansion is slower. It may also reflect their more pluralistic societies. Growth objectives often have come into conflict with other more pressing political needs, and there has been less opportunity for the development of a strong economic bureaucracy that is autonomous from domestic political forces opposed to growth. Given these constraints they have had remarkable growth and, except for the Philippines where economic technocrats are trying to encourage fundamental reforms in a difficult domestic and international environment, a continuing high growth rate can be anticipated in this region.

Equity and Redistribution

Economic policies in developing nations have strongly influenced the equality of income distribution within their populations. There are significant differences between the levels of income inequality in Pacific Asia and those in Latin America, as illustrated in the above graph. During the period in question, Latin American countries imposed discriminatory taxes on their farmers and protected their industries far more than did most of the Asian countries. Also, the fast developers in Asia invested heavily in widespread public education, regardless of sex or ethnicity. As a result, women in countries such as Malaysia, and Indonesia entered the wage labor force in greater numbers: a factor in improved income distributions. Successful land reform, which raises the incomes of the poor and contributes to social stability, was carried out successfully in Asian economies such as China, Japan, Korea, and Taiwan but not in Latin America or the Philippines.

The conventional wisdom has been that early stages of economic development require a high level of income inequality so that the wealthy elite will boost the nation's capital stock and fast growth will occur. The contrasting growth patterns of Asian and Latin American countries have contributed to a reevaluation of that assumption.

Low-Income Economies of Southeast Asia

More than a hundred million people live in the low-income Southeast Asian economies of Burma (Myanmar), Vietnam, Kampuchea (Cambodia), and Laos. Burma, with more than forty million people, has been pursuing its own brand of socialism since 1962 and has one of the lowest standards of living in the world (less than US$ 250 per capita in 1994). After years of stagnation, in the late 1970s and early 1980s there was a period of growth in Burma exceeding 6 percent annually, fueled by increased rice production and exports. However, exports remained at a third of their highest prewar level. Foreign debt has increased rapidly, reaching more than US$ 4 billion by 1989; debt service payments equivalent to 30 percent of export value have encouraged Burma to diversify exports and increasingly to look abroad for foreign assistance. Until the late 1980s, no foreign investment existed in Burma and the government did not solicit investment despite its foreign capital needs. (Subsequently, companies in Thailand bought major timber-cutting concessions in Burma's rich tropical forests.) The private sector, theoretically nationalized in 1962, still accounts for more than half of production but current economic plans continue to call for a substantial increase in the state sector of the economy and a reduction in the private sector. Other indicators of socioeconomic development, such as longevity, access to clean water, and availability of medical care, are at far lower levels than in the ASEAN countries.

Vietnam also has had a serious foreign debt problem with little success in attracting foreign investment until it altered its investment laws in the 1990s. Early hopes that this country would concentrate on economic reconstruction following reunification were dashed by its 1978 invasion of Kampuchea and by the mid-1980s more than 40 percent of Vietnam's budget was devoted to defense. Among Vietnam's many problems are fertilizer shortages, lack of petroleum for nonmilitary use, a poor transportation network, and inadequate power supplies. The most important economic priority is to continue to boost agricultural production. Like China, Vietnam has introduced a system allowing lands of the cooperatives to be tilled by individual families or small groups under a contract quota system.

Laos and war-torn Kampuchea have limited current economic prospects; maintaining an adequate food supply is the major economic problem for both, and they depend heavily on foreign assistance. Nevertheless, Kampuchea has long-term potential based on its endowment of rich agricultural lands.

Chapter 11: Explaining Asian Business Success

By Nicole Woolsey Biggart and Gary G. Hamilton

The business phenomenon of the decade is obvious: the growth of Asian economies—particularly Japan, Taiwan, and South Korea. Both Japan and Taiwan were destroyed by World War II, and Korea was leveled by a civil war that killed 1.3 million people. Yet all three of these countries—ravaged by war—are booming after little more than a generation. In 1984, Japan's gross national product was the second highest in the world, and Japan has growth and investment rates twice those of the United States. Taiwan's GNP grew an average of 10.6% a year in the decade 1963–1972, and from 1973 to 1982—a period that included a world recession—it still grew 7.5%. South Korea did not begin industrializing until the 1960s, but from 1963 to 1972 its manufacturing exports grew an amazing 52%. From 1962 to 1984 South Korean industrial production increased 17%. In comparison, the U.S. gross domestic product grew an average of 3.2% between 1976 and 1985. In the same period, Great Britain's grew 1.8%. The figures are clear and confirm our observations: Asians have become world-class manufacturers and exporters.

The second-biggest business phenomenon of the decade is related to the first: the explosion of books and theories that try to explain Asian business success. One can go into any bookstore, and many supermarkets, and find a dozen books that claim to unlock the secret to Asian management. Although there are many theories, we can put them into three categories.

THEORY NO. 1: CULTURE

First, there is Theory No. 1, the culture theory. This theory claims that the Confucian ethic is the key to understanding Asia, and it is certainly true that most Asian nations have been influenced by Confucianism. Confucianism stresses the importance of family, of obedience to superiors, of hard work and self-discipline. It is also an ethic that promotes education. Anyone who has been to Asia cannot help but be impressed by the willingness of people there to work extremely hard for very long hours, often for very little pay. The crime rates are low and literacy rates are high, consistent with the Confucian values of self-control and obedience to authority. Clearly all of these factors help the economy.

Culture theory books usually have two lessons for people in the West. The first lesson is that success comes to those who are willing to work for it. Second, Westerners are exhorted to return to traditional values of family thrift, hard work, and education. Europeans and Americans had better revive the Protestant ethic if they are going to compete with the Confucian ethic according to this perspective.

THEORY NO. 2: MANAGEMENT

Theory No. 2 explains Asian success in a different way. This theory argues that the problem really is not cultural differences. After all, many people in the West work very hard, too, and Western nations also have high literacy rates. The problem is not laziness and disinterest, but rather poor organization and management. According to Theory No. 2, the large and small enterprises of Europe and America are simply not put together correctly. The problem is simply one of misorganization and economic mismanagement.

For example, there are books like William Ouchi's *Theory Z* (1982) that discuss the effectiveness of Japanese consensus management, of getting everyone involved in decision making. Or of the *kanban* system, the just-in-time inventory system that reduces production time and links assembly plants with smaller subcontractors who are outside their back doors. Here the lesson is that Westerners must reorganize factories and even whole economies—if Western organizational arrangements were efficient, like those in Asia, then presumably they would remain competitive in world markets.

THEORY NO. 3: GOVERNMENT

The next explanation, Theory No. 3, is not so popular, perhaps, but still important. It argues that although there are certainty differences between Asian and Western cultures, and between Asian and Western business organizations, these differences are not decisive. What is decisive is the relationship between government and business. In all Asian countries, Theory No. 3 argues, the government takes a prominent role in planning and executing economic policy. The government coordinates the domestic economy, controls crucial economic institutions such as banking, and actively promotes industries that are on the rise in the world economy. The lesson is that Asian governments, through smart industrial planning and economic coordination, have created their own economic successes.

What is the message of Theory No. 3? It is grim for people in the United States, whose federal system is hopelessly outdated. They have no economic planning, no centralized mechanism to promote selected industrial sectors, and—if Americans could somehow agree on a plan—virtually no mechanism to coordinate the economy. Instead, the U.S. government is constitutionally divided, with checks and balances that prevent centralized decision making. Branches of government—Congress, the White House, the judiciary—are pitted against each other. State governments contend against Washington, and cities and counties fight with each other and with states for a share of revenue. The United States, where economic coordination is institutionally impossible, must confront capitalist economies that are highly coordinated and strategically planned.

European nations have more centralized authority and planning structures than the United States, and the anticipated unified European economy could be a powerful force. But countries such as Britain and France have a tradition of debate, of loyal opposition, that makes the orchestration of political and management decisions difficult. It also remains to be seen if nations as diverse as Spain, the Netherlands, Germany, and Greece will coordinate their economies.

So what is the solution for politically fragmented societies committed to public debate? Books espousing Theory No. 3 often argue for major political reform.

WHICH CULTURE?

We have described above three different theories about what is right with Asia and, implicitly, what is wrong with the West. We, however, believe that Theories 1, 2, and 3 are built on shaky premises—not that they're all wrong, but they make generalizations that simply do not hold when Asia is closely examined.

Consider again Theory No. 1, the culture theory. This explanation assumes that Asian cultures are all alike. Japan, Taiwan, and South Korea share a Confucian and Buddhist heritage. Through trade, ideas and practices have diffused throughout Northeast Asia for millennia. China, especially, has had an influence in the region. For example, Japanese writing uses Chinese script, as did Korean writing until the sixteenth century. It is also true that as Confucian countries, they all place great emphasis on family, work, education, obedience, and self-discipline.

It is not true, however, that they are culturally all alike any more than England, Italy, Sweden, and France are the same. The Japanese, Koreans, and Taiwanese all speak different languages that are mutually unintelligible. They have different cuisines, different political systems, and different dress and manners.

For example, they all believe in the importance of family, but "family" means something quite different in each nation. In Japan the eldest son inherits everything. He keeps the family wealth intact, whereas younger sons must establish their own fortunes. If a man does not have a son, he will frequently adopt one in order to pass on his wealth. Japanese family relations tend to be harmonious or at least strive toward that ideal.

In Chinese societies such as Taiwan, wealth is divided equally among all sons, so families are often concerned with building a separate business for each male heir. Unlike in Japan, adoption is rare in China—only blood relations have a place in the lineage. No one ever accused the Chinese of harmony: Families squabble and rivalries among sons are commonplace.

The Koreans are different yet. Like the Chinese, they are outspoken and do not adopt outsiders into the family. But they give the lion's share of the inheritance—usually about two-thirds—to the oldest son, and smaller shares to younger brothers. The Korean inheritance pattern is like neither the Chinese nor the Japanese.

One could continue by comparing education, hours of work, and other cultural expressions, and would find that they, too, differ substantially among the three countries. The point is that although there are certainly cultural continuities throughout East Asia, just as there are throughout Europe, Asians are not culturally all the same. Therefore, one cannot explain the success of Japan, Taiwan, and South Korea using a cultural argument—there is no single culture that explains their common success.

WHICH ASIAN MANAGEMENT?

Theory No. 2 suggests that Western businesses, and Western economies, need to reorganize and adopt Asian management practices. Usually this means Japanese management practices. But in fact, the Korean and Taiwanese economies are organized very differently from the Japanese and seem to be doing well without adopting consensual decision making or just-in-time inventory systems.

The Japanese economy is dominated by large business groups such as Sumitomo and Mitsubishi. The Sumitomo business group, for example, is a group of firms in insurance, banking, heavy industry, shipping, and a variety of other industries. Other business groups, like Mitsubishi and Mitsui, also have member companies in diversified businesses. These business group firms are all legally independent, but they work together to aid each other by pursuing joint ventures, lending managers to each other, and financing promising ideas initiated by member firms. It is as though the U.S. companies AT&T, Xerox, Bank of America, and Chevron had formed a mutual aid society.

The large firms in Japanese business groups are linked to smaller subcontracting firms through very stable long-term relations. They try to help each other by improving product designs and sharing economic downturns. In sum, the Japanese economy is characterized by networks of large companies connected to each other by stable relations and to smaller companies through similarly stable subcontracting ties. Even the large business groups like Sumitomo and Mitsubishi have ties to each other through the common ownership of financial institutions.

Koreans also have large business groups, such as Daewoo, Hyundai, and Lucky-Goldstar. But these are not networks of companies that come together for mutual assistance, as in Japan. Instead, each of these business groups is a giant conglomerate owned by a single patriarch and his family. None of the firms in the Hyundai group—or *chaebol,* as such groups are called in Korea—would think of meeting together in the absence of the patriarch. These are highly centralized groups of firms that report only to the man at the top, who runs them with a very authoritarian management style. There is no consensus management in South Korea, no subcontracting relations of any importance, and Korean *chaebol* compete fiercely with each other.

Taiwan is organized differently yet. Taiwan has business groups also, but they tend to be networks of small to medium-sized family firms. There are almost no large companies in Taiwan that could rival those in Korea and Japan Firms are established in one generation only to break apart and re-form in the next. The stability of Japanese companies and the size of Korean companies are unthinkable in Taiwan.

When books based on Theory No. 2 espouse that the United States organize its economy like Asian economies, or that U.S. firms borrow Asian management practices, one must ask which Asian economy and practices—Japan's, South Korea's, or Taiwan's? They differ dramatically one from the other, and yet each has been successful.

Consider again Theory No. 3, which says Asians have been successful because their governments are active participants in economic planning. In fact, in all of the three countries we are considering, government and business have very different relationships. In Japan, the state acts as a negotiator of business interests. Businesses are reluctant to depart from government plans, but agreement is reached through negotiation and consensus building, not through direct orders. The Japanese government does not run the economy, although it plays an oversight function and encourages investment in promising industries.

In South Korea, government does run the economy. It targets industries for development, picks the companies that will develop them, approves their plans, and lends them money. Until recently, Korean businesses could not get money without going to the government—the state owned all the banks. If the government disapproves of the way an industry is run, financing dries up.

In Taiwan, the government takes care of industrial infrastructure such as transportation and energy. As in Korea, the Taiwanese government was authoritarian throughout the period of rapid industrialization. But aside from providing infrastructure and a lot of rhetoric, it tends to keep out of the economy. Milton Friedman, the conservative American Nobel laureate in economics, is said to approve of Taiwan's free market environment.

So, if one is going to explain Asia's success according to Theory No. 3, government activism in the economy, which government is to serve as a model? Each is different from the others.

THEORY NO. 4

So what are we left with? If it's not culture, management, or government that explains Asia's obvious business success, what is it?

We believe that Japan, Taiwan, and South Korea have done very well not because they have been attempting to do the same Asian thing, but because they have been pursuing different industrial strategies. Each has a culture, organizational arrangements, and a government-business relationship that suits its national strategy for success in the world economy.

Theory No. 4 says very simply that Asian economies have worked so well because they have created organizational arrangements and management practices that give them a competitive advantage. Japan, South Korea, and Taiwan all pursue business strategies that suit their social arrangements—their cultures, their traditional ways of organizing and managing, and their government structures. None of these nations attempts to do everything, and none has attempted to imitate the West. Instead, each has focused on industries and processes in which it has a particular social advantage.

Consider Japan first. Before World War II, Japan's economy was dominated by large enterprise groups called *zaibatsu*. *Zaibatsu* were groups of firms owned by families. The firms in the groups kept separate books, but in fact were related to each other through shared investments and common ownership. The *zaibatsu* firms coordinated their business plans with each other, shared personnel, and even entered into common financing arrangements.

The *zaibatsu* grew very large and powerful and in fact dominated the Japanese economy by the time of World War II. When the United States occupied Japan in the late 1940s and helped to orchestrate that country's recovery from war, one of the first things the Americans did was take apart the *zaibatsu*. *Zaibatsu*, from a Western perspective, look like a terrible way to organize. They were essentially cartels and impeded competition. Their management practices were very paternalistic and rewarded seniority, not merit. The Americans made the *zaibatsu* companies independent firms and forbade all but the smallest cross-holdings of shares between companies in Japan. The United States wanted Japan to establish an economy of independent firms that competed aggressively with each other. The Americans wanted a Japanese economy that looked like theirs, then the strongest economy in the world. They attempted to rout out cooperation and collusion among firms.

The *zaibatsu* are gone. There are no more powerful family-owned business groups in Japan that control large portions of the economy. But who dominates the Japanese economy today? Groups of firms like Sumitomo, Mitsui, and Mitsubishi—groups of firms that look much like their pre-war predecessors. In fact, the Japanese did not take long in reconstructing their prewar organizational patterns.

Today's business groups, such as the Sumitomo group, are typically composed of a couple of dozen firms that—although legally independent—act together for their mutual advantage. They enter into joint projects, plan common business strategies, and share personnel. They act like a *zaibatsu* community of firms.

There was a period during the 1960s when this reversion to traditional patterns of organizing, and to traditional paternalistic management practices, was soundly criticized by both Westerners and some Japanese. The critics said that competition and individualism were the only ways to compete successfully in the modern world economy. Critics predicted that Japan would do well only as long as its labor costs were low, but that it could not compete in technologically advanced industries. In fact, Japan did well by adapting its traditional business patterns to a modern economy. Indeed, it is clear that some Japanese methods work especially well in a modern international economy.

What are the competitive advantages of the Japanese pattern? First, there is a commitment to the organization that is conspicuously absent in the West. Paternalism—treating workers as family, as the *zaibatsu* did—develops a loyalty to the products and success of the firm. Quality control experts say that this human commitment—as much as technical superiority—is responsible for the low error rates of Japanese manufacturing. Japan has become known for its high-quality products.

Second, cooperative relations among legally independent firms create financial and managerial synergies. Most of the stock of Sanwa Bank is owned by Sanwa business group firms. If the bank wants to invest in a project that has good long-term payout, it has only to convince the other members of the group that this is a worthy idea. The group will forgo short-term profits and be patient, waiting for a more substantial reward over the long-term. Because stock ownership is more diffuse in the West, Western firms feel greater pressure to seek quick returns to keep investors happy.

Cooperative relations—not just competition—can cut costs. For example, just-in-time inventory systems can mean considerable savings. The Japanese keep their subcontractors near the back doors of their assembly plants. They do not need to stockpile, at great expense, large inventories of small parts and materials. This system is possible in Japan because of the close cooperative relations that exist between manufacturers and parts suppliers. A large firm works closely with smaller firms, often helping them out with financial problems. The small firms know that the large firm values their relationship and will work to keep it profitable for both parties.

Contrast this with the West, where competitive bidding dominates. If a given firm can beat last year's supplier by a dollar, there is a new supplier. Suppliers are constantly looking for multiple outlets for their goods, so that in case one company abandons them, they will not go out of business. Companies can lose suppliers, too, if the suppliers find other companies that will pay a dollar more. As a result, in the West there is the just-in-case inventory system—large, expensive stockpiles of parts kept on hand, just in case.

Third, cooperative relations between business and the Japanese government have enabled the country to target areas for development and to direct R&D money to especially promising projects.

These are examples—there are many more—of ways in which cooperative relations and paternalistic management have helped the Japanese to develop a healthy economy. They were given the opportunity to develop Western patterns, but opted for doing what made sense to them culturally. The Japanese have certainly borrowed technology and management techniques from the West, but they have imported new ideas without changing their basic framework.

South Koreans also have large business groups, but they are very different from the Japanese groups. In South Korea, most of the stock of Hyundai, Samsung, Lucky-Goldstar, and each of the other *chaebol* is owned by a single man—a patriarch and his heirs. All of the companies within a *chaebol* report to the man at the top, and most of the firms are run by members of the family, who exert very tight control. There is no consensus decision making in Korea. There is centralization and rigid hierarchy within each *chaebol*.

How did the Koreans come up with these patriarchal conglomerates as a way to organize their economy? After all, Korea was colonized by the Japanese until World War II, and Koreans knew all about *zaibatsu* organization; further, the United States tried to teach them Western management techniques after the Korean War.

In fact, the *chaebol* is reminiscent of preindustrial political organization in Korea. Korean society—for hundreds of years—was organized into patriarchal clans. These clans were located in geographic regions and sent emissaries to the Korean dynastic court in Seoul. It is a very ancient form of organizing that the Koreans reverted to when they planned their economic recovery. Even today, the *chaebol* have regional roots—most of the top executives in any *chaebol* come from the same province as the patriarch who owns it.

Nor does the South Korean government sit down to coordinate national business planning the way the Japanese government does. Instead, the Korean government dictates what business will do in much the way the Korean kings attempted to dictate their political will. The government decides which sectors of the economy will grow and selects businesses to develop those sectors. It lends money to the businesses—the government owns all the banks—and then often tells them what price they can charge.

How can the Koreans have succeeded, given these rigid, hierarchical organizations that are owned by families? What competitive advantages do the *chaebol* offer? First, the *chaebol* are a very effective way to keep large amounts of capital together. These are huge conglomerates with large sums of money under their control—given the watchful eye of government. The *chaebol* have been able to invest in highly capital-intensive industries such as steelmaking, shipbuilding, and automobile manufacturing. The amounts of money these industries require would have been very hard for independent entrepreneurs to raise without the backing of government. The limited amount of competition that the government allows assures that Korea will have viable businesses in some core industries.

Second, worker discipline has been maintained by the rigid hierarchy of Korean management. Americans work about 38 hours a week, Japanese about 42 hours a week, and Koreans nearly 58 hours a week. These are incredibly long hours, often under difficult circumstances. Korean management style stresses self-discipline and obedience to superiors. Unlike the Japanese, who encourage workers to master several jobs, even on assembly lines, the Koreans want dedication to a position.

Is this a good organizational strategy for development? Probably in the short term, yes. South Korea has become a major competitor in capital-intensive industries, such as heavy construction, equipment manufacturing, and steelmaking. It is also giving Japanese shipbuilding a tough time. Moreover, South Koreans have enjoyed a rising standard of living even while working hard.

No doubt there will be a modification of this harsh strategy as workers demand more pay and as Koreans need more advanced technology. Rigid hierarchy and centralization are poor ways to encourage innovation. Nonetheless, the South Koreans have achieved an amazing level of success by using traditional organizing strategies—strategies that made sense to them. They developed a competitive advantage not by copying the West or the Japanese, but by figuring out what they could do well given the kind of society they had.

The Taiwanese borrow organizationally from neither the Japanese nor the South Koreans. The Taiwan example shows that remarkable development can occur in the absence of huge corporations. Although Taiwan certainly has large firms, few Westerners could name a single company there or identify a single Taiwanese brand name. Yet Taiwan's economic success in recent years is second to none, with monetary surplus matching even that of Japan.

Westerners are unfamiliar with Taiwanese companies because the majority of export goods to the West enter under local brand names or are insignificant component parts of larger items. Taiwan sells few expensive consumer items to the West—no cars, robotic systems, supercomputers, high-grade steel, or computer chips. Instead, Taiwan sells inexpensive consumer non-durables such as toys, small electronics, furniture, shoes, and watches.

The typical production system in Taiwan, as in other Chinese societies, is a cooperative network of small and middle-sized firms that join together to produce commodities on demand. These production systems are extremely flexible and respond quickly to market forces. For example, Taiwan is the world's largest producer of bicycles for export, yet has not a single large bicycle factory. Instead, there are firms that manufacture parts and others that assemble them to meet retailers' specifications.

These "satellite assembly systems" dissolve when the orders stop. The individual firms seek new product orders and form a new satellite assembly system with the next wave of orders. Flexible, undercapitalized, and extremely sensitive to market demand, this type of production system creates a sort of capitalism that rolls with market forces and does not attempt to control them. Several people have called the Chinese industrial system "guerrilla capitalism."

Like the Korean and Japanese systems, this type of capitalism rests on the distinctive features of Chinese society. In Taiwan, where each son gets an equal share of his father's estate, animosity among male heirs can be great. Rather than having a large corporation that breaks up at the father's death, it is a reasonable strategy to start several small independent firms so that each son will have a business to manage. Over the centuries, Chinese people have developed social rules that allow for the formation of cooperative networks of related and unrelated people, called *guanxi* networks, which promote the mutual well-being of their members. These network patterns, with origins in imperial China, have been adapted to the modern world economy. Taiwan's competitive advantage in the international marketplace is based on the ability to form socially binding, but economically flexible, production systems quickly and reliably.

SOCIETAL COMPARATIVE ADVANTAGE

Most analysts see comparative advantage as a product strategy, but if we employ a broader conceptualization, it is clear that comparative advantage also applies to societies. Theory No. 4 tells us that different societies have distinctive social patterns that lend themselves to particular organizing strategies.

What lessons are there in Theory No. 4 for the West? First is the obvious point that there is no one necessarily right way to further economic development. Instead, many possible strategies can be successful. This lesson would suggest that Western nations need not be concerned with following Asian management practices because they are "best."

Second is a less obvious point: The Asian cases show that one should organize in a way that makes sense to the people being organized. Culturally familiar organizing strategies promote control, especially self-control, because people can intuitively understand what is expected of them, even if they do not always like it. Asian nations have drawn on their own social and cultural repertoires to create new economic organizations.

The lesson to be understood from this conclusion is that the United States needs to build on its own traditions. We need to diagnose our own weaknesses dispassionately and to understand the sources of our own shortcomings. From that knowledge we should build upon the repertoire that exists within our own society. If we decide a more cooperative and less competitive economy is needed, then we should remember that ours is not a shallow tradition, but is rather a full and complex one that provides many examples of cooperation. Remember it was Alexis de Tocqueville in the 1830s who marveled at the organizational complexity of American society, a society filled with all manner of voluntary associations. Have we lost our capacity to organize such associations, to form groups such as the so-called friendly societies that filled our country in the nineteenth and early twentieth centuries?

The third point is implied by the second. One can adapt techniques and import technologies from other societies, but the success of these in large part depends upon how well they blend into the organizational structure of the host society. After all, the Japanese took their idea for quality circles from the United States, and these were successful in large part because the Japanese have an affinity for techniques that reinforce group solidarity. Asian societies, however, have uniformly rejected the radical individualism that is characteristic of behavior within and between American firms.

The lesson to learn from this conclusion is that the successful importation of technology is not independent of the social organization of the host society. If Americans expect to import Asian technology and managerial techniques, they should do not do so mechanically and without thinking about how these will fit into or can be adapted to our own society.

Finally, the fourth point is more sobering. The Asian successes ride on the backs of people who earnestly desire to improve themselves and their families. These people desire to raise their own standards of living by raising the standards of their entire societies, by pushing those societies into the ranks of the industrialized nations. They have been successful in part because they were hungry for success, and they were patient and worked hard for small gains. The patience and hard work of Asians have paid off in terms of a more advanced material life for most of these Asian nations' populations. Will that Asian hunger for well-being continue, or will future generations become complacent? That answer is for the future.

The lesson for the United States right now is that Americans must be willing to work for their society's, as well as for their own individual, benefit. No amount of leadership and no management technique will succeed if people will not follow, or refuse to be organized. Are the truly visionary economic and political leaders in the United States without followers? And for the moment have Americans grown weary of working so hard? Have they lost the will and patience to attain difficult goals? These answers, too, are for the future, but in these particular answers lies hidden the secret of America's economic success or failure in the next century.

GROWTH INTERRUPTED

The Asian Currency Crisis

Chapter 13: The Roots of the Crisis

By Karl D. Jackson

F rom 1945 to 1997 the Asian economic miracle fueled the greatest expansion of wealth, for the largest number of persons, in the history of mankind. Prognosticators spoke confidently of the advent of "an Asian century." By 2020 Asians were expected to produce 40 percent of the world's GDP while the U.S. and European shares would recede to 18 percent and 14 percent, respectively. Some market researchers predicted that Asia's middle and lower middle classes would grow to more than a billion people by the turn of the century, powering the greatest explosion of consumption the world had ever seen (see Rohwer 1995).

REGIONAL IMPACT OF CRISIS

In mid-summer 1997, a half-century of economic progress came to a crashing halt. In direct contradiction to conventional wisdom, several Asian economies previously praised for balanced budgets, high savings and investment rates, low inflation and openness to the world marketplace, went into free fall. What became a region-wide panic struck first in Thailand before spreading to Malaysia, the Philippines, Indonesia, and eventually to Korea. Stock markets and currencies plummeted, prompting central banks to mount expensive currency defenses through buying forwards, raising interest rates to unprecedented levels, or both. The magnitude and volatility of the crisis dealt a sharp blow to fragile and overextended banking systems, while devastating those manufacturing establishments dependent on cheap capital and foreign inputs for their production. During the first year of the crisis, the currencies of the five affected countries depreciated by 35–80 percent, diminishing substantially the wealth of the five miracle economies (Table 13.1).

TABLE 13.1 Impact of the Crisis: Exchange Rates and GNP.

Country	Exchange Rates to U.S. Dollars		GNP in U.S. Billion Dollars	
	June 1997	July 1998	June 1997	July 1998
Thailand	24.5 baht	41	170	102
Indonesia	2,380 rupiah	14,150	205	34
Philippines	26.3 peso	42	75	47
Malaysia	2.5 ringgit	4.1	90	55
Korea	850 won	1,290	430	283

Source: Updated version from a table in R. J. Cheetham, "Asia Crisis," June 1, 1998.

On a human scale, the Crash of 1997 shook the confidence of foreign investors and domestic entrepreneurs, while decreasing the wealth of the newly emergent middle classes and impoverishing the non-agricultural labor force. The number of people living on less than one U.S. dollar per day in the five affected countries was approximately 40 million prior to the crisis, and they were concentrated in Indonesia and the Philippines (Cheetham 1998). During the first year of the crisis the number of Asians living in absolute poverty more than doubled in countries without elaborate social safety nets, and pockets of absolute poverty reappeared in Korea and Thailand. In Indonesia, the "good news" was that the government and the international agencies were actively moving to acquire the millions of tons of rice needed to prevent starvation.

The affected middle classes had formerly been known for their automobiles, cell phones, and a materialistic lifestyle that had never been available before in Southeast Asia outside of the narrowest upper reaches of the elite. The middle classes of the affected countries worked hard, and their upwardly mobile children were acquiring educational tools in universities at home and abroad. Educational statistics are not yet available on the impact of the crisis, but the number of families incapable of paying school fees has escalated rapidly, thereby diminishing the prospect for white collar jobs for a whole generation of citizens who realistically expected them. If economic nationalism results from the Crash of 1997, it will be generated by formerly upwardly mobile people who have suddenly been denied access to the status, power, and wealth they had come to expect.

As a result of the crisis, governments throughout the area now find their political legitimacy challenged by groups and individuals who, until recently, had been willing to tolerate cronyism and familism so long as governments delivered the economic goods.[1] With remarkable speed, democratic and non-democratic governments were overturned during the first twelve months of the crisis. In Korea, former political prisoner Kim Dae Jung ousted the ruling political party, even though he had long been considered too extreme to be acceptable to important factions of the Korean elite. In Thailand, the dominance of up-country rural politicians was at least temporarily eclipsed with the promulgation of a new constitution and the installation of the government of Chuan Leekpai in November 1997. In Indonesia, a thirty-two-year regime ended abruptly when the military asked for President Suharto's resignation in the wake of student protests and urban looting directed against the Indonesian Chinese community. In the Philippines, the electorate rejected the chosen successor of President Fidel Ramos and chose the most anti-establishment candidate, Joseph Estrada, over the objections of the Catholic Church and the traditional elite power holders. As a result of the LDP's poor showing in Japan's Upper House elections on July 12, 1998, Prime Minister Ryutaro Hashimoto was forced to resign from office. Depending on the duration and severity of the crisis across Asia, other formerly secure governments may be toppled at the ballot boxes or in the streets in the political aftermath of the severe economic downturn.

ROOTS OF THE CRISIS

Initially, the financial crisis was perceived almost exclusively as an exchange rate problem, being blamed alternatively on governments (for maintaining fixed exchange rates and allowing currencies to become overvalued) or on greedy foreign speculators who, in a matter of days, supposedly had undone the hard work of generations of Asians. In the early months of the crisis, commentators clung to the language of the Asian miracle by depicting the crisis as temporary, chanting the mantra of the "strong fundamentals of the Asian Tigers." At the same time, some Asian nationalists voiced conspiracy theories suggesting Asia was being put in its place by wily global capitalists using sophisticated speculative tools to deflate the value of all Asian assets in a plot to buy everything Asians had built but at fire sale prices. The frustration and resentment of Asian nationalism is captured in Mahathir's August 23, 1997, statement, "All these countries have spent forty years to build up their economies and a moron like Soros comes along" (Loh 1997).

In reality, the simultaneous crises affecting much of Asia are as multifaceted as they are tied to fundamental problems within the economic structure of each country. Excessive borrowing abroad (primarily by the private sector) is the hallmark of this crisis. In the five years prior to the crisis, the borrowings of banks and non-banks in the affected countries grew very rapidly. In particular, banks in each country rapidly increased their net foreign liabilities by large percentages during the four years prior to the crisis. By the time the crisis broke in mid-July 1997, total external indebtedness had reached large proportions, exceeding 50 percent of GDP in Thailand, Indonesia, and the Philippines (Figure 13.1).

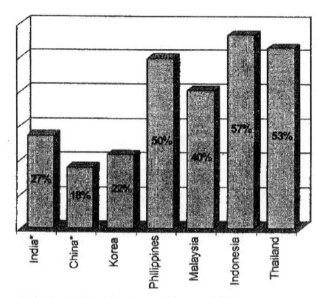

Source: World Bank, Global Development Finance; *JP Morgan

FIGURE 13.1 External Debt as a Percent of 1996 GDP.

Particularly in Thailand, Malaysia, and the Philippines it was the private sector, rather than the governments, who were responsible for incurring these large overseas obligations.

As reflected in Figure 13.2, not only was the amount of foreign indebtedness large as a proportion of GDP, but in several instances there were large amounts of short-term borrowings. As Korea, Indonesia, and Thailand approached the year of crisis, they were burdened by short-term loans equal to 13, 14, and 22 percent of their respective GDPs. In the ensuing period of plummeting currency values, these short-term loans, with principal and interest due in less than one year, became a crushing burden for all three countries.

Although external aspects (fixed exchange rates, high interest rates, and excessive borrowing from abroad) are among the important causal factors in this crisis, the crisis would not have occurred without internal weaknesses as well: inadequate supervisory institutions, traditional banking practices, and, most of all, poor investment decisions made by the private sector of each country. Foreign borrowing led to a domestic lending boom across all of Asia, which generated multiple asset bubbles, especially in stock markets and real estate.[2] If it had not been for pre-existing internal weakness throughout the private sector, the Asian contagion would never have spread so far or had such a lasting impact in individual countries. The variants of corporate familism found in Asian businesses, pre-existing forms of business-government relations, and a tendency to follow investment fads rather than market demand created over-capacity in production in similar sectors across Asia. There was simply too much foreign money chasing too few sound investments that were capable of earning foreign exchange sufficient to service the principal and interest on the debt. Instead of exercising restraint, local banks re-lent monies borrowed abroad to speculative investments in real estate (which earned no foreign exchange) or to protected and noncompetitive enterprises such as steel and petrochemicals. The speed of the investment buildup can be seen in Figure 13.3, which shows domestic credit expansion as a percentage of GDP for several Asian countries.

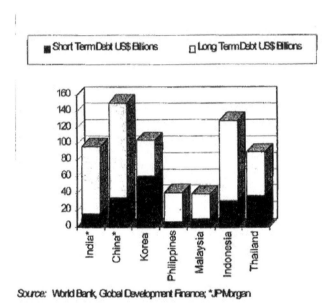

Source: World Bank, Global Development Finance; *JPMorgan

FIGURE 13.2 Total External Debt in US$ Billions in 1996.

The failure of entire business sectors to meet global standards regarding financial regulation, auditing, and corporate governance became critical in undermining foreign confidence once earnings began to fall rapidly as a result of glutted markets in real estate, steel, automobiles, petrochemicals, and semiconductors. Domestic investors were first to react to the downturn. As they became unable to meet payments to domestic bank creditors on stalled or unprofitable projects, they also began pulling capital out of local stock markets. These factors became exacerbated by capital flight in Indonesia, Thailand, Malaysia, Korea, and the Philippines once foreign and domestic investors sensed the deep-seated weakness of the financial sector in each country. Sharply falling stock and property markets reinforced one another in a downward spiral that devastated local financial systems.

Asia had profited greatly during the late 1980s and early 1990s from massive amounts of domestic and foreign investment. Across the region governments maintained fixed exchange rates minimizing the foreign exchange risk for domestic borrowers and foreign investors.[3] Local banks borrowed offshore at low, short-term rates and lent the money for long-terms at a substantial premium to manufacturers and real estate developers. Unfortunately, the abundance of inexpensive capital, in combination with local bank loans based on personal relationships rather than real business plans, resulted in the widespread misallocation of capital into speculative and noncompetitive sectors and enterprises. Returns on investments fell steadily during the 1990s in Korea, Indonesia, and Thailand until large numbers of projects no longer generated income sufficient to meet born principal and interest payments.

Asian firms often perceived market share to be the most important indicator of success. In their search for increased market share, firms borrowed heavily to fund plant expansion and acquired unsustainable debt/equity ratios. Heavy debts meant that a slight downturn in national or regional economic growth (not to mention the possibility of currency devaluation) would mean insolvency. The worst examples of excessive borrowing prior to the crisis are found in Korea, when in 1996 the five largest *chaebols* (producing 30 percent of the GDP) had debt/equity ratios averaging 3.9. As a group, the top thirty *chaebols* had even higher debt/equity ratios along with barely positive returns on capital. High debt/equity ratios, when combined with wafer thin profits, were simply unsustainable. Seven of the *chaebols* folded during the first year of the crisis (Pyo 1999).

Before the currency crisis struck the region, poorly conceived investments turned into non-performing loans, effectively curtailing the ability of banking systems to maintain the economic expansion through continued lending. In Thailand, Indonesia, and Korea the proportion of bank loans that became non-performing skyrocketed, probably reaching more than 20 percent of the total loan portfolio of many banks and finance companies, rendering them technically insolvent prior to the advent of the currency crisis.[4] The combination of unhedged foreign liabilities, non-performing domestic assets, and the absence of institutions capable of supervising the banks and protecting small depositors created near perfect conditions for a classic banking panic. In essence, most of the banks in Asia were technically insolvent before the run on the baht in mid-1997.[5]

The oversupply of Asia's export markets in the late-1990s also contributed to the Crisis of 1997. Three factors account for this oversupply:

1. capital from Western Europe, North America, and especially Japan, flowing into Asia as foreign direct investments designed to produce exports;[6]
2. the assumption of foreign and domestic investors that expansion of inter-Asian trade would continue to boost exports at double digit figures for the foreseeable future; and
3. a belief that the marketplace could absorb an almost infinite supply of shoes, textiles, semiconductors, petrochemicals, steel, automobiles, and automobile parts.

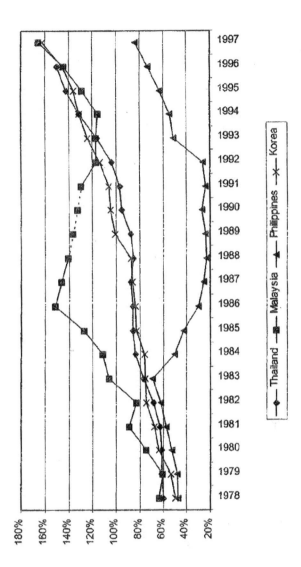

Figure 13.3 Domestic Credit, 1978–1997 in Percent of GDP.

Source: IMF International Financial Statistics. Data for Malaysia between 1989–1991 is incomplete and has been estimated using trend.

The seemingly endless export boom began having problems in the mid-1990s.[7] Thailand was the first country in Southeast Asia to experience virtually zero growth in its export markets, signaling to speculators the vulnerability of Thai foreign exchange reserves that had become dependent on foreign borrowings rather than on foreign trade earnings.

In Thailand, only one-third of the non-performing loans that crushed the financial sector came from investments in property. An additional one-third originated from manufacturing. Although not directly related to export industries, estimated levels of industrial oversupply for Thailand in early 1997 indicate a manufacturing establishment poised on the brink of collapse. According to Saicheua (1997), Thailand's automotive industry had an oversupply level of 192 percent; modern housing in Bangkok had an oversupply of 200 percent; petrochemicals an oversupply of 195 percent; steel bar production an oversupply of 150 percent; and private hospital beds had an oversupply of 300 percent.

If misjudging the markets had been characteristic of only Thai entrepreneurs and their bankers, the financial crisis would not have become a region-wide event featuring an eventual collapse of inter-Asian trade. Rapid expansion of domestic lending in similar industries also led to excess capacity in China, where a 1995 survey of capacity utilization showed 60 percent utilization rates for 900 major industrial products (see Lardy 1999). Part of this stemmed from the chronic inefficiency of the older, state-owned enterprises (SOEs). Serious oversupply conditions also were apparent in more recent investments such as automobile production and the varied products of the township and village enterprises (TVEs) that had been responsible for most new employment opportunities in China during the late 1980s and 1990s. One seasoned observer estimated production levels in the TVEs had fallen approximately 50 percent by the end of 1997. The construction boom, especially in Shanghai and Beijing, had far exceeded market demand by late 1996. By 1999, Shanghai will have as many upscale office spaces as Hong Kong, with most financed by domestic lending. The conclusion of the construction boom caused an immediate contraction in employment, while sharply elevating non-performing loans of the major Chinese banks.

Chinese auto production slowed prior to the advent of the Asian crisis, working at only half capacity in late 1996 (Wards Auto World December 1996). Likewise in Thailand, car buying dropped off at the beginning of the year before the outside world sensed any serious economic downturn. In Korea, domestic sales of automobiles and commercial vehicles had fallen by 13 percent in the first five months of 1997, well before the crisis. After the crash these markets became chronically saturated with automobiles. In Japan, by the first half of 1998 domestic automobile production on a monthly basis had declined by 25 percent in comparison to the year before. Toyota's exports to ASEAN in January 1998 fell by 42 percent from the same period in 1997, while Nissan's sales to ASEAN shrank by 40 percent and Mazda's by 52 percent (Indonesian Commercial Newsletter, March 16, 1998). Likewise, Japanese machine tool domestic sales were down by more than 15 percent in the first half of 1998 compared to a year earlier.

Neither Asian entrepreneurs nor major Western investors should have been caught unaware by the events of 1997. By the early 1990s the misallocation of investments that would bring the great Asian boom to a halt was visible to the naked eye in cities such as Bangkok and Shanghai (see Ramo 1998).[8] In early 1995, Bangkok was becoming a city of dark towers, where completed buildings stood empty against the night sky while finance companies and real estate developers continued to borrow and build (Figure 13.4). Everyone assumed the expansion would never stop, and many assumed that an 8.5 percent annual expansion of the GDP had become a permanent parameter of the business environment. Such a high rate of expansion could absorb any number of office spaces and condominiums, petrochemical complexes, steel plants, and semiconductor factories. Practically down to the month the balloon burst in Bangkok, macro economic statistics (with the exception of the current account deficit) continued to mislead observers because glutted real estate and manufacturing markets were masked by balanced budgets, low inflation, and high rates of savings and investment.

THEORIES OF CAUSALITY

The Asian financial crisis illustrates the absence of unified theory among social scientists. Each discipline remains tied to its own partial explanations, rejecting the explanations drawn from other disciplines. In reality, there are three complementary streams of causality rising from political science, economics, and investment banking.

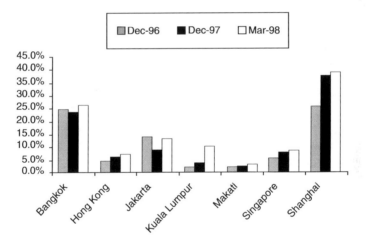

FIGURE 13.4 Asia Pacific Office Vacancy Rates, 1996–1998.

Source: Jones, Lang, Wooten

For example, political scientists and journalists tend to depict the crisis in Jakarta as being almost solely the product of familism and cronyism. According to this logic, if only the Suharto family had not taken so much, for so long, from so many, and had not concentrated such a large portion of the national wealth in its own hands, then the Indonesian economy might not have collapsed. This represents, at best, only part of the story. Primitive business practices (e.g., absence of accounting standards, overestimation of asset values, and disguised liabilities) are found throughout the Indonesian business and banking systems; they are not limited to institutions controlled by the Suharto family and its cronies.

On the other hand, economists saw the plummeting rupiah as the product of a regional panic and an overvalued currency. Relatively scant consideration was given to either the internal economic weaknesses flowing from gross misallocation of investments or the political interests which both facilitated the misallocation and precluded unwinding them prior to a political transition. Especially during the initial stages of the crisis, economists portrayed the crisis as a panic and assumed things would calm down quickly once the market realized the underlying macro-economic strengths of the economy and recognized that the market had overshot in devaluing the rupiah. Concentration on macroeconomic models tended to blind economists to the microeconomic mess which, on a firm-by-firm basis, had undermined the foundations of the Asian economic miracle.[9]

Finally, market analysts perceived the crisis as involving weak banks and real estate speculation, in addition to fixed exchange rates, partially overvalued currencies, and political uncertainty. More than others, market analysts sensed the degree to which the Asian miracle was, in fact, a house of cards. By virtue of being directly involved in commerce, financial analysts sensed glutted markets and vulnerable financial structures. Market analysts and foreign exchange traders have been special targets of economic nationalists like Prime Minister Mahathir, but it was the financial analysts who first predicted boom turning into gloom and rapidly moved their resources elsewhere. They did not cause the crash but simply identified it, and, through their reactions, further accelerated it.

Market analysts, however, were not without their own blinders. They were often the other half of loans that should not have been made, either because they believed biased information provided by corporations and governments or because they believed (quite amorally) that there was one last deal to be made before rushing for the market exit. Market analysts tended to neglect good governance issues ranging from the underdeveloped government regulatory and supervisory capacities, the absence of modern planning and control mechanisms at the corporate level (detailed business plans based on realistic projections, transparent auditing procedures, etc.), and the ways in which competition among interest groups can immobilize governments in the early stages of a financial crisis, thereby precluding a soft landing.

Both economists and market analysts tended to be relatively insensitive to the political dimensions that would exacerbate the crisis once it broke. In Thailand and Indonesia, for instance, the most acute aspects of the crisis might have been avoided if each country, in its own way, had not been politically immobilized. As the crisis broke, Thai democracy was controlled by a coalition of up-country politicians who had little interest in fixing Bangkok's financial institutions and protecting the Bangkok middle class from economic ruin. Only after a new constitution had been adopted and a new government had taken office in November 1997 did Thailand begin to put in place the painful reforms required to regain the confidence of the international marketplace. In Indonesia, no Suharto cabinet could unwind the special interests choking the marketplace, because the web of special interests constituted almost the entire base of the government's political support. Reforms could not be adopted because their content threatened the regime's very existence.

A Comprehensive Approach

Understanding and explaining what came to be known as the Asian contagion requires abandoning the certainties of disciplinary parochialism in favor of a more comprehensive approach to all facets of the Asian crisis. Since no single cause is both necessary and sufficient to explain the contagion's spread within or among countries, this volume contains several case studies. Included are the country where the first symptoms of the crisis appeared in the early 1990s (Japan); three of the most prominent victims of the Asian crisis (Thailand, Indonesia, and Korea); two of the most notable exceptions (China and India); the Philippines, where reforms instituted during previous crises partially precluded a disaster of the proportions experienced in Thailand and Indonesia; and an economy partly insulated from the Asian contagion by it own isolation and relatively low level of economic development (Vietnam).

Understanding why some countries became victims while others remained relatively healthy requires analyzing the political, economic, and financial aspects of each case. Thailand, Indonesia, and Korea fell victim because all five of the following factors were present simultaneously:

- Capital account convertibility
- Fixed exchange rates
- Excessive expansion of domestic lending accompanied by gross misallocation of investments by the private sector
- Absence of regulatory and supervisory capacities to control excesses in the financial sector
- Paralysis of political decision making at the onset of the crisis.

Thailand, Indonesia, and Korea manifested all five elements, whereas China and India shared several but not all of the same characteristics. For this reason, China and India have not fallen victim to the Asian financial crisis, but each remains susceptible because it possesses several of the main underlying weaknesses. The Chinese economy, for example, suffers from misallocation of investments and massive insolvency within its banking system; but it has remained economically stable during the first year of the crisis for several reasons. First, its currency is not freely convertible and therefore is not susceptible to attack by speculators (except by proxy via the Hong Kong dollar). Second, although China—like Thailand, Indonesia, and Korea—has expanded its domestic lending at a torrid pace, its banking system is saddled with relatively little short-term foreign debt. Third, China has emphasized foreign direct investment and accumulated record trade surpluses and foreign reserve holdings. Finally, China has benefited from relatively decisive political leadership, which has reacted to the Asian crisis by undertaking financial reforms designed to preempt any onset of the crisis inside China itself.

China has not yet fallen victim to the Asian financial flu, but it might do so in the future because of misallocation of investment, overproduction, insolvent banks, and declining rates of internal economic growth.

Likewise, the Indian economy hosts a fragile banking system and the inefficient post-infant industries that are the products of forty years of centralized planning in combination with isolation from the global economy. Only in the 1990s, under the reforms initiated by the Rao government, have large amounts of foreign direct investment begun to flow into India. The speculative boom characterizing much of Asia simply did not have sufficient time to develop the excesses necessary to bring down the entire economic system. Also, the group of technocrats guiding the Indian economy have been particularly adept during the 1990s, creating high levels of growth which have legitimized the whole process of internal economic reform. Further, India (like China) has the stability conferred by the size of its internal market as well as the relative isolation of its economy. India and China (like Vietnam) had no capital account convertibility. The economic isolation of India may have constrained the upside of economic expansion but it also limited the downside of potential economic catastrophe.

Lessons from the Afflicted Asian Tigers

Thailand, Indonesia, and Korea illustrate the combination of external and internal factors that have created Asia's worst economic decline in three decades. First, all three countries had overextended banks, which were caught in a vice between domestic borrowers who could not pay, and foreign lenders who became increasingly reluctant to lend. Second, all three countries experienced massive capital flight as soon as the crisis began. Credit lines dried up and foreign banks became increasingly reluctant to roll over previously extended short-term loans. Third, all three countries had relatively immobilized political systems at the time the crisis struck. The constellation of vested interests in these counries precluded bold policy responses which might have mitigated the sharp decline in domestic and international confidence.

In Thailand, Korea, Malaysia, and the Philippines (although not in Indonesia), the fall in the stock market was one telltale sign of the coming of the overall crisis (Figure 13.5). By January 1997, well before the baht came under pressure, the Stock Exchange of Thailand (SET) had already fallen 51 percent from its 1993 high. Likewise, the Korean stock market fell 36 percent between 1994 and 1996. Although the stock market of Malaysia had fallen by 24 percent in 1994 and remained down in 1995, it had almost recovered in 1996 before falling again at the beginning of 1997—months prior to the crisis.[10]

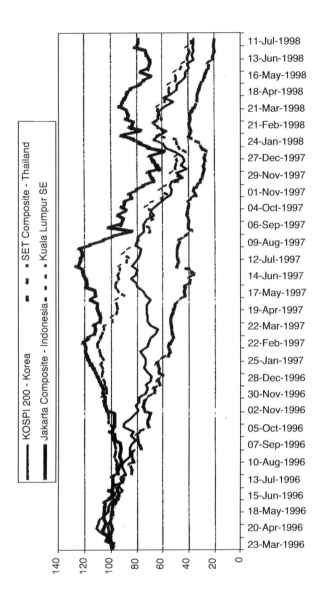

FIGURE 13.5 Stock Market Indices for Korea, Thailand, Indonesia, and Malaysia March 1996 to July 1998 (March 1996=100).

The fate of property market indices, rather than indices for whole markets, proved an even more reliable predictor of the oncoming crash. Between 1993 and 1996, property stocks in Indonesia, Malaysia, and Thailand had fallen 33 percent, 20 percent, and 73 percent, respectively, before plunging into oblivion in 1997.[11] The rapid decline of property stocks was a harbinger of doom for finance companies and those banks which had lent heavily to property companies during the late 1980s and early 1990s. The fact that property stock fell earlier and more steeply than stock markets in general probably means that domestic capital began to exit the stock markets first. In more general studies, declining equity prices have also been shown to correlate with the breakdown of fixed exchange rate systems (Kaminsky, Lizondo, and Reinhart 1997; Taylor 1998).

The movements of international capital, in turn, multiplied the impact of the crisis once it had begun. There was a contagious loss of confidence by domestic elites across Asia, leading them to move liquid assets to more secure havens in Norm America and Western Europe. Within the first year of the Asian crisis, over $200 billion had fled from the five affected Asian markets, amounting to roughly 18 percent of the combined GDPs of the five countries (Severino 1998). Markets can punish and they can forgive; restoration of foreign confidence had been partially achieved by Thailand, and Korea in early 1998 before local equity markets returned to record lows in early summer.

Thailand, Indonesia, and Korea were all required by the IMF to adopt policies that were more appropriate to Latin America in the 1980s than to Southeast Asia in the 1990s. In spite of the fact that before the crisis the Asian Tigers had balanced budgets, the IMF required belt-tightening monetary and fiscal policies, including budget surpluses. This requirement crushed consumer demand and brought the current account rapidly into surplus—but at the expense of kindling a deep recession and a substantial decline in inter-Asian trade. Subsequent discussions led the IMF to relax the budget surplus requirements, but not before unemployment in the major cities had spiked to record levels.

Both Thailand and Indonesia were at the end of a building boom when the crisis struck. Poorly financed property companies had built too many upscale offices and high-priced condominiums on the assumption that rapid economic expansion was a continuing certainty. When growth collapsed, even existing office space began to empty with the result being that central business area office vacancy rates in Jakarta and Bangkok will be approximately 20 percent in 1998–1999. Once the pain of the property companies was transferred to the banking system, non-performing loan balances resulted which precluded further loans to virtually any business by any bank. Non-performing loan balances were already critically high prior to the onset of the crisis; and when foreign credit lines and domestic deposits both dried up, the banking systems melted down. Loans for normal business activity became almost impossible. Banks, with inadequate capital reserves, simply could not lend and normal commerce stopped. Even export financing for businesses with signed contracts could not be obtained from the banks, thereby limiting the ability of each country to export its way out of the crisis.

Thailand and Indonesia both suffer from a legacy of political clientelism. Until 1973, when the students first brought down the military, Thailand was a bureaucratic polity, that is, a state ruled by and for the benefit of a narrow circle of officials, both uniformed and civilian, who comprised the upper levels of the civil and military bureaucracies. Neither political parties nor voluntary organizations existed which were capable of disciplining or sharing power with the civil and military bureaucrats. In the 1940s and 1950s, the entire Sino-Thai business community was exploited as a source of rent by the ruling bureaucratic elite. The expansion of the Thai economy was brought about in an atmosphere of "competitive clientelism" in which different portions of the business elite competed for the patronage from different parts of the bureaucratic elite (see Doner and Ramsay 1999).

During the 1950s and 1960s, the wealth of the Bangkok business elite grew substantially. Prestige eventually flowed toward money, even while the essence of political power remained in the Thai bureaucratic community. The expansion of university education, the growth of the Thai middle class, and the extension of economic and communication networks into the hinterland, all further populated the Thai political stage with new actors. In a gradual process, extending from the student uprising of 1973 through the democracy movement of 1992, these new forces seized control of the Thai political system. In doing so they transformed it from a bureaucratic polity into a democracy. The basis of modern Thai democracy remains clientelist, however. Politics is based on neither ideology nor permanent organizational membership, but on constantly changing cliques of patrons and shifting groups of clients. Politics in present-day Thailand remains democratic and particularistic, a search for benefits for one's own patron-client grouping, rather than the pursuit of generalized legal change designed to benefit all members of a wider social grouping.

The expansion of participation beyond the confines of narrow elite politics has had two important effects on Thailand. First, military rule has ceased being a long-term option. Although military rule might not be out of the question if Thailand descended into chaos, it is no longer the normal form of government that it was from 1932 to 1973. Second, democracy has meant one-man, one-vote and this has shifted power away from the civilian side of the Bangkok bureaucracy to political party leaders drawn largely from the provinces (Robertson 1995). Technocrats can now wield real power only if they are also political leaders with genuine, grassroots constituencies. Three-quarters of the wealth of Thailand is located in the cities (primarily Bangkok), while three-quarters of the votes remain in the countryside (Laothamatas 1996). Under democracy, Bangkok has lost its automatic preeminence, and unsophisticated rural politicians have dominated three out of the five democratic governments. The Bangkok elite, as reflected by the Bangkok mass media, refused to accept the leadership or legitimacy of the Chatchai, Banham, or Chavalit governments. The very acceptability to Bangkok of the first and second Chuan governments provides one important root of ongoing political instability. Paradoxically, in the past it is His Royal Majesty, King Bhumiphol, who has been absolutely critical to insuring the survival of clean governments that were backed by Bangkok, and thus far he seems to be quietly using his immense authority to support the second Chuan government.

Suharto's Indonesia was a presidential variant of bureaucratic polity in which power to influence the most important decisions of the state was concentrated almost exclusively in the ruling circle of officers and bureaucrats in nearest proximity to the President (Jackson 1978). Patron-client relationships were the most important form of political glue tying Suharto's Indonesia together. State enterprises and the state budget were dispensed as the personal largesse of the President. While clientelism in Thailand featured competitive bureaucratic and business cliques, clientelism in Indonesia became monopolistic. In the end, this is what dramatically weakened President Suharto along with the economic modernization which had bred the beginnings of a middle class. At the end of the day, President Suharto had very few clients who were actually willing to fight to maintain his power. The problem was that corruption had ceased being sufficiently widespread. When it became limited to cronies and family members only, the power base of the regime shrank dramatically. After thirty-two years in power, Suharto had become so weak that not even a significant armed confrontation proved necessary to bring down the regime. President Suharto in the aftermath of the Crash of 1997, like Ferdinand Marcos in the Philippines in the wake of the commodities recession of the early 1980s, fell rather quickly: performance regimes that lack other (noneconomic) sources of legitimacy tend to collapse during sharp economic downturns.

THE FUTURE

The relative emphasis here on domestic factors is not meant to deny the relevance of international sources of the contagion. Bhalla (1999) has written extensively concerning the degree to which China's exports undercut Southeast Asia's after China's devaluation in 1994. According to his theory, the financial crisis in Southeast Asia was set in motion when Southeast Asian export markets were undercut by China's 7 percent devaluation on January 1, 1994. By contrast, Ferald, Edison, and Loungani (1999) contend the sharp downturn in demand for ASEAN exports had relatively little to do with China's 1994 nominal devaluation, which was actually a minor downward adjustment in a 60 percent appreciation of the Chinese currency in real exchange rate terms during 1993–1996. They argue that slower economic growth rates in Japan and Western Europe, a downturn in world wide demand for computer chips, and the depreciation of the yen were more directly related to the declining rate of ASEAN export growth. Furthermore, China's gains in the export markets have come at the expense of the newly industrialized economies (Korea, Singapore, and Taiwan) rather than at the expense of Thailand, Indonesia, Malaysia, and the Philippines.

Each of these theories may be partially true. China's 100 percent increase in exports from 1993 to 1996 may have caused significant problems for Southeast Asia, but mainly because of a general oversupply in Asia rather than as a result solely of falling exchange rates. Support for this compromise interpretation can be found in the list of industries where China accumulated excess capacity in the 1990s: office buildings, automobiles and auto parts, steel, petrochemicals, and so forth. These are precisely the areas into which Southeast Asian nations, like Thailand, were mistakenly pouring investments during the 1990s.

This is not to deny the destabilizing impact, especially in the short term, of competitive devaluation. During the first stage of the Asian crisis, Singapore and Taiwan both refused to protect the value of their currencies and allowed them instead to depreciate by approximately 20 percent. This preserved their international competitiveness but also created pressure on the Hong Kong dollar and the Korean won. A major destabilizing factor in 1998 will continue to be the weakening yen and the increasing pressure this is creating for a Chinese devaluation at the beginning of 1999 (Figure 13.6).

Although the conventional wisdom during the first half of 1998 assumed China would not devalue its currency, the continuing slowdown of the Chinese economy, sharply declining production in the employment-producing township and village enterprises, and the collapse of much of inter-Asian trade have forced analysts to reassess this line of thinking. Virtually all agree there are circumstances under which the yuan will be devalued. In what may have been a trial balloon to condition the international marketplace, a high-ranking official of the People's Bank of China wrote on May 6, 1998:

> There are difficulties associated with the strategy of maintaining the exchange rate and the consequences of slowing exports to the domestic economy could be far-reaching. First, falling export competitiveness may affect those foreign investors, particularly small and medium size firms, who use China mainly as an export production base. As a result, inflows of foreign investment may slow down. Second, with a drop in export revenue and a slowdown in capital inflows, supporting an overvalued exchange rate could be costly and result in a substantial reduction in official exchange reserves. Third, a setback to export growth is likely to cap economic growth in the next two years making the current structural adjustments even more difficult (Yi Gang 1998:5–6).

The most powerful arguments against further devaluation of the yuan are that many of China's exports are based on foreign inputs and that a Chinese devaluation also would imperil the prospects of Hong Kong. According to this argument, a Chinese devaluation would be followed by competitive devaluations throughout the rest of Asia, which would prevent China from gaining any real advantage from a devaluation. Unfortunately, these arguments are more frequently voiced in New York, London, and Washington than in Beijing. On the eve of President Clinton's July 1998 trip to China, the U.S. government initiated a large-scale intervention in the currency markets to prop up the value of the yen in order to stave off a devaluation of the yuan during the president's visit. The joint American and Japanese intervention was prompted by statements from Beijing indicating that China would not be able to maintain the yuan if the yen continued to depreciate against the dollar.

The near universal fear among policy-makers and currency traders alike is that a Chinese devaluation, perhaps combined with an adjustment of the Hong Kong dollar peg, would lead to a further round of downwardly cascading exchange rates throughout Asia. A Chinese devaluation in late 1998 or early 1999 might set off another set of devaluations in Asia. This would continue until valuations were reached at which world markets would absorb a sufficient portion of the overcapacity produced throughout Asia by the heady investment boom of the 1990s. Such an event would probably mark the bottom of the Asian financial crisis from which the recovery of drastically devalued Asian assets would begin.[12]

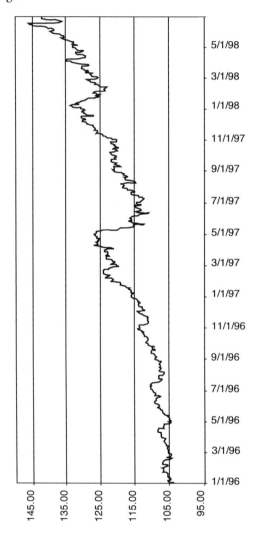

FIGURE 13.6 U.S. Dollar / Japanese Yen Exchange Rate, January 1996–June 1998.

In any case, the Asian crisis is now more than a year old and appears far from over. Fixed exchange rates have been replaced by floating ones, and current accounts have moved from deficit to surplus. The afflicted economies remain in deep recession, bordering on depression (see Severino 1998). The standard IMF medicine did not work well in Thailand, where it has been the most successful, or in Indonesia where the results, for both political and economic reasons, have been disastrous. The economies under the direct care of the IMF doctor currently remain in the economic equivalent of an intensive care ward.

Talk of the crisis being over in eighteen months now seems far-fetched. Asia, unlike Mexico, does not border on the most dynamic economy in the world, and Asia is not likely to be admitted to NAFTA any time soon. The logical engine for pulling Asia out of the crisis is Japan, but this would-be economic locomotive is itself stalled at the station. It suffers from the "Five-Ds": debt, deflation, default, demography, and the absence of deregulation (see Asher and Smithers 1999). Both government and corporate debt have reached levels that will be difficult to sustain in the long run. Average debt/equity ratios in corporate Japan at present are at least 4 to 1, resembling more closely Korean rather than U.S. corporations. In 1997 real public debt in Japan (from all sources) probably exceeded 150 percent of GDP, higher on a per capita basis than the public debt of Italy. The assets of Japan will continue to deflate, especially domestic real estate and the stock market, as will the holdings of corporate Japan in Southeast Asia and Hong Kong. At present the sum of bankruptcies, as a percentage of GDP, have reached a post-World War II high; the current level exceeds that in the U.S. at the depth of the Great Depression. The banks are encumbered with $600 billion to $1 trillion in non-performing loans, and the government has yet to chart a clear course for auctioning non-performing loans to clear the markets to allow economic growth to begin again.

With Asia's fastest aging population, new entrants to the economy will not be a stimulus for a high rate of growth. Although Japanese manufacturing institutions are highly efficient, labor productivity elsewhere, particularly in services and in agriculture, remains low in comparison to the remainder of the industrial world. Nowhere is low efficiency more crippling than in the Japanese financial sector, which needs to be de-bureaucratized rather than just de-regulated (see Dattel 1999). Land, labor, and capital—as factors in production—must be deregulated, exposing them to levels of competition capable of creating world-class performance standards. In spite of having saved more than any economy in the world, Japan must either embark on fundamental economic reform or it will be condemned to a slow but inexorable decline (Asher and Smithers 1999).

Lurking behind the "Five D's" is a sixth D: indecisiveness. Since the end of the bubble economy, the Japanese political system has been incapable of extricating the system from crisis. This is partly because the vast majority of Japanese do not perceive the fundamental ills of the system and partly because "the 1955 system" (comprised of a dominant, multi-factional Liberal Democratic Party and an unelectable Socialist Party) has ended, but with no strong system of government to take its place. Japan remains basically a one-party system in search of a viable alternative governing party. Furthermore, the bureaucrats, who along with the major corporations ran Japan during the post-World War II era, have lost prestige and power because their leadership has been inadequate in coping with the demands of a highly competitive, globalized economy, especially in the field of finance (see Dattel 1999). In addition, scandals have destroyed the legitimacy of Tokyo bureaucrats as a group for honest public service. In sum, MOF no longer rules, but nobody else does either. The result is policy paralysis rather than the kind of decisiveness required to move the world's second largest economy back to the path of robust growth.

In Thailand, Indonesia, and Korea (and one suspects, Japan), macroeconomic policies alone have not brought and will not bring recovery rapidly enough to quell pressures for more radical change (economic nationalism of the left or right). The financial crisis was basically caused by a defective Asian banking system, which led to vast misallocation of investments by the private sector. As a result, the banking systems deserve a significant share of the blame, but their recovery requires public resources, and without state-induced recovery of the banking system general economic recovery will be impossible. Only when the banks are healthy and begin to lend again to private businesses can the economies return to growth and industrial workers to their jobs.

In Thailand, Indonesia, and Korea, the size of the hole in the financial system created by domestic and foreign debt remains enormous. Non-performing loans in Thailand equal approximately one-quarter of the GDP. In Korea, returning private firms to a 2:1 debt/equity ratio would require in excess of $400 billion in new equity. Japan has both the largest banking problem (measured in absolute size) and the largest savings resources with which to deal with it. China, on the other hand, carries a massive load of bad bank debt on the books but as yet has not faced a crisis of confidence internationally or among its depositors (see Lardy 1999).

One solution is nationalization of the banking systems. This is being done partially in Korea and Thailand. Moral hazard notwithstanding, the only workable alternative may be to nationalize some of the banks, while simultaneously guaranteeing the savings (at least of small depositors), stripping out the bad assets of the banks, and clearing the markets by selling these assets. In addition, the newly nationalized banks should themselves be privatized at the earliest possible moment. The budgetary resources of most nations will not be sufficient to accomplish these arduous tasks. Furthermore, in each of these newly democratic societies, there is substantial popular resistance to bailing out banking institutions widely perceived to have been both incompetent and corrupt.

POLICY IMPLICATIONS

What is to be done? There are at least seven requirements. First reality must be recognized. The Asian crisis is a threat to global economic well-being, and governments in Washington and Tokyo must move beyond denial. The problems described above are found in virtually every Asian financial system, with the partial exceptions of Hong Kong, Singapore, and Taiwan, and the impact will continue to spread unless a credible multinational effort is mounted by the capital rich countries.

Second, policy-makers must squarely confront the primarily private sector nature of this crisis. Not only must the banks be fixed, but also the problems of the real sector must be dealt with through complex restructuring that only the private sector can adequately accomplish. Beyond the banking sector, only company-by-company restructuring, complete with management changes and loan write-downs, can return companies and employees to work. This requires a massive recapitalization effort, a partnership between the state (changing regulations and the economic parameters) and the private sector (both foreign and domestic). Recovery must primarily be a private sector solution. But resolution cannot come without a strong public policy component, because current owners will not sell out at rock bottom prices and need the state to shoulder, at least temporarily, part of the debt burden to facilitate fast, as well as fair, restructuring.

Third, the private sector *alone* cannot supply all of the answers, at least not in sufficient time to preclude a more generalized global slowdown and the possible political instabilities that would flow from it. Private capital from Europe and North America remains reluctant to reinvest the $200 billion withdrawn from the five affected Asian countries during the last year until it can see at least the beginning of the end of the crisis. An initial wave of recapitalization was undertaken during the first half of 1998. The losses (in share values) to the new investors of early 1998 in several instances exceed 50 percent after just three months. Major intermediaries, burned in early 1998, will be twice reluctant later in the year unless new international measures are adopted to reassure the market.

Fourth, Washington must recognize that not one of the economically afflicted systems—not Japan, not China, not Korea, not Indonesia, and not Thailand—has the political will, *on its own*, to make the necessary financial changes rapidly enough to preclude its own destruction at the polls. Good governments and bad tend to lose elections when economies collapse. Altering the national leadership may lead to an improved response to the financial crisis (as in Thailand, and Korea) or to continued drift (as in Indonesia and Japan). An appropriately designed multilateral institution could bolster economic reform policies regardless of which political party or faction comes to power.

Fifth, Asian elites can only enforce the required sacrifices if a new international financial institution is created to support the tough decisions necessary to restructure broken banking systems.[13] The day-to-day workings of an international restructuring agency would alter the culture of Asian finance, requiring it to move away from the personalism/familism of relationship-based banking to credit-based decisions emphasizing independent audits and honest asset evaluation. The new international structure should be designed to transfer to Asia the financial technologies created by the private sector during the 1980s and 1990s. Bringing new financial vehicles to Asia (from venture capital funds to leveraged buy outs) is at least as important as transferring particular lessons learned from the Swedish banking crisis and the American S & L debacle of the 1980s.

Sixth, the United States should take the lead in organizing such a new financial institution by rallying the resources of the G–7 to supply the capital inputs necessary to prevent the Crash of 1997 from becoming an Asian depression.

Seventh, the alternative to bold action may be a depth of socioeconomic and political instability in Asia in the next twenty years that will be reminiscent of the period 1930–1960. Can anyone conceive of a decade long depression not creating an outburst of economic nationalism in Indonesia? Likewise, would it not be prudent to create an international institution capable of dealing with a massive banking crisis before, rather than during, the next banking crisis (perhaps in China in 2001)?

Even though at present public opinion throughout the G–7 countries remains riveted on the reality of its own prosperity, the long-term global political risks of the Crash of 1997 remain of historic proportions. Economic liberalization of the global marketplace is already threatened, and if only one of the major political systems (for instance, Indonesia or China) becomes radicalized as a result of an unchecked crisis, the levels of expenditure required to contain the political consequences will dwarf the scale of preventive measures that might now be token.

The years 1997 and 1998 have witnessed a vast reversal of economic fortunes in Asia. The worst may be yet to come, depending on when, whether, and how the yuan is devalued. The political stability and long-term economic viability of Asia in the first quarter of the twenty-first century will depend on the quantity and quality of the international public and private response. At this point the stakes are very high, but policy-makers, at least in Washington, remain remarkably uninvolved, believing the crisis will take care of itself or that acting incisively might involve them in "moral hazard," or that as leaders, they are simply powerless to act internationally in the post-Cold War world. Unfortunately, it may be too late politically in Asia before the West fully realizes that neglect is not benign at this historic juncture, and that an opportunity to establish itself as the model for politics and commerce for the next century may be lost for lack of insight and fortitude.

NOTES

1. Familism is defined as a disproportionate attention to the interests of the nuclear, (and in Asia, the extended) family at the expense of considering the good of the community as a whole. The predatory behaviors of the Marcos and Suharto families remain difficult to comprehend without reference to amoral familism, the tendency to maximize only the wealth and well-being of one's family and to behave largely without scruples whenever something comes into conflict with the interests of the family. On the concept of amoral familism, see Banfield (1958).

2. The magnitude of the boom in the stock markets of Southeast Asia was obvious in the early 1990s. The indices of the stock exchanges of Indonesia, Malaysia, the Philippines, and Thailand for 1991–1993, increased by 37 percent, 50 percent, 58 percent, and 56 percent per annum for three consecutive years. In this casino-like atmosphere, all manner of phony valuations and chain listings of the same assets for multiple companies created massive equity bubbles based on unrealistic valuations. Of the five affected

economies, only Korea showed moderate increases of 8 percent per annum for the period 1991–1994. Interestingly, the very markets that ascended so quickly leveled off and, with the exception of Indonesia, moved systematically downward. This indicated the boom had really begun to fade domestically in 1994, long before the collapse of the currencies in mid-1997. For a diametrically different view regarding asset bubbles and the import of private sector mismanagement, see Bhalla (1999).

3. The truly pernicious interaction between managed exchange rates and responsible fiscal polices is described in detail by Bhaila (1999).

4. Precise figures on the proportion of non-performing loans remain elusive because each banking system had its own criteria for defining them. The 20 percent figure seems reasonable, however, if non-performance is defined as non-payment of principal and interest for ninety days and if finance companies are included in the calculation.

5. If 50 cents on the dollars can theoretically be recovered on the 20 percent of loans that are non-performing, this means a loss of 10 percent of total loan portfolio—which is probably more than the total equity of most banks at a given point in time.

6. Declining economic growth and low rates of return in both Europe and Japan in the early 1990s made Asia a particularly attractive alternative, and over time hundreds of billions of dollars in outside private capital became available to the emerging markets. Japanese government attempts to escape from slow growth included lowering interest rates to near zero. This meant that Japanese seeking returns needed to look abroad for higher returns on loans than could be obtained onshore in Japan.

7. Bhalla (1999) strongly believes that the Chinese devaluation of 1994 led directly to the collapse of Southeast Asian export growth and that this, in turn, set off the Crisis of 1997.

8. After a trip to Bangkok in December 1994 and as a result of analyzing the Jones, Lang, and Wooten data on the office real estate market, my colleague at FX Concepts, Inc., R. Roderick Porter, and I passed a letter indirectly to the Governor of the Bank of Thailand. It stated: "As of 9/30/94 the supply of office space in the Bangkok area was 4,054,582 square meters. Of that, 2,528,730 square meters (62%) was completed since the beginning of 1992. Even more extraordinarily, an additional 3,087,730 square meters is likely to enter the market before the end of 1997. That will bring the supply to 7,142,325 square meters of which 79% will have been completed since 1992."

"With Bangkok's current office vacancy running at around 20%, it is clear that it will be difficult to absorb the additional space no matter how fast Thailand's economic growth proves to be. These statistics indicate the Bangkok may be on the verge of a real estate crisis like the Savings and Loan crisis in the United States and the non-performing real estate loan problem currently crippling banks in Japan. We believe that devising a game plan early which utilizes the experience gained in the American real estate/banking crisis could minimize the damage to Thailand."

9. Eugene Dattel's work places emphasis on the importance of firm-by-firm analysis and the degree to which each country's business organizations and practices are an outgrowth of their own culture (see Dattel 1994 and 1999).

10. With floating exchange rates there is virtually no correlation on a day-to-day basis between the strength of a currency and the fluctuations of its stock market. As John R. Taylor (1998) has pointed out, in countries which are capital poor and which have fixed exchange rates, the local stock market serves as a proxy for the strength or weakness of the currency. Government operations to maintain the peg suppress any movement in the currency's value until it suddenly explodes out of the official band. Equity markets are not as controlled by the government, and the end of the game is nigh when the stock markets move precipitously downward, indicating that investors have withdrawn their vote of confidence from the business sector and that, if given the chance, they will move a substantial portion of their investments into liquid assets or actually move them out of country.

11. Interestingly, the Shanghai building frenzy also peaked in mid-1993 (see Ramo 1998:68).

12. This optimistic view rests on the assumption of continued robust economic growth in the United States. A sharp stock market correction or a recession in the United States would greatly complicate and delay the reemergence of Asian economic growth.

13. Although an independent agency might be ideal, the most important thing is to make restructuring the banks and closing those that are beyond help the number one priority of the international financial system. Neither the IMF (whose charter is to maintain currency stability) nor the World Bank (a development institution) was designed to act as an international equivalent of the Resolution Trust Corporation. Neither institution has the specialized experience or the skilled manpower required to produce the desired outcome.

REFERENCES

Asher, D., and A. Smithers. 1999. Japan's Key Challenges for the 21st Century. In *The Asian Contagion*, ed. K. D. Jackson. Boulder, CO: Westview.

Banfield, E. 1958. *The Moral Basis of a Backward Society*. New York: Free Press.

Bhalla, S. S. 1999. Domestic Follies, Investment Crises: East Asian Lessons for India. In *The Asian Contagion*, ed. K. D. Jackson.

Cheetham, R. 1998. Asia Crisis. Paper presented at conference, U.S.-ASEAN-Japan Policy Dialogue. School of Advanced International Studies of Johns Hopkins University, June 7–9, in Washington, D.C.

Dattel, E. R. 1994. *The Sun That Never Rose: The Inside Story of Japan's Failed Attempt at Global Financial Domination*. Chicago: Probus.

———. 1999. Reflections of a Market Participant: Japanese and Asian Financial Institutions. In *The Asian Contagion,* ed. K. D. Jackson.

Doner, R., and A. Ramsay. 1999. Thailand: From Economic Miracle to Economic Crisis. In *The Asian Contagion*, ed. K. D. Jackson.

Ferald, J., H. Edison, and P. Loungani. 1999. Was China the First Domino? Assessing Links Between China and the Rest of Emerging Asia, Board of Governors of the Federal Reserve System, International Finance Discussion Paper No. 604.

Indonesian Commercial Newsletter. 1998. March 16.

Jackson, K. 1997. Thailand and the Crash of '97. Unpublished monograph. December.

———, ed. 1999. *The Asian Contagion: The Causes and Consequences of a Financial Crisis.* Boulder, CO: Westview.

Jackson, K., and L. Pye, eds. 1978. *Political Power and Communications in Indonesia.* Berkeley, CA.: University of California Press.

Kaminsky, G., S. Lizondo, and C. Reinhart, 1997. Leading Indicators of Currency Crises. Working Paper of the International Monetary Fund. July.

Kindleberger, C. 1996. *Manias, Panics, and Crashes: A History of Financial Crises.* New York: John Wiley.

Laothamatas, A. 1996. A Tale of Two Democracies: Conflicting Perceptions of Elections and Democracy in Thailand. In *The Politics of Elections in Southeast Asia.* ed. R. Taylor. New York: Cambridge University Press.

Lardy, N. R. 1999. China and the Asian Financial Contagion. In *The Asian Contagion,* ed. K. D. Jackson.

Loh, Hui Yin. 1997. Mahathir Calls Soros "Moron" in War of Words. *Business Times.* August 25.

Pyo, H. K. 1999. The Financial Crisis in South Korea: Anatomy and Policy Imperatives. In *The Asian Contagion,* ed. K. D. Jackson.

Ramo, J. 1998. The Shanghai Bubble. *Foreign Policy.* Summer.

Robertson, P. 1996. The Rise of the Rural Network Politician: Will Thailand's New Elite Endure? *Asian Survey* 36, no. 9.

Rohwer, J. 1995. *Asia Rising: Why America Will Prosper as Asia's Economies Boom.* New York: Simon and Schuster.

Severino, J. M. 1998. Speech at the International Herald Tribune Summit, June 16, in Melbourne, Australia.

Sicheua, S. 1997. The Way Out of the Economic Crisis. Unpublished paper. September 30.

Taylor, J. R. 1998. Paper presented at conference, The Dilemma of Emerging Markets Currency Risk Management. International Foreign Exchange Concepts Conference, June 22, in Auckland, New Zealand.

Wards Auto World. 1996. December.

Yi Gang and Song LiGang. 1998. East Asia in Crisis: From Being a Miracle to Needing One? Paper presented (The full text of a paper given by Yi Gang from the People's Bank of China and Song Ligang from Australia National University.) May 6.

Chapter 14: Asian Values and the Asian Crisis

By Francis Fukuyama

A MERE decade ago, Americans at every level of business and government were being chided for their failure to emulate the example of Asia. The key to that region's economic success was said to be its cultural values—a combination of the work ethic, respect for community and authority, and a tradition of paternalistic government—all of which were contrasted invidiously to the rampant dysfunctionality then plaguing the American economy and American society alike.

Today, as the International Monetary Fund (IMF) imposes Western, market-oriented rules on one desperate Asian country after another, the mood has shifted to the other extreme. Asian values, we are now told, are what led to nepotistic credit allocation, an overly meddlesome state, and a disastrous lack of transparency in financial transactions. From being the cause of Asia's success, Asian values are now seen as the root of last summer's currency crisis and of the ensuing economic meltdown across nearly the whole region. Neither reading is correct.

II

THE SUBJECT of Asian values emerged in the early 1990s thanks largely to two politicians: Lee Kuan Yew, then Prime Minister of Singapore, and Prime Minister Mahathir Mohamad of Malaysia. Each was in pursuit of a relatively narrow agenda. Lee, seeking to improve his ties with China, hoped to gain favor in Beijing by promoting a mildly anti-Western sense of Chinese cultural identity. Mahathir, for his part, wanted to fend off the Bush administration's push to create a forum known as Asia-Pacific Economic Cooperation, in favor of a new Asian political bloc that would exclude "white" powers like Australia and the United States.

But the idea of a distinct Asian cultural and political identity had a larger resonance as well. In part, it reflected the genuine pride felt by many people in the region at the stunning success of their economies over the previous two generations. It also, however, served the interests of states eager to shield themselves both from Western criticisms of their human-rights practices and from pressure to open their protected domestic markets to imports and foreign investment. To the "soft" authoritarian governments ruling Singapore, Malaysia, Indonesia, and increasingly the People's Republic of China, "Asian values" offered an apparently principled defense of their reluctance to broaden political participation.

The idea of Asian values was, however, problematic from the start. As anyone knows who has spent time in that part of the world, there are huge cultural differences not only among the various countries but also among the ethnic groups that make up multicultural societies like Singapore and Malaysia. In southern China, families are both large and cohesive; in Japan, much less large and socially less significant. Whereas in Japan, South Korea, and Taiwan the state has traditionally commanded substantial respect, in many parts of Southeast Asia it has been historically weak or nonexistent. Confucian societies tend to invest more resources in education than do Islamic, Malay, or Catholic ones—indeed, Lee Kuan Yew was forced to pull back from his embrace of Confucianism for the simple reason that it did not reflect the cultural heritage of the 15 percent of Singapore's population that is of Malay descent.

As for the relationship between Asian values and economic success, that is dubious at best. Not only have attitudes toward work and money varied tremendously from one part of Asia to another, but Asia as a whole was rightly regarded as an economic basket-case for much of the first half of the 20th century. As Max Weber pointed out in 1905, no Asian society had ever produced indigenous capitalist institutions; economic growth became possible only after contact with the West and with Western ideas of property rights, the rule of law, scientific rationalism, modern state institutions, and the like. To put it another way, economic growth was contingent on the rejection by Asians of important elements of their own cultural heritage, including the Mandarin disdain for commerce and physical labor.

This is not to say that Asian values did not also turn out to be economically valuable: the Confucian emphasis on education and meritocratic advancement, for example, happened to dovetail very nicely with the requirements of a modernizing society. But as in the case of the impoverished Asian immigrants who came to Canada and the United States and made a success there, those values could come into play only when combined with other values and institutions imported from the West.

Aside from inculcating good work habits, Asian values have also been said to have a political dimension. Thus, Lee and Mahathir have argued that their brand of authoritarian government is well-suited to Confucian traditions of hierarchy and enables the state to focus its resources on economic development while avoiding the high degree of social disorder characteristic of Western democracies.

Unfortunately, the alleged cultural fit between Asian values and authoritarian government is a matter more of convenience than of principle. In any old and complex cultural system—whether Confucianism or Christianity—it is possible to find sources legitimating totally contradictory practices. Historically, Christians reading the same Bible have both promoted and condemned slavery. Similarly, if Lee Kuan Yew can cite Confucian sources to support rule by benevolent authoritarianism, Taiwan's Lee Teng-hui has cited other sources to prove the compatibility of Confucian tradition with the kind of democratic institutions he has sought to build in his island nation. All cultural systems evolve. Given the examples of Japan, South Korea, and Taiwan, who is to say that "Asian values" constitute an insuperable obstacle to the establishment of Western-style democracy?

Nor is the economic efficacy of authoritarian government clear-cut, as the careful studies of Robert Barro and others have shown. When such governments function well, as in the case of Singapore and of South Korea under military rule, they can indeed be very effective at promoting rapid growth; but when they function badly, like Brazil or Peru during the 1970s, their economies tend to perform much more poorly than democracies.

It is true that Asian authoritarians have, on the whole, been more competent and honest than Latin American ones, but, as the current crisis already suggests, there can be no assurance this will continue to be the case over the long run. In the absence of adequate feedback mechanisms and institutional controls on state power, it ends up being a matter of luck whether authoritarian institutions are turned toward the single-minded pursuit of investment and growth or become vehicles for padding the bank accounts of the politicians in charge.

III

If Asian values are not the cause of either rapid growth or of a superior form of governance, are they, instead, a catalyst of excessive state intervention and "crony capitalism"? And if so, can they be blamed for the economic debacle that occurred in the wake of the collapse of the Thai baht and other regional currencies in the summer of 1997? Alas, in sickness as in health, Asia is a very diverse place, and the causes of crisis vary from country to country.

The trouble in Thailand began when the government's efforts to defend the baht's link to the dollar came under attack in international currency markets. But it was the very stability of that link that had encouraged private firms, in Thailand and abroad, to borrow and lend short-term funds to finance speculation in real estate and other questionable ventures. If there was failure at the government level, it lay not in excessive interventionism but in an insufficiency of regulatory power: the Thai state was unable to impose proper reporting, disclosure, and reserve requirements on its banking system. And if there has been longer-term failure at the government level, it is again one of omission rather than commission—a failure, that is, to invest adequately in public education and physical infrastructure.

The problem facing Thailand—overzealous speculative investment fueled by cheap credit—has been a feature of capitalist markets for as long as they have existed. Nor is Thailand alone in the region in this respect. Most Southeast Asian governments have opened their economies to foreign investment and trade, and some, like Singapore and Hong Kong, have been models of state minimalism in the economic realm—not that this has saved them from being buffeted in the global financial markets.

Of course, the crisis today is centered not in any of these places but in Japan and especially South Korea. In both countries, state agencies for the past 45 years have indeed played a hyperactive role in guiding economic life, primarily through the allocation of credit.

Intervening on both a macro- and microeconomic level, the Korean government protected domestic producers from foreign competition and created a government-industry machine that resembled a time bomb waiting to go off. The large Korean conglomerates known as *chaebol* became addicted to cheap, often subsidized credit for ambitious expansion projects. While these paid off during the country's high-growth period from 1961 to 1987, the absence of constraints, either in the form of hard budgets or in the form of shareholder demands for a return on equity, led to spectacular mistakes, as in the 1996 decision by the Samsung conglomerate to become the sixth major Korean automobile manufacturer. The tremendous power vested in government also led to cases of massive corruption; former President Roh Tae Woo stole some $600 million, and politics played a role in the recent collapse of Hanbo Steel.

Japan's sins are by now familiar: lack of openness, regulation, and transparency in the financial sector, coupled with a penchant for keeping faltering firms alive at all costs rather than letting managers and shareholders absorb the consequences of failure. All this has led to a rolling seven-year crisis in the banking system that has seriously weakened the country's still-competitive manufacturing firms. As in the case of Korea, government intervention in markets has persisted long past the point where it makes economic sense.

But the fact that government intervention is no longer functional in places like Japan and South Korea does not mean that it served no purpose in the past. Although many American economists assert dogmatically that state intervention always produces inefficiencies, the fact is that these same meddlesome Asian governments presided over periods of growth that were historically unprecedented anywhere in the world. Perhaps one might argue that, in the absence of state intervention, Asian growth from 1950 to the 1990s could have been even higher than it was; but to imagine that one period of unprecedentedly high growth should have yielded to another and even higher one is to indulge in fantasy.

WHICH BRINGS us to the other frequently-named culprit for Asia's present troubles, "crony capitalism." If Northeast and Southeast Asia share a common failing, it is that business decisions are frequently made by other than market criteria. The entire region is permeated with personalistic ties of all sorts, ranging from the mutual obligations that Japanese managers feel toward their workers or their business-network (*keiretsu*) partners to the forthrightly corrupt dealings of Indonesia's Suharto family. In Southeast Asia, family connections link the far-flung overseas Chinese communities; in Northeast Asia, there are long-term corporate alliances or informal connections between government overseers and the firms they ostensibly regulate.

Greater formality, based on the strict rule of law, is a pressing need everywhere in Asia. Nevertheless, "crony capitalism" is a misnomer. The term was initially coined to describe the Philippines under the late Ferdinand Marcos, a place where huge amounts of money were being siphoned off by the dictator's close associates. Historically, despite exceptions like the Philippines, China, and Indonesia, East Asia boasted astonishingly *low* levels of corruption. In light of the huge regulatory powers vested in Japanese, Korean, and Taiwanese bureaucrats over the past two generations, one might reasonably have expected to see nepotism, influence-peddling, and stagnation in these countries on the level of, say, Mobutu's Zaire. Instead, while major scandals have emerged over time, all three countries have demonstrated an ability to build strong, competent, and reasonably honest government institutions that can stimulate a high level of savings and direct them to productive investment.

No society can expect to keep this going forever, which is why formal institutions are critical in the long run. But few countries outside Asia have shown an ability to make "personalism" pay off so spectacularly even in the short run.

In any case, is it so obvious that "personalism" is always a bad thing? Ironically, business-school professors and information-technology gurus have been urging *American* firms to move in precisely that direction. In a sophisticated economy, we are told, work is done by highly educated professionals who must be allowed to organize themselves. To that end, American companies are being advised to replace their large, bureaucratic, hierarchical structures with smaller, flatter ones linked by informal networks. Many high-tech firms have also adopted a policy of "relational contracting," basing their business decisions not on price and performance criteria but on relationships of trust with suppliers or with clients that resemble nothing so much as the Japanese *keiretsu*.

IV

IF ASIAN values are not central to the saga of Asia's economic rise and recent decline, and will not, in and of themselves, determine the kind of political system that ultimately prevails in that part of the world, what, then, *is* their significance? The answer lies in the sphere of social relations.

Among all the criticisms of the West lodged by proponents of Asian values in the early 1980s, the most cogent focused on the effects of excessive individualism in Western societies, and particularly in the United States. The concept of the autonomous individual as the ground of all rights and duties is indeed unique to the liberal West; it has no counterpart in Asia, where people are born into the world encumbered with a whole series of obligations to others, from the family to the state. This encumbrance can inhibit their ability to take advantage of the good things that we associate with individualism, like innovation and entrepreneurship; but it can also reduce their susceptibility to the bad things, like crime and illegitimacy.

How does this play out in practice? Many modern Asian societies have followed a completely different evolutionary path from Europe and North America. Beginning approximately in the mid-1960s, virtually every country in the industrialized West experienced a rapid increase in crime rates and a breakdown in the nuclear family. The only two countries in the Organization for Economic Cooperation and Development *not* experiencing this disruption were the Asian ones, Japan and Korea.

Since the end of World War II, Japan has shown but a slightly rising divorce rate, while its rate of illegitimacy has been both low and flat, and its crime rate, already one of the lowest in the world, has trended slightly *downward* for the past three decades. Korea underwent a slight rise in crime in the 1970s and has experienced periodic outbreaks of political violence, but there, too, very little social dysfunction has attended industrialization.

Similarly with the countries of Southeast Asia. As their per-capita income has risen, they have experienced *declining* rates of both divorce and illegitimacy. To be sure, traditional family structure has changed dramatically, as joint and multigenerational families have turned into nuclear ones; but the breakdown of the nuclear family that is so notable in the West has been all but absent.

Any number of factors may be adduced to explain why these social trends in Asia differ from those in the United States and other Western countries. But, from the perspective of "Asian values," the most important difference—and the one that has yet to be confronted squarely—has to do with the role of women. Here, indeed, is an example of a social value with large effects both in economic life and in politics.

To a much greater extent than in the West, women in Japan and Korea, not to mention in other, less-developed Asian societies, continue to be treated differently from men both in social custom and in law. While female labor-force participation can be high, girls generally work only until they are married, and then drop out to raise families. Women across Asia are also less able to control their own reproductive cycles. Even in Japan, the pill was only recently made legally available.

Until recently, too, Japanese labor laws prohibited women from working double shifts in factories; they were thus effectively barred from the fabled lifetime-employment system of large Japanese corporations. And what has been true of Japan tends to be even truer in the more socially conservative parts of Asia: in one way or another, women are prevented from earning enough to support themselves and their children without a husband.

When Asian spokesmen (at least the male ones) say they do not like Western values, what they often mean is that they do not like Western sexual roles; the individualism that is problematic for them includes not only freewheeling political protest but freewheeling protest within the family. And no wonder: family structure has implications for education, for economic performance, for public safety, and for government investment in such things as crime prevention and health care. Through the selective application of "Asian values," Asian societies have so far preserved the coherence of the nuclear family and have spared themselves the social disruption that has attended economic change in the West.

V

BUT WHAT of the future? In the long run, there is no reason to think that the nations of Asia cannot resume, if at a slower pace, the trajectory they were on prior to last summer's crisis. It is much less certain, however, that their economic and political institutions will be able to withstand the powerful forces of globalization. If they are to remain competitive, for example, the Japanese *keiretsu* and the Korean *chaebol* will have to undergo massive changes in the next decade. In Northeast Asia, the regulatory hand of the state will have to be relaxed; in Southeast Asia, in order to guarantee the soundness of the financial sector, it will have to be strengthened. All Asian countries will need to rethink the wisdom of pegging their currencies tightly to the U.S. dollar.

A likely result of these and other changes will be an erosion of Asia's social distinctiveness, which is already under siege by a variety of factors. Fertility rates in Japan and Korea are far below replacement levels, and Japan in particular faces not only an older but a dramatically shrinking population. If the country wants to see some semblance of economic growth, it will have to expand its labor force, either through immigration or through allowing more women to work. Caught between these two choices, many Japanese would, I suspect, opt for the latter. But this means that, over time, Japan too will begin to experience Western-style family disruption, and the social problems that grow out of it.

In short, what the current crisis will end up doing is to puncture the idea of Asian exceptionalism. The laws of economics have not been suspended in Asia; as the economies of the region catch up to the West, growth rates will slow and social problems will accumulate. And neither have the laws of politics: the well-documented correlation between stable democracy and a high level of development surely applies to a region where rising educational achievements and the complex nature of industrial or post-industrial societies will increasingly favor the rule of law and greater popular participation.

In order to get to the long run, however, we must first survive the short run. In the near term, most countries in Asia will face a severe challenge restructuring their economies without generating a political backlash, and all sorts of uncertainties may complicate the process of recovery. The likely future behavior of the PRC and North Korea is one such unknown. Another is the reaction in the United States. As Asia's fallen tigers try to export their way back to health on the basis of depreciated currencies, America's trade deficit will swell, increasing the pressure for protectionism already evident in the defeat of the Clinton administration's effort to secure "fast-track" trade legislation. On top of all that, there has already been an upsurge of resentment against the IMF and the United States in Korea, Thailand, and other economically prostrate countries.

The remaining years of the 20th century thus promise to be difficult and eventful ones for people on both sides of the Pacific. It would be nice if, for the duration, we could be spared further lectures either about the special advantages or about the special deficiencies of Asian values.

FRANCIS FUKUYAMA is Hirst professor of public policy at George Mason University and director of its International Transactions program.

Chapter 16: Post-Crisis Asia— Economic Recovery, September 11, 2001 and the Challenges Ahead

By Shalendra D. Sharma

To the extent that Asia is recovering, no one can claim the credit. The amazing thing to me—if you leave Indonesia out—is how similar the performances are, regardless of the policies. Korea took the IMF's advice and it's bouncing back. Thailand took the IMF's advice and it's starting to come back. Malaysia defied the IMF and did everything the IMF told it not to—it's coming back fast. Everybody's contemplating success for their policies: Mahathir said he did it, the IMF said they did it. The truth is the natural resilience of economies did it (Paul Krugman, August 25, 1999).[1]

In the aftermath of East Asia's spectacular economic collapse in mid-1997 even the most optimistic predictions gave at least a decade before Asia could fully recover.[2] Yet, in early 2000, an IMF study triumphantly noted that "the financial crises that erupted in Asia beginning in mid-1997 are now behind us and the economies are recovering strongly" (IMF 2000a). Indeed, the economic recovery between the second quarter of 1999 and the last quarter of 2000 was simply astounding. South Korea, Thailand, Malaysia, and the Philippines notched growth-rates equal to or above those just before the crisis. South Korea made the biggest gain, its GDP growing by a whopping 10.7 percent in 1999 and 11.2 percent in the first half of 2000, from a contraction of –6.7 percent in 1998. Also, by October 2000, Korea had already surpassed its pre-crisis per capita income peak.[3] In September 1999, the IMF-prescribed programs for South Korea (and Thailand) were brought to an end after being in effect for two years. South Korea also stopped drawing from the IMF, and in August 2000 completed repayment of a US$19.5 billion IMF loan, almost three years ahead of schedule. By March 2000, South Korea had accumulated substantial enough reserves (from US$9 billion at the end of 1997 to about US$83 billion) to provide it with reasonable insulation against shocks. In October 2001, Korea's foreign-exchange reserves stood at US$100.4 billion, and in November 2001, the international rating agencies restored the country's sovereign rating to investment grade.

The recovery in Hong Kong, China has been equally impressive. The first-quarter growth in 2000 was 14.3 percent, followed by 10.8 percent in the second quarter. GDP growth in Singapore of 5.4 percent in 1999 was partly due to rising productivity levels. Moreover, Singapore experienced a rapid growth of its information technology industry— no doubt benefiting from the government's policy of transforming the island republic into a "wired" economy. Malaysia, the Philippines, and Thailand grew at 5.4, 3.2, and 5.2 percent respectively in the first quarter of 2000 (ADB 2000). Only Indonesia continues to lag behind. However, considering the fact that Indonesia experienced a dramatic output contraction of –13.2 percent in 1998, its real GDP growth of 0.23 percent in 1999 was a significant milestone (ADB 2000). Moreover, the rupiah strengthened to about 7,450 per U.S. dollar in mid-2000. Also, inflation, which peaked at 82 percent in September 1998, has declined to about 1.7 percent in December 1999.[4] At the end of June 2000, Indonesia's gross external reserves stood at US$27.4 billion (ADB 2000b, 31). The more recent figures show that in the first quarter of 2000 real GDP growth in Indonesia reached 3.0 percent.

Other indicators of the region-wide recovery included the steady return of capital. For example, portfolio equity investment flows have stabilized and turned positive with US$8 billion in aggregate inflows in 1999–2000. FDI flows have been also positive, largely owing to sharply depreciated asset values and exchange rates and also to the relaxation of foreign ownership rules, which has encouraged mergers and acquisitions. The latter factor has been most pronounced in South Korea. In fact, South Korea, almost closed to foreign direct investment before the crisis, received US$15.5 billion in outside investment in 1999, five times the 1996 inflow. By early 2000, the current accounts of South Korea, Indonesia, Thailand, and Malaysia were all positive, foreign-currency liabilities, especially those with short maturities, had fallen, and the exchange-rate misalignments have largely been corrected. By mid-May 2000, the value of local currencies (in nominal terms) had stabilized, although they still bought 20 to 35 percent fewer U.S. dollars than before the crisis in South Korea, Malaysia, the Philippines, and Thailand, and 50 percent fewer dollars in Indonesia. Overall, these positive developments reduced the region's external vulnerabilities substantially.

What explains this remarkable economic recovery? There are several interrelated factors. *First*, the massive financial injection, totaling some US$35 billion, provided by the IMF in 1998–99, and some US$85 billion committed (although not all of this actually materialized) by other multilateral and bilateral sources helped to restore investor confidence and stop any further economic hemorrhage, and in particular the massive currency depreciation. In South Korea, an increase in foreign equity participation in the financial sector has provided an additional source of inflows. Balance-of-payments surpluses have allowed the crisis-hit countries to accumulate additional international reserves and let currencies appreciate gradually. *Second*, it is important to recognize that financial crises do not necessarily destroy the capacity for economic growth. Although the Asian financial crisis exacted a heavy toll in terms of lost output and socioeconomic dislocations, it did not destroy the industrial and manufacturing infrastructure and the productive capacities of these economies. The significant investments these countries made in physical plant and equipment served them well as the global economy picked up. *Third*, domestic fiscal stimulus and a rebuilding of inventories combined with favorable external developments provided Asia's sagging export sector with a much-needed boost. Specifically, the global output growth of 3 percent greatly stimulated the initially suppressed demand for goods and services produced in Asia. Most importantly, as the negative effects of the global electronics downturn that occurred from 1996 through to 1998 were gradually reversed, this boosted the South Korean, Malaysian, Thai, and Singaporean economies, which depend heavily on the manufacture and exports of electronics, including information-technology-related products. The Korean recovery was also helped substantially by the external demand for cars and semi-conductors. Moreover, in all four countries service-sector output grew strongly, owing to growth in telecommunications, wholesale and retail trade, and financial services.

Prior to the global economic slowdown (which began ostensibly in the last quarter of 2000, compounded by the uncertainty produced by September 11, 2001), the U.S. economy played an important role in supporting global demand—accounting for more than 50 percent of the growth of global demand. While this was reflected in record U.S. current-account deficits, these deficits proved to be an important buffer against global recession. Japan, on the other hand, has failed to live up to expectations as the engine behind the regional economies. Although positive growth in Japan in the first half of 1999 began to stimulate recovery in the region, it was short-lived.[5] The return to negative growth (0.5 percent in 2001) weakened the stimulus to regional exports that otherwise would have been created by the stronger yen. Moreover, the Japanese government's growth stimulus from the 1999 fiscal package has petered out. The growth forecast for 2002 has been marked down to 0.5 percent, reflecting in part the global economic slowdown, but also the continuing weakness of consumer confidence and underlying problems with the financial system. While the Japanese government has the resources to introduce another fiscal stimulus plan, given the high level of public debt, at 125 percent of GDP, there is little scope for reflationary fiscal policies. Indeed, given Prime Minister Koizumi's plans to curb government spending, the economy is not likely to be stimulated by fiscal policy. Japan is therefore unlikely to provide much support to the regional economies this year through demand for their exports. Although it is expected that the growing intra-Asian trade and demand from the European Union will help to fill the void, there is little doubt that Japan's recovery is crucial (at least, in the short term) to the region's recovery. Over the long-term, Japan's importance as a market for Asian exports and a source of long-term direct capital to the region will gradually diminish.

Fourth, the Asian crisis was not a current-account, but a capital-account crisis. Conventional current-account crises are caused by the deterioration of domestic macroeconomic fundamentals, such as price inflation, fiscal deficits and low rates of saving. A capital-account crisis is characterized by massive international capital inflows, usually large enough to surpass the underlying current-account deficit, and composed mainly of short-term borrowing denominated in foreign currencies. This leads to currency and maturity mismatches, which adversely affect the balance-sheets of domestic financial institutions. There is thus a dual financial crisis—a currency crisis due to currency mismatch that leads to international liquidity problems, and a domestic banking crisis resulting in credit contraction. During the Asian crisis, the swing of international capital from inflows to outflows amounted to more than 20 percent of GDP in Thailand. Currency depreciation further worsened the balance-sheets of corporations by inflating the value of liabilities in domestic currency terms, thereby precipitating a currency and banking crisis. Further, there was an imbalance between high levels of short-term foreign debt and low foreign-exchange reserves. However, as investor panic (both foreign and domestic) that partly triggered the crisis abated, capital once again started to return—with FDI dominating the composition of net private flows, representing about 82 percent of the total (World Bank 2000c, 154). This allowed the economies to rebuild their official international reserves, reduce their external liabilities, and strengthen their currencies and external current-account positions.

Fifth, prudent monetary and fiscal policy—some domestically inspired and some promoted by the IMF—have acted as important catalysts for recovery. For example, in South Korea, Thailand, and Malaysia, money-market interest rates have been broadly unchanged since mid-1999, at levels significantly below those observed before the crisis.[6] Lower interest rates helped reduce the pressure on heavily indebted corporations and contain the non-performing loans problem.[7] with regard to fiscal policy, in Korea a supplementary budget adopted in August 1999 provided a much-needed additional stimulus, while targeting a consolidated central government deficit of 5 percent of GDP for 1999. And *sixth*, luck has played an important role in Asia's recovery, just as it compounded underlying problems in 1997. In particular, while the El Nino and La Niña weather phenomena devastated agricultural production in 1997–98, the favorable weather conditions in 1999 and the first half of 2000 have helped Indonesia and the Philippines to reap bumper crops of rice and other basic agricultural commodities. In addition to creating agricultural employment, this has also eased burdens on the overstretched social safety nets and enabled vulnerable households better to meet their consumption needs.

THE GLOBAL ECONOMIC SLOWDOWN AND SEPTEMBER 11, 2001

Most Asian countries experienced a sharp economic slowdown beginning in the last quarter of 2000. The problems of a deteriorating external environment due in large part to the downturn in the U.S. economy were exacerbated by the September 11 terrorist attacks. Countries that are closely linked to the global economy through trade and capital flows were more adversely affected than those where these linkages are weaker. In particular, Asian countries with heavier dependence on manufacturing, in particular the production and export of electronics, saw a larger decline in growth. For example, South Korea's manufacturing sector grew only by 1.5 percent in the first three quarters of 2001, compared to an average growth of more than 18 percent between 1999 and 2000. Similarly, in Malaysia the manufacturing sector actually shrank by 4 percent in the first three quarters of 2001, whereas the average growth rate was 17.4 percent in the preceding two years. Singapore's manufacturing shrank by 9 percent in the first three quarters of 2001, from an average growth of more than 14 percent in the preceding two years (ADB 2001, 4). To varying degrees, the decelerating export demand has been accompanied by softening domestic demand. Indeed, slowing growth and the sharp decline in stock prices have adversely affected both consumer confidence and business investment. The impact of the economic slowdown has been reflected in the growth-rates. In the first three quarters of 2001, Indonesia, South Korea, Malaysia, the Philippines, and Thailand taken together grew only by 2.5 percent. This represents a sharp deceleration from the 7.8 percent growth they achieved in the first three quarters of 2000 (ADB 2001, 4). Even resilient Singapore saw its GDP decline by 0.6 percent in the first three quarters of 2001, compared to 9.5 percent growth in the corresponding period in 2000. The impact of the global slowdown on China has been moderate, partly because of its lower dependence on information technology exports, and partly because of a series of substantial fiscal stimulus measures that have been implemented over the last four years. Thus, China posted a growth of 7.6 percent in the first three quarters of 2001 (ADB 2001, 4).

Another negative impact was the result of the sharp rise in oil prices in the first six months of 2001. Although prices have since leveled off, the potential oil-price instability (compounded by the uncertainty in the Middle East) remains a major concern. However, the price-rise was something of a mixed blessing. It has worked in favor of net exporters of oil such as Indonesia and Malaysia, but against net importers, such as South Korea, Taiwan, the Philippines, and Thailand.[8] Korea is more vulnerable to rising international crude oil prices than most other Asian countries. Clearly, Korea's current-account balance would deteriorate significantly if oil prices were to rise sharply.

Third, the rebounds in East Asian equity markets in 1999 declined gradually in 2000, but were further sharply eroded following the September 11 attacks. In local currency terms, as of end-September 2000, Korean, Indonesian and Thai equities had fallen by almost 40 percent, while losses in the Philippines were just under 35 percent since early 2000 (ADB 2000b, 4). The drop in equity markets has been influenced by external and domestic factors. Externally, rising U.S. interest rates triggered downward adjustments in global equity markets, while increased capital outflows have contributed to the decline in stock prices. Overall, all this has had an adverse impact on regional markets. Another factor that has influenced regional equity markets is the worldwide corrections in prices of information-technology stocks since the second quarter of 2000. Since the information technology sector in the affected Asian countries has expanded in recent years, this has also increased their exposure to fluctuations in information-technology stock prices.[9]

THE CHALLENGES AHEAD

The palpable concern that the drop in equity markets and the currency depreciations would trigger another crisis have since subsided—in large part because gross domestic product growth picked up in much of Southeast and East Asia in the first quarter of 2002. Taken together, Indonesia, Malaysia, the Philippines, Singapore, Thailand, the PRC, and Korea grew by 5.3 percent, representing an improvement from the 3.8 percent growth achieved in the last quarter of 2001 and the 4.3 percent growth for the entire year 2001. This resurgence in growth is driven primarily by a rise in global demand for the region's exports. This positive development notwithstanding, it is important to recognize that the crisis-affected countries are now more resilient to shocks than before. First, almost all the crisis-affected countries now run current-account surpluses. Second, foreign-exchange reserves have improved significantly, and more than cover the entire short-term external debt. In fact, the short-term to total debt ratios and total external debt to GDP ratios are now lower than those seen at the height of the 1997 crisis. Third, the magnitude of net private capital outflows is nowhere near as large as it was in 1997 and 1998. Fourth, the composition of capital being withdrawn is also different. In 1997–98 the main problem was the non-renewal of short-term credit by banks and investor panic. Now the problem is scheduled debt repayments and slowdown or withdrawal of foreign direct investment and portfolio capital. Fifth, the ratio of money supply to foreign-exchange reserves (another indicator of the vulnerability of a country to a currency crisis) has improved, and capital adequacy ratios and the profitability of banks are slowly recovering. Finally, as was noted earlier, the 1997 crisis was primarily a capital-account crisis that was exacerbated by pegged—and ultimately unsustainable—exchange rates. Currently, most Southeast and East Asian countries have adopted more flexible exchange-rate regimes. This should enable them to adjust to external shocks more smoothly.

Yet the crisis-affected countries still face some daunting challenges. For example, in order to deal with the social costs of the crisis and then the subsequent economic slowdown, governments responded with a series of fiscal stimuli measures to boost the economy. For example, between August 1998 and August 1999 the Thai government launched three fiscal stimulus packages, including tax and tariff reductions, to boost domestic demand. Consequently, it ran a large deficit which, on a cash-balance basis, reached a cumulative 79.4 billion baht in the first half of fiscal year 1999/2000 (ending September 30). The overall public-sector deficit, including interest costs of financial sector restructuring for the fiscal year 1999/2000 was around 7 percent of GDP. Total public debt was estimated at about 2.6 trillion baht (US$67.7 billion) in 1999, equivalent to around 56 percent of GDP (ADB 2000c, 37–38). Thus rising deficits in combination with very substantial financial sector restructuring costs have contributed to a rapid increase in public-sector debt since the onset of the crisis. Although China, South Korea, Malaysia, Singapore and Thailand introduced the stimuli measures in their 2001 budgets, the sharp downturn following September 11 forced them to announce supplementary spending packages. As a result, fiscal deficits have further increased in each country. Bringing these deficits to a manageable level remains a major challenge.

Since weaknesses in the financial and corporate sectors were at the heart of the crisis, reforming them has been a top priority. There are broadly two phases in resolving financial system distress: containment and restructuring. The containment or distress-resolution phase occurs with the onset of a financial crisis, when there is a major loss of confidence in the financial system. The aim during this phase is quickly to stabilize the financial system and prevent a credit crunch. The usual strategy is to provide large-scale liquidity support to the financial institutions and to limit losses by closing down unviable banks. The countries are now beyond the containment stage. Now in the restructuring and rehabilitation phase, the governments of Indonesia, Korea, Malaysia, and Thailand have all intervened in non-viable financial institutions and re-capitalized some of the viable, but weak institutions, and have begun to take steps to improve prudential regulation and supervision. Yet inadequate regulation, weak supervision of financial institutions, poor accounting standards and disclosure rules, outmoded laws, and weak corporate governance continue to pose problems. Moreover, since financial restructuring has involved the governments' injecting a large amount of capital into or nationalizing troubled banks, this has resulted in the state's owning a high proportion of the banking sector. Although governments are committed to privatizing the nationalized banks and divesting state ownership, the process has been slow—owing in large part to unstable market conditions and political sensitivity in selling bank assets to foreign buyers. Of greater concern is the fact that most banks remain heavily burdened with large volumes of non-performing loans, many of which may ultimately have a relatively low recovery rate.

Governments have pursued various approaches to corporate restructuring. One popular voluntary method has involved mergers and acquisitions (M&As). The number of M&As,

particularly those that are cross-border, has increased sharply. That is, total cross-border M&As, defined as acquisitions of more than 50 percent of equity by foreign investors, increased from some US$3 billion in 1996 to about US$22 billion in 1999. The largest rise was in Korea, accounting for roughly US$13 billion of M&As in 1999 (ADB 2001, 123). While M&As have been triggered by important policy changes, including the liberalization of investment in non-traded sectors and changes in competition policy, it is important to note that much of the M&A activity has been concentrated in such activities as wholesale and retail trade, real estate, and financial services. Overall, progress in corporate restructuring has been modest. There are several reasons for this. First, asset disposition has been slow, owing to the difficulty in valuing assets, thin markets for selling assets, and fear of selling them too cheaply. Secondly, many banks not only have insufficient capacity to absorb losses without facing a serious threat of closure, but in most countries operate with a full government guarantee on their liabilities, reducing any real incentive to undertake fundamental restructuring. Third, most banks have a limited technical capacity to restructure, while their long-standing links with corporations have complicated the restructuring process. Finally, the needed restructuring and asset sales have been hampered by disagreement between creditors over loss-sharing, and weak insolvency procedures, including creditors' reluctance to write down losses, have prolonged the liquidation of unviable companies.

Compared to their peak levels during the crisis, non-performing loan ratios have fallen in most of the crisis-hit countries. However, caution should be exercised in interpreting this decline. The reductions in non-performing loan ratios have been brought about by the transfer of such loans from banks' balance sheets to the government-owned asset-management companies (AMCs). While this has enabled banks to resume lending and support recovery, the real test of restructuring also hinges on the progress made in asset-disposal by AMCs.

Finally, the financial crisis left widespread socioeconomic distress in its wake, with massive job losses and bankruptcies. The resultant sharp rise in inflation (in the context of a considerably weakened labor market) exacted a heavy toll in terms of falling real wages and incomes. The combined effects of higher unemployment, inflation and the absence of a meaningful social safety net pushed hundreds of thousands, if not millions, of people into poverty. While the various social support systems introduced in Thailand, Malaysia, South Korea, and Indonesia helped to protect the most vulnerable sectors of society, much more needs to be done. In the immediate term, given that the scope for expansionary macroeconomic policies is greatly limited, it is imperative to develop a means-tested social assistance that provides minimum income support to the most needy. Only Korea has come close to developing such a system, in the long-term, sustained economic growth and continuing investments in health, education and social services are a must.

A NEW EAST ASIAN REGIONALISM?

Does East Asia's long-term salvation lie in a new East Asian regionalism? Obviously many East Asian governments think so. The single greatest push for East Asian regionalism has been the Asian financial crisis. The commonly held view in Asia (especially Korea and the ASEAN countries) was that they were let down by the West (in particular, the United States and Japan) during the crisis. In their view, since Western banks and financial institutions from the G-7 countries had created and exacerbated the crisis by suddenly pulling their funds from the region, it was only appropriate for Western governments to provide assistance. The fact that G-7 governments either declined individually to take part in the rescue operations (as was the case of the United States and Japan with Thailand), or required excessively stringent demands through the IMF, only served to aggravate the feelings of let-down and betrayal. At the same time it was widely believed that the United States (through the IMF) was not only dictating flawed policy responses to the crisis, but also that these self-serving policies had worsened the crisis by pushing Asian economies into a deeper economic recession. As Bergsten (2000, 24) notes:

> The single greatest catalyst for the new East Asian regionalism, and the reason it is moving most rapidly on the monetary side, is the financial crisis of 1997–98. Most East Asians feel that they were both let down and put upon by the West. In their view, western banks and other lenders created much of the crisis by pulling out. The leading financial powers then either declined to take part in the rescue operations, as the United States did in Thailand, or built the much-bally-hooed "second lines of defense" so deviously that they could never be used. At the same time, the IMF and the United States dictated much of the Asian response to the crisis.

Whatever the merits of such thinking, it is clear that Asian governments now agree that they must reduce their dependence on the G-7 countries and multilateral financial institutions like the IMF and the World Bank. Perhaps, most significantly, the celebrated APEC (Asia Pacific Economic Cooperation) has been severely compromised. APEC's failure at its Vancouver Leaders' Meeting in November 1997 to support Japan's proposal for an Asian Monetary Fund and its endorsement of the centrality of the IMF to the resolution of the crisis alienated many Asian governments from the organization. However, one cannot conclude that Asian countries are rejecting multilateralism and global economic integration. Rather, it seems that they want their own institutions and a bigger say in regional economic matters. More diplomatically, Asian countries claim that a regionally focused facility might be able to design more appropriate conditionality than the IMF because of the former's presumably superior regional expertise and its closer geographical proximity to its member countries.

The Asian Monetary Fund

The idea of the Asian Monetary Fund (AMF) dates back to August 1997, when Thailand approached the Japanese government for financial assistance. In response, Japan, along with several member countries of ASEAN, proposed setting up a separate monetary fund to provide emergency financing to countries affected by the economic crisis. The proposal was enthusiastically welcomed, as the ASEAN nations were only too eager to see Japan take on a greater leadership role (i.e. in the economic sphere) in the region. Moreover, there was an anticipation that the conditionality attached to AMF resources would not be nearly as strict as that imposed by the IMF. However, in its public relations campaign, ASEAN claimed that the AMF would not only promote regional cooperation and trust, but that there was a real economic rationale for such a body. Specifically, since trade tends to be regional, the affected region loses disproportionately from trade disruptions caused by currency crises. Thus it made sense that the regional governments work in unison to prevent the spread of financial crises. It was also argued that the AMF, like the Arab Monetary Fund and the Latin American Reserve Fund, would complement the IMF (Sussangkarn 2000).

By the end of September 1997, it seemed that the AMF would be a reality. The Japanese government pledged an initial US$50 billion, while an additional US$50–60 billion was to be raised through contributions from the PRC, Taiwan, Hong Kong, and Singapore (Yoshitomi and Shirai 2000, 67–9). It was argued that the AMF and its financing arm, the Regional Financing Facility, would provide sufficient liquidity that could be quickly mobilized to forestall speculative attacks on the region's currencies. Also, unlike the IMF assistance, funds from the AMF were to be unconditional, taking into account the individual needs of the member countries. As expected, the United States and the European Union were unequivocal in their objections. First, they argued that unconditional financial assistance would increase the risk of moral hazard, and second, that an independent AMF would undermine the IMF, because of the potential conflicts in their policy guidelines for member states. In the end "Japan decided to give up the proposal in November 1997, owing to the opposition by the United States and the IMF on the grounds that such an arrangement would enhance the problems of moral hazard and double-standards" (Yoshitomi and Shirai 2000, 68). Wade and Veneroso (1998b, 19), more bluntly note that "the United States Treasury pulled out all the stops to kill the proposal, and it died."

Although the proposal for the AMF did not get off the ground, the ASEAN finance ministers at the November 1997 APEC Summit in Vancouver agreed to establish a cooperative arrangement of regional surveillance (called the Manila Framework Group) through a better coordination between the member states' finance ministries and central banks. The Framework included the following initiatives: (1) a cooperative financing arrangement that would supplement IMF resources, (2) enhanced economic and technical cooperation, particularly in strengthening domestic financial systems and regulatory capacities, and (3) a mechanism for regional surveillance to complement the IMF's global surveillance. To enhance cooperation further, the ASEAN finance ministers (on October 4, 1998), formed the ASEAN Surveillance Process (ASP) to promote closer consultations on economic policies. The ASP has two major elements: (1) to monitor global, regional, and national economic and financial developments, and (2) to provide a forum where ASEAN finance ministers can share information and jointly develop collective action programs to counter potential threats to any member country and the region.[10]

On October 3, 1998, Japan formally proposed a "New Initiative to Overcome the Asian Currency Crisis." The most ambitious element was the "Miyazawa Initiative." Under this initiative, Japan pledged US$30 billion to support the crisis-hit countries. Half the pledged amount was to be dedicated to short-term capital needs during the process of implementing economic reforms. The rest was earmarked for medium- and long-term reforms. By February 2000, US$21 billion had been committed, with US$13.5 billion for medium- and long-term reforms. Korea has been the largest recipient (US$8.4 billion), followed by Malaysia (US$4.4 billion), and Indonesia and Thailand with US$2.9 billion each, and the Philippines (US$2.5 billion). The initiative has supported economic adjustment, financial and corporate restructuring, social safety nets, infrastructure, and export financing. In the second phase of the initiative, Japan has partially guaranteed sovereign debt issues, enabling countries to use limited public resources to mobilize private capital, thereby promoting private debt markets (World Bank 2000b, 152–3).

The Chiang Mai initiative

About a decade ago, Malaysian Prime Minister Mahathir Mohamad proposed the creation of an exclusive "East Asian Economic Group" (EAEG) comprising the ASEAN countries, China, Japan, and South Korea. Concerned as he was about the emerging trade blocs in Europe and North America, Mahathir's undeclared objective was to persuade the mentioned countries to shift their economic strategies along the lines of his own "look East" policy—with Japan as the economic focal point. While the EAEG proposal received lukewarm support from Asian countries (including Japan), it was vigorously opposed by the United States, Australia and New Zealand, because they felt that the EAEG would undermine the incipient Asia–Pacific Economic Cooperation (APEC) forum.[11]

However, the organization that actually expanded (with strong American backing) was the broad-based APEC (Asia–Pacific Economic Co-operation). However, in the aftermath of the Asian financial crisis, the ASEAN countries hastily created the "ASEAN+3" (comprising the 10 member countries of ASEAN, plus China, Japan, and South Korea) as envisaged earlier by Mahathir. Since December 1997, informal ASEAN+3 summits have been convened on an annual basis. They have already set up a "vision group" to explore ideas for cooperation, and have been holding regular meetings of their finance ministers.

However, the central task of ASEAN+3, besides setting up the vision group, has been to establish a surveillance mechanism to try to anticipate and head off future financial crises. Top-level discussion has also taken place regarding common currency baskets and joint intervention arrangements—to replace both the discredited dollar pegs of the past and the costly free floats imposed by the crisis.[12] Most dramatically, at the thirty-third annual meeting of the Board of Governors of the Asian Development Bank meeting in Chiang Mai, Thailand in June 2000, the finance ministers of ASEAN+3 committed their countries to even greater regional cooperation under the new "Chiang Mai Initiative." Specifically, they announced their agreement to share foreign-exchange reserves (through a region-wide system of currency swaps and repurchase arrangements) in order to defend their currencies against speculative attacks. The finance ministers reasoned that providing countries under pressure with short-term hard-currency liquidity would act as a firewall against future financial crises. To show their commitment, the ASA (ASEAN Swap Arrangement) was endowed with US$1 billion effective November 17, 2000. While the repurchase agreements (repos) are designed to allow ASEAN members with collateral like U.S. Treasury Bills to swap them for hard currency, and then repurchase them at a later date, it is hoped that hard-currency lines of credit can be made available to members without strict linkages to repos. Indeed, under the initiative, ASA is to be made available for two years and is renewable upon the mutual agreement of the members. Each member is allowed to draw a maximum of twice its committed amount from the facility for a period of up to six months, with the possibility of a further extension, which is not to exceed six months. In addition to ASA, members are encouraged to establish bilateral swap arrangements. In April 2001 Japan signed a bilateral swap arrangement with Malaysia, Thailand, and Korea totaling some US$6 billion. While the maximum amount that can be withdrawn under the bilateral swap will be determined by the two countries, in the spirit of regional cooperation all member states will be fully consulted when deciding the size of the disbursements.

Moreover, in keeping with the signed Chiang Mai Initiative, ASEAN+3 have committed themselves to work towards cooperation. In March 2001, the ASEAN Task Force on the ASEAN Currency and Exchange Rate Mechanism was established, with the ambitious task of working towards harmonizing the macroeconomic and exchange-rate policies of the member countries. Moreover, there is agreement to work towards a common market and a single Asian currency unit on the euro model. Even the IMF has given its blessing to this goal. In fact, the fund has expressed support for any regional initiative as long as it is complementary with the policy of the IMF. The IMF recently noted that "regional initiatives can be helpful in supporting sustained economic growth and stable financial relations among participating countries. In this vein, the recent Chiang Mai Initiative among ASEAN members and China, Korea and Japan is an important example of enhanced regional cooperation through which countries in temporary financial difficulties will be able to obtain foreign exchange from their neighbors through swap and repurchase arrangements" (IMF 2000d, 9). In this context, some have argued that the Chiang Mai Initiative is like the European Monetary System (EMS) arrangement. However, this seems to be a bit of an exaggeration. After all, the exchange rate mechanism (ERM) of the EMS provided for automatic and unlimited support of bilateral pegs. That is, the arrangement conveyed an essential message to the markets: any attempt at tearing apart any one currency from the others is bound to face strong official resistance, since the central bank is committed to put up unlimited amounts of its currency as a defense. In contrast, the amounts to be swapped within the Chiang Mai arrangement are limited and unlikely to be commensurate with the amounts that markets can mobilize.

In the end, how all these initiatives will actually work in practice remains to be seen. However, what once seemed a pipe-dream is now no longer that. The growth of cross-border trade is driving Asian economies inexorably towards closer cooperation. Suffice it to note that, the demands for regional arrangements to ensure currency stability and more efficient regional exchange transactions will grow. The Asian financial crisis vividly underscored the fact that Asian countries have a vested interest in cooperating with one another to minimize the systemic risk now inherent under globalization.

NOTES

1. Cited in DeRosa (2001, 186–7).
2. The Asian Development Bank (ADB) defines East Asia as the 10 Association of Southeast Asian Nations (ASEAN), including Brunei Darussalam, Cambodia, Indonesia, Laos, Malaysia, Myanmar, the Philippines, Singapore, Thailand and Vietnam), plus China and South Korea.
3. International credit-rating agencies such as Moody's, Standard and Poor and Fitch IBCA have raised their credit ratings for South Korea, Malaysia, and Thailand. Most importantly, in all three countries the capital inflows have been mostly non-debt-creating. Thus these countries have been able further to reduce their external liabilities. With short-term liabilities being redeemed, the maturity profile of the external debt has improved significantly.
4. Although the rupiah now seems to be less vulnerable and volatile than before, trading levels during the last week of February represent a depreciation of about 67 percent in U.S. dollar terms from its end-June 1997 level.
5. In the second half of 1999, Japan's GDP growth fell to 0.9 percent and to a negative 0.3 percent in the third and fourth quarters respectively. For details, see ADB (2000c, 5).
6. In Indonesia, a market-led decline in short-term interest rates resumed in the late 1999 as political uncertainty eased, but interest-rate levels continue to exceed those elsewhere in the region.

7. Short-term nominal interest rates have come down sharply and are now either below their pre-crisis level or close to it.

8. In the case of Indonesia, the net effect of higher oil prices on the government's fiscal position is unlikely to be substantial, as increased government revenues will be partially offset by the higher costs of the government fuel subsidy.

9. Prices of IT stocks tend to be more volatile and more closely correlated internationally than those of traditional non-IT stocks.

10. In addition to the usual monitoring of exchange rates and macroeconomic aggregates, the ASP also monitors sectoral and social policies, including provisions for capacity-building, institutional strengthening and sharing of information.

11. Although some Japanese officials viewed the EAEG proposal favorably, the Japanese government had to oppose it publicly in the face of strong opposition from the United States.

12. Although the finance ministers of ASEAN+3 met for the first time in Manila in April 1999, top-level discussions have been taking place since mid-1997.

THE CHINA MODEL

Chapter 17: The Era of Market Socialism 1978–1996

The death of Mao in 1976, and Deng's seizure of power in 1978, ushered in what has justly been described as a new era in Chinese development. The 'Gang of Four' Chen Boda (Mao's secretary) and five officers accused of plotting to assassinate Mao in 1971 were tried and imprisoned after a Stalinist show trial in November 1980 which was little more than a demonstration of the justice of the victors. The Party was purged of those, like Hua Guofeng and Chen Yonggui, who had been committed to the late Maoist development model. And late Maoist economic structures were progressively abandoned. Instead, China moved unequivocally in the direction of creating a market-orientated economy based on private ownership and presided over by an authoritarian state.

Nevertheless, there was nothing abrupt about this process of transition. On the contrary, its hallmark was gradualism.[1] This gradual process of change distinguished China from (say) Russia and the nations of the former Soviet Union, where moves towards democracy and privatization were abrupt. As a result, whereas the epithet 'capitalist' can justly be applied to these countries by the middle of the 1990s, the Chinese economy of the mid-1990s was still in all essentials a market socialist system. In other words, China began its transition much *earlier* than Russia, but it was well *behind* in terms of privatization and marketization by the time of Deng's death in 1997.

This chapter charts the unfolding of Chinese policy after 1978. However, because the progressive opening-up of the Chinese economy, and its extraordinarily rapid industrial development, have garnered so much attention. In this chapter, I focus on the debates

Chris Bramall, "The Era of Market Socialism, 1978–1996," from *Chinese Economic Development*, pp. 325–359. Published by Routledge. Copyright © 2009 by Taylor & Francis. Permission to reprint granted by the rights holder.

Chapter 17: The Era of Market Socialism 1978–1996 | 251

about which path China should take, the evolution of macroeconomic policy and the agricultural revolution.[2] Implicit in the time frame of 1978–96 adopted here is the assumption that Deng's death in early 1997 marks the beginning of a new era, during which the policy of gradual transition was abandoned in favour of a breakneck rush to embrace capitalism

ALTERNATIVE MODERNITIES

The Third Plenum of the Eleventh Central Committee of the Chinese Communist Party in December 1978, to give the full and tedious title of the meeting, confirmed Deng's accession.[3] The Plenum also ushered in a new phase in China's political and economic development. However, the Plenum itself did little more than lay the groundwork. The Party had to face up to the complex task of how to assess the history of the previous twenty years in such a way that the Cultural Revolution (and much of the late Maoist development strategy) could be repudiated without undermining the hegemony of the CCP. A communiqué on some of these issues was released at the end of the Plenum, but the definitive pronouncement did not appear until June 1981.[4] Note too that the Plenum did not announce a radical new economic policy; there was no real agreement amongst the leadership on the way forward at that time.

In some respects, in fact, there was continuity across the 1978 divide: Deng Xiaoping showed no inclination to promote Western-style democracy in the 1980s and no disinclination to persecute dissident Party members. The members of the Gang of Four were duly tried for their supposed 'crimes', Hua Guofeng was retired, Hu Yaobang was summarily dispensed with during 1987 for failing to combat 'bourgeois liberalism' and Zhao Ziyang was placed under permanent house arrest for his part in 'encouraging' the Tian'anmen protesters in 1989.[5] Some writers have made much of the supposed change in style in the treatment of Party opponents, but in fact the fate of the Gang was little different from that of Liu Shaoqi or Peng Dehuai during the Cultural Revolution. Moreover, the hand of retribution extended down to lower levels within Chinese society. Many of those seen to have profited 'unfairly' during the late 1960s and 1970s were purged and imprisoned during 1983 and 1984 (Unger 2007: 116). The justice of the 1980s was in truth little different from that of the 1970s; in both cases, it was the justice of the victors. Moreover, the Party remained only too willing to encourage mass protest by students whenever it served their purposes; the racist demonstrations directed against African students studying in China during 1985–6 are but one example. If the late Maoist era was marred by violence, the 1980s were little different.

Nevertheless, policy changed in many respects after 1978. For one thing, the post-1978 era was one in which economics, rather than politics, was in command. Deng's approach was thus much closer to the orthodox Marxian notion that the development of the forces of production should take priority, and that superstructural (political) change was subordinate to that goal. In concrete terms, this meant the repudiation of class struggle.[6] However, and in a clear break with Marx, the working assumption was adopted that China was in the primary stage of socialism: 'socialism' because the bulk of industry was in public ownership and exploitation had been ended, 'primary stage' because the development of the productive forces was essential and therefore a range of material incentives (inequality) was functionally necessary to raise productivity.[7] Whereas Marx had argued that capitalism had to precede socialism, the CCP took the view in the 1980s that a primary stage of socialism could serve as a substitute for capitalism. Zhao Ziyang (1987) summarized the approach thus:

> China is now in the primary stage of socialism. There are two aspects to this thesis. First, Chinese society is already a socialist society. We must persevere in socialism and never deviate from it. Second, China's socialist society is still in its primary stage. We must proceed from this reality and not jump over this stage [p. 641] … precisely because our socialism has emerged from the womb of a semi-colonial, semi-feudal society, with the productive forces lagging far behind those of the developed capitalist countries, we are destined to go through a very long primary stage. During this stage we shall accomplish industrialization and the commercialization, socialization and modernization of production, which many other countries have achieved under capitalist conditions [p. 642] … The principal contradiction we face during the current stage is the contradiction between the growing material and cultural needs of the people and backward production. Class struggle will continue to exist within certain limits for a long time to come, but it is no longer the principal contradiction [p. 644].

On all this, there was wide agreement within the CCP during the 1980s. The economics of late Maoism needed to be abandoned and replaced by some sort of strategy of *gaige kaifang* (reform and opening up). For all their disagreements, Deng Xiaoping, Chen Yun, Li Peng, Zhao Ziyang, Hu Yaobang, Zhu Rongji, and Jiang Zemin shared a common desire to repudiate many of the key tenets of Maoism. And yet, if the leading members of the Party were clear on what they were against, there was little agreement on what they were for. In particular, there was great uncertainty as to the scope of *gaige kaifang,* and considerable disagreement over the pace of the transition process. It is in this sense that Chinese economic policy-making after 1978 has been characterized as *mo shitou guohe* ('crossing the river by feeling for the stones').[8] In principle, three choices were open to China. It could revert back to the economic system of the earliest Maoist era (socialism). It could make a rapid transition to a market-orientated economic system (capitalism). Or it could put in place a system which combined elements of markets and planning (market socialism).

Back to the future? A return to the early Maoist model

The logic behind the first of these strategies would be to reform the system of central planning in an attempt to make it function more effectively. This was in essence the 'Old Left' view advanced by Chen Yun at the end of the 1970s, and it amounted to a return to the structures of the 1950s. More concretely, it would involve the restoration of family farming in agriculture, the removal of many of the restrictions on private industry and commerce and—perhaps most importantly for Chen—a reallocation of state investment away from defence, metallurgy and machine building, and towards light industry, and agriculture. This was the policy of 'Readjustment' which was pushed between 1978 and 1982. The focus was on structural rather than systemic change; private ownership would be countenanced, but the dominance of the state sector was to be preserved. In some ways, the model here was the New Economic Policy pursued in the U.S.S.R. between 1921 and 1928.9 Markets would be allowed to function, but this NEP model was not some form of market socialism, because price-setting would remain in state hands.

The NEP model continued to have its adherents throughout the 1980s. Readjustment (which, as we will see, was in many respects an attempt to restore the pre-1955 system) was abandoned after 1982, and in retrospect 1978–82 was the swansong for the Old Left; even the Tian'anmen massacre and the economic debates of that period did not lead to any significant policy reversal. Nevertheless, the Leninist NEP model continued to attract Old Left intellectuals such as He Xin well into the 1990s. For example, He Xin and others famously characterized the attempts by the World Bank to impose neoclassical economics on China as 'cultural imperialism' on the part of the U.S. establishment and as economic suicide for China. When allied to He Xin's fierce nationalism, this doctrine made for a powerful cocktail and attracted many adherents. The survival of some of these ideas was further strengthened by the emergence of a New Left, as represented by *(inter alios)* Wang Shaoguang and Cui Zhiyuan, during the 1990s. Both offered coherent and searching critiques of the market socialist model. Wang, for example, has argued powerfully against decentralization; only fiscal centralization (and hence central government transfers from east to west) offers a viable solution to the problem of regional inequality. And Cui's support of workplace democracy in the mid-1990s—his model was based on Mao's famous Angang Constitution -offered an appealing solution (not, however, to the Old Left) to the problem of SOE inefficiency. In a sense, Cui takes the democratizing logic of the Cultural Revolution one stage further. Thus the left was never entirely marginalized during the 1982–96 period and as inequality increased, so the appeal of its underlying message grew.[10]

The capitalist alternative: Anglo-Saxon, Rheinish and neoauthoritarian capitalism

The second theoretical possibility in the early 1980s was to make a complete transition to some form of capitalism. One variant on this theme, and the most radical solution, was of course to adopt the Anglo-Saxon model, in which state ownership was all but non-existent. The Japanese, French, and West German 'Rheinish' model of indicative planning, plus state ownership of some key industries, was also attractive. But the adoption of either form of capitalism would require a massive programme of privatization, and it was obvious that such a step might lead to very big rises in unemployment and hence threaten regime stability. Unlike many of the Western economists who have advised post-socialist regimes, the Chinese leadership was entirely realistic about the social consequences of privatization and hesitant about proceeding down that path. There was also a recognition that the underpinning of property rights by parliamentary democracy, a free media and an independent judiciary—all hallmarks of the Western democracies—would be impossible to combine with a one–party system. Accordingly, the models of authoritarian capitalism (or neoauthoritarianism as it was usually called in the debates of the late 1980s and early 1990s) adopted in Singapore, Taiwan and South Korea appealed much more, especially to Zhao Ziyang.[11] The Russian failure to prosper under an essentially democratic regime in the early 1990s served only to strengthen the position of the neoauthoritarians. Its central tenet was set out by Wu Jiaxiang: 'neo–authoritarianism is an express train toward democracy by building markets' (Wu 1989: 36). The long-run objective was democracy, but neoauthoritarianism was seen as the means to that end in the short run. This model thus combined a market economy—that is, essentially private ownership and market-based price-setting—with continued CCP rule. It would not be possible to combine authoritarian rule with a *fully* market-orientated economy because the property right uncertainty for private agents resulting from authoritarianism would lead to sub-optimal levels of investment. Private entrepreneurs would not invest if they risked profit and property confiscation, as they would in an authoritarian state. Accordingly, some state-led investment would be a necessity under this sort of system—as it is in Singapore. Nevertheless, compromise or not, such a system of authoritarian capitalism would be a world removed from the Maoist economic system which Deng inherited.

Chinese market socialism

The final alternative was to move much further down the path of market socialism than envisaged by Chen Yun or as practised in the early Maoist era. Chen's NEP model was built around the principles of extensive state ownership and price-setting by the state. However, one could in principle combine extensive state ownership with *market*-based price determination; this is the type of model which features prominently in John Roemer's (1994, 1996) conception of market socialism. Such a decentralized approach to price-setting would, at a stroke, remove the informational problems which had bedevilled central planners in the U.S.S.R., Eastern Europe and indeed China itself and thereby improve allocative efficiency. However, by retaining a large measure of public ownership, the equity objectives that are integral to socialism could nevertheless be realized. In effect,

Roemer's vision of market socialism does away with inequalities which derive from share ownership and from profits. Inequalities are allowed to exist, but only in so far as they reflect differences in productivity in the labour market.[12] Although few of China's planners consciously conceptualized the issues in this way, it was—as we shall see—precisely the model with which the People's Republic ended up in the mid-1990s.

THE EVOLUTION OF POLICY

In practice, the CCP chose to adopt the early Maoist model in the aftermath of the 1978 Third Plenum. Late Maoism was repudiated, and so to Chairman Hua's 'foreign leap forward.' However, there was no attempt at privatization in either urban or in (most of) rural China. Nevertheless, the set-up of new non-state firms was allowed, prices were altered by the state to more closely reflect notional market conditions and the more relaxed international environment meant that the defence industrialization of the late Maoist era could be brought to a conclusion. By 1982, however, there was a general perception that the more market-orientated of China's experiments had been most successful, and therefore that a more radical strategy was possible, and indeed desirable.

Between 1982 and 1989, therefore, policy-making became much more radical. Ownership reform was very much on the agenda as a wholesale process of agricultural decollectivization was pushed through across the Chinese countryside. Many price controls were lifted, as market forces were given an increasingly free rein. The process signalled the abandonment of the Leninist model, and a recognition that nothing less than some form of market socialism—characterized by liberalization and by the retreat of the state to occupy only the commanding heights of industry and infrastructure—would serve to generate rapid growth. However, price reform combined with macroeconomic expansion ignited an inflationary bubble which led directly to the democracy movement, and ultimately to the Tian'anmen massacre and the fall of Zhao Ziyang in 1989.

The drift towards market socialism began anew in the early 1990s. Price reform was completed between 1991 and 1996; the Tian'anmen repression and more contractionary macropolicy made that easier to accomplish by holding down demand and by cowing the workforce into accepting rises in the prices of key wage goods. In many ways, this was a classic neoauthoritarian programme. At the same time, many of the restrictions on foreign trade and inward investment were removed in the wake of Deng's 'southern tour' in 1992, which extolled the virtues of the special economic zones. However, macroeconomic policy again became overly expansionary, leading to a new inflationary bubble in the mid-1990s. For all that, a genuinely market socialist economy had been created by the time of Deng's death in 1997. Large swathes of the industrial sector remained in state hands, but virtually all prices had been liberalized and the open door policy had been implemented so fully that membership of the WTO became a realistic policy option.

Box 17.1 Chinese economic policy, 1978–1996

Phase	Title	Policy
1978–82	Readjustment	Industrial liberalization Readjustment of fiscal priorities Changes in the state-set relative price structure SEZs established
1982–9	The beginnings of market socialism	Decollectivization Further industrial liberalization Beginnings of market-based price determination
1989–91	Rectification: the Tian'anmen massacre and macro contraction	Suppression of student and worker dissent Cuts in government spending Transition to market socialism halted
1991–6	Completion of the market socialist project	Pause in the policy of opening-up Price liberalization completed Acceleration in the pace of opening-up Introduction of stock markets Fiscal and monetary expansion

This rather chequered path demonstrates one of the key truths about this era: there was no blueprint for reform, and no country which China could easily copy. The experiences of the East Asian newly industrializing countries were instructive, but the legacies of Maoism made China's situation unique. A new Chinese model of development had to be developed from scratch. It is therefore worth looking in more detail at the way in which policy unfolded after 1978.

READJUSTMENT, 1978–1982

Economic policy-making between 1978 and 1982 was dominated by the theme of 'Readjustment.' More precisely, Party policy was encapsulated in the slogan 'readjusting, restructuring, consolidating and improving the national economy' approved by the Central Committee in April 1979.[13] The central idea was that the growth rate could be accelerated by reallocating state investment from less efficient sectors (defence, metallurgy and machine-building to name but three) to more efficient sectors (in particular those which produced inputs for agriculture and consumer durables). The corollary was that ownership change was unnecessary. Structural change rather than systemic reform was all that was needed to accelerate the growth rate. Nevertheless, even though Readjustment was not an especially radical policy initiative, its adoption heralded the end of Hua Guofeng's 'foreign leap forward.'[14]

Several areas were identified for Readjustment: the ratio of agricultural to industrial production, the ratio of light to heavy industrial production, the structure of heavy industry itself (meaning increased production of inputs destined for agriculture and light industry) and the structure of agriculture (meaning less attention to grain production). Self-evidently, this was an agenda for balanced growth which was directed primarily towards the task of raising living standards by increased production of (non-grain) agricultural commodities and industrial consumer goods (Liang 1982).

The other key component of the Readjustment strategy was a change in the relative price structure. Policy here was designed to align state-set prices more closely with social marginal costs in an attempt to provide incentives to producers. This was a particular concern in respect of agriculture, where state procurement prices were so low by the late 1970s that it was impossible for communes to make any sort of profit on the production of a wide range of agricultural commodities; these included wheat, corn, vegetable oil and cotton, all of which were unprofitable to produce at some point or other during 1975–8 (Han and Feng 1992). This pro-industry bias in the internal terms of trade meant that there was little incentive for peasants to increase production, and it is therefore fair to conclude that one reason for slow agricultural growth under Mao was this distorted price structure.[15] China's planners sought to address this issue early in the Readjustment period. Accordingly, procurement prices were increased on average by 22.1 percent in 1979, the margin between the quota and above-quota price was increased and the state paid still higher 'negotiated' prices on still higher sales (Sicular 1988, 1989). This shift in the terms of trade towards agriculture continued thereafter. If the index of the terms of trade is set at 100 in 1978, it had risen to 150 by 1985 and to 189 by 1996 (Bramall 2000a: 315). However, more general attempts to estimate an 'optimal' relative price structure which could simply be imposed by the planners on the economy were far less successful. The central problem of how to calculate prices in a non-market economy without reference to demand remained (Naughton 1995: 129–30). Indeed it is revealing that very little attempt was made to adjust the price of energy even though Chinese energy prices were well below world levels. The coal price rose by about 6 percent in 1980, and it increased by more than the average for industrial products during 1980–2 (ZGTJNJ 2000: 305). Nevertheless, this change was far smaller than the adjustment required, and the price of energy was actually allowed to fall in 1980 and 1982 even though there was massive excess demand across the economy.

The period 1978–82 also saw considerable change in the structure of ownership, even though there was no attempt at privatization. By October 1981, nearly 40 percent of production teams had abandoned the collective and restored family farming. Controls on the operation of private industry were tacitly lifted in some parts of the Chinese countryside in the late 1970s. Wenzhou municipality in Zhejiang province was the pacesetter here; by 1982, about 12 percent of total gross industrial output value was being contributed by the private sector (WZTJNJ 2001: 203).[16] Some attempts were also made to reinvigorate state-owned enterprises. For one thing, the freeze on urban wages in force between

1963 and 1977 was lifted.[17] In addition, SOEs were allowed to retain a large proportion of their profits, and were granted much more autonomy in respect of the wage scales and the payment of bonuses; launched in Chongqing in 1978, these reforms were extended across most of the state sector during 1979 and 1980 (Wu 2005: 145). Furthermore, SOEs were allowed to sell some of their products at market-determined prices once they had met the requirements of the plan, an issue discussed further below. Still, it is worth emphasizing that no attempt was made to promote privatization during the Readjustment period. It was simply not on the agenda in the early 1980s.[18] The aim of industrial policy during this period was liberalization, not privatization.

The other important initiative in the Readjustment period was the establishment of four Special Economic Zones (SEZs) in Shenzhen, Shantou, Zhuhai (all in late 1979) and in Xiamen (October 1980). The aim was to attract foreign direct investment, and hence promote both exports (from newly established joint venture companies) and technology transfer. In order to do that, a relatively relaxed regulatory regime was established and tax holidays were granted. Two important but often neglected points about the SEZs need to be made.[19] First, the decision to establish the SEZs in south-east China—rather than in the key industrial centres of Shanghai and Liaoning—was only partly motivated by the proximity of Hong Kong. As importantly, it was a deliberate attempt to avoid 'capitalist contagion.' Guangdong and Fujian, the two provinces which hosted the SEZs, were comparatively under-industrialized and therefore little damage would be done if the SEZ programme spiralled out of control. Interestingly enough, Deng Xiaoping seems later to have concluded that it had been wrong not to have given SEZ status to Shanghai:

> In retrospect, one of my biggest mistakes was leaving out Shanghai when we launched the four special economic zones. If Shanghai had been included, the situation with regard to reform and opening in the Yangzi delta, the entire Yangzi river valley and, indeed, the whole country would be quite different. (Deng 1992: 363–4)

Second, the construction of the SEZs was financed to a very considerable extent by central government. For example, as well as direct financial subsidies, some 25,000 PLA engineers and workers were sent to Shenzhen (Kleinberg 1990: 58). Foreign investors certainly contributed, but the SEZ programme would simply not have happened without central government investment in infrastructure.

The macroeconomic aggregates show the impact of these various Readjustment policies (Figure 17.1). In fact, Chinese Readjustment was almost a classic example of a World Bank structural adjustment programme in that it cut government spending and shifted resources away to a more 'efficient' sector of the economy. Government spending as a proportion of GDP was cut sharply, falling from 31.5 percent in 1979 (when it was partially inflated by the war against Vietnam) to just over 22 percent in 1982. At the same time, the balance of industrial production shifted sharply away from heavy industry and towards light industry.

As a result, the share of light industry in industrial output rose from 43 percent in 1978 to 51.5 percent in 1981. In some of the provinces, the change was even greater. In Beijing, Liaoning, Sichuan, Jiangsu, Shaanxi, and Shandong, the light industry share rose by 10 percentage points or more between 1978 and 1981 (SSB 1990).

Particular sectors singled out for investment cuts were defence (especially Third Front projects), rural education and the production of agricultural machinery. For example, the abandonment of the campaign to 'learn from Dazhai,' at the heart of which had been the promotion of agricultural mechanization, led to a sharp fall in the production of agricultural machinery; its share in total industrial production more than halved between 1977 and 1981. Textiles were the main beneficiary; production as a percentage of gross industrial output value rose from 12.4 to 16.7 percent during 1977–81 (SSB 1985: 34–5). The Readjustment programme made itself felt particularly strongly in the rural CBE sector. The number employed in agricultural enterprises fell from 6 million in 1978 to 3.4 million in 1982, a period during which total employment in the sector rose from 28 to 31 million (MOA 1989: 292). However, the CBE industrial sector experienced extensive restructuring. The production of building materials and electrical equipment was sharply reduced, as was that of nitrogenous and phosphate fertilizers. By contrast, the production of textiles in CBEs greatly increased (XZNJ 1989: 44, 56, 59; MOA 1989: 298–9). In the process, labour productivity increased significantly; it more than doubled in agricultural enterprises and rose by over 50 percent in industrial CBEs.

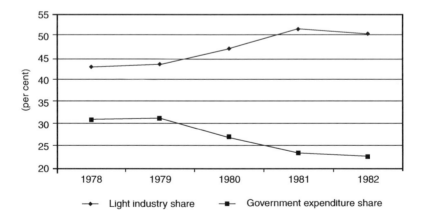

Figure 17.1 The impact of Readjustment.

(**Sources:** SSB (1990: 10); SSB (1999: 6 and 8).

Note: The government (budgetary) expenditure share is as a percentage of GDP at current prices. The light industry share is the share of light industrial production in the gross value of all types of industrial production (GVIO) at current prices.

The most visible short-run consequence of the Readjustment programme was a reduction in the growth rate of GDP. As Figure 17.2 shows, the rate of growth dipped from nearly 12 percent in 1978 to a mere 5.2 percent in 1981. This was well below the post-1978 trend and in fact, as we shall see, only in 1988 and 1989 was the annual growth rate below this for the entire 1978–2005 period. The readjustment may have been necessary, but the loss of output (relative to potential) that occurred during 1979–81 was very considerable for a comparatively poor country.

The long-run impact of the Readjustment programme is much more difficult to gauge. In part, this is because of the rash of systemic changes which occurred after the middle of 1982. It is therefore very hard to judge whether post-1982 trends reflected the medium-term impact of Readjustment or the accelerating rate of systemic change. Nevertheless, the impact on industrial structure was relatively long-lived. To be sure, the light-industry share fell back from over 51 percent in 1981 to 47 percent in 1985, but it was back up to 49 percent by 1988. In any case, even the 1985 nadir of 47 percent was still well up on the 43 percent of 1978. It therefore seems fair to conclude that the balance of Chinese industrial production was permanently altered, and there is little doubt that the increased supply of consumer goods did much to raise material living standards and to build a coalition of support behind Deng's reform programme.

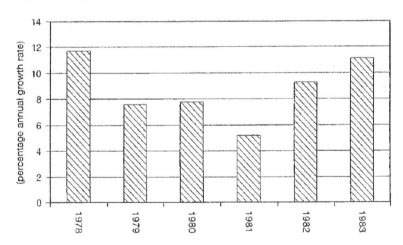

Figure 17.2 Annual growth rate of GNI during Readjustment (percentage change; comparable prices).

(**Source:** ZGTJNJ (2005: 53).

For all that, the consensus amongst most Chinese and Western economists is that the Readjustment programme did not go far enough to reinvigorate the economy. Even those sympathetic to the notion that extensive state intervention is a *sine qua non* for rapid growth have noted that the policies of 1978–82 left China with an economy which was still very recognizably Leninist: price-setting remained in state hands and only very limited privatization had been carried out. Much more change was needed if China was to create a genuinely market socialist economy. Those of a neoclassical persuasion within the Chinese policy-making bureaucracy itself were even more critical: for them, capitalism was the only way to guarantee rapid growth, and accordingly the reforms of 1978–82 were derisory in scope and impact. The Readjustment programme (similarly structural adjustment programmes) may have been essential to restore macroeconomic stability, but it did not go far enough in addressing the issue of continuing state ownership. Only privatization could resolve the fundamental problem of inefficiency caused by soft budget constraints.[20] The scene was thus set for a more neoliberal approach to economic policy-making after 1982.

DECOLLECTIVIZATION, PRICE REFORM AND THE ROAD TO TIAN'ANMEN, 1982–1991

As has been seen, economic policy-making between 1978 and 1982 focused on Readjustment rather than on systemic reform. After 1982, however, the advocates of Readjustment were increasingly marginalized, and the reformers assumed centre stage. The guiding principle for them was that it was entirely possible to combine a market economy with socialism. A number of Deng's speeches and statements during 1985 set out this agenda, which was to guide policy-making throughout the remainder of the 1980s and during the early 1990s (Deng 1985: 152):

> It is clear now that the right approach is to open to the outside world, combine a planned economy with a market economy and introduce structural reforms. Does this run counter to the principles of socialism? No, because in the course of reform we shall make sure of two things: one is that the public sector of the economy is always predominant; the other is that in developing the economy we seek common prosperity, always trying to avoid polarization. The policies of using foreign funds and allowing the private sector to expand will not weaken the predominant position of the public sector, which is a basic feature of the economy as a whole. On the contrary, those policies are intended in the last analysis to develop the productive forces more vigorously and to strengthen the public sector. So long as the public sector plays a predominant role in China's economy, polarization can be avoided.

Nevertheless, and it is a point that has often been made, the process of Chinese transition was gradual, and stands in sharp contrast to events in Russia (Nolan 1995). Not only did China travel a much smaller distance down the path towards a market economy in the 1980s and early 1990s (especially in that privatization was largely avoided), but also, in so far as China did liberalize, the pace of change was slow. In a very real sense, therefore, it makes sense to describe Chinese reform as gradualist, a process of 'crossing the river by feeling for the stones' *(mo shitou guohe)* or 'growing out of the plan' (Naughton 1995).

The result of this progressive reorientation of policy was a dramatic acceleration in the pace of change after 1982, at least compared to what had happened between 1978 and 1982. The two most dramatic changes were agricultural reform and the removal of price controls. Other changes did occur. Decision-making and fiscal powers were decentralized; China increasingly opened itself up to foreign trade; controls on private industry were progressively relaxed; and attempts were made to improve the performance of urban industry. However, the significance of some of these changes can easily be exaggerated. China remained only partially integrated into the world economy before 1992; little FDI was attracted during the 1980s and tariffs remained high. The changes in the urban industry sector fell far short of anything that could be styled privatization. Most would-be Chinese entrepreneurs were very reluctant to establish large industrial enterprises; they worried about being labelled as capitalist loaders. The private industrial sector therefore remained small. And the impact of fiscal decentralization has been exaggerated in much of the literature. It was less important in driving the growth of rural industry than has sometimes been claimed. The really significant changes in the 1980s were in agriculture and in price-setting. Let us consider these in turn.

The agricultural revolution

The Third Plenum of 1978 was chiefly important in an economic sense because it gave approval to a number of experiments. For all the continuities between the early 1970s and the era of Hua Guofeng, Hua's time in office was one of significant experimentation in economic policy-making. For example, the Plenum gave approval to small-scale attempts to invigorate state-owned industry by providing managers with greater decision-making power; Sichuan was in the vanguard.

However, experimentation was most dramatic in the sphere of agriculture, where the introduction of family farming and private markets in poor regions were more or less condoned by local officials.[21] This process of agricultural experimentation was especially marked in Anhui under the leadership of Wan Li, and in Sichuan province (presided over by Zhao Ziyang). The reforms there were judged to be a great success by 1978; the famous slogan *yao chifan Zhao Ziyang; yao chimizhao Wan Li* ('if you want to eat grain, call Ziyang; if you want to eat rice, call Wan Li') was already in wide circulation.

The initial reforms in agriculture, especially in Anhui and Sichuan, focused not on changing ownership or even the management of collectives but rather on reducing the tax and procurement burden, and giving teams much more discretion over cropping patterns. For example, many aspects of Maoist agricultural policy were reversed under the slogans of *fangkuan zhengce* ('relax government controls') and *tiyang shengxi* ('recuperate and multiply'), which were popularized across Sichuan as early as the spring of 1977. Private commerce, for example, was encouraged. Triple cropping of grain was largely abandoned; it had proved impossible to achieve in many areas because of labour shortages and because the growing season was too short. Instead, communes were given much more freedom over the range of crops cultivated.[22] And the policy of *tiyang shengxi* led to big reductions in taxation and procurement quotas in poor areas. In conjunction with better weather (1976 was a particularly bad year) and the introduction of the full Green Revolution package, the effect was to bring about a surge in agricultural production in 1977 and 1978.

Indeed, although the restoration of private farming occurred in some poor parts of China during 1976–1982, there was no *general* programme of decollectivization in the late 1970s and indeed the process of decollectivization was very slow.[23] Accordingly, although some (for example Sachs and Woo 1994) have characterized Chinese agricultural reform as an example of shock therapy or big bang, it actually makes more sense to characterize the process of change as gradual (Box 17.2).

Box 17.2 Agricultural institutions, 1976–1964.

Chinese name	Translation	Peak year
baochan daozu	contracting production to work groups	1980 (25 percent)
baochan daohu	contracting production to households	1981 (26 percent)
baochan daozu (or dabaogan)	contracting everything to households	1983 and after (94 percent in December 1983)

Source: Chung (2000: 64–5).

Note: The peak year data, refer to tile year in which the highest percentage share of teams using that system was recorded.

The initial management reforms divided production teams into smaller units or groups. This was the system of *baochan daozu,* and in its essentials was little different from collective farming.[24] The logic behind *baochan daozu* was that the problems of supervision and control of the labour force which afflicted Chinese collectives could be obviated by creating smaller units of production. Production groups, being smaller than teams, would ensure that the value of each work point would be much more closely related to labour productivity, and hence discourage shirking (Liu 1994). The system *of baochan daohu* was much more of a hybrid because it restored most management decisions to households even though decisions concerning income distribution remained in the hands of the collective. Only the system of *baogan daohu* was family farming proper, because, as the name suggests, this involved contracted all decision-making, and transferring assets, to households.[25] This system has also often been called the household responsibility system because it delegates the responsibility for farm management to households.

Anhui is the province usually credited with pioneering reform, and there is no doubt that decollectivization did occur early in some of it as counties; the case of Fengyang, where decollectivization began in 1977, is the best-known example, However, Anhui as a whole moved rather slowly to embrace family farming. In fact, Guizhou was the only province where more than 50 percent of production teams had adopted family fanning by the end of 1980. Nationally, the 50 percent figure was reached only in December 1981, and even this figure included households practising *baochan daohu* (which was not family fanning at all). Sixty-seven percent of teams had introduced the *baogan* system prior to June 1982, and given that the bulk of the harvest is sown and collected during the summer and early autumn, we are justified in seeing 1982 as the first year in which a preponderance of the harvest was produced on family farms. Only by December 1983 was the process of decollectivization complete; by then, 94 percent of teams had restored family farming (Chung 2000: 64–5). The following year, the final step in the process was taken when it was announced that communes, production teams and the production would be abolished, their administrative functions being taken over by the newly restored *xiang* (township) and *cun* (village). The agricultural system has remained largely unchanged ever since.

Given this relatively slow pace of change, there is an argument for seeing the entire period between December 1976 and December 1983 as a transition period between collective and family farming. Alternatively we can use December 1981 as the point at which the dominance of family farming was restored.[26] Yet however we date it, evidently the second land reform was a gradual process, certainly much more so than the introduction of collective fanning during 1955–6. Family farming—the system of *baogan daohu*—had been adopted by less than 40 percent of production teams even as late as the autumn and winter of 1981. In other words, the Chinese countryside was still dominated by collective farming at the end of 1981.

It remains a matter for debate whether this process of Chinese decollectivization was spontaneous or pushed from above.[27] My own interpretation is that much of the initial decollectivization, especially in mountainous and poor areas, was driven by popular demand and encouraged by local leaders. Given that material living standards and yields had risen only very slowly in these areas in the late Maoist era, it was almost inevitable that a return to family farming would be looked upon favourably; almost anything was deemed worth trying. In more prosperous parts of China—the counties on the Chengdu plain (Endicott 1988: 134), Sunan, Yantai in Shandong and virtually the whole of Manchuria—decollectivization was widely resisted. In Heilongjiang, for example, only 9 percent of teams had adopted *baogan* even as late as May 1982, by which time the national figure was around 70 percent (Bramall 2000a: 328–9). In part this resistance reflected the hostility of provincial leaders, but it was grounded in a recognition that a return to small-scale farming would hamper mechanization and the maintenance (still more the expansion) of irrigation systems. As a result of the 1979 price change, the introduction of new seeds and greater availability of chemical fertilizer, the agricultural sector was booming in many parts of China during the early 1980s and it is therefore far from obvious that collective farming was an obstacle to agrarian progress. Thus, as Hinton (1990) argued so eloquently, decollectivization imposed real costs on the Chinese countryside, and its universal imposition across China was arguably as unwise as the earlier decision in 1955–6 to impose collectives.

(a) Agricultural performance after 1978

There is no doubt that the *package* of agricultural reforms was very successful in the sense that output surged in the late 1970s and early 1980s.[28] Table 17.1 brings together data on the growth of overall agricultural output and grain production. It shows that there was a period of very rapid transitional growth between 1981 and 1984, reflecting a combination of weather (1980 and 1981 were years of flooding whereas 1984 was a very good year), a reduction in underreporting of output and a range of policy changes, both institutional and structural.

Table 17.1 Agricultural growth rates, 1963–2006 (percent per annum).

	Growth of agricultural GVA	Growth of farm sector output	Growth of grain production
1963–81	2.9	3.3	3.5
1981–84	10.6	9.5	6.8
1984–2006	3.9	4.3	1.0

Sources: SSB (1999: 4 and 31); ZGTJNJ (2006: 59, 462 and 466); SSB (2000a: 37 and 462); ZGTJNJ (2007: 465 and 478).

Note: GVA is at 1980 prices. Farm sector output refers to the gross value of farm output (not value-added), measured at 1980.

But the sort of miraculous growth achieved between 1981 and 1984 was not sustainable; the trend rate of growth between 1984 and 2006 fell back to about 3.9 percent per year.[29] Of course this was considerably faster than the trend growth rate between 1963 and 1981 of about 2.9 percent per year; as Figure 17.3 shows, the growth rate was clearly faster (the trend line is steeper) after 1984 than it had been between 1963 and 1981. Nevertheless, the difference in growth rates between the two periods is by no means as dramatic as often suggested.

Why did growth accelerate in the 1980s? In essence, the explanation lies in the package of agricultural reforms introduced in the late 1970s and early 1980s. The combination of decollectivization, new seed varieties, the completion of irrigation projects, greater supplies of chemical fertilizer and more favourable relative prices proved highly effective. One part of this package particularly deserves emphasis because it is often neglected, namely the changing composition of agricultural output. A change in macroeconomic priorities, in conjunction with the decentralization of decision-making to farm households, led to far less emphasis on grain production, and indeed less emphasis on farming in general. As Table 17.1 shows, the rate of growth of grain production was much slower after 1984 than

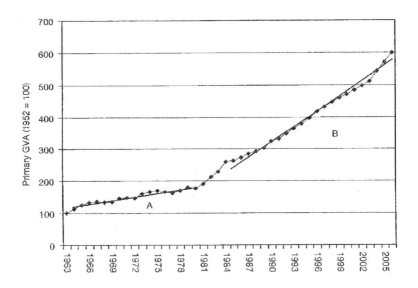

Figure 17.3 The growth of agricultural value-added, 1963–2006.

(**Sources:** SSB (1999: 4); ZGTJNJ (2007: 59).

Note: The solid lines A and B indicate approximate trends during the periods 1963–81 and 1984–2006 respectively. They are provided for illustrative purposes only. Agricultural GVA is at comparable prices and calculated by aggregation of subsectors.

it had been during the Maoist era. This provides a clue as to what has going on. In effect, China has been shifting its rural labour force and its inputs away from grain farming and towards more profitable subsectors such as animal husbandry and fisheries. In 1978, farming accounted for 80 percent of GVAO, and animal husbandry and fisheries for 15 and 2 percent respectively. By 2006, farming was down to 51 percent whereas husbandry stood at 32 percent and fisheries at 10 percent (ZGTJNJ 2007: 465). Thus the rapid growth of agricultural GVA reflects not so much the dynamism of the individual agricultural subsectors, but rather the increasingly greater weight of animal husbandry, fisheries and non-grain crops in total output. None of this is to criticize the post-1984 agrarian strategy, but we do need to recognize that agricultural growth has been driven as much by a change in policy objectives as it has by the reform package per se.

(b) Continuing agricultural problems

Chinese agriculture has grown quite quickly during the 1980s and 1990s, as we have seen. However, its efficiency remains low and it is beset by a range of problems. Even relatively optimistic scholars such as Rozelle and Huang (2006) have drawn our attention to some of China's failures (and its productivity implications) even whilst emphasizing the more positive aspects of China's record on technical progress in the farm sector.

For one thing, Chinese agriculture has become very reliant on massive inputs of chemical fertilizer. Total usage in 1975 was 5.5 million tonnes but this had risen to 17.4 million by 1984, 40.8 million in 1998 and to 47.7 million tonnes by 2005 (SSB 2005b: 44; SSB 2006: 469). As a result, China's per hectare usage was second only to Japan by the mid-1990s (Maddison 1998: 113). The People's Republic is nearing the point where further growth will lead to declining yields, and the environmental consequences (especially in terms of pollution of water) are already apparent (Smil 2004: 118–19). Widespread use of plastics is also causing considerable problems, not least for the use of agricultural machinery, and declining use of organic fertilizers is likely to produce declining soil fertility in the near future (Veeck and Wang 2000: 66 and 76).

A second problem is the deterioration of China's irrigation system, which had a seriously adverse effect on total factor productivity in the rice sector and offset the positive effects of the introduction of new varieties. The Green Revolution technologies introduced across the world in the late twentieth century comprised a package of technology: irrigation improvement (such as tube wells, drip irrigation systems, and large-scale water control projects), high yielding (and increasingly GM) varieties and increased use of chemical fertilizer. Without increased water availability to complement the other elements in the package, the rise in yields is typically small. Irrigation is therefore crucial, and in this regard the decollectivization of the early 1980s caused a range of problems. In particular, it fragmented control of the irrigation system and made it difficult to mobilize labour for irrigation maintenance and construction, which produced a growing number of disputes between households over access to water, especially in the north of China. Many scholars have drawn attention to the problem (Vermeer 1997; Nickum 1990b; Watson 1989; Nickum 1995: 67–70; Hinton 2006: 194), and whilst Vermeer is right to caution against the conclusion that the water conservancy system has collapsed, there is no doubt that it has deteriorated significantly in quality as structures (including tube wells) have been neglected or abandoned. In addition, although the introduction of water fees in the 1980s may well have encouraged a more efficient use of water—a point celebrated by some authors (Johnson *et al.* 1998)—the reduction in consumption has delayed the introduction of high-yielding new varieties which are water-using.

The third key problem is that of small farm size, compounded by the fragmentation of holdings (Hinton 2006: 193). This problem dates back to the decollectivization settlement of the early 1980s, which sought to equalize the quantity and quality of land allocated to households by dividing village land up into small plots. The net result was that a typical household received plots of land which were scattered across the village. The data for 1986 show that 51 percent of farms were less than 0.3 hectares in size, and this figure had gone up to 54 percent in 1990. And the comprehensive Agricultural Census of 1997 found that no less than 79 percent of holdings were of less than 1 hectare in size; the comparable Japanese figure was 71 percent in 1986. In fairness, however, it remains a matter for debate whether average farm size is too small. For example, some studies have found little evidence of economies of scale (Wan and Cheng 2001), though these types of studies do not properly allow for the gains from the mobilization of labour for infrastructural projects.

The case against parcellization is much more generally accepted. The data show that a typical farm was divided into nearly ten non-contiguous parcels in 1984–5. This had fallen to around six plots by 1990, about the same degree of fragmentation as reported in Buck's prewar survey (Bramall 2004: 125–6). A number of recent studies confirm that parcellization hampers technical efficiency (Nguyen *et al.* 1996; Tan *et al.* 2006); one estimate suggest that an end to fragmentation might increase grain output by as much as 70 million tonnes (Wan and Chen 2001: 192). Other trends associated with parcellization are also a cause for concern. Small-scale tractor use increased more than tenfold between 1978 and 2005, and the usage of agricultural machinery has increased approximately sixfold since 1978. However, small tractors were used as much for transport purposes as for agricultural work; China's agricultural parcels were too tiny even for small tractor use in many cases. More significantly, the number of large and medium-sized tractors increased very slowly after 1983 and peaked in 1987 at 881,000. Thereafter it declined, to reach a low of 671,000 in 1996. The total has increased since; the figure for 2005 was 1.4 million (SSB 2005b: 36; SSB 2006: 467). Nevertheless, the slow overall pace of growth serves to underline the way in which decollectivization recreated small-scale farming and thereby slowed down the release of labour. Decollectivization has served to recreate the prewar agricultural landscape, with all its embedded inefficiencies.

The conundrum which confronts the Chinese authorities is the same as that with which the governments of Taiwan and Japan have wrestled since the end of the Second World War. The solution lies in land consolidation schemes. But the difficulty is in devising policies and institutional structures which will promote such consolidation. Even in Japan, and despite much postwar effort, the percentage of farms of less than 1 hectare in size fell from 73 percent in 1955 to only 71 percent in 1986 (Kojima 1988: 733–34). In Taiwan, considerable energy has been put into carrying out what has been styled a second land reform based around land consolidation, but the process has been very slow (Liu *et al.* 1998).

The final constraint that China confronts is that large-scale agricultural imports are not really an option, and therefore the need to ensure food security by means of domestic production remains. It is true that the political constraints on China's foreign trade have eased immeasurably since the late 1970s. Furthermore, reductions in transport costs (especially within China as a result of Maoist investment in railways) and the development of international grain markets make large-scale grain imports an altogether more plausible proposition. Nevertheless, China's policy-makers continue to shy away from reliance on large-scale imports of food, principally because that would entail dependence on the U.S.A. That is not surprising given that the two countries are fast becoming global competitors. In principle, however, China could significantly increase its dependence on imports and at the same time ensure diversity of supply by reliance on Canada, Brazil and southeast Asia as well as the U.S.A. In fact, the problem is more economic. Precisely because China is not a small country, it is not a price-taker in world markets. Accordingly, even a comparatively slight rise in imports would exert significant upward pressure on world food prices, thus adversely affecting China's terms of trade. That in turn would require China to export every increasing quantities of industrial goods, at falling prices and against a background of all the protectionist concerns that this type of policy would ignite in industrialized countries. Moreover, China's entry into the World Trade Organization has restricted its freedom for manoeuvre because it limits the extent to which barriers to imports, whether tariffs or subsidies, can be utilized.[30] It therefore seems likely that China will become a growing net importer of grain over the decades ahead.[31] The rise in net imports during 2004–5 therefore seems to offer a portent of what is to come.

(c) A property rights solution?

It is relatively easy to enumerate the problems faced by Chinese agriculture. It is much harder to identify the solutions. In essence, however, we can think of two different approaches to the agricultural problem. One sees the solution in more secure property rights and improved market functioning. The other regards the state as part of the solution rather than the essence of the problem.

The market-led approach sees agricultural inefficiency in China as rooted in insecure property rights and malfunctioning markets. This insecurity discourages investment and technical progress.[32] In particular, it discourages land sales and the creation of larger farms operating non-fragmented plots of land. Larger farms would make it easy to resolve irrigation problems (by reducing the collective action problems which inevitably stem from having a myriad of small family farms), as well as allowing the exploitation of those economies of scale which do exist in farming. The creation of proper land and rental markets, as well as the development of rural labour markets, is therefore crucial to agrarian progress. From this perspective it also follows that the development of capital markets is necessary so that farmers can borrow the funds required for land purchase, and for agricultural investment.

From this market-led perspective, Chinese decollectivization did not go far enough, because it did no more than transfer land management rights, rather than ownership, to households. And fifteen-year land management contracts introduced after decollectivization did little to encourage investment. Even though many were replaced by thirty-year year contracts in the late 1990s, many villages continued to award comparatively short-term (five- to ten-year) contracts (Krusekopf 2002). At the same time, the Chinese state did little to encourage the development of rental and finance markets, both necessary concomitants for land consolidation to occur.

These problems persisted into the 1990s (OECD 1997; Nyberg and Rozelle 1999). However, a number of academics have argued that the functioning of Chinese rural markets has improved significantly in recent years. Commodity markets are well integrated, land markets have developed quickly since the 1990s and many of those left behind by the process of out-migration have benefited from the increased scope for renting arable land (Carter and Rozelle 2001; Brandt *et al.* 2002; Rozelle and Huang 2006). From this perspective, China is moving in the right direction but a good deal more needs to be done if the productivity of agriculture is to be increased significantly.

Part of the solution to the problem of insecure property rights lies in reduced government intervention. It is argued that the problem is not merely that local government across China is guilty of sins of omission but that it has committed sins of commission. That is, farm land continues to be owned by village-level government, and this level of government has periodically redistributed land from household to household ensuring that even land management rights were insecure (Judd 1992; Zhu and Jiang 1993). In part the aim has been to hold inequality in check by ensuring that even the poorest households continue to have access to land. But, perhaps more importantly, China's villages have tried to allocate land in such a way as to concentrate it in the hands of the most efficient farmers. The most common system of land management is the *liangtianzhi* (two-field system). This involves households being allocated two types of land in addition to private plots First, households received *kouliangtian* (grain ration land) as part of the decollectivization settlement. This land was usually allocated on a per capita basis, the aim being to ensure that each household managed enough land to meet its subsistence requirements. Second, and in addition, households could usually sign a contract with the village to manage additional land (responsibility land or *zerentian)* in return for agreeing to meet a part of the procurement quota imposed by central government. In 1990, *zerentian* land accounted for 360 million *mu* in those parts of China using the *liangtian* system; *kouliangtian* accounted for a further 180 million *mu*. In addition, Chinese villages retained a reserve of land. Some of this was used to provide feed for pigs. And some was rented out *(chengbaotian)* in return for a fee and the households agreeing to take on an additional part of the village's procurement quota. Crucially, the allocation of land was not set in stone at the time of decollectivization. As households have died out or migrated, *kouliang* land reverts to the land reserve controlled by the village government. Conversely, the village allocates more *kouliang* land to households which are growing in size. Additionally, it is village government which makes decisions about how much land would be contracted out and whether households wishing to contract land represent a good or bad risk. To be sure, a secondary land market exists whereby households which have contracted land in turn lease out that land to other households. Nevertheless, it is local government which continues to exercise control. As a result, the market for land in rural China is far removed from that found in most other countries, whether developed or underdeveloped. Usufruct rights are to some extent permanent and heritable, but the system is altogether less market-driven than is the norm in both developed and developing countries.[33]

(d) Beyond property rights: the role for the state

The market-driven perspective on China's agricultural challenges outlined in the previous section is problematic. Some scholars are sceptical as to whether insecure property rights are holding back agricultural investment (Kung 1995). More fundamentally, secure property rights would not circumvent collective action problems and coordination failures: market failure is inevitable, and there is thus a *prima facie* case for state intervention. The development, maintenance and expansion of irrigation networks provides a classic example of a collective action problem which is not easily resolved by reliance on market-led interaction amongst small family farms. It is for precisely this reason that the expansion of irrigation in India was less rapid than in China in the late Maoist era. It is also telling that the introduction of a land law in Vietnam in the early 1990s explicitly designed to promote land sales has largely failed to increase farm size (Ravallion and van de Walle 2001). Landlessness has increased (mainly because well-to-do farmers have sold their land, rather than because of distress sales), but small-scale farming and fragmentation remains a severe problem, especially in the relatively fertile rural region around Hanoi.

The market-driven perspective is also problematic because, as noted above, the redistribution of farmland by the state between households has played a key role in holding income inequality in check. Any move towards a fully market-based system would run the risk of producing big differences in income from farming, and thus exacerbating the high pre-existing level of inequality in the countryside (which stems from differences in the amount of income derived by each household from the non-farm sector). In short, China's pressing need is for *more state intervention* in the rural sector rather than for less. That need not presage a return to collective farming but it does suggest the need for a very different state-led approach if the problem of agricultural inefficiency is to be resolved.

The logical conclusion to draw from this critique of the market-led approach is that the solution to China's continuing agricultural problems lies in increased state intervention designed both to hold down inequality and to promote farmland consolidation schemes. The logic here is clear: market-led solutions may push the process of consolidation along in the right direction, but are unlikely to be carried out as quickly or as effectively as they can be by a proactive state. The same is true of essentially cooperative solutions aided by state funding, as in Taiwan's second land reform of the late 1970s and early 1980s. These schemes did help to increase farm size and yields (Liu *et al.* 1998) but in general have been only a partial success, seemingly because of the reluctance of governments to fully commit to consolidation schemes (Bain 1993). The Chinese government has also been rather reluctant to proceed too rapidly down this route, even though the evidence points strongly to the benefits from the Comprehensive Agricultural Development programme which was introduced in the late 1980 (Wu *et al.* 2005).

Implementing a state-led solution to China's agricultural problems will not be easy. In particular, a renewed attempt by the state to boost agricultural output by increasing farm prices seems unlikely to succeed. Trends in relative prices between the late 1970s and the

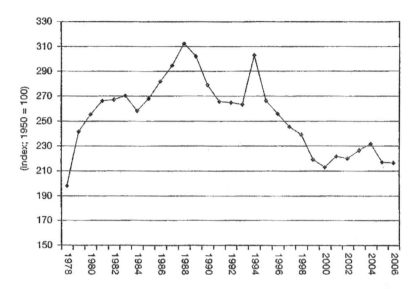

Figure 17.4 The internal terms of trade, 1978–2006.

(**Sources:** SSB (2005a: 32–3); SSB (2005b: 203); ZGTJNJ (2007: 325 and 327).

Note: The internal terms of trade is the index of agricultural product prices (procurement prices before 2001) divided by the index of agricultural producer good prices (industrial goods selling in rural areas before 1978).

late 1980s were largely favourable to agriculture; as Figure 17.4 shows, the internal terms of trade were on an upward trajectory throughout the 1980s. This helped to maintain the growth of the early 1980s. After 1988, however, agriculture did much less well. In that year, the terms of trade reached their highest level in the post-1949 era, and thereafter prices shifted against agriculture. The trend between 1994 and 2000 was particularly unfavourable, the index declining from 303 to 213. In no small measure, this was because of big rises in agricultural production, which depressed product prices in the market-orientated environment of the late 1990s. But in a sense, it was almost inevitable that relative farm prices would fall as China became more integrated into the world economy. Grain prices were typically well above world prices at the end of the 1970s, and even in 2000 that remained true for many commodities when differences in quality are taken into account.[34] The Chinese wheat price, for example, only appears to be lower than the world price because Chinese wheat is of much lower quality than the high-grade wheat which is imported; contrast the results in Huang *et al.* (2004: 89) and Carter (2001: 80). It is therefore likely that the long-run effect of WTO accession will be to depress the price of maize, cotton, sugar and soybeans, though meat, rice, and horticultural prices will probably rise (Huang *et al.* 2004: 89 and 94).

There has been some revival in the terms of trade since the nadir of 2000, but it is clear that China's agricultural sector has been operating in a much more hostile macroeconomic environment during the last two decades than in the halcyon days of the late 1970s. These adverse price trends have impacted severely upon farm incomes, as will be discussed below. Worse, there is no easy solution to this problem. A policy of direct price-based subsidies to farmers seems to offer an obvious way forward; this was the course followed by the E.U. in the postwar era. However, this type of policy is largely ruled out by the terms of WTO accession. In any case, it would be extremely expensive given the size of China's farm sector, and arguably of doubtful utility because the subsidies would probably be 'captured' disproportionately by richer farmers. Pricing policy may have been effective in accelerating growth in the late 1970s, but the scope for such a policy no longer really exists. The agricultural problem will have to be solved by other means.

Fiscal policy offers one such means, not least because the state's treatment of agriculture has not been especially generous since 1978 (Huang *et al.* 2006). Measured purely in terms of financial flows (and thus ignoring any resource extraction via the terms of trade), agriculture was a net contributor to the rest of the economy. These flows were partially via the fiscal system. The contribution of agriculture to total state revenue rose during the post-1978 period, mainly because higher taxes on fruit and vegetable production offset declining income from grain. Mandatory procurement quotas also imposed an implicit grain tax on the farm sector.[35] Furthermore, state investment in agriculture hardly changed between 1978 and 1997; a significant decline in irrigation investment is especially apparent. Nevertheless, total state investment in agriculture exceeded taxation and in that sense the priorities of the Chinese state were clear. The primary channel for financial outflows was in fact the banking system, and in this way a very substantial proportion of agricultural savings financed investment in the industrial sector. Nor is it evident that things have changed dramatically in response to the perceived crisis of the late 1990s. For example, the share of state spending on agriculture rose substantially in 1998 but, taken as a whole, there was no real trend between the late 1980s and 2004; the figure remained at around 8 percent (SSB 2005b: 77).

The other possible solution is to reduce the price of agricultural inputs. The Chinese industrial sector has of course become much more market-orientated since 1978 as SOEs have faced growing competitive pressure from imports, from TVEs and from the private sector. Nevertheless, the rapid pace of productivity growth has not translated into substantial price falls for agricultural means of production such as plastics, chemical fertilizers, and machinery. This suggests that Chinese manufacturing continues to enjoy a considerable degree of protection and monopoly power—as it has done since 1949. In other words, the problem of unequal exchange remains. Further liberalization in this area may be the best way forward for a China serious about promoting the development of agriculture.

Price reform

The second main focus of policy between 1982 and 1989 was price reform. There were two obvious differences between China and Western economies in the late 1970s. For one thing, asset ownership was vested in the Chinese state, and little changed in this regard until the late 1990s. Second, Chinese prices (including wages and interest rates) were set by the state instead of by market forces. The relative price structure was altered during the Readjustment period, as we have seen, but the fundamental approach remained: prices were set by the state rather than by market forces. All this changed during the mid- and late 1980s (Chan 1989; Yabuki 1995).

There were several arguments in favour of a move towards price-setting by market forces. The main problem for economic planners in the 1970s was the impossibility of determining whether a sector was efficient. This was because profit rates were far more closely related to the prices which enterprises were allowed to charge than to underlying economic performance. For example, mining and large swathes of agriculture were unprofitable because the prices set by the state for their products were far too low.[36] By contrast, enterprises which manufactured consumer goods were immensely profitable by virtue of the high prices which could be obtained. There were thus vast differences in profit rates in 1984 which largely reflected the distorted price structure. The rate of pretax profit in light industry was 56 percent and 76 percent for chemicals, whereas that for the coal industry was only 3 percent (Zhang 1988: 90–1).

One solution to this problem was for the state to alter the price structure; there was no need to introduce a market-based system of price determination simply to deal with this problem. Indeed Oscar Lange famously argued in the mid-1930s that it was quite possible for a socialist state to set prices. The central planning bureau only needed to start with prerevolutionary prices and then adjust them to reflect the evidence of shortage and oversupply; it need not compute the price for every good at every moment in time. By the late 1970s, however, it was clearly recognized that the whole business of state price-setting was a much more complex process.[37] For one thing, a vast range of commodities (each of different qualities and specifications) existed. Even if the state responded to shortages and surpluses only in the manner prescribed by Lange, the costs involved in setting prices for all these commodities were very high and therefore the inevitable tendency was for prices to be changed only very slowly—which meant that prices were out of line with those that the planners felt desirable. In addition, it made for an exceptionally difficult planning process. Precisely because so many goods were inputs into other types of production, the planners needed to consider very carefully the impact of any given price change. For example, increases in agricultural prices necessarily cut urban wages and reduced profitability in the food-processing sector. That was not necessarily a bad outcome, but there were clearly both economic and social consequences which needed to be considered. A big increase in coal prices also had profound ramifications for the rest of the economy. The obvious alternative approach was to leave price determination to market forces, though that too was not without its costs. That was because a shift to a market-based system of price determination would inevitably reintroduce a high degree of uncertainty into economic life as a result of speculation and fluctuations in both demand and supply.

Yet, and irrespective of whether the solution adopted was price adjustment by the state or reliance on market forces, the main problem posed by price reform was that it would produce general inflation. Relative price adjustment would invariably take the form of price increases rather than falls; a cut in the average price level would require a cut in money wages, the hardest of all things to achieve given worker resistance. These price increases would feed into inflation directly, and any attempt to cushion the blow by providing price subsidies would have fiscal implications—and as likely as not fuel demand-pull inflation. Of course inflation could in principle be controlled readily enough by complementing relative price adjustment with contractionary fiscal and monetary policy, but that would tend to depress the growth rate.

In the mid-1980s, the CCP took the view that inflation was a price worth paying for the allocative gains that would follow from adjusting the relative price structure, and for the maintenance of rapid growth. Influential here was the view of Li Yining, who was a close adviser to Hu Yaobang (the Party secretary) and Hu Qili. Li saw little cause for concern in inflationary pressures. He perceived the increase in the money supply, which was the consequence of pressure on the state budget, as largely benign in that it was growth-promoting; much better, he argued, for demand to exceed supply than the converse (Li 1990). Li doubted that the Chinese population had a high degree of 'social tolerance' for inflation but was even more sceptical of the utility of combining price reform with macroeconomic contraction.

The centrepiece of the price reform strategy of the mid-1980s was the dual-track pricing system. There were two elements to this. First, enterprises were allowed to sell a significant (and rising) proportion of their output outside the plan. Second, the price at which extra-plan sales could take place was allowed to diverge from planning prices. Between 1982 and 1984, the permitted range within which above-plan sales could take place was plus or minus 20 percent of the centrally-determined price. However, it was increasingly recognized that this type of restriction was unworkable. In October 1984, therefore, this restriction was removed; the 'Decision of the Central Committee of the CCP on Reform of the Economic Structure' effectively allowed above-plan sales at *market* prices. This policy certainly had the effect of providing an incentive to firms to increase production. However, it also created abundant opportunities for corruption; by buying commodities at central planning prices and selling at market prices, speculative profits could be made; thus was born the phenomenon of *guandao* (profiteering) and spiralling income inequality. Moreover, the scope for making speculative profits was very large indeed because of the divergence between market and plan prices. In December 1988, for example, the average market price of steel was, *yuan* compared to a plan price of 592 *yuan*. As for trucks, the price for a *Dongfang 12o* selling in Shenyang was 63,800 *yuan* compared with a plan price of 25,800 *yuan* (Yabuki 1995: 130).

The dual-track pricing system was only one part of the price reform process. In addition to introducing the dual-track approach, the number of commodity prices subject to any form of state control was reduced. The prices of 160 commodities were fully liberalized in September 1982, and another 350 in the autumn of 1983 (Chan 1989: 312). More agricultural and light industrial products were liberalized in January 1985. Most radically of all, the prices of non–staple consumer goods -including vegetables, fish and meat—were significantly increased in 1985 (Shirk 1993: 301). In the main, however, these price rises were offset by subsidies to the urban population, and the net effect was a combination of rapid growth but spiralling inflation. The steady post-1979 increase in farm procurement prices had not been accompanied by any corresponding increase in the consumer prices charged to urban residents. In effect, therefore, the state was paying a growing price subsidy to the urban sector, and the scale of these subsidies was running at around 30 billion *yuan,* or 13 percent of government spending by 1988 (SSB 1999: 8). Although the subsidy burden in percentage terms had not increased since 1981, the need to finance a growing absolute volume of spending inevitably put great pressure on public finances and contributed to inflationary pressure within the Chinese economy. Indeed it was only with some difficulty that the inflationary bubble of 1985–6 was brought under control, albeit at the cost of abandoning the big change in industrial producer prices which had been initially planned for) 986 (Shirk 1993:296–309).

The apparent insouciance of Hu Yaobang over the effects of rising prices (like Li Yining, he saw moderate inflation as a price worth paying for rapid growth), as well as his perceived failure to act more decisively against the student disturbances of 1986, left him politically isolated even though the inflation rate in 1985 was still running at less than 10 percent (Figure 17.5). Hu was replaced as Party secretary in early 1987 by Zhao Ziyang, who had successfully portrayed himself as a relative conservative in abandoning the mooted 1986 price reforms (Shirk 1993: ch. 13). Under Zhao, and acting on the advice of Wu Jinglian, China sought to combine continuing relative price reform with a more contractionary macroeconomic stance after 1986. In this, Zhao was backed by Deng Xiaoping (1988: 257–8): 'We cannot speed up the reform without rationalizing prices … we have no choice but to carry out price reform, and we must do so despite all risks and difficulties.'

Zhao's strategy focused on lifting controls on four non-staple commodities, namely meat, eggs, vegetables, and sugar, without any attempt to cushion the blow by paying subsidies. Moreover, it was announced that these changes were but the beginning of a more extensive process of price reform, and indeed much of this was accomplished; by the end of 1988, only 25 percent of commodities were subject to full-scale state control, leaving around 25 percent subject to floating prices (i.e. prices were allowed to vary within a specified band) and the remaining 50 percent being market-determined (World Bank 1990: 59). In retrospect, it was a mistake to announce such radical price reform in advance. Its effect, combined with actual price rises, fuelled panic buying and this served only to intensify inflationary pressure. In February 1988, retail prices were 11 percent higher than they had been in January 1987. By August, the inflation rate was running at 23 percent and in February 1989 it peaked at 27.9 percent. For some goods, the inflation rate was much higher; the inflation

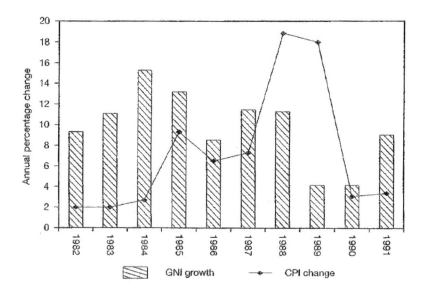

Figure 17.5 Growth of gross national income and the consumer price index, 1982–1991.

(**Sources:** ZGTJNJ (2005: 5): SSB (1999: 21).

Note: The growth of GNI is at constant prices. The CPI is the official consumer price index.

rate for vegetables peaked at 48 percent (August 1988) and that for meat, poultry, and eggs at 44 percent in October 1988 (World Bank 1990: 165).

With the CCP bent upon pushing through these relative price changes, the only way to deal with the inflationary spiral was a process of fiscal and monetary contraction.[38] This was the approach adopted during 1988–9, and it triggered a collapse in output growth. As Figure 17.5 demonstrates, macroeconomic contraction was ultimately successful in that sense that the inflation rate was brought down; from a peak of nearly 19 percent in 1988, the rate fell back to a mere 3 percent by 1990. However, the cost in terms of growth was very considerable. Deng Xiaoping (1988: 258) had hoped as late as May that 'the growth rate for 1988 may still exceed 10 percent' and in that respect he was right; actual growth exceeded 11 percent. But growth slowed markedly thereafter, with GNI registering increases of only a little over 4 percent in both 1989 and 1990.

The contraction of 1988–90 was costly in terms of bankruptcy and rising unemployment in the small–scale private sector. More importantly, the price rises of 1988 and 1989 fuelled the democracy movement by encouraging urban workers to join with students, culminating in the great demonstrations and massacre at Tian'anmen Square in June 1989.[39] This was the classic demonstration of Deng's new authoritarianism: an increasingly market–orientated economy underpinned by an authoritarian and ruthless state. Hu Yaobang had been purged in 1987 for his support for bourgeois liberalism, and Zhao Ziyang paid the same price in 1989. For those who died in Tian'anmen Square and the subsequent witch hunt, the penalty was much greater. In addition, the need to deal with the political turmoil necessarily brought the process of economic liberalization to a halt. The process of reform was not to resume until 1991.

THE LAST HURRAH: DENG'S SOUTHERN TOUR AND BEYOND, 1991–1996

The transition to market socialism was relaunched in 1991. The background to this was the collapse of the Soviet Union (and the failure of the attempted coup there in August 1991), and the triumph of the coalition forces in the First Gulf War, which provided a startling demonstration of U.S. military capability. These events made it clear that the CCP faced a stark choice if it was to remain in power. It could reverse the transition process, attack corruption and inequality and recentralize the planning process—thus preserving the sort of Leninist state which Gorbachev had dismantled in the U.S.S.R. during the late 1980s but running the risk of halting the growth process in its tracks. Alternatively, the CCP could attempt to rally popular support by abandoning the contractionary macroeconomic policies of 1988–90 (thus increasing the pace of economic growth) and using some of the fruits of growth to promote defence modernization and hence a nationalistic agenda.[40]

Deng's choice was to accelerate the pace of economic growth and to relaunch the marketization process. He signalled this course during his trip to Shanghai (February 1991), and his *nanxun* (southern tour) to Shanghai and to Shenzhen in February 1992. Many parts of his 1992 speeches reveal Deng's intent very clearly, namely to push ahead with reform, to secure socialism by means of authoritarianism and state ownership of the key industries and to increase the growth rate:

> We should be bolder than before in conducting reform and opening to the outside and have the courage to experiment. We must not act like women with bound feet … So long as we keep level-headed, there is no cause for alarm. We have our advantages: we have the large and medium-sized state-owned enterprises and the rural enterprises. More important, political power is in our hands … Right tendencies can destroy socialism, but so can Left ones. China should maintain vigilance against the Right but primarily against the Left. The Right still exists, as can be seen from disturbances. But the Left is there too … Our three-year effort to improve the economic environment and rectify the economic order was a success. But in assessing that effort, we can say it was an achievement only in the sense that we stabilized the economy. Should not the accelerated development of the preceding five years be considered an achievement too? (Deng 1992: 360, 361, 363 and 365)

Two of the main themes of the 1990s were the rapid opening-up of the economy to foreign trade and investment, and renewed attempts to enhance the efficiency of the industrial sector. Yet more important than anything in rekindling the growth process was monetary and fiscal expansion, and Deng (1992: 364–5) seems to have regarded it as perfectly normal to have periods of rapid growth (such as 1984–99) broken up by short periods of rectification and stabilization. The government accounts show the renewed expansion very clearly (Figure 17.6). State capital construction, which had stagnated in the late 1980s, helped to pull the economy out of the doldrums in 1990, and accelerated the pace of growth during 1994–5. Government consumption expenditure helped to moderate the downturn in 1989 and provided a massive stimulus in 1991 and 1992, when it grew by 20 percent in each year. At the same time, and in order to prevent the central government deficit spiralling out of control, a process of fiscal recentralization was initiated by Zhu Rongji, the new Premier, starting in 1994. Its central aim was to reverse the trend whereby central government budget revenue had fallen from about 35 percent of GDP to only 15 percent between 1979 and 1993.[41]

The net result of all this was accelerating growth. In each of the years 1992–4, the growth rate of real GNI comfortably exceeded 12 percent, well up on the 4 percent recorded in 1989 and 1990 (ZGTJNJ 2005: 53). That the inflation rate also spiralled—the consumer price index rose by 15 percent in 1993 and 24 percent in 1994 (ZGTJNJ 2005: 301)—suggests that these sorts of growth rates were unsustainable, and Zhu Rongji moved quickly to take the growth rate down to around 9 percent by the late 1990s. For all that, the achievement of such rapid growth points to the underlying vitality of the Chinese economy right up to the time of Deng's death in early 1997.

It deserves to be emphasized that the rebound of the economy, as well as the rapid growth which had been achieved between 1982 and 1988, was achieved under a system of market socialism. The 'market' features of the system were market-based price determination and the liberalization of entry by private firms. By 1995, for example, 78 percent of the value of producer good sales, 89 percent of retail sales and 79 percent of farm commodity sales were at market prices (OECD 2005: 29). By that time, too, the intensity of competition was high across the whole economy as the result of entry by private and foreign-owned firms. And the People's Republic was deeply embedded in the world trading system. In all these respects, it makes sense to describe the Chinese system using the word market. But in many key respects, this was still a socialist economy. As we have seen, the industrial sector continued to be dominated by state-owned enterprises operating in both rural and urban areas. Tariff barriers, though lower than they had been in the 1980s, were still high; in that sense, China's international economic integration was only partial. Controls on the migration of labour between urban and rural China were easing, but they were still powerful in the mid-1990s. Stock markets had been created in Shanghai and Shenzhen, but these were weak and sickly things. And the extent of income inequality, though much higher than it had been in the early 1980s, was not extreme by international standards. By the end of 1996, the transition to capitalism had not been completed, and there is every reason to suggest that this was by design, and not by accident.

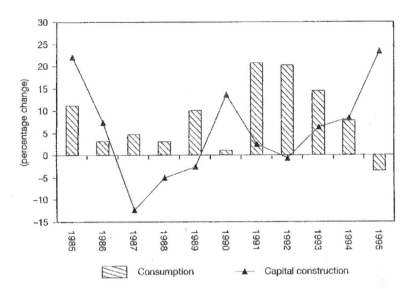

Figure 17.6 Growth of government consumption and capital construction expenditure.

(**Sources:** World Bank (1997a: 124); SSB (1999: 11).

Note: 'Consumption' is the annual growth of real general government consumption expenditure (GDP basis), measured at 1990 prices. The growth of capital construction expenditure by government is measured at current prices.

CONCLUSION

The Chinese economy of 1996 that Deng surveyed from his deathbed was recognizably different from that he inherited in 1978. Collective fanning had been swept away and replaced by a system of small-scale family farming. China had opened up further to the world economy, and was increasingly a magnet for foreign direct investment as well as a supplier of cheap but low-quality manufactured exports. Rural industry had enjoyed more than a decade and half of extraordinary growth. Virtually all prices were determined by the market instead of being set by the state.

Yet the China of 1996 was still far removed from being a market economy. Property rights were vague and insecure, posing a threat to investment in agriculture and industry alike. The average rate of tariff protection on imports continued to be high, and levels of inward investment were still very low. Guangdong province was relatively open, but the rest of China bore the characteristics of a closed economy. Perhaps most importantly, the bulk of the industrial sector remained firmly in the hands of the state. In fact, the role of the state had actually expanded in the Chinese countryside: the most numerous industrial enterprises were those owned by townships and villages, not those owned by the nascent private sector. And in the cities, large state-owned enterprises continued to hold sway. To be sure, the official data show a slightly different picture (Jefferson and Singh 1999: 27). By 1996, those enterprises formally designated SOEs produced only 29 percent of gross industrial output. But when one adds to this the output of collective enterprises—urban collectives, county-owned collectives, township enterprises and village enterprises—the true share of the state sector rises to around 70 percent.[42] Given that SOEs and urban collectives were larger and boasted higher productivity than household industries, their share in value-added was even higher. Some of the collective enterprises may have been private enterprises in disguise; many private sector capitalists feared a policy reversal which might leave them vulnerable. But even allowing for this, we still have the conclusion that the state sector was producing well over 50 percent of industrial output in 1996. This is far above the share controlled by the state in advanced capitalist economies.

We are therefore entitled to regard the Chinese economy of 1996 as still recognizably different from that to be found in other countries. The drift to capitalism in China had gone far, but this was still a market socialist economy at the time of Deng's death. The very fact that it was a hybrid—that it combined elements of state and market in a way that was different from both the China of 1978 and the America of 2007—helps to explain why it was able to generate such rapid growth in the two decades after Mao's death. That, however, takes us ahead of our story and to an assessment of China's performance as a market socialist economy. Before moving on to that, we need to document the extraordinary changes which occurred in the industrial sector, and in China's relations with the world economy, between 1978 and 1996.

NOTES

1. For some of the literature and debates about the extent to which the Chinese model was characterized by gradualism, see Sachs and Woo (1994), Nolan (1995), Naughton (1996) and Bramall (2000).

2. I take the story on agriculture all the way through to 2006. There has been no real change in agricultural policy or performance since 1996 and therefore it makes little sense to impose such an artificial dividing line.

3. A useful, though necessarily partial, biography of Deng is that of Yang (1998). For a summary of Deng's reacquisition of power during 1977–8, see Huang (2000: ch. 7). The 1978 'truth criterion' debate is discussed in Schoenhals (1991). It is sometimes suggested that policy after Mao's death was dictated by the 'Eight Immortals' (Deng Xiaoping, Chen Yun, Peng Zhen, Yang Shangkun, Bo Yibo, Li Xiannian, Wang Zhen and Song Renqiong), a phrase traditionally used to refer to eight Daoist deities, but now used by some Chinese scholars in a more contemporary context. All eight certainly played a role in the Chinese Revolution but, Deng and Chen aside, this was a group of mediocrities. This was undoubtedly one of the reasons Mao was content to dispense with their services during the Cultural Revolution; indeed, Li Xiannian's disastrous handling of the economy in the early 1970s forced Mao to recall Deng Xiaoping (MacFarquhar and Schoenhals 2006: 377–9). As for the contribution of the others, Song Renqiong's

very status as one of the eight is uncertain (some accounts list Wan Li), Yang Shangkun was purged in the early 1990s for attempting to usurp power, and seven of them (Deng was the exception) were part of the Readjustment faction which vehemently opposed marketization in the early 1980s (see below). The part played by Zhao Ziyang, Zhu Rongji and even Li Peng in formulating and executing the development strategy of the 1980s and 1990s was far greater than that of the 'Immortals' (again Deng is the exception). In short, the contribution of the 'Immortals' to Chinese economic development was as negligible as that of the Daoist sages on whom they were modelled. It is for this reason that the phrase is used much more by Western journalists than by Chinese scholars.

4. This was the document 'On Questions of Party History,' which has been reprinted in translation in a number of sources, e.g. Liu and Wu (1986).

5. Hua 'volunteered' his resignation as Premier in September 1980, and was forced to resign as Chairman of the Central Committee and of the Central Military Commission in June 1981.

6. As noted in the previous chapter, the notion of self-reliance was progressively abandoned after 1972. Although post-1978 policies are often called *gaige kaifang* (reform and opening up), the process of *kaifang* had been initiated by Mao and continued by Hua Guofeng.

7. According to Zhao (1987: 644), the 'primary stage of socialism' would last for about a hundred years (starting from the 1950s, when socialism was established). The term itself first seems to have been used by Su Shaozhi. The phrase 'primary stage of socialism' does not feature in Marx's writings.

8. There is now an extensive literature on the post-1978 policy package. For a variety of perspectives, see Naughton (1995), Nolan (1995), Bramall (2000), Lin *et al.* (2003), Wu (2005) and Hart-Landsberg and Burkett (2005). For a good diagnosis of many of the problems faced by China in 1980, see Xue (1981). For the policy debates of the 1980s, see Sun (1995), Hsu (1991) and Shirk (1993). Most of the best Chinese literature focuses on the problems which have emerged in the late 1990s as a result of this transition strategy, and will be discussed in the next chapter.

9. For an introduction to NEP in the Soviet Union, see Davies *et al.* (1994).

10. The problem for the Old Left was its inability to articulate a plausible economic alternative to traditional state ownership in the industrial sector. As Cui Zhiyuan has argued, some form of worker management constitutes a plausible alternative in one sense (cooperative management certainly can work), but that was not really acceptable to the Old Left, because it amounted to conceding state control to the working class. It did not help that He Xin's intellectual background was in literary studies, though paradoxically it allowed him to understand rather better than most economists the manner in which the master discourse cloaks its true agenda beneath the mantle of

freedom and choice. For the views of such critically engaged intellectuals, see Fewsmith (2001) and Zhang (2006).

11. Key advocates of neoauthoritarianism in the circles around Zhao Ziyang were Wu Jiaxiang, Zhang Bingjiu and Xiao Gongqin.

12. It is simply not true that Chinese inequalities by the 1990s reflected no more than differences in productivity. However, the Dengist conception of *an lao fenpei* (distribution according to work done) was unambiguous enough in principle.

13. For discussions of the economics and politics of readjustment, see Xu (1982) and Fewsmith (1994).

14. In political terms, we can think of 1978–82 as a period of struggle between the 'readjustment' (*tiaozheng*) and the 'reformist' (*gaige*) factions within the CCP over the degree to which systemic (ownership) change to the economic system was needed. The readjustment faction was led by Chen Yun and the grouping included Li Xiannian, Peng Zhen, Wang Zhen, Bo Yibo, Deng Liqun, Hu Qiaomu and Yao Yilin. Its economic analysis was supported by the bulk of economists based at the State Planning Commission and the People's University in Beijing. Zhao Ziyang, Hu Yaobang, Wan Li and Hu Qili were much more closely associated with the notion that reform was needed, and economic advice was provided to them by *(inter alios)* Xue Muqiao, Dong Fureng, Yu Guangyuan, Sun Shangqing, Liu Guoguang and Chen Yizi. This group increasingly advocated a neoclassical policy solution: only privatization and a hardening of budget constraints offered a proper and lasting solution to the problem of industrial inefficiency.

15. The extensive literature on intersectoral resource flows and pricing issues includes Ishikawa (1967), Nakagane (1989), Karshenas (1995), Sheng (1993) and Knight and Song (1999).

16. For an introduction to the development of Wenzhou, see Nolan and Dong (1990).

17. Urban incomes did increase during this period, but only because of growing participation rates amongst women.

18. One of the best accounts of initial industrial reform in China is that given in Chai (1998). See also Naughton (1995: ch. 3) and Otsuka *et al.* (1998: ch. 2).

19. One of the very few useful accounts of the SEZ programme is that of Kleinberg (1990).

20. From a theoretical viewpoint, there is a recognition that a readjustment programme almost inevitably leads in the long run to the collapse of planning. Kornai (1992) is the classic source here. Leninist systems have a coherence about them, but attempts to make incremental changes will lead to their collapse because of the emergence of all manner of contradictions between the market and non-market sectors. China's dual-track pricing system, for example, was a recipe for corruption and could lead only to pressure for further, more dramatic, changes.

21. Agriculture is divided into four subsectors in China: farming, animal husbandry, forestry and fisheries. Household sideline activities (such as handicraft production), though a separate category during the 1980s, are now included within farming.

22. Triple cropping of grain—two rice crops and one wheat crop—was widely promoted in the late 1960s and early 1970s. The literature on these agricultural reforms includes Shambaugh (1982), Donnithorne (1984), Wang (1988), Bramall (1995) and Chung (2000).

23. For a discussion of the reform process, see Ash (1988), Du (1996) and Bramall (2000). For discussions of decollectivization, see Chung (2000), Kelliher (1992), Zhou (1996) and Unger (2002).

24. This sort of system was by no means uncommon in the late Maoist period. Magaoqiao production brigade in Sichuan, for example, used it in the early 1960s, and reintroduced it again after 1971 (Endicott 1988: 127 and 129). In that sense, the continuities between the Maoist era and that of Deng are much stronger than is usually recognized.

25. It needs to be emphasized, however, that full ownership rights—especially the right to sell assets—were not transferred to households, something which has arguably caused problems in the late 1980s and during the 1990s (as will be discussed below).

26. There is no sense, however, in seeing 1978 as the turning-point, at least as far as output trends are concerned.

27. For some of the literature, see Watson (1984), Zhou (1996), Kelliher (1992) and Chung (2000). For all the brio of Zhou's account, I find it very hard to take seriously her notion that it was 'a spontaneous, unorganized, leaderless, non-ideological, apolitical movement' (Zhou 1996: 15).

28. I stress 'package' here because there is much debate about the role played by decollectivization in the process of accelerating output growth.

29. Inspection of the data suggests that there was a clear break in the series in the early 1980s, with comparatively steady growth on either side. The trend growth rate was undoubtedly higher after 1984, indicating an apparent step-change in agricultural performance.

30. For international trade issues and the effects of WTO entry on Chinese agriculture, see Gamaut et al. (1996), Garnaut (1999), OECD (2001), OECD (2002b), Diao et al. (2003), and Bhattasali et al. (2004).

31. The picture, however, is complex. Rice and wheat were not subject to much protection in 2001, whereas maize and cotton both benefited from export subsidies; imports of these last two are likely to increase. However, the Chinese government retains a good deal of discretionary power to limit imports, especially via the way the way in which VAT is levied on imports but not on many agricultural commodities traded on the domestic market (Bhattasali et al. 2004: 5–7 and 81–98). Given that the level of protection on Chinese imports has declined steadily since 1978, WTO entry should be conceived of as being another step in the liberalization process, rather than a climacteric.

32. This approach is typical of much contemporary development theorizing, as exemplified by Ray (1998). The development 'problem' is reduced to one of incomplete or missing markets, an approach which grapples adequately with neither the problem of

pervasive uncertainty (which ensures that markets will always fail to generate efficient outcomes) nor that of the ways in which class relations bias market outcomes against both efficiency and equity. The very possibility that the only way to deal with market failure is to eliminate the market in question is rarely considered. Ultimately, of course, the problem is to identify the second-best solution: is it a badly functioning market or ill-conceived state intervention? There is no theoretical high ground to be seized here; that which works in practice is inevitably very context-specific, depending as it does on state capacity and the quality of governance.

33. The property law passed by the NPC in March 2007 is unlikely to change the situation very much, because its focus was essentially on urban property rights. It does help somewhat by allowing leases on farmland to be renewed when they expire. However, the power to appropriate land enjoyed by local government remains, and the law does not allow the mortgaging of land, which is a necessary step if a land market is to develop properly.

34. The crux of the problem for Chinese farmers in the late 1970s was that input prices were too high (as reflected in the high rates of profit being made in the industrial sector), not that product prices were too low.

35. The rate of extraction from the rural sector (as opposed to the agricultural sector) was much higher because of taxation levied on township and village enterprises.

36. According to Wright (2006: 165): 'up to the mid-1990s, the state's economic priorities expressed through the fixing of prices were the most important negative influence on coal mining profits.'

37. This formed the basis for the critique of price-setting (and hence the very concept of socialism as an operational economic system) by von Mises and Hayek. For a discussion of the Lange model and criticism thereof see Gregory and Stuart (1974: ch 9), and Nove and Nuti (1972).

38. The process of rectification also led to the reimposition of controls on some prices. By 1990, the prices for seventeen agricultural products were still set by the state and a further eleven were subject to state guidelines. The prices of twenty-four primary products or processed agricultural products (e.g. wheat flour) were similarly controlled. As for industry, the prices of some 742 products were subject to state control (Yabuki 1995: 128).

39. The massacre was applauded by a number of Western academics, who dismissed the suggestion that the number of deaths ran into the thousands as exaggeration, and argued that it was functionally necessary to uphold the authority of China's neoauthoritarian state.

40. For the politics of the revival of the reformist agenda, see Fewsmith (2001: ch. 2).

41. The Chinese fiscal system and the 1994 reforms are usefully discussed in Brean (1998).

42. China's collective enterprises were *de facto* state enterprises. Many of them were actually more closely controlled by the state than the SOEs themselves.

Chapter 18: Chinese Capitalism Since 1996

BY CHRIS BRAMALL

I t is not difficult to argue that the death of Deng Xiaoping in February 1997 was a climacteric in Chinese economic policy. His death, one might argue, removed the last check on the growing authority of Jiang Zemin and resulted in the abandonment of the market socialist vision articulated by Deng for so long.[1] Whether one dates the change from the articulation of the policy of radical industrial restructuring *(zhuada fangxiao)* at the 14th Party Congress (1995), the start of the Ninth Five Year Plan period (1996) or from the death of Deng himself, there is little doubt that economic policy changed significantly in the mid-1990s. Most obviously, China has joined the WTO, privatized many of its SOEs and TVEs and abandoned its attempts to control internal labour migration. The rhetoric of socialism may have been retained, but the true goal of the CCP over the last decade has been to effect a rapid transition to a full-blown capitalist economy; the decision to allow private-sector capitalists to become Party members in 2001 at the urging of Jiang Zemin was the most symbolic step.[2]

An alternative reading of the evidence would be that the commitment of the CCP to socialism remains undiminished. Although Jiang moved China in the direction of capitalism, his socialist credentials remain evident from the energy injected into the west China development programme, and continuing state ownership of around 30 percent of the production of the industrial sector. And the commitment of Hu Jintao, Jiang's successor, is even more apparent. He has, for example, articulated a vision of 'a harmonious society' and the creation—based around *(inter alia)* the abolition of school tuition fees in rural areas—of a new socialist countryside. Moreover, the strategy of breakneck growth has

Chris Bramall, "Chinese Capitalism Since 1996," from Chinese Economic Development, pp. 469–496. Published by Routledge. Copyright © 2009 by Taylor & Francis. Permission to reprint granted by the rights holder.

been modified by a new emphasis on energy conservation and on environmental protection. How then can it be fair to argue that China has moved decisively towards the creation of a capitalist economy? This chapter addresses this central question as part of a more general summary of evolving macroeconomic policy after 1996.

STABILIZATION POLICY

A central precondition for structural change is macroeconomic stability, and this has been an abiding concern of the CCP leadership throughout the post-1996 period. To that end, the target growth rate has been relatively low, and five-year plans have continued as a framework within which policy objectives could be formulated and realized.

Macroeconomic policy

As we saw in the previous chapter, the Chinese economy at the time of Deng's death was in a relatively healthy state. Zhu Rongji's recentralization of the fiscal system and contractionary monetary policy served to reduce the rate of inflation from about 20 percent in 1994 to 5 percent by 1996. A price was paid in the sense that the rate of job creation slowed down and the growth rate of GDP declined. Nevertheless, it was hardly a catastrophic downturn. The growth rate for 1996 was down on the 14 percent real growth rate achieved in 1992, but the 10 percent increase recorded was hardly a failure.

The central macroeconomic task for planners during the remainder of the decade and the first years of the new millennium was to ensure that the growth rate remained at around 10 percent. This conclusion as to the target growth rate was based on the experience of the early 1990s, which suggested that a rate of 14 percent was unsustainable in that it served to ignite inflation. With that in mind, the investment rate as a share of GDP was held below the 43 percent recorded in 1993. Only in 2004 did the investment rate return to these dizzy heights, and the result—prices began to rise quite sharply in 2006 and 2007—seems to confirm the notion that a growth rate of over 10 percent is simply not sustainable.

The macroeconomic challenge which confronted policy-makers in China after 1996 was of course very different from that faced in other parts of Asia, where 1997–8 saw startling falls in GDP caused by capital flight, rising domestic interest rates and a consequent wave of bankruptcy. China avoided these problems for two reasons: controls on the flow of foreign capital were still in place, and China's trade integration with the rest of the world economy was still quite limited. The first ensured that China (like Taiwan) was immune to the financial crisis that engulfed countries like Malaysia, and South Korea. China before 1997 had attracted little speculative capital in the first place, and controls prevented large-scale outflows from occurring. The second Dengist legacy ensured that China was largely unaffected by contagion. Precisely because Chinese growth was not export-led, the big falls in GDP across East Asia had only modest effects on the Chinese economy. Only relatively export-orientated Guangdong was hit hard, and even there the pain was far from insupportable. In short, China's limited integration into the world economy has meant that macroeconomic policy-making was comparatively easy even in the late 1990s.

China's success in maintaining a high rate of growth over the last decade is evident from the data (Figure 18.1). There is no sign that the growth rate is slowing; Chinese rates of growth have accelerated over the period since 1999. And if the current pace of convergence between China and the U.S. is maintained, there is every chance that China will become the largest single economy in the world (when measured using purchasing power parity GDP) by 2040. Moreover, it has achieved these rates of growth without very high rates of inflation. Even in 2007, when GDP growth reached a peak, the consumer price index rose by only 4.8 percent.

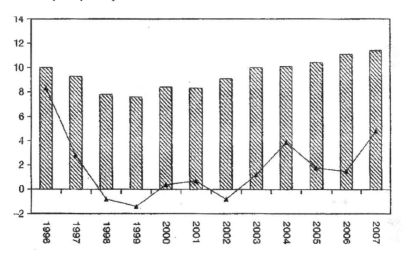

Figure 18.1 Growth of real GDP and the consumer price index, 1996–2007.

(**Sources:** ZGTJNJ (2007: 59 and 309). The figure for 2007 is a preliminary estimate by the SSB.

For all that, policy-makers in China and abroad have increasingly viewed growth as unbalanced in the sense that the investment share is too high and the contribution of the service sector too low. According to Hu Jintao (2007):

> We must keep to the new path of industrialization with Chinese characteristics, pursue the policy of boosting domestic demand, particularly consumer demand, and propel three transitions in the mode of economic growth: the transition from relying mainly on investment and export to relying on a well coordinated combination of consumption, investment and export, the transition from secondary industry serving as the major driving force to primary, secondary and tertiary industries jointly driving economic growth, and the transition from relying heavily on increased consumption of material resources to relying

mainly on advances in science and technology, improvement in the quality of the workforce and innovation in management.

There is something in this notion that Chinese growth was unbalanced between 1966 and 2008. As far as investment is concerned, there is no doubt that its share in GDP in the decade after 1996 was very high by international standards (World Bank 2007: 218–20). Gross capital formation accounted for 44 percent of GDP in 2005 (compared to 36 percent in 1990). By comparison, the average for middle-income countries across the globe was only 27 percent, and China was well ahead of other large developing economies such as India (33 percent), Indonesia (22 percent) and Nigeria (21 percent). Of course China's high investment rate was one of the reasons for its rapid rate of growth, but it is nevertheless fair to wonder whether it made sense to keep it above (say) 35 percent. Not only can one argue that investment was increasingly subject to diminishing returns, but also the cost of investment was suppressed consumption—no small consideration for a country which remains relatively poor. It follows from this that China would do better to shift towards productivity-based growth, and, as Hu's speech suggests, this was one of the aims of macroeconomic policy in the years after Deng's death.

Nevertheless, it is far from clear that China would do well to follow this advice. From a theoretical viewpoint, there are good reasons to reject a neoclassical perspective in which the contribution of technical progress can be separated from investment. The neoSchumpeterian view that most technical progress is endogenous and needs to be embodied in new equipment—as a range of economists from Kaldor (1961) and Scott (1989) to De Long and Summers (1991) have suggested—is far more plausible. It follows therefore that there is a real possibility that cuts in the investment share will lead simply to slower technical progress. It is all very well to suggest that China needs to shift towards a more productivity-based growth path in the medium term if growth is to be sustained. However, there is much in the evidence to suggest that Chinese growth has been based around productivity growth ever since the early 1980s precisely because of its high investment rate and growing competition in domestic markets, and therefore that no fundamental change is needed. The very fact than even economists using a neoclassical growth accounting framework (for example Bosworth and Collins 2007) have found that productivity growth has made a big contribution to growth suggests that the notion of a dichotomy between investment- and productivity-based growth is overstated. IMF and World Bank advice to rebalance growth towards consumption may be well intentioned (though we do well to remember that both organizations are financed mainly by the U.S. government, and it is far from obvious that U.S. strategic interests are served by a successful Chinese economy). However, Chinese planners would do well not to respond with alacrity to this sort of suggestion; with growth in excess of 10 percent the need for drastic action plainly does not exist in the short run.

As for the notion that the service sector is too small, there is again something to this charge. Between 2000 and 2005, for example, the service sector grew less quickly than manufacturing (10 percent per annum compared to over 11 percent). Moreover, the share of services in Chinese GDP was only 40 percent compared with an average of 53 percent in middle-income countries (World Bank 2007: 190–6). The contrast with India is especially striking given the similarities of the two countries in other respects (notably size and level of development); in India, services accounted for 54 percent of GDP in 2005.[3] One consequence of this structure of output for China is that the growth of employment—services are of course relatively labour-intensive—is slower than it might be in the short run, thus contributing to China's unemployment problem. Again, however, a good deal of caution is in order. A large manufacturing sector is essential for growth, and it may well be that the push for Chinese deindustrialization is premature. China and India are certainly very different, but it is at least arguable that the large number of English speakers in India makes a development strategy more reliant on IT-intensive services far more sensible than in the Chinese case.

The Five Year Plans

It is commonplace for Western academics to regard Chinese policy-makers as having abandoned planning since 1978, and to some extent this is true. The very fact that so much of the economy is subject to market forces makes traditional-style allocation of inputs and outputs across sectors rather meaningless. For exactly this reason, Chinese planning in practice is indicative. Targets are set and the government uses a range of fiscal and financial instruments (primarily taxes and interest rates) to achieve those targets.

Nevertheless, thinking about Chinese development in terms of Five Year Plans is useful because it is evident that economic policy variation occurs across these planning cycles (Table 18.1). Thus the Eighth Five Year Plan (1991–5) marked a sharp deviation from the previous period in that it was an era of very rapid growth which began in 1991. Deng's *nanxun* in 1992 has garnered much attention, but it is evident from the data that the recovery of GDP began in 1991.

The themes of the Ninth Five Year Plan (1996–2000) were very different from those of the Eighth. Instead of growth, the focus was on macroeconomic contraction (to squeeze inflation out of the system) and the wholesale restructuring of the industrial sector under the slogan of *gaizhi* and *zhuada fangxiao*. It is no accident that the key policy announcements were made in 1996, the start of the planning cycle. The Ninth Plan was a very poor period for China's farmers, in contrast to both Eighth and Tenth Plan periods. Wage income (mainly from industry) continued to grow rapidly, but per capita income from farming declined in nominal terms. As for urban China, the impact of the policy of industrial restructuring is painfully apparent in the data on industrial value-added and employment. Value-added growth halved compared with the Eighth Five Year Plan even after adjusting for inflation, and secondary employment growth was almost non-existent, in contrast to the significant rates of growth achieved during the Eighth and Tenth Plans. The Tenth Five Year Plan (2001–5) marked a return to growth promotion. It was recognized that agricultural performance had been poor in the late 1990s, and there was growing concern about the level of urban unemployment. The very fact that WTO entry might lead to further unemployment added more weight to these concerns. The solution to both problems was to accelerate the growth rate, and this is precisely what happened: the growth of farm income, industrial value-added and secondary employment were all well up on the rates during the Ninth Plan.

Table 18.1 Variation in growth rates across plan periods.

		Rural growth rates		Industrial growth	
		Farm income	Rural wage income	Industrial value-added	Secondary employment
Eighth Plan	1991–5	+25.3	+22.7	+8.7	+2.9
Ninth Plan	1996–2000	−3.3	+11.5	+9.4	−0.1
Tenth Plan	2001–5	+7.0	+10.7	+11.6	+2.8

Sources: ZGTJNJ (2006); SSB (2006c).

Note: Rural growth rates are at current prices. The high inflation rate of the Eighth Plan period means that the absolute data are misleading, but it is the relative rate of farm and rural wage growth that is of interest. Industrial GVA growth rates are at constant prices; industry excludes construction.

None of this is to say that important macroeconomic changes did not occur *within* plan periods. The 1994 fiscal recentralization and the programme of macroeconomic contraction introduced by Zhu Rongji in the middle of the Eighth Five Year Plan show that very clearly. Nevertheless, trends during plan periods after 1991 display a degree of coherence which suggests that Chinese macroeconomic planning was by no means dead even in the new millennium. It may not have been the planning of old, but it is evident that the government sought, and to a considerable extent succeeded, to control the pace and pattern of development.

THE TRANSITION TO CAPITALISM

The main theme, however, of economic policy-making after 1996 has not been stabilization policy so much as structural change on an unprecedented scale. Many of the events of the last decade suggest that the Dengist strategy of market socialism has been abandoned and the CCP has instead opted to make the transition to capitalism.

By the late 1980s, many elements of the late Maoist development model had already been jettisoned. Collective farming had long since been abandoned. The hegemony of urban state-owned industry was being challenged by local state-owned enterprises (TVEs) based in the countryside, and by a vibrant private sector. Inequality was spiralling. Any notion that superstructural change was a necessary condition for economic change had long since been abandoned. In so far as this strategy had an ideological underpinning, it was based around the idea of creating a market socialist economy which combined elements of authoritarianism (CCP rule) with state control over key economic sectors and a vibrant market economy.[4]

At the end of the 1980s, however, the doctrine of neoauthoritarianism was becoming increasingly attractive to Chinese intellectuals as an alternative to market socialism. Most of these intellectuals if asked would have styled themselves as neoauthoritarian. That is, they saw a combination of a market-driven economy and an authoritarian state as offering a better path to modernity than the market socialist vision of a mixed economy.[5] The rapid growth of the economy seemingly confirmed the effectiveness of market-led solutions. And the 'chaos' threatened by the demonstrators in Tian'anmen square in 1989 affirmed their conviction that only a strong state stood between them and barbarism. Democracy was a desirable long-run objective, but the basic premise of neoauthoritarianism was that economic change was a necessary condition for political change, thus reversing the late Maoist notion that causality runs as much from the superstructure to base as in the opposite direction. During the early 1990s, this neoauthoritarian doctrine increasingly infiltrated the upper echelons of the Communist Party. For example, Wang Huning (a leading advocate of neoauthoritarianism in the 1980s) became a close adviser to Jiang Zemin. The seeming failure of democracy in Russia and the continuing resilience of Singapore's economy attracted new adherents to the neoauthoritarian cause.

Nevertheless, Chinese praxis in the mid-1990s was arguably still closer to that of market socialism than it was to the neoauthoritarian vision of strong state and free market. The Chinese state was certainly 'strong' enough for it to be classified as neoauthoritarian and the commitment to income equality was admittedly very hollow by then. However, the extent of state ownership in China was still far greater in 1996 than in any of the other East Asian economies, China's commitment to free trade and capital movements remained luke-warm and the internal labour market was still heavily controlled, especially via continuing restrictions on internal labour migration. The drive to create a neoauthoritarian state was seemingly tempered by Deng Xiaoping's commitment to retaining state control over the commanding heights of the economy. Deng's death in February 1997 therefore broke the log-jam because it removed the last check on the neoauthoritarian instincts of Jiang Zemin.

The waning of the market socialist vision

Events since 1996 point towards the conclusion that the aim of policy-making was to create a neoauthoritarian system by maintaining China's strong state, and simultaneously making a thoroughgoing transition to capitalism. One feature of the years after Deng's death was the continuation of the process of price liberalization begun in the late 1970s.

In fact, the data suggest that price liberalization was largely complete by 2003. In that year, 87 percent of producer good sales, 96 percent of retail sales and 97 percent of farm commodities were at market prices (OECD 2005: 29). To all intents and purposes, therefore, price determination was by market forces—a characteristic feature of capitalist economies across the globe. Similarly, the rise of the private sector continued. By 2003, private sector companies accounted for 57 percent of value-added in the non-farm business sector, up from 43 percent in 1998 (OECD 2005: 81).

Price liberalization and the removal of restrictions on the growth of the private sector were merely a continuation of a policy begun in the early 1980s. However, the same cannot be said of other aspects of the constellation of policies implemented after 1996. There are continuities across the 1996 divide, but we should not underestimate the extent to which the death of Deng Xiaoping was a climacteric in Chinese economic policy-making.

Box 18.1 Key events of the post-1996 era.

1995	*zhuada fangxiao* slogan first appears at 5th Plenum of the 14th Party Congress; privatization of small SOEs and TVEs begins in earnest in the autumn
19 February 1997	Death of Deng Xiaoping
July 1997	Asian financial crisis begins in Thailand
September 1997	Jiang Zemin announces decision to cut back the state sector to the 15th Party Congress. Importance of private sector formally recognized Policy of *zhuada fangxiao* re-articulated
April 1999	U.S. and China fail to agree terms for Chinese entry to World Trade Organization
May 1999	Bombing of the Chinese embassy in Belgrade
11 December 2001	Chinese accession to WTO
October 2002	Hu Jintao becomes Party leader in succession to Jiang Zemin
July 2005	*Renminbi*—U.S. dollar exchange rate peg abandoned
March 2007	New property right law passed by the NPC allowing children to inherit wealth made by insider privatizations and fraudulent share dealing

Three new initiatives signalled the end of the Chinese attempt to steer a third way to modernity between national communism and international capitalism. First, the programme of industrial privatization launched initially under the banner of *zhuada fangxiao* ('grasp the large, let go the small') in 1995 and accelerated after September 1997. Whereas industrial policy before 1996 focused on restructuring and liberalization—encouraging, for example, the growth of private and foreign enterprises—policy after 1996 centred around privatization of state-owned industries in the cities and in the countryside. Second, China's accession to the World Trade Organization in December

2001, which heralded the demolition of most of China's remaining tariff and non-tariff barriers to international trade. This was seen as enhancing the impact of privatization by exposing Chinese industrial enterprises to more intense competition. It also served a political purpose: restrictions on the scope for industrial policy implied by WTO membership meant that there was no way back to the market socialist model. Third, and as is discussed in the next section, barriers to internal labour migration were largely removed with a view to reducing the income gap between Chinese regions and ensuring an abundant supply of cheap labour in China's cities.

The growth of internal labour migration

Between the death of Mao and the middle of the 1990s, extensive labour migration occurred between the countryside and China's cities. Some of this was permanent migration (*qianyi*) involving a change in the place of a person's registration (*hukou*).[6] However, an increasing proportion of migrants were temporary, and these made up an increasingly large floating population (*liudong renkou*) across China. It is difficult to be absolutely certain about the size of this floating population because of changing definitions.[7] Nevertheless, most estimates put the number of floaters at around 30 million in the early 1980s, rising to 70 million by the late 1980s and to around 100 million by the end of the 1990s (Chan 2001: 130–1). This growth has continued largely unchecked in recent years.

The 2000 Population Census, undoubtedly the most reliable of any of China's surveys, came up with a figure of no less than 144 million migrants (ZGTJNJ 2002: 102–3). The census data are very revealing (Table 18.2). First, they show that around 79 million of the floaters were long distance migrants; that is, they had migrated across county or provincial borders. This was well up on the figure of 22 million recorded in the 1990 census (Liang and Ma 2004: 470) and demonstrates the extent to which China's population became increasingly mobile as the economy became more market-orientated. Second, the data show clearly that the migration was largely rural to urban and from west to east. Thus the jurisdictions with the largest percentage of floaters were Beijing, Tianjin and Shanghai (the big prosperous urban centres), Zhejiang (where TVEs and private industry had flourished) and Fujian and Guangdong (both of which had attracted abundant FDI). The frontier provinces (Xinjiang, Inner Mongolia and Manchuria), which were still seen as offering opportunities for migrant workers—especially in their resource extraction sectors—also attracted above-average numbers of floaters. Third, the experience of Guangdong stands out. Not only did it attract a large number of floaters, but a disproportionate number of them were long-distance migrants; no less than 15 million of China's 42 million trans-provincial migrants were living in Guangdong in 2000. They were of course attracted to Guangdong's manufacturing industries, especially the dynamic centres of the Pearl river delta in cities such as Dongguan and Shenzhen (Yeung 2001; China Labour Bulletin Research Report 2006).

Table 18.2 The floating population in 2000.

Province	Total floaters	Share in provincial population	Inter-provincial floaters	Share of inter-provincial floaters in national total
	(million)	(percent)	(million)	(percent)
Beijing	4.64	33.6	2.46	5.8
Tianjin	2.18	21.8	0.74	1.7
Hebei	4.88	7.2	0.93	2.2
Shanxi	3.72	11.3	0.67	1.6
Nei Menggu	3.83	16.1	0.55	1.3
Liaoning	6.48	15.3	1.05	2.5
Jilin	2.95	10.8	0.31	0.7
Heilongjiang	3.77	10.2	0.39	0.9
Shanghai	5.38	32.1	3.13	7.4
Jiangsu	9.10	12.2	2.54	6.0
Zhejiang	8.60	18.4	3.69	8.7
Anhni	3.56	5.9	0.23	0.5
Fujian	5.91	17.0	2.15	5.1
Jiangxi	3.36	8.1	0.25	0.6
Shandong	7.47	8.2	1.03	2.4
Henan	5.20	5.6	0.48	1.1
Hubei	5.70	9.5	0.61	1.4
Hunan	4.40	6.8	0.35	0.8
Guangdong	25.30	29.3	15.06	35.5
Guangxi	3.23	7.2	0.43	1.0
Hainan	0.98	12.5	0.38	0.9
Chongqing	2.63	8.5	0.40	0.9
Sichuan	6.67	8.0	0.54	1.3
Guizhou	2.42	6.9	0.41	1.0
Yunnan	3.87	9.0	1.16	2.7
Tibet	0.21	8.0	0.11	0.3
Shaanxi	2.37	6.6	0.43	1.0
Gansu	1.56	6.1	0.23	0.5
Qinghai	0.52	10.0	0.12	0.3
Ningxia	0.67	11.9	0.19	0.4
Xinjiang	2.83	14.7	1.41	3.3
Total	144.39	11.4	42.43	100.0

Source: ZGTJNJ (2002: 102–3).

Note: The data here include both intra-county migrants (who were not included in the 1990 census as migrants; they numbered 66 million in 2000) as well as inter-county migrants. For a discussion, see Liang and Ma (2004).

Nevertheless, although these migrant numbers are large in absolute terms, the rates are still relatively small compared with Europe or North America. It is therefore not surprising that many Western economists were arguing that it was time to remove the remaining residual controls on internal labour migration by the mid-1990s. The World Bank (1997c) was very positive on the benefits to be expected. Knight and Song (1999) argued that Chinese policy had long been characterized by urban bias, and that one feature thereof was the creation of an 'invisible Great Wall' between urban and rural sectors by means of the erection of barriers to rural-urban migration. Khan and Riskin (2001: 155) also argued in favour of migration, maintaining that the government policy should aim to:

> liberalize control of population movement so as to permit a freer flow of people in search of economic and social opportunity. We have argued that liberalized policies toward population mobility have helped reduce rural poverty, and we favor furthering this process—including the phasing out of physical restrictions on population movement—to eliminate the inequitable segmentation of the urban labor market and the second class status of rural-urban migrants.

The Chinese government has increasingly heeded these sorts of policy recommendations. Temporary residence permits and identity cards were granted to migrants after 1985, and these allowed them to live legally in urban areas. However, the process went a stage further in the mid-1990s, when local government (at the behest of the CCP) started to award 'blue' *hukou* status to temporary migrants to large cities. So-called because it involved a blue rather than red stamp on the *hukou* card, the blue *hukou* granted a range of rights to migrants in exchange for the payment of a fee to local government. It thus had the effect of integrating migrants further into urban communities, even if discrimination remained (Gaetano and Jacka 2004: 18–20; Dutton 1998; Wong and Huen 1998). It has also become easier to reside in small towns as a result of legislation passed by the State Council in June 1997 and March 2001. In addition, local governments across China have played a key role in helping to export labour, which they have seen as a means towards the end of poverty reduction; the process has been well documented in Anhui province, which has exported large quantities of labour to Shanghai in recent years (Lei 2005).

Nevertheless, there is evidence that these migration-promoting policies have not worked in the sense that there was growing evidence by around 2003/4 of shortages of unskilled labour in the Pearl river delta and in Jiangsu (Inagaki 2006). Guangdong was said to be short of a million workers in 2004, and the deficit in Fujian and Zhejiang was around 2 million; Dongguan alone was predicted to have a shortage of 1 million workers in 2005 (Shao et al. 2007: 10). These shortages continued into 2006 and 2007. Given that most scholars believe that there is still a large number of relatively underemployed workers in the countryside, these shortages are widely seen as reflecting labour market failures. More precisely, low wages and discrimination against migrants—such as restrictions on the jobs open to migrants and attempts by local government to limit access to social insurance and public goods—have been seen as discouraging migration (Shao *et al.* 2007). Yet it is not just discrimination. The one-child policy has also played an important role in restricting the supply of young workers. Indeed the very fact that shortages of young female workers are most acute demonstrates very powerfully the discriminatory impact of that policy (Inagaki 2006).

It also needs to be recognized that there is no evidence that the Chinese government is bent upon abolishing the *hukou* system. As Chan and Buckingham (2007) point out, recent changes have had the effect of delegating decisions about migration to local government. And local governments have typically responded by encouraging in-migration by the educated, the wealthy and the skilled, but simultaneously retaining powerful barriers when it comes to in-migration by the poor and the unskilled. For example, by requiring migrants to have worked in the city for two years and to be the owners of a residence before granting *hukou* status, the government of Shijiazhuang has effectively closed the door (Chan and Buckingham 2007: 29).

The intent of central government is clear, such local interference notwithstanding. Controls on labour migration are far less strict than they were even in the early 1990s, and barriers continue to come down. China is still a long way from having created a well-functioning labour market, but it has moved far in that direction. Despite labour shortages in some regions, the scale of migration has increased dramatically over the last decade. And in that the migrants are typically better educated and wealthier than those who do not migrate, the Chinese labour market has many of the features seen in market-orientated OECD economies.

AN ENDURING COMMITMENT TO SOCIALISM?

Much of the evidence discussed earlier in this chapter, certainly suggests that China has abandoned market socialism. However, even though there is much to suggest that the Chinese leadership is bent upon (and has gone far towards) creating a capitalist economy, some have argued that the true intentions of the CCP are not easily assessed. Die Lo and Li Guicai (2006: 16), for example, argue that China is still on some form of heterodox trajectory, pointing to 'the fundamental importance which the Chinese state leadership, and the society as a whole, attach to the objective of "constructing a harmonious society."' What, then, has been the goal of the CCP leadership since 1996?

Official rhetoric and Chinese realities

In answering this question, it is undeniable that Party rhetoric suggests a continuing ideological commitment to socialism; see for example Hu (2007). Moreover, the Eleventh Five Year Plan (2006–10) does seem to have articulated a rather different vision of the Chinese future from those which preceded it, and some have argued that we need to take all this very seriously. According to Lin (2006: 276):

Although such efforts are still short of being a grand vision of socialism for missing the dimension of democracy, redefining development is nevertheless an honourable and ambitious goal in a country of China's size and in the face of its formidable obstacles. The official statements about readjusting development deserve serious treatment.

Lin certainly has a point. The need to protect China's environment has been recognized, and attempts to calculate green GDP have been made. Restrictions on the inflow of foreign capital and on currency movements remain; in that sense, the globalization of the Chinese economy still has some distance to travel. The policy objective of creating a *xiaokang* (comfortable) standard of living is routinely mentioned, and some efforts have been made to define it in terms of both opulence and human development indicators. Macroeconomic policy emphasis has shifted away from growth and towards redistribution. Much stress has been placed on creating a harmonious society.[8] Perhaps evenly more significantly, the need to develop the rural sector has been stressed repeatedly. Here the aim is to create a 'new socialist countryside' and to solve the *sannong* ('the three rural problems': the problem of agriculture, the problem of rural areas and the problem of the peasantry). This pro-rural vision has been given teeth in the policy announcements of 2006—the abolition of the agricultural tax and the end of tuition fees for rural children aged between six and fifteen.

All these policy aims were reiterated by Hu Jintao at the start of the 17th Party Congress in October 2007. Few concrete announcements were made, but three aspects of his speech stand out. First, Hu announced that the aim of policy was to quadruple per capita GDP between 2000 and 2020. Although this was more ambitious than the previous aim (which was to increase total GDP by that amount over the same period), it nevertheless implies an annual growth target of only around 6 percent between 2007 and 2020. Given that the economy was growing by over 10 percent during 2007, this amounted to an apparent scaling back of China's growth ambitions and by implication a commitment to broader social development. Second, a feature of Hu's speech was a recognition of the environmental implications of rapid growth and the need for conservation. In the introduction to his speech, he even admitted that 'Our economic growth is realized at an excessively high cost of resources and the environment' (Hu 2007). Third, there was not only a recognition that income disparities had widened dramatically, but also a commitment to reducing them:

> A relatively comfortable standard of living has been achieved for the people as a whole, but the trend of a growing gap in income distribution has not been thoroughly reversed, there are still a considerable number of impoverished and low-income people in both urban and rural areas, and it has become more difficult to accommodate the interests of all sides [Section III]. … We will protect lawful incomes, regulate excessively high incomes and ban illegal gains. We

will increase transfer payments, intensify the regulation of incomes through taxation, break business monopolies, create equal opportunities, and overhaul income distribution practices with a view to gradually reversing the growing income disparity [Section VIII].

Nevertheless, it remains to be seen whether any of this rhetoric means very much. For example, it is hard to see how the creation of a 'new socialist countryside' is going to be financed. The same caveat applies to the provision of free tuition to rural children. To be sure, this is not merely posturing. According to Wen Jiabao's *Report on the Work of Government* (March 2007), 'A total of 184 billion *yuan* was allocated by both central and local governments to fund rural compulsory education, enabling us to pay tuition and miscellaneous fees for the 52 million rural students receiving compulsory education throughout the western region and in some areas in the central region ...' during 2006 (Wen 2007). However, it is doubtful that these types of policies will address the underlying problems. The agricultural tax has long been a very small part of the 'burden' carried by the peasantry, and its abolition will therefore make little difference to peasant incomes. Low enrolment rates in the rural schools certainly have something to do with the cost of education. But at least as big a problem is low demand for education, especially for girls. Wen Jiabao recognized the point. Although the CCP had committed itself to 'completely stop collecting tuition and miscellaneous fees from all rural students receiving compulsory education' in 2007, Wen recognized that this would only 'ease the financial burden of 150 million rural households with children attending primary and middle schools' (Wen 2007). More generally, endemic discrimination by parents against their daughters in the Chinese countryside is the crux of the educational problem, and that is not likely to be addressed by modest subsidies.

Developing western China

Perhaps the clearest sign of the Parry's vestigial commitment to some sort of egalitarian vision has been its apparent determination to reduce the regional income gap between eastern and western China.[9]

This certainly had not been the case in the 1980s, when the income gap between the coastal and the interior provinces probably widened. In part this was a consequence of both history and geography interacting with the liberalization of the economy and the decentralization of the fiscal system—which allowed regions well favoured by history and geography to forge ahead. The coastal provinces were certainly favoured by their geography. For one thing, intra-provincial transport costs were very low within the coastal provinces. For another, the great metropolitan centres of Shanghai, Beijing and Hong Kong offered large external economies of scale because they supported both a large pool of skilled labour and offered an immense market to local producers. Perhaps most importantly of all, the

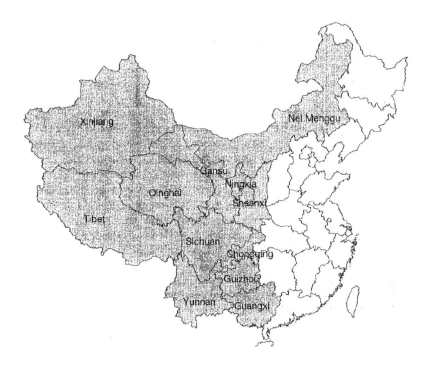

Figure 18.2 The western region of China, 1997.

Note: This is the official CCP definition of western China, the provincial boundaries are those of 1997 showing Chongqing as a separate municipality.

eastern provinces were coastal. That reduced long-distance transport costs to other Chinese coastal provinces, but it also gave them easy access to the fast-growing economies along the Pacific Rim, and to the more distant markets of the U.S.A., Australasia and Europe. History too was in their favour. China's railway network was much denser in the eastern provinces than further west, and industrial development before 1949 and under Mao had led to the creation of a skills base and to the establishment of a range of industrial infrastructure. The late Maoist Third Front programme did little more than hold inequalities in check. It could not eliminate them.

However, the widening of spatial income inequalities owed as much to CCP policy as it did to historical legacies and physical geography. For one thing, the fiscal system in operation during the 1980s was characterized by coastal bias. At root, the problems were caused by fiscal decentralization, a process which favoured the more prosperous provinces. Decentralization (*fangquan rangli*) was pioneered in Jiangsu in 1977, where the introduction of *guding bili baogan* (fixed-rate contact) specified that the province was to be allowed to retain 42 percent of revenue raised over the following four years. The key national reform did not occur until 1980. That year saw a lump-sum system introduced in Guangdong and Fujian and a fixed-rate system (based on the Jiangsu model) put in place in the great metropolitan centres and in Jiangsu itself, while all the remaining provinces operated a system under which specific types of revenue were shared between province and centre (Shirk, 1993: 166–8). The effect of the 1980 reform was to replace a system of *chi daguo fan* (eating out of the same big pot) with that of *fen zao chifan* (eating in separate kitchens)—that is, the provinces were given much greater control over how much revenue they retained and how they allocated it.

Further fiscal reforms followed in sharp succession, and they reinforced regional bias. The 1988 reform, for example, treated fast-growing provinces even more favourably by specifying that a certain proportion of revenue would be handed over to central government but that the contribution rate would be reduced once a target level of revenue had been remitted (Shirk, 1993: 192–3). This *shouru dizeng baogan* system was designed to provide provinces with the incentive to increase revenue by reducing the marginal remittance rate. The system was formalized in the early 1990s. It involved two distinct elements: contracted transfers and earmarked transfers (Wong *et al.* 1995: 90–8) On the one hand, all China's provinces had agreed a fiscal contract which specified that they remitted a certain amount to the centre (rich provinces) or that they received an agreed subsidy (poor provinces). On the other hand, every province received earmarked transfers from central government. Some of these earmarked subsidies were for capital construction. However, it is remarkable that no less than 59 percent of all earmarked grants took the form of price subsidies. These necessarily benefited affluent, urbanized, areas. As a result, for example, Guangdong's 1990 contracted remittance of 5.2 billion *yuan* was partially offset by an earmarked inflow of 1.24 billion yuan (Wong *et al.* 1995: 98).

The net effect of these changes was to reduce the extent of transfers from coastal to interior provinces. The total figure remitted to the centre declined in absolute terms between 1985 and 1990. The seven jurisdictions remitting most to central government (Shanghai, Jiangsu, Liaoning, Tianjin, Shandong, Zhejiang and Beijing) made contracted transfers of 33 billion *yuan* in 1985 but only 28 billion *yuan* in 1990. Looked at over the entire 1978–93 period, the decline was much more steep. Shanghai's surplus of revenue over expenditure fell from 51 percent of GDP in 1978–80 to only 8.5 percent in 1991–3. The comparable declines for Beijing and Tianjin were from 26 percent to 1 and 4 percent respectively (Wang and Hu, 1999: 190). With less money available to central government, transfers to poor provinces declined. Guizhou's subsidy of 11.7 percent of GDP in 1978–80 dwindled to only 3.3 percent by 1991–3 and the decline for Xinjiang was from 24 to 7 percent. The full details on the five provinces with the biggest (percentage) surplus and the five with the biggest deficit are summarized in Table 18.3. These data show very clearly how some of China's richest areas were able to retain an increasing proportion of tax revenue, thus reducing the ability of central government to transfer funds to poor hinterland areas.

The data given in Table 18.3 undoubtedly need to be qualified in several respects. First, it is unclear whether these official data include financial flows earmarked for military purposes. As all but Guizhou of the poor provinces listed here were frontier provinces, these military flows could well have been significant. Second, and following on from this, it may well be that transfers to poor provinces declined after 1978 because of the termination of the Third Front programme and the ending of the short confrontation with Vietnam. If so, at least part of the decline in subsidies (in particular funds made available for investment in physical capital) represented little welfare loss to their populations. Even declines after 1985 may have reflected continuing fluctuations in military spending. Third, it is hard to believe these data include the full range of flows between provinces, especially (non-military) extra-budgetary transfers and subsidies. Finally, the data exclude loans. In the case of the rich provinces, loans to central government tended to be the norm. The reverse was true for the poorer provinces. But, and notwithstanding these qualifications, it is hard to believe that the official data do not provide at least a qualitatively accurate picture of the pattern of intergovernmental flows over the first decade of the transition era. The very fact that numerous Party officials went on record between 1989 and 1994 to state that central government was becoming increasingly paralyzed by fiscal weakness suggests that there undoubtedly was a crisis caused by the fiscal federalism of the 1980s.

Table 18.3 Fiscal surpluses as a share of GDP, 1978–1989 (ranked by surplus in 1978)

	1978	*1989*
Shanghai	52	13
Tianjin	30	3
Beijing	28	3
Liaoning	28	2
Jiangsu	13	3
Yunnan	–9	–5
Guizhou	–13	–6
Ningxia	–20	–15
Nei Menggu	–20	–9
Xinjiang	–25	–10

Sources: by calculation from SSB (1990a; 2005a).

CCP policy also exacerbated regional inequality because its focus was on a coastal development strategy. The Third Front was abandoned and instead emphasis shifted towards the promotion of rapid growth in the provinces along the Pacific seaboard. Still, and despite the creation of four special economic zones in 1979 and 1980, the coastal development strategy was initially very tentative. In no small measure, this was because of the resistance (or at least caution) of Chen Yun. Nevertheless, the documents setting out the Sixth Five Year Plan (1981–5), published in 1983, made clear the intent of the leadership: the continuing development of the Chinese interior was not an end in itself, but should merely serve the purpose of *promoting* economic growth along the coast (Yang, 1997: 83). By the mid-1980s, the rhetoric had softened a little; development in eastern

China was to help serve the needs of the interior rather than the reverse.[10] Nevertheless, it was commonplace for CASS economists to put forward the proposition that it was a 'law' of economic development that rapid growth in the coastal region had to precede growth in the interior:

> China's economy can be divided into three major geographic regions: eastern, central and western, and the objective tendency of development is to push from east to west. (Central Committee 1991: 501)

The best-known justification for a pro-coastal strategy was put forward by Wang Jian, who was based at the State Planning Commission. His idea of a grand international cycle (*guoji da xunhuan*) envisaged an initial phase of export growth based upon the labour intensive industries of the coastal region. The export earnings of the coastal region would in turn help to finance capital deepening and the development of the interior in a later phase (Hsu 1991: 9). By 1987, the theory had won favour with Zhao Ziyang, and it was adopted as official Party policy in February 1988. Deng, too, was an ardent supporter.

> The development of the coastal areas is of overriding importance, and the interior provinces should subordinate themselves to it. When the coastal areas have developed to a certain extent, they will be required to give still more help to the interior. Then the development of the interior provinces will be of overriding importance, and the coastal areas will in turn have to subordinate themselves to it. (Deng 1988: 271–2)

Zhao's fall and the Tian'anmen massacre put a break on the momentum of the coastal development strategy. Moreover, it appears that Deng Xiaoping was himself becoming increasingly concerned by the gap between coast and interior. The spur for this was a belief that the gap in terms of per capita GDP had widened excessively during the 1980s. One obvious way to see this is in terms of the difference in per capita GDP between Guangdong (one of China's richest provinces) and Guizhou (probably the poorest). A simple comparison of per capita GDP between the two (Figure 18.3) appears to show that the ratio widened from around 2 to 1 at the start of the 1980s to over 3 to 1 by the time of the Tian'anmen massacre, a dramatic increase by any standard.

Deng and the CCP were also concerned that regional inequality would interact with ethnic tensions in western China. This held out the possibility of some of fragmentation of the People's Republic itself, and the concerns of the CCP were allayed neither by the close relations between the Dalai Lama and the U.S. administration, nor the collapse of the Soviet Union. Nevertheless, it is unlikely that the creation of breakaway republics Is a real concern for the Chinese leadership, not least because the control of the PLA in Xinjiang and Tibet is tight and because the presence of Han settlers in these outposts of

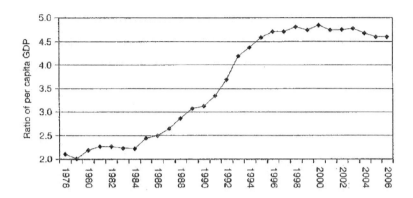

Figure 18.3 The ratio of per capita GDP in Guizhou to per capita GDP in Guangdong.
(**Sources:** SSB (2005a); ZGTJNJ (2007: 67 and 106); ZGTJNJ (2006: 63 and 100).

Note: Data on GDP are at current prices. The population denominator takes no account of the floating population. I discuss some of the limitations of this analysis below.

empire serves to moderate any separatist push. In practice, the worries of the CCP centred much more on the implications of slow growth in the western provinces for migration. Its abiding fear appears to be a tidal wave of uncontrolled emigration from the west into China's cities, creating enormous social and economic tensions. The best way to prevent such a flood was by means of promoting faster economic growth in the western provinces, thus encouraging migrants to stay put.

Nevertheless, and though Deng was anxious to avoid polarization, he was by no means in favour of egalitarianism. His spring tour of 1992 gave renewed vigour to developing the coastal region, and Deng was at pains to promote the idea of regional comparative advantage (*yindizhuyi*). Certainly he did not see a growing income differential between rich and poor areas as a requiring immediate redistribution via the tax system. Extracts from his speeches of 1992 make this plain:

> If the rich keep getting richer and the poor poorer, polarization will emerge. The socialist system must and can avoid polarization. One way is for the areas that become prosperous first to support the poor ones by paying more taxes or turning in more profits to the state. Of course this should not be done too soon. At present, we don't want to dampen the vitality of the developed areas or encourage the practice of having everyone 'eat from the same big pot.' We should study when to raise this question and how to settle it. I can imagine that the right time might be the end of the century, when our people are living a fairly comfortable life. … In short, taking the country as a whole, I am confident that we can gradually bridge the gap between coastal and inland areas. (Deng 1992: 362)

> [T]hose areas that are in a position to develop should not be obstructed. Where local conditions permit, development should proceed as fast as possible. There is nothing to worry about so long as we stress efficiency and quality and develop an export-oriented economy. Slow growth equals stagnation and even retrogression. (Deng 1992: 363)

Deng's answer to the regional problem was therefore suitably modest in scope The solution, he argued, was to 'twin' coastal cities and provinces with western provinces, thereby promoting a transfer of skills and finance. This was called creating *duikou zhiyuan* (sister city relationships). An example was aid from Shenzhen to Guizhou for school building (Wright 2003: 52). To all intents and purposes, this was a strategy which aimed simply to make trickle-down more effective.

By the middle of the 1990s, however, the gap had continued to widen and the rhetoric amongst CCP leaders became increasing shrill.[11] According to Li Peng, the then prime minister, action was imperative:

> We must admit the east–west gap. We must create conditions so that the gap can gradually close. The central government cares very much about this problem and has determined that the West's development is a major issue that must be addressed through policy, funding, and technological support. (Li Peng 1993, cited in Wright 2003: 55)

The Ninth Five Year Plan (1996–2000) gave expression to these concerns. The CCP leadership proposed as the solution to the problem an extension of the open-door policy to encompass the interior and an intensification of Deng's twinning solution, this time under the name of *hengxiang jingji lianxi* (horizontal economic cooperation). Under this arrangement, Beijing was twinned with Inner Mongolia, Shanghai with Yunnan, and the special economic zones with Guizhou. A further policy initiative was the decision to designate Chongqing as a provincial-level municipality in 1997, thus putting it on a par with Beijing, Tianjin and Shanghai. In part this was a way of dealing with the relocation of the population displaced by the Three Gorges dam. As a result, the new municipality is much bigger than Chongqing city and its outlying counties; it also included the poor prefectures of Wanxian to the north-east and Fuling to the south-east. It was hoped that placing all these areas under an administrative jurisdiction which included a large urban centre would make it easier to move displaced peasants into urban jobs. As importantly, however, the new dam would improve navigation along the Yangzi river by increasing its depth. This in turn would allow the Yangzi shipping route to be opened up much further and reduce transport costs. Thus Chongqing would become the hub of development for the entire western region, and it was fitting that it should have municipality status.

Whether the solutions implemented during the Ninth Five Year Plan were successful is moot. Wright (2003: 56) argues that they were not, and he may well be right. Certainly there is no doubt that it is much too early to judge either the impact of the Three Gorges dam or the upgrading of Chongqing to municipality status. Part of the problem is that the only way to measure the benefits generated by the programme is to look at the extent to which the per capita income gap between coast and interior has changed over time, and it is very difficult to track the trajectory of the per capita GDP gap during the 1980s and 1990s. To be sure, Figure 18.3 seems to tell a very clear story. However, there are three problems with these data. First, the Guizhou–Guangdong comparison makes no attempt to adjust for regional price differences. According to the recent analysis offered by Brandt and Holz (2006: 78), this might reduce Guangdong's per capita GDP by around 24 percent in 2000 relative to Guizhou.[12] Second, the time series data are distorted by the revaluation of GDP following the 2004 Economic Census, which (taken alone) served to widen the gap between the two provinces. This affects the data for 2005 and 2006, and in that sense the series shown in the figure is not consistent. Third (and to some extent offsetting the revaluation of GDP), the data are based upon permanent provincial populations prior to 2005. Taking the floating population into account has the effect of cutting Guizhou's population by around 2 million between 2004 and 2005, whereas Guangdong's population increases by no less than 9 million.

If we take these factors into account, it seems likely that the Guangdong–Guizhou gap was in the order of 2 to 1 at the start of the 1980s, a time when GDP overvaluation, provincial price variation and labour migration was of relatively little import.[13] If we adjust the gap shown in Figure 18.3 for the floating population, use revised official estimates of GDP and accept the Brandt–Holz view of regional price differentials, this rise to around 3.7 to 1 by 2006. But when exactly the increase occurred is moot. It is probable that most of it occurred during the 1990s; Guizhou benefited from the surge of agricultural production in the 1980s, whereas Guangdong gained ground in the 1990s as a result of big inflows of foreign investment and relatively lower rates of price inflation than Guizhou. Out-migration may have benefited Guizhou in absolute terms in the 1990s (though I rather doubt it given that migrants are preponderantly the young and the better educated), but Guangdong almost certainly gained far more from attracting a pool of relatively well-educated workers (at least by the standards of western China) who were willing to work for low wages in the labour intensive industries in the special economic zones and across the Pearl river delta.

Whatever the actual trajectory of regional income differentials, the CCP leadership seems to have concluded by the end of the 1990s that these income gaps could not be allowed to increase any further. This led to the programme of 'Developing the West.' Zhu Rongji set up the Leading Group on Western Development in 1999, which initiated a Develop the West programme (*Xibu da kaifa*); the phrase was seemingly first used by Jiang Zemin in June 1999. This Leading Group was formally placed under the State Council on

16 January 2000 as the Leading Group to Develop the Western Region (*Xibu diqu kaifa lingdao xiaozu*).

As conceived, the Develop the West programme covers the eleven provinces and autonomous regions of western China, though the State Council circular of April 2002 also included the three ethnic prefectures of Xianxi (Hunan province), Enshi (Hubei) and Yanbian (Jilin). The programme drawn up in 2000 envisaged five ways by which development could be promoted (State Council 2002). The first was to increase spending on centrally funded projects. These were primarily infrastructural projects. The most famous is the Qingzang railway linking Qinghai and Tibet (completed in July 2006). Equally important, however, is the east–west natural gas pipeline linking the gas fields in the Tarim basin (Xinjiang) and the Changqing (centred on Jingbian in northern Shaanxi) with Shanghai, which became operational in 2004. Also of great significance is a series of power transmission projects (collectively labelled the east–west power transmission project), which transfer electricity produced at hydrostations on the Jinsha, Lancang and Yellow rivers to eastern China. But spending did not only focus on infrastructure. For example, for every *mu* of cultivated land withdrawn from use, the farmer received a grain subsidy of 150 kg per annum. Furthermore, the central government provided a subsidy of 20 *yuan* for every mu of cultivated land converted to forestry or pasture as well as a seedling subsidy of 50 *yuan*. This latter was even classified as infrastructural spending (State Council 2002).

Second, transfer payments to the governments of the provinces of western China were increased. The western provinces were already receiving large fiscal transfer from the centre in the 1990s to cover their budgetary expenditure. These were increased very substantially between 1995 and 2004 as Table 18.4 (covering some of the provinces) shows. These numbers should not be taken too literally. Chinese fiscal data are remarkably opaque, excluding many types of extra-budgetary and off-budget revenue and expenditure. Nevertheless, the data probably give a fair indication of the scale in the increase in fiscal transfers.

Three other policies are integral to the Develop the West programme. First, the central government instructed the State Development Bank of China to provide cheap loans and credit for infrastructural projects. The Agricultural Bank of China was also instructed to provide easier credit. Moreover, the restructuring and privatization of SOEs in the western provinces was accelerated and many of them were privatized. There was a perception in China (and amongst Western economists) that the western provinces had been very slow to promote privatization, and therefore efforts were made to accelerate the privatization process after 2000. Third, in an attempt to encourage more FDI into the western region, corporate income tax was reduced to 15 percent for the period 2001–10.

Many academics continue to be sceptical as to whether any of this will be successful. Lai (2002: 459) argued that 'predatory and wasteful habits, inefficiency, and unfamiliarity with the market and legal norms hinder the building of a favourable investment environment in the west.' This type of allegation has frequently been made, and in fact many Han Chinese scholars offer a discourse that is at best chauvinistic and at worst racist. One example of

Table 18.4 Budgetary revenue and expenditure in a sample of western provinces (billion yuan).

| | *1995* | | | *2004* | | |
	Revenue	*Expenditure*	*Subsidy*	*Revenue*	*Expenditure*	*Subsidy*
Sichuan	12.1	21.2	9.1	38.6	89.5	50.9
Yunnan	9.8	23.5	13.7	26.3	66.4	40.1
Gansu	3.4	8.1	4.7	10.4	35.7	25.3
Xinjiang	3.8	9.6	5.8	15.6	42.1	26.5

Source: SSB (2005a: 853, 921, 1021 and 1123).

Note: Data are in current prices. The ail-China consumer price index increased by only 15 percent in total (not per annum) between 1995 and 2004, so subsidies increased very substantially in real terms over the period. These data cover only local government budgetary revenue. Substantial sums were raised outside the budget by provincial governments.

this is Wang and Bai (1991), but it is a routine for Han Chinese to lament the drunkenness, sloth and incompetence of ethnic minority and other cadres across the western provinces. For writers like Wang and Bai, both subsidies and expenditure on infrastructure will fail because the main problem in the western region is the quality of 'human resources' and the nature of 'socioeconomic relations.' According to them: 'the rural inhabitants of backward regions are clearly characterized by a general lack of entrepreneurial spirit and an excessive adherence to old ways [p. 38]. ... the real problem in China's backward regions ... [is that of] ... reversing the attitude of the local inhabitants towards social wealth and changing their traditional ways of exploiting natural resources' (p. 92). There is no doubt that labour productivity in western China is lower than in the east (Demurger 2002; Hare and West 1999).

It is also fair to say that a number of Western scholars are profoundly sceptical as to whether aid offers much of a solution to the problem of underdevelopment in developing countries.[14] But to jump from this to the conclusion that culture is to blame is a step too far. In fact, the attitude of Han scholars and policy-makers is arguably one of the principal obstacles to the development of the western provinces.

However, the main critique of the Develop the West programme is that the only reason the western provinces are being developed is to supply raw materials to the coastal region. In a sense, this is a classic example of imperialism, whereby the metropolitan centre extracts resources from the periphery via a process of unequal exchange in which the west loses its skilled labour and natural resources for a derisory amount of financial recompense. And woven into this 'development of underdevelopment' is a process of colonialism. Han settlers continue to 'flood' into Xinjiang, and Qinghai—historically part of Tibet—is now a Han Chinese province.[15] In short, a discourse of development cloaks a process of exploitation. It remains unclear whether this type of allegation is correct. Many emotive passages have been written about western China. However, the issue awaits a proper scholarly treatment and the results will be very sensitive to assumptions made about the price paid for raw materials exported to other Chinese provinces, and whether this constitutes a process of unequal exchange. It is clear, however, that the apparent enthusiasm manifested by the Chinese government for the development of the western provinces (an enthusiasm reiterated by Hu Jintao) cannot be taken as signifying any clear commitment to egalitarian development.

ASSESSING POLICY SINCE 1996

It is true that, even in 2008, the Chinese economy still differs markedly from that of the U.S.A. The extent of state ownership of industry is much greater despite the privatizations of the last decade. And the rhetorical commitment of the CCP to socialism remains undiminished. According to Hu (2007):

> [W]e have adhered to the basic tenets of scientific socialism and in the meantime added to them distinct Chinese characteristics in light of China's conditions and the features of the times. In contemporary China, to stay true to socialism means to keep to the path of socialism with Chinese characteristics.

My own view is that much of this is little more than empty posturing. The Party is of course keen to maintain its hegemony, and mere self-preservation dictates that it should advocate 'social harmony', the creation of 'ladders for social mobility' via free education and a regional development strategy designed to appease indigenous ethnic minorities and Western observers alike. But much of this is a sham. A commitment to the genuinely progressive income taxation needed to ensure social harmony is lacking. It is unlikely that the central government will be able to finance 'free' education; tuition fees may be abolished but the likelihood is that they will be replaced by some other form of tax. As noted earlier, the abolition of the agricultural tax, a much-heralded part of the programme to build a new socialist countryside, is of little significance because it has been only a very small proportion of farm income since the early 1960s.[16] And the western China development programme, ostensibly designed to accelerate the pace of development, is in reality little more than an attempt to make full use of the region's mineral resources and to use it as a dumping ground for the polluting industries of the east.

In view of all this, it is not surprising that a number of the characteristics of Chinese neoauthoritarianism have come in for heavy criticism in the West. For Hutton (2007: 117), for example: 'The Chinese economy and Chinese Communist Party are in an unstable halfway house—an economy that is neither socialist nor properly capitalist.' Beset by social tensions, a lack of democratic pluralism, a failure to create global brands, endemic state predation and growing inefficiency of investment, China's Leninist state, he argues, is certain to collapse unless the Enlightenment institutions developed in the West are adopted.

More importantly, Chinese neoauthoritarianism has been attacked within China itself. Many intellectuals have been blind to the failings of the Chinese state, not least because most of them were making money on the Chinese stock market by exploiting insider knowledge and inadequate legal safeguards. But Chinese liberals have been much less charitable towards the regime, and have published a wide range of critical pieces directed against state corruption, malfeasance and incompetence. The best known of these critiques is He Qinglian's (1998) *Pitfalls of Modernization*, in which she documented a wide range of corrupt practices. Nevertheless, critics like He have largely accepted the desirability of a market economy, and it is in that sense that the term 'liberal' is entirely appropriate as a descriptor for these writers. Much of their criticism has focused on the impossibility of creating such an economy without a well-defined system of property rights. Moreover, very few of China's liberals have taken issue with the notion that an authoritarian state is a necessary condition for growth in the *short* term. Here He Qinglian and Yang Xiaokai are unusual in that they advocate a rapid transition to democracy; in so doing they are the true heirs to the May 4th movement of 1919. But for most, democracy is more in the nature of a long-term aspiration for the People's Republic, and in that sense their perspective is in the neoauthoritarian rather than the liberal tradition.

The late 1990s have also seen the emergence of a group of intellectuals who espoused a return to some form of socialism.[17] The best known is that group of scholars often called the New Left, which includes Cui Zhiyuan, Wang Hui and Wang Shaoguang. These scholars have advocated a more positive appraisal of the Maoist era as well as fiscal reform as a means towards strengthening the Chinese state, which most of them see as an essential condition for modernization.[18] They fear that the CCP might go the same way as its Soviet cousin unless an effective programme of state strengthening can be accomplished.[19] But there are other strands of opinion as well, including neo-Maoists (such as Li Xianyuan and Huang Jisu), and the neostatist He Xin. Li and Huang became famous in 2000 for staging the play *Che Guevara*, which praised revolution and the revolutionary vision of Mao and *Che Guevara*. He Xin gained notoriety for the support he offered to the Chinese state in suppressing the Democracy Movement, but he has also been a powerful critic of marketization and globalization, arguing that both have adverse implications for welfare, unemployment and living standards. A strong Chinese state is therefore functionally necessary for the realization of He Xin's social market vision (which is based on the German economic model of the 1950s).

Despite their differences, these left-leaning intellectuals have been united in their condemnation of state corruption and its implications for both urban inequality and stability in the countryside, the drift towards capitalism, and in their advocacy of greater state intervention as a solution to China's continuing search for a viable path to modernity.

More precisely, the left's critique has focused on three developments since Deng Xiaoping's death: China's entry into the WTO, the mass privatization of state-owned industry and the creation and expansion of the Chinese stock market. As Lin (2006: 268) puts it:

> The reform in effect legitimized much of what socialism stood against in terms of values and practices. Workers, while losing state protection, found no space to organize themselves outside of official trade unions; and farmers remained in a situation of 'taxation without representation.' ... Thus polarization, money fetishism, greed, and corruption poisoned social cohesion. [China] ... became at the same time vulnerable to foreign dependency, private domination, rent seeking, and short term behaviours largely due to state failures.

Nevertheless, the advocates of a return to socialism within China remain handicapped by the narrowness of their vision. The main problem they face is how to deal with the Cultural Revolution, because it is easy for neoliberals to portray that as the inevitable culmination of any programme of mobilizational socialism—and by implication that any form of socialist experimentation is to be avoided. The typical response on the left is simply to avoid the issue and argue that what matters is merely to criticize the current regime (Kipnis 2003). But that does not get the left very far. It is not enough to criticize Chinese capitalism; the real challenge is to outline a viable alternative strategy. One solution to the conundrum is to outline a leftist vision which rejects the Cultural Revolution because of its violence and anarchic quality. Some on the left have taken this approach, advocating in effect a return to Leninism. A more interesting approach—which recognizes that Leninism is a *cul-de-sac*—is that taken by Cui Zhiyuan. He has interpreted the Cultural Revolution as a form of mass democracy, and hence a check on the development of interest groups within the Party; Mao's notion that 'it is right to rebel' thus has much to recommend it in Cui's view. As significantly, Cui has argued that the Cultural Revolution was also an attempt to create workplace democracy (along the lines set out in the Anshan constitution) in which management participated in labour, and this offers a means by which traditional socialist practice can be reinvigorated. Cui's influence within China has admittedly been much circumscribed by his seventeen-year period of residence in the West.[20] Nevertheless, this type of assessment chimes with some of the writings of Western scholars, who have argued that the real failure of the Cultural Revolution was that it did not go far enough.[21] Lin (2006) has also taken a more positive view of the Cultural Revolution:

> For all its faults and horrors, the Cultural Revolution in its ideological originality and historicity was as much a democratic revolt against privilege, bureaucracy, and perversions of revolution as it was a mass mobilization opportunistically used for power struggle [p. 170]. ... equally important were the egalitarian and populist drives to reduce the gaps between urban and rural lives and between

cadres and ordinary people, and to curtail the rigid sectoral and gender divisions of labor [p. 164].

Lin and Cui in effect argue that, instead of using the army to suppress the Red Guards in 1968, the movement should have been encouraged.

That still leaves open the question of alternatives. Lin argues in favour of what she calls *xiaokang* socialism, which is a programme designed to meet basic meets, develop democracy and promote community—and clearly also a linear descendant of the Cultural Revolution model. For her, a Chinese alternative to traditional state socialism and globalization is eminently feasible. China enjoys the advantages of backwardness, has a tradition of pioneering alternative paths—what was Maoism if not that?—and has the advantage of being a large country and therefore better able to engage with the world economy on its own terms. It is hard to disagree with this analysis. China, almost alone amongst nation-states, can resist the influence of globalization, and it is a prosperous enough country to guarantee income security for its population. The unfolding Chinese tragedy is that its leaders have set their face against such a path.

NOTES

1. Jiang represented the 'third generation' of CCP leaders, following Mao and Deng. Officially, he assumed power at the Fourth Plenum of the 13th Central Committee in June 1989 (a chronology reiterated by Hu Jintao at the 17th Congress in October 2007) but in practice his authority was limited until Deng's death.

2. Jiang's justification was framed in terms of his theory of the 'Three Represents' (first articulated in 1998 and accommodated into the 2003 Constitution). The idea here was that the Party represented advanced forces of production, advanced culture and the 'overwhelming' majority of the population. According to this last element in the trinity, the Party came to represent workers, peasants, intellectuals, cadres, soldiers—and capitalists. Where once the Party had been the vanguard of the working class, by 2003 only criminals were excluded from its ranks.

3. For a comparison of China and India, see Wu (2007).

4. A 'strong' state is needed for the implementation of a market socialist model because the state needs to be selective in its industrial policy—that is, it needs to subsidize potentially successful industries, and close down losers (those with a poor productivity record and with limited long-run potential). Advocates of this type of approach, and the closely related 'developmental state' model (Johnson 1985; Chang 2002), have long recognized this. However, the developmental statists typically miss the point that an authoritarian state is not necessary strong; the example of sub-Saharan Africa since 1980 illustrates that rather clearly. More generally, it needs to be recognized that there is no correlation between rates of economic growth and the presence of authoritarian

regimes; the international evidence suggests that democracy is usually better for growth (Halperin *et al.* 2005).

5. Amongst Chinese economists, the leading advocates of the neoauthoritarian paradigm in the late 1990s were Dong Fureng, Lin Yifu, Fan Gang and Li Yining. Advocacy of neoauthoritarianism was also of course politically expedient for intellectuals in the aftermath of Tian'anmen because it did not require an attack on Party rule.

6. For concepts and definitions of migrants, see Chan (2001) and Liang and Ma (2004). The origins of the *hukou* system are discussed in Cheng and Selden (1994). For useful discussions of post-1978 migration patterns, see Bakken (1998), Solinger (1999), West and Zhao (2000), Murphy (2002), Gaetano and Jacka (2004) and Fan (2005). Pre-1978 migration is discussed in Shapiro (2001) and Bernstein (1977).

7. The authoritative and generally reliable decennial population censuses themselves adopted differing definitions. The 1990 census defined floaters as those living away from their place of registration for more than a year but included only persons living outside their county or city of origin. By contrast, the 2000 census used a six-month cut-off line and included both intra-county and city and inter-county and city migrants (Liang and Ma 2004).

8. Even under Jiang Zemin, attempts were made to reduce the length of the official working week from forty-eight to forty-four hours in 1996 and to forty hours since 1998 (Lin 2006: 279)

9. For some of the literature on regional inequality and attempts to Develop the West see Wright (2003), Goodman (2004), Lai (2002), Bao *et al.* (2002), Demurger (2002), Démurger *et al.* (2002) and Yeung and Shen (2004).

10. 'Although there should be an order of priority in the economic development of various areas, that does not necessarily mean that development of one area must be postponed pending development of another. The eastern region should take the initiative and consider how to assist the central and western regions to develop' (Central Committee 1991: 501).

11. The writings of Wang Shaoguang and Hu Angang in the mid-1990s (translated in Wang and Hu 1999, 2001) were also influential in redirecting the attention of policy-makers to the problems faced by western China.

12. According to their computations, prices increased much more quickly in Guizhou than in Guangdong between 1990 and 2000, such that the cost of a basket of goods fell from being 37 percent higher in Guangdong in 1990 to being 24 percent higher by 2000.

13. Even this assumes negligible regional price differences, and that is rather a strong assumption. Prices were set by the state, but variation in (for example) the prices paid by the state for the procurement of grain was still considerable even between provinces as close as Sichuan and Yunnan. On the other hand, the variation in the price of industrial goods in rural areas was fairly small. I know of no systematic study of the net effect of this on provincial costs of living in the early 1980s.

14. For a recent summary of this literature on the impact of aid to LDCs, see Collier (2007). He concludes that aid does have positive effects, perhaps in the order of a growth boost of 1 percentage point per annum, but this is hardly enough to remedy the problem of underdevelopment.

15. The extent of Han settlement can, however, be easily exaggerated. The official data from the 2000 census show that, if we exclude the military presence (and that does make a considerable difference), the Han population of Qinghai was 54 percent in 2000, and the figures for Xinjiang and Tibet were lower at 41 and only 6 percent respectively (RKTJNJ 2003: 52).

16. The programme also involves increased investment in health care, rural infrastructure and on supporting farm prices. These goals will no doubt change as the results of the second agricultural census, conducted during 2007, become available.

17. This, and the following, paragraph are heavily based on the work of Zhang (2006).

18. Almost all Chinese intellectuals are nationalists, both out of conviction and from a belief that this is a way to promote stability and hence hold the fragile Chinese state together.

19. Many of the views of the New Left were put forward in the book *China and Globalization: Washington Consensus or Beijing Consensus?* (Huang and Cui 2005). For some of their English-language writings, see Wang C. H. (2003) and Wang H. (2003).

20. For some of Cui's writings in English, see Unger and Cui (1994) and Cui (1997). Liu Kang's writings are also of great interest (Liu 1997, 2004).

21. For some of these ideas, see Dirlik *et al.* (1997).

Chapter 19: The China Model

BY ROWAN CALLICK

Economic freedom plus political repression. That's the sinister, sizzling-hot policy formulation that's displacing the 'Washington Consensus' and winning fans from regimes across Asia, Africa, the Middle East, and Latin America. But, Rowan Callick asks, for how long?

From Vietnam to Syria, Burma to Venezuela, and all across Africa, leaders of developing countries are admiring and emulating what might be called the China Model. It has two components. The first is to copy successful elements of liberal economic policy by opening up much of the economy to foreign and domestic investment, allowing labor flexibility, keeping the tax and regulatory burden low, and creating a first-class infrastructure through a combination of private sector and state spending. The second part is to permit the ruling party to retain a firm grip on government, the courts, the army, the internal security apparatus, and the free flow of information. A shorthand way to describe the model is: economic freedom plus political repression.

The system's advantage over the standard authoritarian or totalitarian approach is obvious: it produces economic growth, which keeps people happy. Under communism and its variations on the right and left, highly centralized state-run economies have performed poorly. The China Model introduces, at least in significant part, the proven success of free-market economics. As citizens get richer, the expectation is that a nondemocratic regime can retain and even enhance its power and authority. There is no doubt that the model has worked in China and may work as well elsewhere, but can it be sustained over the long run?

The Communist Party of China, or CPC, rose to power in the mid-20th century after decades of civil war, starvation, and eventually the invasion of the Japanese. But under Mao, communism fell far short of its economic promise. Then, after the bitter chaos of the Cultural Revolution, which began in 1966 and culminated with the death of Mao in 1976, Deng Xiaoping carefully devised and implemented the formula through which the CPC today retains its legitimacy: the party ensures steadily improving living standards for all, and, in return, the Chinese people let the CPC rule as an authoritarian regime. This economic basis for the party's power gives it a credibility that is being projected well beyond its own borders, with all the more success because of the recent decline in the international standing of the United States, focused as it is on its tough and increasingly lonely task in the Middle East.

The economic portion of the model works like this: open up the doors—*kai fang*—and let in foreign capital, technology, and management skills, guiding the foreigners to use China initially as an export base. Engage with global markets. Let your manufacturing and distribution sectors compete with the best. Give farmers control over their own land, and support the prices of staples.

Do everything you can to lift living standards. Give your middle class an ownership stake in the newly emerging economy by privatizing most of the government housing stock for well below the market price. Corporatize as much of the state sector as you can, and then list minority stakes on the stock market to provide a new outlet for savings. But don't let the central bank off the leash; use it to maintain a hold over the currency exchange rate and other key policy levers. Keep ultimate control over the strategic sectors of the economy; in China's case, these include utilities, transportation, telecommunications, finance, and the media.

The leaders of the Deng and post-Deng years have mostly been engineers, people of a practical bent with a particular enthusiasm for pouring cement and building infrastructure. The salient features of China's economic system, which is still evolving, include increases in inputs, improvement in productivity, relatively low inflation (with the state maintaining a grip on some prices while others are gradually exposed to the market), and rising supply, especially of labor. The country has a large pool of surplus rural workers, as well as many millions more who were laid off as state-owned enterprises underwent rapid reform, emerging from welfare-focused loss centers to become market-focused profit centers.

As it became easy to import sophisticated components from elsewhere in Asia and assemble them in China, most of the Asian neighborhood has been earning bilateral trade surpluses, becoming intimately enmeshed in the Chinese economy. The services sector remains undeveloped, a massive field awaiting investment and exploitation. Huang Yiping, chief Asia economist of Citigroup, says, "The mutually enhancing effects of reform and growth were probably the secret of China's success." The regime has succeeded in one of its prime goals, to generate sufficient surplus value to finance the modernization of the economy. China holds $1.3 trillion worth of foreign reserves.

Even after 30 years of the *kai fang* strategy, however, the Chinese economy remains only selectively open. For instance, although the currency, the yuan, can be converted on the current account, chiefly for trade, its conversion on the capital account, for investment, remains strictly controlled. China is still substantially a cash economy, with little use made of Internet banking or even of credit cards or mortgages.

The People's Bank of China remains a tool of government rather than an autonomous institution, as most Western central banks now are. A large range of core industries are, by policy, fully or majority-owned by the government, and although the four "pillar banks" have attracted massive investments from Western corporations and from international shareholders, their boards and management are regularly shifted according to the needs of the party-state. Foreigners are free to establish fully owned firms in a fast-growing range of activities from manufacturing, processing, and assembly to banking and leasing, rather than being required, as before, to enter joint ventures with local partners. But the regulatory hurdles to register such companies usually take many months to negotiate. Indeed, much of China's business environment is negotiable. There appear to be few absolutes.

Nontariff barriers to trade are declining, but they remain legion, especially in the services sector. Still, more and more foreigners are successfully doing business in China "below the radar" with small operations, such as restaurants, art galleries, and marketing firms, while the latest American Chamber of Commerce survey says that 73 percent of American companies operating in China claim they are operating profitably, with 37 percent adding that their profits in China are higher than their average global profits.

This steady but cautious opening of the economy to foreigners and to domestic entrepreneurs to a defined degree has ensured that as global liquidity has soared, much of it has found its way to China. The country's very scale, with a population of 1.3 billion, is a lure in itself, but it is the nation's convulsive arrival as not merely a receptacle but a driver of globalization that best explains its attraction to international business.

Many of China's global partners require transparent governance, independent courts, enforceable property rights, and free information. None of these is present in China today, or will be unless the party surrenders a degree of political authority it has so far regarded as inconceivable. Won't pressure for these four requirements in itself apply sufficient pressure to force liberalization? Not necessarily—because China meets all four, plus a freely convertible currency and a free port, in its own city of Hong Kong, governed under the "one country, two systems" format devised by Deng. Hong Kong is a valve to release pressures that might cause a rigid centralized economy to explode.

Nor does China seem especially vulnerable to outside shocks. Daniel Rosen, principal of China Strategic Advisory, says that at the time of the Asian financial crisis a decade ago, which China largely sailed through, "the country had not opened its

320 Growth and Crises in the Asian Pacific Rim

capital account, relied on foreign debt, floated its currency, freed monetary policy from political control, or even relinquished the role of the state as a predominant force in financial flows. A decade later, with a new sort of financial crisis unfolding in the United States subprime mortgage market, many believe the factors that insulated China in the past still buffer it today." However, he concludes, this isn't the final word: "The macroeconomic outlook is strong not because China is immune from adjustment pressures amplified by global credit conditions, but because it has a demonstrated willingness to accept adjustment where necessary."

The China Model is demonstrating this cautious adaptability by shifting its focus from inward investment to outward investment—making its foreign reserves start to build the returns it will need as it faces the demographic jolt caused by the shift in policies from Mao's "populate or perish" to the one-child urban family. "In addition," says Italian journalist Francesco Sisci, "the party has shown itself adept at co-opting potentially troublesome private sector businesspeople by recruiting them into the National People's Congress and the Chinese People's Political Consultative Conference."

When previous leader Jiang Zemin opened the Communist Party to such people, many commentators saw capitalists taking over the party. The reverse has happened, with the party extending its controls into the thriving private sector, where growing numbers of party branches are being established. But, Sisci concludes, "it is very hard to believe that in 15 to 20 years, when the middle class could be asked to pay 30 percent or more of its income in taxes, and both Chinese society and the world at large have become more open, that this middle class will remain content to stay out of politics."

No one, however, is anticipating such a shift anytime soon. In the 1990s, a presumption grew that the crowds of well-connected young Chinese returning with their Ivy League MBAs would not acquiesce to the continued unaccountable rule of the cadres. But many of them instead joined the party with alacrity. A striking example is that of Li Qun, who studied in the U.S. and then served as assistant to the mayor of New Haven, writing a book in Chinese on his experiences. After his return to China, he became a mayor himself, of Linyi in Shandong Province in the Northeast. There, he swiftly became the nemesis of one of Chinas most famous human rights lawyers, the blind Chen Guangcheng. First, Chen was placed under house arrest and his lawyers and friends were beaten because of his campaign against forced sterilizations of village women. Then Chen was charged, bizarrely, with conspiring to disrupt traffic when a trail of further arrests led to public protests. He was jailed for four years.

Thus, best of all, in the view of many of the international admirers of the China Model, is that the leaders, while opening the economy to foster consumption, retain full political control to silence "troublemakers" like Chen. Indeed, the big attractions of China to capital from overseas has been that the political setting is stable, that there will be no populist campaign to nationalize foreign assets, that the labor force is both flexible and disciplined, and that policy changes are rational and are signaled well ahead. Economic management is pragmatic, in line with Deng Xiaoping's encomium to "cross the river by feeling for stones," while political management is stern but increasingly collegiate, the personality cult having been jettisoned after Mao and factions having faded together with ideology.

The CPC is replacing old-style communist values with nationalism and a form of Confucianism, in a manner that echoes the "Asian values" espoused by the leaders who brought Southeast Asian countries through their rapid modernization process in Singapore, Malaysia, Thailand, and elsewhere. But at the same time, in its public rhetoric, the party is stressing continuity and is assiduously ensuring that its own version of history remains correct. Historian Xia Chun-tao, 43, vice director of the Deng Xiaoping Thought Research Center, one of China's core ideological think tanks, says, "It's very natural for historians to have different views on events. But there is only one correct and accurate interpretation, and only one explanation that is closest to the truth." The key issues, he says, are "quite clearly defined" and not susceptible to debate. "There is a pool of clear water and there's no need to stir up this water. Doing so can only cause disturbance in people's minds. ... However much time passes, the party's general judgment" on such key events won't change.

The party, for example, required its 70 million members to view, late in 2006, a series of eight DVDs made by the country's top documentary producers about the fall of the Soviet Union. The videos denigrated the Khrushchev era because it ignored the crucial role of Joseph Stalin and thus "denied the history of the Soviet Union, which in turn triggered severe problems." Young Soviet party members who grew up in this atmosphere lacked familiarity with the party's traditions, and "it was they who went on to bury the party." According to the CPC version of history, Stalin was wrongly viewed in the Soviet Union as the source of all sins, "in spite of the glories of socialism."

But the documentary series ended on an upbeat note: the Russian people are rethinking what happened, and two-thirds of those surveyed now regret the fall of the Soviet Union. "When Vladimir Putin stepped in, he reestablished pride in the country," according to the videos. For Stalin, of course, read Mao. The CPC has no intention of taking Mao's vast portrait off the Tiananmen Gate, nor burying his waxed corpse, sporadically on view at the Soviet-style mausoleum whose construction destroyed the *feng shui*, the harmony, of Tiananmen Square that Mao himself created.

In the May/June edition of the American, Kevin Hassett, director of economic policy studies at the American Enterprise Institute, explained that evidence is emerging that developing "countries that are economically and politically free are underperforming the countries that are economically but not politically free." China, of course, is in the lead of the economically free but politically unfree nations. Hassett wrote, "The unfree governments now understand that they have to provide a good economy to keep citizens happy, and they understand that free-market economies work best. ... Being unfree may be an economic advantage. Dictatorships are not hamstrung by the preference of voters for, say, a pervasive welfare state. So the future may look something like the 20th century in reverse. The unfree nations will grow so quickly that they will overwhelm free nations with their economic might."

The kleptocrats who have ruled many developing countries in past decades have tended to come unstuck when Western aid dwindles, their own economies falter and then fall backward, and all too often rivals emerge within their armies. The China Model presents the possibility that such rulers can gain access to immense wealth through creaming off rents while at the same time their broader populations become content, and probably supportive, because their living standards also are leaping ahead. This formula also entails hard work, application, policy consistency, and administrative capacity spread through the country—hurdles where followers of China are likely to fall. But for now, they're lining up in hope and expectation.

Even some Westerners are impressed by the new China. American swimming superstar Michael Phelps said on a visit to Beijing, the host city of the Olympic Games next August, "Going to the hotel, we see Subway, 7-Eleven, Starbucks, Sizzler, McDonald's. It's like a big American city. They have everything we have in the States." In fact, they don't. They lack basic freedoms.

It is true that the Chinese people are free to consume whatever they can afford. That's novel. They have also gained in the last three decades the freedom to travel where they want, at home and abroad. They can now work for whom they want, where they want. They can buy their own home, and live where they choose (the *houkou* system of registration is breaking down). A Chinese woman can marry the man she loves, though in the cities the couple can still only have one child unless they can afford the fine for having more. The Chinese can study at any institution that will have them. They can meet anyone they like, but not in a suspiciously large group.

The emerging middle class also benefits from a "gray economy" that, a recent survey by the National Economic Research Institute led by Wang Xiaolu has discovered, is worth a breathtaking $500 billion a year, equivalent to 24 percent of China's GDP. That's why new graduates clamor for government jobs ahead of those with glamorous international corporations—because the opportunities to get rich quick during this transitional period of asset transference from the state, and to benefit hugely from rent-seeking, are so great.

But Chinese citizens can't form a political party, or any other organized group, without official permission. They can't choose their leaders. Even the ordinary CPC members have no say in their hierarchy. Sisci, Beijing correspondent of the Italian newspaper La Stampa, writes in the China Economic Quarterly that "there is something like a 75 percent avoidance rate on personal income tax" because few people anywhere choose to concede taxation without any representation. "There is a political pact," he writes. "The government allows tax evasion in return for political obedience. So far, the middle class has acquiesced: it prefers to pay less taxes and not vote, rather than buy its right to elect the government by paying more taxes."

Phone calls, text messages, and emails are likely to be screened, and many Internet sites—such as Wikipedia and BBC News—are blocked or filtered by the 30,000 "net police." Bloggers must give their real names and identity card numbers to their Internet service providers, which must in turn make them available to the authorities when asked. Tim Hancock, Amnesty International's campaign director in the UK, says, "The Chinese model of an Internet that allows economic growth but not free speech or privacy is growing in popularity, from a handful of countries five years ago to dozens of governments today who block sites and arrest bloggers."

All books published in China must bear a license code from a state-owned publishing house. Books under question are sent out to groups of retired cadres to censor. Before art exhibitions, says painter Yao Junzhong, who now sells most of his work over-seas, the local cultural bureau usually sends a list of taboos to the organizers, and through them to the artists: "You will be told not to attack communism, not to attack the party. Sex is sensitive. So is violence. But not as much as politics." He recently had to send three photos of a painting, ready for an exhibition, to a gallery owner, the cultural bureau, and the exhibition organizer. The picture showed his young son holding a gun, set in a renminbi coin. "I named it 'Qianjin,' which means advance, and also means money." A cadre couldn't put his finger on it, but felt "there must be a political element," so the organizer was told it was not appropriate.

All films must be vetted by the State Administration for Radio, Film, and Television. All print media are government- or party-owned. The party's propaganda department has recently introduced a penalty scheme for media outlets that deducts points for defying government guidance. Twelve points means closure. Every inch of public territory remains tightly defended, although warnings are usually not explicit, leaving maximum space for artists to choose to censor themselves. Leading new-wave filmmaker Jia Zhangke, winner of the top award, the Golden Lion, at last year's Venice Film Festival, says, "If we don't touch the taboo areas, we will have a lot of freedom. But then those areas grow larger. If your tactic is to guess what the censors are thinking, and try to avoid their concerns, you are ruined as an artist."

Chinese people do not expect to obtain justice from the courts, which are run by the party, the judges answerable to the local top cadres. Ordinary people, the *laobaixing*, have to negotiate their way out of any troubles if they can. They have grown accustomed to, but not accepting of, widespread corruption. They are meant to report to the neighborhood police whenever someone new comes to stay with them. A file is kept on Chinese citizens, which follows their work and home moves, but they cannot see it. There are only two legal churches that the Chinese can join, the Catholic and the Three Self (Protestant) organizations; the leaders of both are ultimately responsible to the party. Evangelism is not permitted. There are no church schools.

Freedom House, in its annual survey, gives China a ranking of "7" for political rights—the organization's lowest rating and the same as that of North Korea, Burma, and Cuba (Japan ranks "1"). China ranks only slightly higher, at "6," for civil liberties, the same as Iran, Saudi Arabia, and Zimbabwe.

In the 1980s, wishful thinking on the part of some Western observers, combined with a form of historical determinism that was, in its way, a tribute to the thinking of Hegel and Marx, had China inevitably becoming more free and democratic as it became more of a market economy. The Tiananmen massacre caused some head-scratching for a while, but Western business, in particular, tended to take the public view, when pressed, that a semicapitalist country was bound to evolve in time into a democracy, because the emerging middle class would demand it.

Now, such views have faded. Premier Wen Jiabao said during the last annual session of China's version of a parliament, the National People's Congress, that the country would remain at the present "primary stage of socialism," during which it would require continued guidance by the party, for at least another 100 years. This model of the state has power going from the top down, and accountability from the bottom up. It also leans heavily on the seductive story of China's ancient uniqueness, its serial defiance of foreign prescriptions.

This story of cultural heroism, even though it is bound up in the China Model, with its far warmer embrace of globalization than most other developing nations have conceded, has acquired a glossy appeal because of the sheer, palpable success of China's modernization drive. The nation's gross domestic product has grown at an average annual rate of more than 10 percent since 1990.

When 21 leaders controlling three-fifths of the world's economy met at the latest Asia Pacific Economic Cooperation summit in Sydney in September, The Nation newspaper in Thailand editorialized: "One could easily spot who the real mover and shaker among them was. It used to be that what the leader of the U.S. said was what would count the most. That is no longer." The new mover and shaker is China. The entire piece was reprinted by The Statesman, an influential English-language newspaper in India. Developing nations believe that, as an ideal, the China Model has replaced the American Model, especially as embodied in the "Washington Consensus," a set of 10 liberal democratic reforms the U.S. prescribed in 1989 for developing nations.

Last November, 41 African heads of state or government were flown by China to Beijing for a summit hosted by President Hu Jintao. The government ordered most cars to stay off the roads as the leaders sped to meetings and banquets. One million security forces were deployed for almost a week to ensure the summit went smoothly. Abundant affirming slogans such as "La Belle Afrique" and attention to ingratiating detail—hotel staff learning African greetings, rooms decorated with African motifs, magnificent gifts even for the thousands in the presidents' and prime ministers' retinues—marked a contrast with concerns about corruption, crime, and cruel civil war that comprise most Western encounters with Africa.

Premier Wen said that two-way trade between China and Africa would double to $110 billion by 2010, after soaring tenfold in the last decade, with fuels comprising more than half of China's imports from Africa. China is canceling its debts due from the least developed countries in Africa, setting up a $5.5 billion fund to subsidize Chinese companies' investments in the continent, and increasing from 190 to 440 the number of items that Africa's poorest countries can export to China tariff-free. Already, by a large margin, China is the biggest lender to Africa, providing $8.9 billion this year to Angola, Mozambique, and Nigeria alone. The World Bank, by contrast, is lending $2.6 billion to *all* of sub-Saharan Africa.

The Western requirement that good-governance medicine must be consumed in return for modest aid is now not only unwelcome but also, as far as many African leaders are concerned, outdated. They are no longer cornered without options. Now they've got China, which is offering trade and investment, big time, as well as aid. And more than that, they've got the China Model itself.

This is no longer the communist program that Mao Zedong tried to export with little success except in places like Peru and Nepal, where Maoists have survived long after they have vanished from China itself. It is, instead, the program that gives business room to grow and make profits, while ensuring it walks hand in hand with big, implacable government. And, of course, the China Model holds out the promise of providing the leaders of developing nations the lifestyles to which they would love to become accustomed.

This is the China Model: half liberal and international, half authoritarian and insular. Can it last?

A few writers have become mildly wealthier by forecasting doom. The best known is lawyer Gordon Chang, whose book, *The Coming Collapse of China*, published in 2001 by Random House, concluded, "Beijing has about five years to put things right." Chang made clear that he did not expect the party to pull it off. His litany of likely triggers of collapse included entry into the World Trade Organization (which happened in December 2001), within whose regulatory structure, he said, China could not remain competitive; the impossibility of reforming the 50,000 state-owned enterprises, which he said sucked up 70 percent of domestic loans while producing less than 30 percent of the economy's output; the failure of the reform of the banking system, with its huge burden of nonperforming loans and planned restructuring through inexperienced asset-management companies; the government's lack of revenues; corruption; and the rush of new global information and views made available on the Internet. Chang's critique was plausible at the time, but now, six years later, it merely underlines how dangerous it is to bet against China's pragmatic economic reform program.

Randall Peerenboom of UCLA describes in his new book—*China Modernizes: Threat to the West or Model for the Rest?*—the country's "paradigm for developing states, a 21st-century, technologically leap-frogging variant of the East Asian developmental state that has resulted in such remarkable success for Japan, South Korea, Hong Kong, Singapore, and Taiwan." China resisted the advice of foreign experts to engage in shock therapy, he says, and has persisted in gradual reform. The state has played a key role in setting economic policy, establishing government institutions, regulating foreign investment, and mitigating the adverse effects of globalization in domestic constituencies. And the strategy has broadly worked: "Chinese citizens are generally better off" than in 1989. "Most live longer, more are able to read and write, most enjoy higher living standards. China outperforms the average country in its income class on most major indicators of human rights and well-being, with the notable exception of civil and political rights."

Where China fails to match up, however, is in creativity and innovation, without which it may have to resign itself to remaining a net importer of new technologies, and a manufacturer under license. It has failed to produce a single global brand to compare with its neighbors. Japan has its Sony, Toyota, Panasonic, Honda, and the rest. South Korea has its Samsung and Hyundai. Taiwan has its Acer, BenQ, and Giant bicycles. China's Haier white goods and Lenovo personal computers remain, for now, wannabes. The controls that China deploys on use of the Internet, the battles it wages with its artists in every field, the focus in its education system on rote learning, the continuing failure to implement its own intellectual property rules, and now the embracing of a new Confucianism—all of these inhibit lateral thinking and invention.

As Maoism and Marxism lose their grip, the dangers of nationalism as a defining value system become apparent, and religion remains under suspicion as a potentially powerful rival to the Communist Party and the authoritarian state, Chinas leaders are eagerly rediscovering the country's 2,500-year-old Confucian tradition.

Contemporary philosophers claim to be reengineering Confucianism to suit the needs of 21st-century China by, for instance, focusing on the ecological potential in its advocacy of "the unity of heaven and humanity" and on its requirement of self-discipline. But the reasons that early-20th-century modernizers and artists, including China's greatest writer, Lu Xun, rejected Confucianism as essentially authoritarian and inimical to modernization remain unaddressed.

Lee Yuan-tseh, the president of Taiwan's top research institute, Academia Sinica, describes how, after a traditional Confucian upbringing, he shifted for postgraduate opportunities to the United States, first at the University of California at Berkeley, then Harvard, then Chicago, and back to California. He says that the inquisitive academic climate there "made me think bad thoughts: that my teacher was wrong." In time, he took what he describes as the biggest step of his life—telling the teacher so. In 1986, he won the Nobel Prize for chemistry. In 2000, Gao Xingjian won the Nobel Prize for literature, but only after he had exiled himself and become a French citizen. No person has ever won a Nobel Prize for work in China; the U.S., by contrast, has won nearly 300 Nobel Prizes, winning or sharing four of the six 2006 awards.

Even in entrepreneurship and wealth creation, the CPC retains its grip. Carsten Holz, an economics professor at the Hong Kong University of Science and Technology, wrote in the Far Eastern Economic Review that "of the 3,220 Chinese citizens with a personal wealth of 100 million yuan ($13 million) or more, 2,932 are children of high-level cadres. Of the key positions in the five industrial sectors—finance, foreign trade, land development, large-scale engineering, and securities—85 percent to 90 percent are held by children of high-level cadres."

Attempts are being made to shift the economy higher up the value-added chain by creating and importing more capital-intensive companies. For instance, on a vast industrial estate southeast of Beijing, Richard Chang, a Taiwan-raised American citizen, has built a $1.5 billion microchip-making factory for his company. Semiconductor Manufacturing International Corporation. The factory employs 2,000 staff who work in "clean rooms" constantly tested for dust and humidity. The machines there cost up to $30 million each. About 55 percent of the staff have undergraduate degrees, and 10 percent are hired from overseas. All have three months of in-house training before they begin work.

In 2006, manufacturers in China bought $64 billion worth of chips, but much of that hardware was imported. Whether SMIC—which Chang founded only in 2000, after working for 20 years with Texas Instruments—can build the research capacity and the skills needed to compete will provide an important test of China's ability to move its model on to a higher plane. China, in typical fashion, threw a heap of incentives Chang's way to ensure he got up and running: free land, syndicated loans, R&D aid, zero tax.

Like most other East Asian states, China's route to development placed economic reforms before democratization. But the China Model differs markedly from most of the region in that it has resisted taking any serious steps down that road to democracy. There is talk of "intraparty democracy" within continued one-party rule, but unsurprisingly, no champions of it have any real influence. There were also some token village elections, but they have remained dominated by the CPC and its cadres. Commentator Shu Shengxiang wrote in July, on the influential website Baixing ("the common people"): "The democratically elected cadres are gouging the people [by corruption] too. They do not know that a democracy which only has elections but not supervision is at best a half-baked democracy, if not a fake democracy. Half-baked democracy not only harms the villagers' personal interests, but even gives them the misconception that democracy is not good."

At the same time, however, the party is refining its contract with the Chinese people to reflect shifting popular concerns about living standards: the quality of growth as well as the quantum. Leading this new agenda is the environment, which surveys show tends to top, together with corruption and access to health and education services, the concerns of most Chinese. The World Bank says China contains 16 of the world's 20 most polluted cities in their air quality, and anxieties about both water and air have triggered a large proportion of China's "mass events"—demonstrations and protests—which even official figures estimated at 87,000 in 2005.

The central government has effectively opened the environment to media commentary and to the establishment of NGOs, and has pinned the blame for the worst environmental disasters on avaricious or neglectful local officials. Ambitious targets have been set, in the five-year plan that began in 2006, for reduction of carbon dioxide and sulfur emissions, and for the use of energy per unit of production. The goals are not being met, and the central government appears determined to impress the whole apparatus that its new green program is not just rhetoric, but that it means business.

This shift from quantity to quality of growth will form the core of the agenda in the second term of the current "fourth generation" of leaders around Hu Jintao and Wen Jiabao. At the party congress, which occurs every five years and started on October 15, their aim is to ensure that only people on board this quality-of-life program get promoted, both in the central institutions and in the provinces. The key principle for their decade in power is the Confucian concept of harmony—as in stability and avoidance of dissent.

This China offers a seductive model that is being eagerly taken up by the leaders of countries that have not yet settled into democratic structures: Vietnam; Burma; Laos; the Central Asian dictatorships that were part of the Soviet Union; a growing portion of the Middle East, starting with the United Arab Emirates, including its glossy new centers like Dubai; Cuba; most of Africa, including South Africa; and even to a degree the hereditary cult that is North Korea. Beijing sometimes gives more than it receives to cement its developing world leadership, according most-favored-nation status to Vietnam, Laos, and Cambodia even before they join the World Trade Organization. In an unsettling way, the China Model is attractive to the leaders of some countries that had already become democratic, such as Venezuela. The model is even inspiring democratic India to compete with its own adaptive version.

The China Model is, of course, admired in the West, too, with business leaders' words (at platforms such as Forbes magazine conferences and the World Economic Forum, which has just instituted an annual summer session in China) providing great reinforcement for Chinese leaders. The World Bank is just one of the international institutions that champion China (its greatest client and in some ways its boss) as a paradigm for the developing world. Also fascinating is the appeal of the China Model to Russia, which as Azar Gat, professor of national security at Tel Aviv University, writes in Foreign Affairs, "is retreating from its post-communist liberalism and assuming an increasingly authoritarian character as its economic clout grows." China is exporting scores of Confucian Institutes, most of them at first just language schools but in the future offering platforms for extending Chinese influence.

But back to our question: Is the China Model sustainable? Two recent books come up with opposite answers. The British center-left economist Will Hutton, author of *The Writing on the Wall*, says China must accede to Enlightenment values or start to fall back again. American journalist James Mann, author of *The China Fantasy*, argues, in contrast, that the Chinese middle class is thoroughly behind the China Model as its major beneficiary, ensuring that the usual source of confrontation with the power elite is not just docile, but eagerly applauding.

It may take a non-Sinologist like Hutton to see how very strange it is that a one-party state that pays lip service (at least) to the doctrines of Marx, Lenin, and Mao should not only survive into the 21st century after all its principal totalitarian and authoritarian peers have collapsed, fallen apart, or been beaten in world wars, but actually prosper, to the degree that its system is starting to gain such currency in the developing world.

"The party is facing a growing issue of legitimacy," he writes. "If it no longer rules as the democratic dictatorship of peasants and workers, because the class war is over, why does it not hold itself accountable to the people in competitive elections?" The answer is in the phrase Hutton himself frequently uses; "party-state." The party won power by force of arms. The People's Liberation Army answers to the party, not to the government or the nation, insofar as those concepts can be levered apart from the party any more. The party's legitimacy, as viewed by most Chinese, lies in its history and past leaders, in its contemporary success at bringing prosperity to a thankful nation, and in its unyielding grip on the trappings of nationalism.

The large gold star in China's flag, for instance, represents the CPC, the four smaller stars the workers, the peasants, the petty bourgeois, and capitalists sympathetic to the party. In the early 1980s, there was some vestigial discussion about separating party and state, but the idea was abandoned as both impractical and undesirable. The party rules today through four pillars—the army, the legal apparatus including the courts and police, the administration, and the state corporations that dominate the "strategic" sectors of the economy. Without cutting away these pillars, without separating the powers, any attempt at "competitive elections" would be hollow. But the pillars appear, to use an understatement, firmly entrenched.

Hutton reiterates the old contention that China's middle class, "more internationalist than its poor," will ultimately insist that the party loosen its political control. James Mann replies that the middle class is doing very nicely, thank you, within the structure as it is. Its members are substantially incorporated into the party and are the structure's biggest supporters, not its underminers.

Hutton's most convincing critique is that "China has no business tradition that understands the moral facet of capitalism, … whose 'soft' institutions (a common culture and shared purpose) are as integral to growth and sustainability as the 'hard' processes." The difficulty Chinese enterprise has in understanding, let alone absorbing and practicing, the morality and trust that are at the root of capitalism and of successful globalization is on display ever more luridly as food, drugs, toothpaste, toys, and a growing list of other products ring international alarm bells and cast a shadow over the "Made in China" brand credibility.

His core conclusion is this: "Welfare systems, freedom of association, representative government, and enforceable property rights are not simply pleasant options. They are central to the capacity of a capitalist economy to grow to maturity. … The party can relax its political control to allow the economic reform process to be completed. Or it can retain political control, watch the economic contradictions build, and so create the social tension that may force loss of political control."

Hutton is not the first commentator to draw up a balance sheet of economic and social pluses and minuses for China, and figure that something has to give politically. "The clock is ticking," he warns. But time keeps passing unremarkably, and one diligent and uncharismatic group of leaders quietly makes way for the next, and the party-state not only remains intact but also appears to flourish.

James Mann, however, says that if China does retain a repressive one-party political system for a long time, this "may indeed be just the China that the American or European business and government leaders who deal regularly" with the country want. The "fantasy" in his book's title is the notion that commerce will lead to democracy or liberalization. One of his scenarios is that the party is still in power 25 years from now, though perhaps called the "Reform Party." But if it is to change names, the CPC will probably find that the "China Party" is the easiest sell.

Leading Australian economist Ross Garnaut, a former ambassador to China, adds an important element of historical perspective—that first Britain, and then the United States, industrialized in a helter-skelter way, which was crucially moderated and channeled by institutional accountability that prevented the industrial-baron entrepreneurs from losing proportion, alienating the population, and misallocating capital disastrously. The institutions that developed to meet this challenge of a rampant new power elite included parliaments, legal structures, and independent regulatory agencies. Will China follow suit, or will its go-it-alone party steer its economy, after three decades of success, into difficult waters (or onto the reefs) because it lacks the true self-confidence to expose itself to other sources of power?

It is almost certain that China will push on with its present structure, but with the prospect of broadening democratic competitiveness for posts within the party, and institutionalizing consultations with more diverse groups in Chinese society, some outside the party. The "ample evidence" that Randall Peerenboom catalogs in his book, "that other countries are looking to China for inspiration," reinforces the CPC's determination to persevere. Laos is following China's lead in implementing market reforms and producing higher growth. Iran and other Middle East countries, including Syria, have invited experts on Chinese law, economics, and politics to lecture to senior officials and academics. They are all attracted by what they see as China's pragmatic approach to reform. The official newspaper China Daily recently hosted on its website a reader discussion on the theme: "China is a role model to all developing nations. After centuries of oppression and domination by Western nations, most developing nations are trying to pull themselves up from poverty. They look at China's rapid progress as an example. China also gives aid and technical help to these nations." The theme attracted a host of supportive responses, such as, "China has shown that you can be successful by expanding through commerce and diplomacy, not by the imperialism demonstrated by the U.S. and UK."

Vietnam, Cuba, Burma, and Venezuela provide good examples of the China Model's attraction. Vietnam, whose economic reform program, *doi moi*, began twenty years ago, has followed China closely, especially replicating its outward-looking foreign investment regime. As a result, strong links have been created between the two communist countries, which are also the fastest-growing economies in Asia. In 2006, China had 377 direct investments in Vietnam. Since China and Vietnam resumed official economic relations in 1991, after Vietnam had allied itself with the Soviet Union, bilateral Chinese-Vietnamese trade has grown at an annual average of 40 percent. Meanwhile, Vietnam maintains a political system as authoritarian as China's, with a ranking of "7" for political rights from Freedom House.

Vietnam's new prime minister, Nguyen Tan Dun, says he wants to ramp up economic cooperation with China, and that the countries "should increase their cooperation to accelerate trade promotion and investment, plus organize trade fairs and exhibitions, to help each other seek more trade and investment opportunities." In Vietnam's north, close to China's booming Guangdong Province, average wages and real estate are much cheaper than in coastal China. Vietnam is the most successful economically of the countries using the China Model, and its entrepreneurial talents suggest that in some areas it could in time even leapfrog it.

China's ability to honor Mao, even as it tears down the economy he set in place, could provide a model for Cuba, says William Ratliff, a research fellow at Stanford University's Hoover Institution who is an expert on both countries. "During the past fifteen years, important members of the Cuban political, military, and business elite, including Fidel and Raul Castro and two-thirds of the members of the Communist Party Politburo, have visited China and remarked with great interest on the Chinese reform experience," Ratliff says. After Raul's visit to China, Zhu Rongji, a leading architect of economic reforms who was then premier, sent one of his chief aides to Cuba, where he lectured hundreds of leaders, with substantial impact.

Ratliff cites a Cuban intelligence official as saying: "Once Fidel Castro is out of the game, other areas of the Chinese experience will most probably be implemented in Cuba rather quickly." Besides the economic model, the Chinese concept of an orderly succession of leaders within an authoritarian system also holds a deep attraction.

Former Chinese Foreign Minister Tang Jiaxuan, often sent as an emissary by President Hu to neighboring countries, said in September that "China wholeheartedly hopes that

Burma will push forward a democracy process that is appropriate for the country." The statement underlines China's crucial support for the ruling military regime, which usurped the election won convincingly in 1990 by Aung San Suu Kyi's party, with 390 of 492 seats. But Tang adds a note of disquiet; China is no longer blasé about being viewed as the main backer of dictatorships, including Sudan and Zimbabwe, and would rather that Burma, like those other outcast countries, worked harder to establish better relations with the rest of the world. In his speech. Tang was supporting the Burmese rulers' plan to introduce a new constitution, and at the same time move toward a market economy, reinforcing the influence of China as their key model.

Since the start of 2007, there has been a surge in diplomatic and business visits by leaders between the countries, with the intention of strengthening economic and strategic ties. As in other countries committing themselves to the China Model, the exchanges entail Chinese businesspeople, technicians, and workers coming to live in Burma for lengthy periods. The South China Morning Post has described three Burmese cities—Lashio, Mandalay, and Muse—as "virtually Chinese cities now." China is building a tax-free export zone for its own industries next to the port of Rangoon.

Meanwhile, Venezuela's regime has become the leader of the hard left's opposition to Western-led globalization. In August 2006, President Hugo Chávez said on arriving in Beijing: "This will he my most important visit to China, with whom we will build a strategic alliance. Our plans are to create a multipolar world, and to challenge the hegemony of the United States." His attempts to enmesh China in his high-stakes campaign against the U.S. were deflected by courteous formalities, but China's economic support—chiefly through investment in energy projects and purchase of oil, despite Venezuela's heavy crude being costly to refine and expensive to transport across the globe—considerably aided Chávez's election campaign last December. Chavez praised China as an economic model for the world: "It's an example for Western leaders and governments who claim that capitalism is the only alternative. One of the greatest events of the 20th century was the Chinese revolution."

Joshua Kurlantzick, the author of *Charm Offensive: How China's Soft Power Is Transforming the World*, writes: "No one has experience with today's China as a global player. ... In a short period of time, China appears to have created a systematic, coherent soft power strategy, and a set of soft power tools to implement it"—particularly public diplomacy, aid, and trade—"though it is still in a honeymoon period in which many nations have not recognized the downsides of Beijing's new power." Those downsides might include a cavalier approach to the environment—other people's as well as China's own—growing military clout, the migration of large numbers of Chinese workers and businesspeople accompanying its trade and investment, harsh labor standards on its projects, and in general a new variant on old colonialism.

Kurlantzick writes: "As China becomes more powerful, other nations will begin to see beyond its benign face to a more complicated reality. They will realize that despite

Chinas promises of noninterference, when it comes to core interests, China—like any great power—will think of itself first.

"China could create blowback against itself in other ways, too. Still a developing country itself, China could overplay its hand, making the kind of promises on aid and investment that it cannot fulfill. And in the long run, if countries like Burma ever made the transition to freer governments, China could face a sizable backlash for its past support for their authoritarian rulers. 'We know who stands behind the [Burmese] government,' one Burmese businessman told me last year. 'We'll remember.'"

The U.S., Japan, and other countries have been urging China to become more transparent about the rapid development of its military capacity, underlined last January by its missile shot that successfully destroyed an aging satellite, and by the sudden surfacing of a submarine, earlier this year, within five miles of the American aircraft carrier *Kitty Hawk*. At least some of the increased military budget is intended to compensate the People's Liberation Army for its lost revenues when it was required, by forceful former Premier Zhu Rongji, to sell off most of its considerable business portfolio.

The principal foreign policy goals appear clear: preventing Taiwan from converting its de facto independence to de jure independence, maintaining a constant capacity to attempt an invasion, extending China's capacity to open up new forms of access to reliable sources of energy and other commodities, and helping safeguard such routes.

China's capacity to project adventurist military power far beyond its borders, or to offer significant help for other countries to do the same—for instance in Venezuela, unsettling the U.S.'s immediate neighborhood—is limited today both by its resources and by its reluctance to leave its heartland short of the muscle the party may need to quell domestic disturbances like those that swept the country in 1989.

To prevent a growing fear of China's economic power, Beijing wants to demonstrate, Kurlantzick points out, that as it grows, it will become a much larger consumer of other nations' goods, creating—in a favorite phrase of the current leadership—"win-win" economics. Chinese leaders constantly talk up the value of likely investments and trade, with total outward investment rising, according to official statistics, 1,000 percent in 2005, though this figure includes mere commitments and the total is only $7 billion, compared with $60 billion in foreign direct investment (excluding the finance sector) flowing to China.

China's soft power offensive and the lure of the China Model remain, however, entirely official government programs. Where soft power has worked durably and has permeated connections among nations and nationalities, it has also involved civil society and the media, the arts, cultural attraction—the broad range of informal human contacts. Beijing will not let such areas of life off the leash at home, let alone license them for export. Thus, its charm in the developing world remains that of the official with his jacket still on, the limousine with darkened windows waiting outside—fully paid for—and the critics regularly, clinically rounded up and removed beyond earshot.

Chapter 20: China's Rebalancing Act

By Jahangir Aziz and Steven Dunaway

n the past 20 years, China has added about $2 trillion to world GDP, created 120 million new jobs, and pulled 400 million people out of poverty. These are big numbers—equivalent to adding a country of the economic size of Portugal every year; creating as many new jobs each year as the total number of people employed in Australia; and eradicating poverty in Ethiopia, Nigeria, Tanzania, and Zambia combined. In recent years, China has grown more than 10 percent annually while keeping inflation below 3 percent. Today, it is the fourth largest economy in the world and the third largest trading nation.

Despite these remarkable achievements, there is growing unease within China and abroad about the state of its economy. At the National People's Congress this March, Premier Wen Jiabao cautioned, "the biggest problem with China's economy is that the growth is unstable, unbalanced, uncoordinated, and unsustainable." More generally, the question is whether the pace of growth is sustainable or whether the imbalances in the economy might slow growth, perhaps significantly. And this is why China's policy-makers are looking to rebalance the economy to rely less on exports and investment and more on consumption as the source of growth.

What are the underlying causes of these imbalances and how should they be addressed? Those are critical questions not only for China but also for much of the rest of the world, whose prosperity is linked to China. For as China has grown, its economic impact on many countries has magnified, whether through its large trade imbalances, exchange rate issues, or its large and growing need for resources and food. There are many suggestions about the policies China should pursue to rebalance its economy—and some even argue that the rebalancing will occur "naturally" as a result of market forces. We believe that a rebalancing will not happen on its own and lean toward an effort that relies on monetary policy, price liberalization, financial market reform, and changes in government expenditure policies.

HOW IT BEGAN

China's liberalization is usually separated into three phases—the reforms of 1978, 1984, and 1994—each of which further opened the economy. The 1994 reforms had three prongs: the unification of the official and market exchange rates and the removal of restrictions on payments for trading goods, services, and income; the opening of the export sector to foreign direct investment; and the reform of the state-owned enterprises (SOEs). The first two changes turned the export sector into a powerful engine of growth, and the third unleashed domestic entrepreneurship.

Foreign enterprises, on their own and in joint ventures, used China's cheap but skilled labor to convert the coastline into the "world's workshop" and a critical node in the global supply chain. Meanwhile, domestic enterprises, relieved of costly social responsibilities and not required to share profits with the government, began to invest in new technologies, expand rapidly, and seek out new markets. Domestic private sector firms also developed. A plethora of incentives from both the central and the local governments—in the form of tax breaks, cheap land, and low utility prices—helped to keep production costs low and raise profits to be reinvested in further expansion.

With capital controls and an underdeveloped capital market limiting investment choices, China's large pool of savings provided these enterprises with a captive and cheap source of financing through a state-controlled banking system. And with this, China began an economic expansion of unprecedented pace driven by investment and exports. But consumption growth, in particular, could not keep pace with the capacity created by rapid investment. As a result, the share of investment in GDP rose, while that of consumption declined, with the difference picked up by a rising trade surplus.

RISING GROWTH, MOUNTING IMBALANCES

The concern is that China's rapid growth could slow, perhaps even sharply, if the continued expansion of capacity eventually leads to price declines that reduce profits, increase loan defaults, and undermine investor confidence. As the imbalances grow, so does the probability of such a development. If the global economy slows at the same time and competition from other countries rises, Chinese firms would find it that much more difficult to sell their products abroad without deep price cuts. Moreover, the risk of rising protectionism in China's trading partner countries could worsen the situation.

But didn't many of today's successful economies sustain such a development strategy for some time? Indeed, an export-based growth-strategy backed by large domestic savings and investment was the right path for China in the early 1990s. And it has been remarkably successful. That said, "much has changed since 1990, when China was a small economy just starting to open up, importing sophisticated inputs and assembling them, into consumer goods for the West. Today this assembly-line business makes up less than 10 percent of China's $250 billion trade surplus. Instead, China's exports have branched into new and more sophisticated products with a growing proportion of domestically made inputs. China also has become a dominant player in many markets. While it was relatively easy to expand market share before, further expansion will likely require Chinese firms to cut prices. If the price cuts needed to sell the created capacity turn out to be deep, many of today's investments could become unviable, turning into tomorrow's loan defaults.

Why is investment high? There is no big mystery here. Profits of Chinese companies have risen sharply over the past several years, suggesting that returns on investment are very attractive. In part this is because key input costs are low—including energy, utilities, land prices, and pollution control. But perhaps most important is the low cost of capital. Investment accounts for nearly 45 percent of China's GDP, and 90 percent of that is financed domestically (the national saving rate is 55 percent of GDP). Foreign direct investment accounts for less than 5 percent of GDP. Domestic bank lending and reinvested earnings of firms share the bulk of the financing needs. Bank lending rates are low because of low deposit rates set by the government.

Since the enterprise reform, the government has not sought dividends from SOEs, not even from those that are listed on the stock exchange and pay dividends to their private shareholders. For these enterprises, profits either are reinvested or sit in low-earning deposit accounts. Rising corporate saving has been the main reason that China's overall savings have gone up. Corporate savings roughly equal household savings—at about 23–24 percent of GDP. Low bank lending rates and retained earnings have kept the cost of investment funds low. Whereas real GDP growth in China has averaged about 10 percent, the real cost of investment has hovered at about 1–2 percent. In advanced economies that gap is negligible. In most emerging market economies it is positive, but in none is it as wide as in China. It is not surprising then that investment growth is so much faster in China and that investment's share of GDP is one of the highest in the world.

The cost of capital is not just low; it has fallen relative to wages, despite China's abundant labor supply. As a result, as economic theory predicts, production has been skewed increasingly toward capital-intensive processes, and job creation has slowed. In most countries, 3–4 percent GDP growth is associated with 2–3 percent employment growth, but in China, 10 percent GDP growth is generating only about 1 percent employment growth. In addition, the undervalued exchange rate and widely held expectations among investors that the currency will appreciate only gradually have biased investment toward exports and import substitution, adding to the rise in the trade surplus.

Why is consumption low? Although consumption has grown at a real rate of 8 percent since the early 1990s, it has lagged GDP growth. Personal consumption's share of GDP has fallen by more than 12 percentage points, to about 40 percent, one of the lowest levels in the world. While household savings in China are high and their rate has increased somewhat in recent years, this can explain only about 1 percentage point of the drop. Nearly all the decline is attributable to a falling share of national income going to households, including wages, investment income, and government transfers. Many countries have seen their wage share decline. But, in most countries, overall household income has held up reasonably well because rising dividend and interest income have offset the falling wage share. In China, though, household investment income has declined from more than 6 percent of GDP in the mid-1990s to less than 2 percent today, mainly because of low deposit rates and limited household equity ownership (directly or through institutional investors). Moreover, in most countries, profits of SOEs are transferred to the government, which uses them to provide consumption goods, such as health care and education, and income transfers to households. But in China the government receives no dividends, and transfers to households and public spending on health and education have declined.

WHY REBALANCING WON'T HAPPEN ON ITS OWN

The way to address these imbalances seems straightforward: switch from investment and exports as the main drivers of growth to consumption. Some analysts question whether there is a major problem and suggest that the normal business cycle will rebalance the economy. During upturns, firms invest and expand, increasing the demand for resources, such as capital and labor, these analysts say. That raises input costs, driving down profits and slowing investment. Less productive firms exit, economic growth slows, and prices stabilize.

In China's case, however, that argument is flawed. Business cycles usually occur in more advanced economies in which markets are well developed and prices provide early signals, allowing firms and households to adjust smoothly. In China, markets are not developed and prices do not provide a true reflection of underlying supply and demand conditions in key markets. Instead they are influenced, to varying degrees, by the government. Consequently, rebalancing requires active involvement by the government in the form of policy changes and reforms. What are those needed policy changes and reforms? There are four principal steps:

First, raise the cost of capital. In the immediate future, interest rates and the exchange rate hold the key to curbing rapid investment growth and the associated rise in bank lending.

Curbing investment has been the main goal of macroeconomic policy over most of the past three years. The Chinese authorities have also tried to control investment directly using a combination of administrative measures and "guided" bank lending, but these have not provided a lasting solution. China must increase its reliance on monetary policy to curb investment and credit growth by raising the cost of capital, the main reason investment is growing so rapidly. But the authorities fear that if the currency is tightly managed, increases in interest rates will encourage capital inflows that will add liquidity to the banking system, requiring further interest rate hikes to absorb it. China's government not only imposes a ceiling on deposit rates, it also sets a floor on lending rates and tightly manages the exchange rate, even after the changes made to the exchange rate regime in 2005.

The obvious way out is to simultaneously raise the floor on lending rates, lift the ceiling on deposit rates, and allow the exchange rate to appreciate more quickly. This will provide the room monetary tightening needs to be effective. Not only will the financial cost of capital increase, but, over the medium term, a stronger currency will help curb investments in the export and import-substituting sectors, while raising household incomes. The objective for economic policy should be that both interest rates and the exchange rate are increasingly determined by the market, so that the right price signals are provided to investors and households.

Second, liberalize prices. Reducing investment growth will require more than just monetary tightening. Other key prices in the economy also need to reflect market conditions and the underlying resource costs. In the past few years, the government has begun to raise the price of industrial land, power, and gasoline, and, importantly, to introduce stricter environmental standards and better enforce pollution controls. The government's goal of cutting energy use per unit of GDP by 20 percent over the next five years should help not only improve energy efficiency and reduce pollution, but also curb investment growth by raising business costs.

On the tax front, the government is unifying the enterprise income tax rate but still must cut tax and other incentives for investment that have proliferated over the past two decades, particularly at the local level. Raising the cost of capital also requires the government to exercise better corporate governance over SOEs, including asking profitable firms to transfer dividends to the budget. A pilot program is planned in which some SOEs would pay dividends to the budget in 2008, the first time since 1994. This is a step in the right direction, but the program needs to be expanded, especially to cover listed companies, which should pay the government the same dividends they pay to their private shareholders.

Third, reform financial markets. While weak corporate governance by the government has allowed SOEs to accumulate large savings, private enterprises, especially the small and medium-scale ones, have done the same because poor financial intermediation has limited their access to bank credit (Aziz, 2006). In the early 2000s, China embarked on an ambitious bank reform program and has made substantial progress in cleaning up nonperforming loans, recapitalizing banks, and opening the sector to foreign participation and competition. But, as a result, banks turned conservative—because of their weak internal risk-management and risk-pricing systems—and have continued to direct most credit to large cash-rich SOEs at the expense of private firms and households. Because capital markets—bond and equity—are also weak, they have not been an alternative source of financing for firms or savings for households. Firms have instead had to rely on internal savings for investment, and consumers have done the same for almost all large purchases-education, health care, pensions, housing, and durable goods (Aziz and Cui, 2007). Greater access to credit and a broader range of instruments to raise funds would reduce the incentives of firms to hold large savings, and better access to credit, insurance, and private pensions would diminish household saving and boost consumption.

Better financial intermediation has thus become the government's top priority. The authorities are pushing for further improvements in the banks' commercial operations, internal controls, and governance. They should also lift the cap on deposit rates, which would not only help push up the cost of capital but also allow smaller and more aggressive banks to compete better against large state-owned banks and provide an incentive for big banks to expand credit to small and medium-scale enterprises. China is also looking to expand its other financial markets, especially bond and equity markets. However, continued government control over bond and equity issuance is a serious impediment to these markets. Raising household consumption requires not only increasing the household share of national income but also reducing the uncertainties that have kept precautionary savings high. For the first, a key factor is increasing households' investment income—through higher deposit rates and greater participation in the equity market, and directly and indirectly through expanded mutual and pension funds. Equity market reforms of the past few years have revitalized a languishing stock market, but the supply of equities needs to be increased.

Fourth, shift government expenditures. The government has another important role in this rebalancing exercise: improving the provision of key social services, especially education, health care, and pensions. Reducing the uncertainties surrounding their provision will substantially diminish the strong precautionary saving motive and give households the confidence to raise their consumption. In the 1994 SOE reforms, the provision of health care, education, and pensions was transferred from companies to local governments. However, in general, local governments were not provided with adequate resources to discharge these new responsibilities. Consequently, households have had to bear an increasing portion of the costs of health care and education. Chinese households pay about 80 percent of health care costs out of their own pockets, one of the highest proportions in the world. They also face considerable uncertainty about pensions, because reforms in this area have not produced a new, viable pension system, although China's one-child policy has intensified the aging of the population and raised the need to save for old age. The government has increased spending for education and health care in recent budgets, but the increases have been limited. In essence, households have self-insured against uncertainties associated with pensions, health care, and education. As a result, they have saved significantly more than they would have were these risks pooled socially.

Rather than provide quick fixes, the government has rightly decided to rebalance the economy by implementing fundamental reforms along several dimensions to shift the economy's heavy reliance on investment and exports toward consumption. China has already made progress on many of them, and most analysts agree on the basic elements of the strategy. However, there is a concern that the current high growth and low inflation in China and a benign world economy may give the false impression that China has time on its side in implementing these reforms. The reality could be different. Unchecked, the imbalances will continue to grow and, with them, the rising probability of a large correction will become a major threat to the country's economic growth and stability.

JAHANGIR AZIZ is a Division Chief and Steven Dunaway is a Deputy Director in the IMF's Asia and Pacific Department.

Chapter 21: Findings and Bottom Lines

CHARLES WOLF JR., K.C. YEH, BENJAMIN ZYCHER, NICHOLAS EBERSTADT, AND SUNG-HO LEE

Our principal findings together with our estimates about the corresponding bottom lines can be summarized as follows.

UNEMPLOYMENT, POVERTY, AND SOCIAL UNREST

Open and disguised unemployment in China totals about 170 million, or about 23 percent of the total labor force in 1999. Moreover, the level of unemployment has been rising due especially to the population increase in the 1980s, as well as to the privatization of SOEs in the 1990s along with the downsizing of these often inefficient, loss-incurring enterprises. Recent and prospective increases in unemployment have not been principally the result of China's efforts to comply with its WTO commitments, although these commitments may engender further unemployment. The aggregate statistics have been accompanied by rising urban unemployment resulting *from* rural poverty, and resulting *in* income inequality between rural and urban areas, rural-to-urban migration, and social unrest.

The *bottom line* in this domain is our estimate of lower total factor productivity, lower savings, and reduced capital formation, causing reductions between 0.3 and 0.8 percent in China's annual growth rate over the next decade.

ECONOMIC EFFECTS OF CORRUPTION

Both the concept and the measurement of corruption are complex as well as more than slightly obscure. Corruption in China as elsewhere includes the circumvention of established rules and laws. But some rules and laws in China as elsewhere may be perverse with respect to economic growth so their evasion may help rather than hinder growth.

In our effort to calibrate corruption in China and to link a possible adverse change in corrupt practices to their impact on China's expected economic performance, we have drawn on two established indices of corruption. These indices are based on polls, questionnaires, and surveys and include such categories as legal structure and security of property rights, regulation of business, and "perceptions" of corruption. In turn, the quintiles of the corruption indices are associated with differing quintile positions in annual economic growth rates of various countries included in the relevant indices We infer that, were corrupt practices in China to increase-thereby lowering the quintile position of China in terms of its associated economic growth—our crude *bottom-line* estimate of the impact on China's expected growth rate would be a reduction of about 0.5 percent.

A recent estimate by Angang Hu has placed the economic cost of corruption in China in a range between 13.2 and 16.8 percent of GDP in the mid- to late 1990s.[1] However, this estimate seems to us to be too high for technical reasons. Moreover the aggregate estimate of 13.2 refers to the *level* of economic cost imposed on the system, rather than the effect of a change in this level on China's growth.

HIV/AIDS AND EPIDEMIC DISEASE

Estimates by the United Nations and other sources have placed the prevalence of HIV/AIDS in China in a range between 600,000 and 1.3 million, with an approximate annual rate of increase between 20 and 30 percent. For the several health scenarios analyzed in this study estimated HIV carriers in the second decade of this century could range between 11 million and 80 million in China. By 2015, China's HIV population would exceed the entire HIV population of sub-Saharan Africa today!

One way of translating these prevalence estimates into economic burdens is to consider the costs of treatment. At a minimum level, based on India's experience, annual treatment costs are $600 per person.

If, for example, the prospectively infected population in China is between 5 and 10 million, the costs of treatment would be $3–6 billion a year at a minimum, and rising. Based on the "intermediate," rather than "pessimistic" scenario, China's population would experience annual deaths from HIV/AIDS between 1.7 and 2.7 million in the second decade of the 21st century, cumulating by 2025 to over 20 million casualties, associated with health-based reductions in productivity and annual reductions in GDP growth between 1.8 and 2.2 percent in the period 2002–2015.

WATER RESOURCES AND POLLUTION

Although China's aggregate water supplies are adequate, China is beset by a perennial maldistribution of natural water supplies. The North China plain, with over a third of China's total population and at least an equivalent share of its GDP, has only 7.5 percent of the naturally available water resources. Subsurface aquifers in North China are near exhaustion, and pollution discharges from industrial and other uses further aggravate the shortage of water available for consumers and industry. By contrast, South China normally has an abundance of natural water supplies, sometimes leading to floods. The dilemma this poses for China's policy-makers is whether and to what extent to push for capital-intensive water-transfer projects from south to north or, instead, to emphasize recycling as well as conservation of restricted water supplies in the north, or to pursue some combination of these alternatives.

This key allocation issue is further complicated by political considerations relating to the relative influence of provinces in the north and south regions. Our analysis examines several different scenarios involving different combinations of water-transfer projects and recycling/conservation efforts which, in general, are more efficient from the standpoint of reducing the short- to medium-term stringencies in water resource availability in the north. If, for various reasons, nonoptimal policy decisions and resource allocations are pursued, a plausible "pessimistic" scenario could result in reducing China's annual GDP growth between 1.5 and 1.9 percent.

ENERGY CONSUMPTION AND PRICES

The risk posed for China's continued high growth rate by availability of oil and natural gas supplies arises from the possibility of major increases in world energy prices, rather than from the fact that China has shifted from being a net exporter of oil in the early 1990s to a current and future situation in which nearly half of its oil and nearly a fifth of its natural gas consumption are derived from imports.

To analyze the fault line that might arise in the energy sector, we posit a scenario in which there is a drastic contraction in global oil supply, for whatever reason or combination of reasons, by about 25 percent and lasting for a decade (2005–2015). Factoring into this scenario a range of plausible demand elasticities, together with a small allowance for increased energy efficiency, we conservatively infer that global oil prices might rise as much as threefold. The resulting effect on China's annual growth rate resulting from a "moderately severe" scenario during the period 2005–2015 would be an average diminution between 1.2 and 1.4 percent.

CHINA'S FRAGILE FINANCIAL SYSTEM AND STATE-OWNED ENTERPRISES

One of the salient indicators of systemic fragility of China's state-dominated financial institutions is the extraordinarily high ratio of nonperforming loans on the balance sheets of the four major state banks. These NPLs have risen and continue to rise as the result of accumulated "policy lending" from the state banks to loss-incurring SOEs. Estimates of total NPLs cover an enormous range, between 9 and 60 percent of China's GDP. The correct figure is more likely to be at the upper end of this range.

Under circumstances, China could experience a "run" of withdrawals from the state banks, large-scale capital flight, a significant reduction in savings rates, and a decline of capital formation. The resulting financial crisis and credit squeeze could plausibly reduce total factor productivity by 0.3 percent, with accompanying reductions in the rates of capital formation and of employment growth that would collectively lower annual GDP growth by 0.5 to 1.0 percent.

POSSIBLE SHRINKAGE OF FOREIGN DIRECT INVESTMENT

Between 1985 and 2001, the annual compound rate of growth in foreign direct investment in China was over 18 percent, rising from an annual rate of about $2 billion to over $40 billion in 2001 (in constant 1995 dollars). Two different mechanisms are generally believed to account for the special importance and leveraging effects of foreign direct investment in contributing to China's high growth rates during the 1985–2001 period.

Yet there are not implausible circumstances under which this pattern of secularly rising FDI might severely contract. These adverse circumstances include both possible *internal* developments (such as tensions accompanying the leadership succession, internal financial crisis, inconvertibility of the RMB, repercussions from a possible HIV/AIDS epidemic, and slow implementation of China's WTO pledges), as well as possible *external* developments (such as improvements in the economic infrastructure and investment climate in other competing countries and regions in Eastern Europe, Russia, India, and elsewhere). To a greater extent than has occurred in the past, future FDI in China is likely to depend critically on the *comparative* risk-adjusted, after-tax return on investment in China compared with that in other countries.

Based on several rough assumptions and crude calculations, a sustained reduction of $10 billion a year in FDI may be associated with a reduction of China's annual GDP growth between 0.8 and 1.6 percent.

TAIWAN AND OTHER POTENTIAL CONFLICTS

The current and recent status of relations between China and Taiwan is characterized as "movement without progress." Yet this status quo entails major benefits for the PRC and Taiwan, as well as for the United States, especially when compared with some of the possible alternatives to it and the paths that might be associated with movement toward them.

There are also significant risks and tensions associated with the status quo, and it is not implausible that these might erupt into possible conflict between the PRC and Taiwan. We consider one scenario involving escalation from provocation by Taiwan as viewed from Beijing, a blockade imposed in response, tangible though limited coercive force to effectuate the blockade, and the resulting effects on China's reallocation of resources to military spending, with ensuing reductions in the rate of growth of the civil capital stock and in the growth of total factor productivity.

The *bottom line* of these adverse security developments would be a conservative estimate of a decline in China's annual rate of economic growth between 1.0 and 1.3 percent.

SUMMARY

Table 21.1 summarizes our rough estimates of the plausible impacts on China's annual growth that could ensue from each of the adversities or fault lines that we have considered separately from one another. As noted earlier, five of these are already present and, in these instances, what we are positing is the possibility of their becoming worse and the economic effects this would entail.

As is evident in Table 21.1, and in the preceding subsections of this chapter, sustaining China's high growth from the past into the period 2003–2010 faces major obstacles, challenges, and what we have called "adversities." These include the several categories of adversities—sectoral, institutional, financial, and security—that we have analyzed in the successive chapters of this study.

The probability that none of these individual adversities will occur is low, while the probability that all will ensue is still lower. Were all of the setbacks to occur, the effect, according to our estimates, would be growth reductions of 7.4–10.7 percent; thus, improbably registering negative numbers for China's economic performance. While the probability that all of these adversities will occur is low, the probability that several will occur is higher than their simple joint, multiplicative probabilities would normally imply. The reason for this multiplication is that their individual probabilities are not independent of one another. Several of the separate adversities may tend to cluster because of these interdependencies. For example, an internal financial crisis would have serious negative consequences for the relative attractiveness of foreign investment in China and would be conducive to shrinkage of FDI. Similarly, tension or conflict in the Taiwan Straight or in other parts of the Asia-Pacific region would very likely seriously diminish FDI in China, as well as increase the likelihood of a financial crisis. Another clustering might arise in connection with the interdependence among unemployment, poverty, and the incidence of epidemic disease, including HIV/AIDS.

Table 21.2 suggests some of the key interdependencies among the several fault lines we have discussed.

Table 21.1 Impacts on China's Growth Arising from Separate Fault Lines, 2005–2015 (Preliminary).

Type of Setback	Separate Effects Diminishing China's Economic Performance (percentage/year)
Unemployment, poverty, social unrest	0.3–0.8
Economic effects of corruption	0.5
HIV/AIDS and epidemic disease	1.8–2.2
Water resources and pollution	1.5–1.9
Energy consumption and prices	1.2–1.4
Fragility of the financial system and state-owned enterprises	0.5–1.0
Possible shrinkage of foreign direct investment	0.6–1.6
Taiwan and other potential conflicts	1.0–1.3

Table 21.2 Interdependences Among Fault Lines

Consequence	Cause							
	Unemployment, poverty, and social unrest	Economic effects of corruption	HIV/AIDS and epidemic disease	Water resources and pollution	Energy consumption and pollution	Fragility of the financial system and state-owned enterprises	Possible shrinkage of foreign direct investment	Taiwan and other potential conflicts
Unemployment, poverty, and social unrest		✓	✓	✓	✓	✓		
Economic effects of corruption	✓					✓	✓	
HIV/AIDS and epidemic disease	✓			✓	✓			
Water resources and pollution	✓		✓		✓			
Energy consumption and prices	✓							
Fragility of the financial system and state-owned enterprises	✓	✓	✓				✓	✓
Possible shrinkage of foreign direct investment	✓	✓	✓			✓		✓
Taiwan and other potential conflicts								

NOTE: ✓ indicates where a fault line (cause/column heading) is likely to affect the occurrence and/or severity of another (consequence/row heading).

NOTES

1. Angang Hu, 2002, op. cit.